NAVAL WAR COLLEGE

NEWPORT, RHODE ISLAND

INTERNATIONAL LAW STUDIES

COLLECTIVE SECURITY UNDER INTERNATIONAL LAW

by

Hans Kelsen

1954

(1956)

NAVPERS 15031

Volume XLIX

THE LAWBOOK EXCHANGE, LTD.

Clark, New Jersey

ISBN 9781584771449 (hardcover)
ISBN 9781616191825 (paperback)

Lawbook Exchange edition 2001, 2011

The quality of this reprint is equivalent to the quality of the original work.

THE LAWBOOK EXCHANGE, LTD.
33 Terminal Avenue
Clark, New Jersey 07066-1321

Please see our website for a selection of our other publications and fine facsimile reprints of classic works of legal history:
www.lawbookexchange.com

Library of Congress Cataloging-in-Publication Data

Kelsen, Hans, 1881-1973.
Collective security under international law / by Hans Kelsen.
p. cm.
At head of title: Naval War College.
Originally published: Washington: U.S.G.P.O., 1957. (International law studies; v. 49).
Includes bibliographical references and index.
ISBN 1-58477-144-5 (cloth: acid-free paper)
1. Security, International. 2. International law. I. Naval War College (U.S.) II. Title.
III. International law studies; v. 49.

KZ5588 .K45 2001
341.26--dc21 00-053507

Printed in the United States of America on acid-free paper

NAVAL WAR COLLEGE

NEWPORT, RHODE ISLAND

INTERNATIONAL LAW STUDIES

COLLECTIVE SECURITY UNDER INTERNATIONAL LAW

by

Hans Kelsen

1954

(1956)

NAVPERS 15031

Volume XLIX

UNITED STATES
GOVERNMENT PRINTING OFFICE
WASHINGTON : 1957

FOREWORD

The following study is an attempt to present a theory of collective security from a legal point of view. Its main purpose is to show that collective security is an essential function of law, national as well as international, and that, therefore, there exists an intrinsic connection between international security and international law; in other terms, that collective security of the state within the international community is, just as collective security of the individual within the state, by its very nature a legal problem.

The study does not intend to describe the historical development of collective security as a problem of international organization; it is restricted to its systematic analysis. Consequently, the material of positive international law referred to in the text and especially in the notes does not lay claim to completeness; but is to be considered as a selection of characteristic patterns illustrating the most important statements.

HANS KELSEN.

Berkeley, Calif.

PREFACE

The publication of this series was inaugurated by the Naval War College in 1894. This is the forty-ninth volume in the series as numbered for index purposes. This title has varied slightly from year to year. The preceding volume, *International Law Documents, 1952–53*, was published in 1954.

The present volume inaugurates a new form for this series. In 1953 a Chair of International Law was established at the Naval War College. One of the duties of the occupant of this Chair is the preparation of a study on a phase of International Law that is of special interest to the U. S. Navy. This volume on the legal theory of collective security, the first of a series sponsored by the Naval War College, was prepared by Dr. Hans Kelsen, the 1953–54 occupant of the Naval War College Chair of International Law.

The many significant events in this era of rapid change in world conditions have prompted the author to insert much new material into this volume before its final release. Thus, although for continuity purposes this volume is entitled *International Law Studies, 1954*, some of the material and notes contained herein represent the views of the author as of about October 1, 1956.

The opinions expressed in this volume are not necessarily those of the U. S. Navy or the Naval War College.

THOMAS H. ROBBINS, JR.,
Rear Admiral, United States Navy,
President, Naval War College.

NEWPORT, 1 December 1956.

TABLE OF CONTENTS

Page

I. THE CONCEPT OF COLLECTIVE SECURITY 1
  1. Individual and Collective Security 1
  2. Security and Law 5
II. THE DIFFERENT DEGREES OF COLLECTIVE SECURITY. 10
  1. The Scope of Protected Interests 10
  2. The Centralization of the Procedure for the Ascertainment of a Delict (i. e., an Illegal Use of Force) and for Determining the Party Responsible for It 12
  3. The Prevention of the Illegal Use of Force by the Peaceful Settlement of Conflicts 15
  4. Legal (Justiciable) and Political (Non-justiciable) Conflicts (Disputes) 19
  5. Removal of the Causes of the Illegal Use of Force 22
  6. The Centralization of the Use of Force as a Sanction 23
  7. Self-Defense 26
  8. The Centralization of the Law-Creating Function (the Peaceful Change of Established Legal Relations) 28
  9. Universal and Regional Security Organizations 29
III. INTERNATIONAL SECURITY 34
  1. Collective Security under General International Law 34
    (a) The *bellum justum* principle 34
    (b) Alliances and the balance of power 39
    (c) The opposition to international security 42
  2. Collective Security under Particular International Law 53
    (a) Defining the use of force to be prohibited 53
    (b) The problem of aggression 58
      (aa) The military concept of aggression and the legal concept 58
      (bb) Aggression and self-defense as a restriction of the prohibition of the use of armed force 59
      (cc) Other exceptions to the prohibition of the use of armed force 62
      (dd) Aggression as conduct not including the use of armed force; indirect aggression 63
      (ee) The definition of aggression 66
      (ff) The attempt to eliminate the problem of aggression .. 67
      (gg) Is the concept of aggression not susceptible to definition? 69
      (hh) The two methods of defining aggression 70
      (ii) The arguments against a pre-established definition of aggression 73
      (jj) Is aggression a political concept and not a legal one? .. 75
      (kk) General or enumerative definition of aggression 78
      (ll) The difficulties in defining aggression and in determining the aggressor 83
      (mm) The problem of provocation 86

III. INTERNATIONAL SECURITY—Continued
2. Collective Security under Particular International Law—Con. *Page*
(c) Sanctions 101
(aa) The concept of sanctions 101
(bb) The execution of sanctions within an international security system 104
(cc) Non-military sanctions 106
(dd) Military sanctions 110
(A) The opposition to military sanctions 110
(B) The organization of military sanctions 111
(C) The international police force organized as a permanent and separate armed force at the direct disposal of a security organization 113
(D) The procedure preceding the execution of sanctions. 120
(E) Sanctions constituting individual responsibility for violations of international law 122
(F) Sanctions consisting of the forfeiture of rights 125
(d) Peace treaties and neutrality 152
(aa) Peace treaties within a system of international security 152
(bb) Neutrality within a system of international security. 154
(e) Preventive measures 171
(aa) Consultation 171
(bb) The peaceful settlement of international disputes 181
(cc) The peaceful change of legally established international relations 194
(dd) Disarmament 197
Disarmament and security 197
Physical disarmament 198
The aim of disarmament 202
Total or partial disarmament 202
Immediate complete or gradual (progressive) disarmament 204
Proportional or balanced disarmament 205
Geographical disarmament 205
Reduction and limitation of expenditures 206
Derogations 207
Control 207
Moral disarmament 210
(ee) Economic cooperation 253
(ff) Universalism and regionalism 258

COLLECTIVE SECURITY

I. THE CONCEPT OF COLLECTIVE SECURITY

1. INDIVIDUAL AND COLLECTIVE SECURITY

Security is the condition of being protected against, or not exposed to, a danger. It is an objective condition of man which, rightly or wrongly, man assumes to exist. The effect of this assumption is a certain state of mind which may be described as freedom from fear, the fear of a danger. There are different kinds of security which may be distinguished according to the nature of the danger. Religion affords a spiritual security, protecting man against the dangers threatening his soul during his lifetime and especially after his death. There is a sanitary security established by health organizations to prevent or restrict, as far as possible, epidemics. To guarantee economic security is the ideal which socialism tries to realize in order to free man from his fear of being deprived of the means for satisfying his most vital needs. The security with which this book deals is the protection of man against the use of force by other men.

"Collective" security is usually distinguished as the security of states in their relation to other states, sometimes called "international" security, from individual security as the security of individual human beings in their mutual, inter-individual, relations.[1] Consequently, the use of force against which states are supposed to be protected by a system of collective, or international, security is the use of armed force, especially that use known as war.

However, it is not quite correct to consider collective security, the security of states within an international community, and individual security, the security of the individual human beings within a state, as opposite concepts. In the last analysis, the security of a state is the security of the individual human beings who are members of a state.

According to a generally accepted view, the state is a political organization. As an "organization" it is a normative order regulating the mutual behavior of men. As a "political" organization it is a coercive order because its specific means is the employment of force, i. e., the threat and use of force. This means that the norms of this order provide for coercive acts as reactions against human behavior considered to be harmful to society. Such reactions are the essence of the law or of a legal order. If a legal order is centralized—that is, if it institutes special organs for its creation and application and, especially, for the execution of the coercive acts, called sanctions—the social order is a state. As a social order, the state is not different from what is usually called the law of the state or the national legal order, for the state is a centralized legal order constituting a legal community.

In the language of political theory, the state is described as not only a social order but also as an acting person. It is said that the state creates, applies and, especially, enforces the law, that is, the norms of the legal order. However, as an acting person, the state is only the personification of this order. In this capacity, the state manifests its existence in acts of state which are always acts of individual human beings determined by the legal order constituting the community. The acts concerned are those by which the coercive order is created and subsequently applied to other individual human beings whose behavior is thus regulated. The individuals performing these acts are "organs," organs of the legal order or, what amounts to the same thing, of the state as a legal order, in contradistinction to the individuals to whom the legal order is applied by the organs. These individuals are the subjects of the legal order, or the subjects of the state as a legal order. The statement that the acts concerned are acts of the state is a figure of speech which metaphorically expresses the idea that the state order is created and applied by these acts, that it operates through the individuals performing these acts in their capacity as organs. This idea implies the personification of the order, the construction of a person to which these acts may be imputed. Since the order is a legal order, the person is a juristic person. The concept of a juristic person is an artificial device used to simplify the description of human relations interpreted according to a normative order presupposed to be valid.

It stands to reason that neither the state as a social order, which means the state as a system of norms, nor its personification can be exposed to any use of force. Physical force can be used only against physical beings, not against an order as a system of norms; and force as a psychic compulsion only against beings endowed with some kind of reason, feeling and will. Hence, as a condition of being protected against the use of force, security can be only the security of human beings. If there is a security of a state, it can be only the security of the human beings who are the members of the state—that is, the individuals whose behavior is regulated by the state order either because they are its organs or because they are its subjects.

The difference which exists between the security of the individual within the state, i. e., the national legal community, and the security of the state (as the security of individuals) within the international community consists in the fact that the former is guaranteed by national law, the so-called law of the state, and hence may be properly called national security, whereas the latter is guaranteed by international law and for this reason is called international security. It is in both cases *collective* security, because it is security afforded by a social order; and a social order always constitutes a certain degree of collectivization.

Collective security must be distinguished from the security which an individual or a state may try to establish for itself. Because it is not afforded by a social order, this latter security may be considered to be *individual* security. It is only in this negative sense of being a non-collective security that individual security can be considered to be the opposite of collective security. However, this individual security is not true security at all, for an individual can never concentrate in his hands a sufficient amount of power to protect himself for any length of time against the united forces of several others. Furthermore, any association with other individuals for the purpose of common defense by mutual assistance is the first step towards a social organization affording collective security. This is precisely the idea which the natural-law doctrine of the 17th and 18th centuries tried to express by inventing the fiction of a social contract. According to this doctrine, men abandoned the state of nature as a state where no positive law was established because of its complete lack of security. They abandoned it by concluding a contract with the main purpose of protecting each member of the community by providing for a collective reaction against any violation of vital interests. In other words, the purpose of this contract was to establish collective security.

The assumption that man existed originally in a state of nature is highly problematical. Men have probably always lived in society, and where there is society there is some kind of law—*ubi societas ibi jus*—although the law may be more or less effective. Transient periods of anarchy are possible and have actually existed in history. However, they are characterized by the fact that no security exists, and the attempts of single individuals to secure themselves against others are in vain. As we shall see,[2] the same is true with respect to any attempt by an individual state to establish a non-collective security for itself. Hence, since security can be only collective, collective security is a pleonastic term.

If the security of the individual within the state (national security) and the security of the state within the international community (international security) are both collective security because they are both guaranteed by a social order, and if this order is in both cases a legal order, collective security is by its very nature legal security in the sense that it is a security established by law.[3] An attempt has been made to distinguished two kinds of state or international security: legal or juridical security and political security.[4] According to this view, legal security is defined as "a condition in which a state that observes the objective law need not fear that its rights as a subject of international law will be violated without redress"; while political security is defined as a condition in which a state "regardless of its conduct, need not fear a successful attack from without." The difference between legal and political security is that only the former is guaranteed by the law. The latter is brought about by the state itself by means which could also be applied if the state were not subjected to a legal order—in other words, if the state existed together with other states in a condition of anarchy. The question of whether so-called political security is achieved in a legal or in an illegal way is irrelevant. Hence, the so-called political security of a state is not collective security but rather a typical case of individual security. The political security of a state is the same kind of security which an individual human being tries to achieve without being protected by a legal order and which, as has been pointed out, is really not security at all.

It has been maintained that the security of an individual within a national community or state (national security) and the security of a state within an international community (international security) are two totally different problems and that there is no real analogy between them, because "the first is a police problem, the latter a problem of social justice finding its protection in legislation."[5] However, as we shall see later, international security is as much a police problem as national security is, and the latter is no less a problem of social justice than the former. There is another argument that has been advanced to justify the view that there is an essential difference between national and international security, and that consequently the latter cannot be modeled exactly after the former. This argument has been formulated as follows: "The State requires of the individual, in case of need, the sacrifice of his life in the interest of the community. In this case individual security is strictly subordinated to collective security. Not so in the international field. Here collective security is the counterpart of individual security and cannot be in opposition to it. The collectivity cannot require a state to sacrifice itself completely in the interest of the collectivity."[6] This argument is based on an erroneous hypostatization of the personification called the "state." An international organization constituting a system of collective security cannot require a state to sacrifice its life because a state is not a living organism like an individual human being. However, there is no reason why an international organization should not require a member state to sacrifice the lives of its subjects in order to guarantee international security. Neither the nature of the state—that is the national legal order constituting the community—nor the nature of the international legal order excludes such a request. As a matter of fact, an international security organization which provides for military sanctions necessarily imposes such an obligation upon the member states. If the proposition that a state sacrifices its life means only that a state which resorts to war against another state may cease to exist as a subject of international law by being defeated and by having its territory annexed by the victorious state, the possibility that a state may lose its life certainly exists if military sanctions are applied. Furthermore, there is no reason why states should not be required to run such a risk in the interest of international security. However, since military sanctions are always organized as collective actions, the risk practically does not exist if a system of international security operates in conformity with its constituent treaty. The statement that "collective security is the counterpart of individual security and cannot be in opposition to it," amounts to a complete rejection of international security.[7]

If it is admitted, first, that the security of the state is the security of the individuals who are the members of the state, and, secondly, that the security of the state within an international community is collective security in the same sense as the security of the individuals within the national community (the state) because both are guaranteed by legal orders, a perfect analogy between them cannot be denied. In both cases, security is established by the specific reaction for which the legal order provides in case of certain harmful behavior by the members of the community. This behavior constitutes a violation of the order, and in both cases the most conspicuous violation is the illegal use of force. To be sure, there is a remarkable difference between the national and the international legal order, especially with respect to this reaction, that is the sanctions stipulated by these orders. However, if the normative order constituting an international community of states is considered to be international "law," and this means law in the same sense as the normative order constituting a state, it must be possible to show that the structure of both normative orders is, at least in principle, the same in all respects relevant to the security they afford; and this *is* possible.

2. SECURITY AND LAW

It is the purpose of any legal order to protect certain interests of the individuals subjected to it by providing for coercive acts as sanctions to be applied as reactions against violations of these interests. In this way, the law tries to prevent such violations. The most important interest protected in this way by the law is man's interest in maintaining his life. Since this interest of the individual is endangered by the use of force on the part of other individuals, the sanctions of law are directed primarily but not exclusively against this use of force (the term "force" meaning physical force). By attaching a sanction to a certain behavior, especially to the use of force by one individual against another, the law forbids this behavior which, as the condition of a sanction, is to be considered as illegal, or, to use a term covering all possible violations of the law or legally protected interests: as a delict. The sanctions consist in the forcible deprivation of life, freedom or property of those responsible for the illegal use of force or other violations of the law. However, these sanctions, too, constitute a use of force. Hence the use of force is not absolutely forbidden by the law. It is even authorized as a sanction; and not all kinds of the use of force are forbidden. But there exists in the evolution of law a tendency to forbid not only the use of physical force destroying or endangering the life of human beings, but also other kinds of the use of force, to restrict, as far as possible, the use of force which has not the character of a sanction by attaching a sanction to it; so that, as a rule, the use of force is to be considered either as a delict, that is, the condition of a sanction, or as a sanction, that is, the reaction against a delict.

Consequently, there can be no law without force. For, by its very nature, the law is an organization of force. The law organizes the use of force in the relations of its subjects by determining the conditions under which definite individuals are authorized to use force. Force used under other conditions is to be considered as a delict. But in using force under the conditions determined by the law, which means in applying the sanction provided for by the legal order, the individuals determined by law execute the order and thus act as organs of this order, or what amounts to the same, as organs of the community constituted by the legal order. Hence the use of force—the legal, but not the illegal use of force—may be imputed to the legal community acting through its organs. If the use of force is legal only as a sanction, the legal order reserves the use of force to the legal community, in other words, the legal order establishes a *force monopoly* of the legal community.

If peace is defined as the absence of force, it is the essential function of the law to guarantee peace in the relations among the members of the community, the subjects of the law. In guaranteeing peace by protecting the members of the legal community against the use of force, the law—any legal order—guarantees its subjects security. Hence, the prohibition of the use of force is an essential element of any system of collective, and that means, legal security. Legal security is identical with peace, or rather with that relative peace which a legal order can secure. It is a relative, not an absolute security. It is relative not only because the use of force is not absolutely forbidden, but also because no legal order can be so effective as to prevent the illegal use of force completely. A system of collective—and that means legal—security, the core of which is the prohibition of the use of force, is meaningful only if the possibility of an illegal use of force is presupposed. However, the legal order which prohibits the use of force may be more or less efficacious. The degree of its efficacy depends—in the first place—on the degree of its centralization.

It follows that, by its very nature, the security afforded its subjects by a legal order is collective security because it is a security established by a social order. By regulating the mutual relations of individuals, every social order creates definite social relations among these individuals and thus brings about a certain collectivization constituting a community as a collective body. The collective character of the security established by a legal order manifests itself, firstly, in the fact that the use of force is forbidden by the legal order which is valid equally for all members of the community constituted by the order, and, secondly, in the fact that the reaction against an illegal use of force is a collective action. It is a collective action because it is an action performed by organs of the community and is therefore imputable to the community, even if the individuals concerned are not special organs, as is the case in both a primitive society under primitive law and the international community under general international law.[8]

In contradistinction to the law of a modern state (the national law), the law of a primitive society does not institute special organs for the creation and application of the law. There are no legislative organs. The general legal norms are created by custom—that is, by the habitual behavior of the individuals subjected to the law. There are no courts competent to ascertain the fact that the law has been violated and to determine the person responsible for the violation. There is no sheriff and no police to execute the law—that is, to apply the sanctions for which the law provides. All these functions are left to the subjects of the law. In case of a murder—that is, in case the members of a group (especially a family) are of the opinion that one of them has been the victim of an illegal use of force by a member of another group—the law authorizes the relatives of the victim to take revenge on the murderer and his relatives, to use force in killing them. In case of other delicts, incest for example, the law authorizes every member of the community to treat the delinquent as an outlaw—that is, to use any kind of force against him so that he is compelled to leave the community, which means to perish. In case of certain material damage by one individual to another's property, the law authorizes the members of the group to which the injured individual belongs to use force to deprive members of the group to which the delinquent belongs of some property as compensation for the damage. In effect, this means that the principle of *self-help* prevails.

The principle of self-help is a consequence of the complete decentralization of a legal order. In a decentralized legal order, the essential legal functions are not conferred upon special—or, what amounts to the same, central—organs which function according to the principle of division of labor but are left to the individual members of the community. This does not mean that there are no legal organs at all under a decentralized coercive order. The coercive acts provided for by this order as reactions against its violation are sanctions, and the individuals authorized by the order to execute these sanctions act as organs of this order or of the community constituted by it. However, these individuals are not special organs who function according to the principle of the division of labor—that is, they are not central organs. In the mind of primitive men living under a completely decentralized legal order, there is a clear distinction between an illegal and a legal use of force, between a murderer who violates the law and an avenger who executes it. However, in a concrete case, it is impossible to give an objective answer to the question of who is a murderer and who an avenger, or, more generally, whether a use of force is illegal (a delict) or legal (a sanction). Nevertheless, the use of force as a sanction is considered to be a reaction by the community against a delict, for even under a decentralized legal order, where the principle of self-help prevails, the use of force having the character of a sanction is considered to be reserved to the legal community. The force monopoly of the community established by a legal order may be decentralized. Even a completely decentralized legal order affords its subjects a certain degree of collective security; but it is the lowest possible degree.

Since under a completely decentralized legal order the question as to who is right and who is wrong in using force cannot be decided in an objective way, the social situation established by such an order is not clearly distinguishable from a situation where no security exists, just as, in its application to a concrete case, a completely decentralized coercive order is hardly distinguishable from a state of anarchy. This is why some writers refuse to consider a social order as law as long as that minimum of centralization constituted by the establishment of courts is not achieved, and also why in traditional terminology we speak of collective security only when the principle of self-help is eliminated and replaced by a legal technique characterized by a certain centralization. Thus the organization of collective security, in the specific or narrower sense of the term, consists mainly, but not exclusively, in the centralization of the coercive order constituting the legal community.

Since the extent of this centralization may vary, collective security may be established in different degrees.

NOTES

1. *Cf.* e. g., Maurice Bourquin, "Le Problème de la Sécurité Internationale." Académie de Droit International. Recueil des Cours. 1934. III. Tome 49, p. 473; and *Collective Security*, a record of the Seventh and Eighth International Studies Conferences of the League of Nations. Paris 1934—London 1935. Edited by Maurice Bourquin. Paris 1936, p. 131.

2. *Cf.* pp. 4, 34 ff.

3. Legal security in this sense must be distinguished from the "legal security" which is the translation of the German term "Rechtssicherheit". The German term designates the principle that the judicial and administrative acts of a state must be determined by pre-established general legal norms. In English terminology, this is called the "rule-of-law" principle.

4. Professor Ludwik Ehrlich in: *Collective Security*, p. 152.

5. Memorandum of the Canadian Institute of International Affairs, submitted to the International Studies Conference 1934–35, *Collective Security*, p. 132.

6. Dietrich Schindler, in a memorandum on "The Notion of Neutrality in a System Including Repression of Resort to War," submitted to the International Studies Conference 1934–35; *Cf. Collective Security*, p. 26.

7. Prof. Schindler advocated the above mentioned doctrine mainly for the purpose of justifying the maintenance of Switzerland's permanent neutrality within a system of international security. *Cf.* p. 169.

8. Collective security is a function of law, regardless of the way in which the law is created, that is to say, with or without the participation of the individuals subjected to the law. In opposition to this view, Sir Alfred Zimmern, "The Problem of Collective Security" (in: *Neutrality and Collective Security*, edited by Quincy Wright, Chicago 1936), asserts: "Collective Security," which means "safety of all by all," "is a democratic notion" (p. 4). "Where there is no freedom [meaning a democratic constitution] there can be no cooperation for collective security" (p. 23). From this view follows that there can be no collective security within a non-democratic state, nor within an international community which is not composed exclusively of democratic states and is constituted by an international order which has not a democratic character. However, Zimmern says also: The principle of collective security "as applied to the world as a whole" means "a condition of law and order for the world" (p. 9). This statement is compatible with the doctrine that collective security is a democratic notion only under the presupposition that law is by its very nature a democratically created social order, that a social order created in another way is no law. Such a concept of law is inadmissibly narrow and in open conflict with the general use of this term; for most of the social orders of the past, and many of the present day, generally called "law" have no democratic character. If collective security is protection against the use of force by one subject of the community directed at another subject, and hence is established by an effective prohibition of this use of force, historical experience does not support the doctrine that collective security can be guaranteed only by a democratic legal order.

II. THE DIFFERENT DEGREES OF COLLECTIVE SECURITY

Since collective security is the function of a legal order, its organization is closely connected to the fundamental relationship established by the law between delict and sanction, the relationship between a definite action endangering the security of the community and the corresponding collective reaction. The action against which the collective reaction of an international security system is directed is usually characterized as "aggression." The definition of this concept may be narrowly or widely delimited. The degree of collective security depends mainly on the extent to which the reaction is centralized. However, the importance of this centralization depends on the scope of the actions against which the more or less centralized reaction is directed. Hence, the degree of collective security increases not only with the extent to which the reaction against certain harmful actions which endanger security is centralized, but also with the scope of the actions against which the reaction of the security system is directed. The definition of aggression [1] is particularly important in this aspect.

1. THE SCOPE OF PROTECTED INTERESTS

With regard to the security which the members of a national community enjoy, it makes a remarkable difference whether the social order constituting this community protects the members against every use of physical force by attaching sanctions to all of them or protects them only against that use of physical force which results in the destruction of life—that is, protects them by providing punishment only for murder. Even under the most primitive legal orders, murder is not the only crime. The development of the law goes hand in hand with an extension of the interests protected by sanctions directed against their violations. These violations may consist of conduct which does not have the character of a use of physical force. For example, non-payment of a debt and slander are both delicts under positive law, but neither constitutes a use of physical force. A legal order which provides for civil execution to be directed against the property of a debtor and imprisonment or fine to be inflicted upon a slanderer guarantees the security of the individual to a greater extent than a legal order which does not react against such conduct. All national legal orders provide for sanctions not only against delicts which consist of a use of force but also against other violations of interests. In other words, these national legal orders also protect interests which may be violated in a way other than by the use of force. However, no legal order can protect all the possible interests of its subjects. It is always up to the legal authority to decide which interests are worth being protected. Hence, there are always interests the violation of which is not a delict. This is another reason why the security guaranteed by the law is never absolute security.

Since the security guaranteed by the law consists of protection against the violation of certain interests,[2] and since this violation is not limited to the use of force, the question arises as to whether or not the concept of legal, and this means collective, security may properly be restricted to protection against the use of force. Such a definition can be maintained only if the term "force" is meant to include not only physical force but any illegal conduct—that is, any conduct by a subject of the legal order which is legally forbidden because of its harmful effect on another subject and which is therefore performed against or without the will of this subject. It is inevitable that this broader meaning of the term "force" be accepted if the sanctions provided for by positive law—the deprivation of life (capital punishment), of liberty (imprisonment), and of property (fine and civil execution)—are to be conceived of as a use of force or as enforcement actions. "Force," in the sense of physical force, is used to overpower an individual who offers resistance. This is normally the case under a primitive legal order when the execution of sanctions is decentralized—that is, when the execution is left to the individual members of the community. However, if the execution of sanctions is centralized, as under the law of a modern state, the individuals on whom these sanctions are inflicted normally offer no resistance, since the centralization of the execution of the law makes any resistance ineffective. Hence, these sanctions are a use of force (i. e., are enforcement measures, or, as it is usually formulated, are enforcing the law) insofar as they are carried out against or without the will of the subject concerned. Consequently, physical force is to be used only in the very exceptional case of resistance. A surgical operation performed by a physican with the consent of a patient is not a use of force. However, an action of the same kind performed against the will of a victim must certainly be considered to be an enforcement action. In this sense, force is implied in any illegal conduct of a person directed toward another person against or without the will of the latter. This means that any delict, just as any sanction, may be considered to be a use of "force." Thus the very concept of force, as it applies to the description of the essential

370624—57——2

function of the law which is to provide for a sanction against a delict—that is, to provide for a use of force to prevent a use of force—changes its meaning under the influence of centralization. Such centralization results in greater effectiveness of the law and the collective security guaranteed by it.[3]

2. THE CENTRALIZATION OF THE PROCEDURE FOR THE ASCERTAINMENT OF A DELICT (I. E., AN ILLEGAL USE OF FORCE) AND FOR DETERMINING THE PARTY RESPONSIBLE FOR IT

This centralization refers to the enforcement measures which are taken under the legal order as a reaction, which means as a sanction, against an illegal use of force, in either the narrower or wider sense of the term. If a sanction is to be taken as a reaction against an illegal act, the existence of such an act must first be ascertained. Only after this function is performed, can a sanction be executed. These are the two stages in which every legal order is applied. The system of collective security established by a legal order operates through the application of this order. Both stages may be more or less centralized, and the centralization of one is not necessarily accompanied by the centralization of the other. In principle, the centralization of the application of the law is independent of the centralization of the creation of the law—that is, independent of the establishment of the general legal norms to be applied in concrete cases. The centralization of the creation of the law is also important in determining the degree of collective security. This aspect of the problem will be discussed later.

The complete decentralization of the first stage of the application of the law is a characteristic feature of a primitive legal order which does not institute special organs competent to ascertain objectively the fact that the law has been violated, i. e., that an illegal use of force, an act of aggression, has taken place; nor are special organs competent to determine the individual or individuals responsible for such an act of aggression. The individuals involved in the conflict arising from a delict, either actually or allegedly committed, the conflict in which the two parties are those violated by the delict and those made responsible for it, must decide the questions concerned themselves. If there is no agreement between them that the law has been violated and no agreement on the compensation for the violated interest, and for various reasons such an agreement is rarely possible, the only way to settle the conflict is by the resort to force by one party against the other. The question remains undecided as to whether this use of force is legal or illegal, whether it is a sanction or a delict, and, consequently, whether it guarantees security or, on the other hand, is a factor of great insecurity. This is the most serious defect of a legal system in which the first stage of the application of the law, the ascertainment of the delict and the determination of the party responsible for it, is decentralized. It is more serious than decentralization in the second stage, the stage in which the use of force is authorized by the law as a sanction, although decentralization in this stage also renders the security function of the legal order problematical. The use of force operates as a sanction and hence acts as a guarantee of security satisfactorily if it normally results in overpowering the party against which it is directed. This result is not secured if the function concerned is decentralized. However, even if it is secured in some way, there must be a certain guarantee that the enforcement measures provided for by the law as sanctions are taken only against the party responsible for the delict, i. e., only against the party responsible for the illegal use of force, that is, against the aggressor. Consequently, first of all, there must be a legal procedure in which the decisive fact of the existence of a delict, i. e., of an illegal use of force, is established and in which the party responsible for the delict, the aggressor, is determined in an impartial way by a decision binding upon the parties. This is done by taking the power of deciding the fundamental questions as to who is right and who is wrong away from the parties involved in a conflict and by conferring this power on a special organ. In other words, this is done by centralizing the legal function which is the basis of all further steps leading to the enforcement of the law.

An essential condition for the impartiality of the organ concerned is that it be independent of the parties to the conflict as well as of other organs of the community, particularly the government of the community. If the organ enjoys such independence, it has the character of a tribunal, and an individual fulfilling this function has the character of a judge. Then the function of ascertaining the existence of the delict and determining the individual or individuals responsible for it is a judicial function. It is hardly possible to overestimate the importance of this step in establishing a system of collective security. As a matter of fact, historically it was the first step in the centralization of this system as applied within the legal community. Tribunals were the first central organs established within primitive society in time of peace. They functioned long before special legislative and executive organs came into existence. They were first created only by agreement of the parties to the conflict and only for particular cases. Later they became permanent institutions and assumed compulsory jurisdiction. This meant that they became competent to decide cases brought before them not only by an agreement of the parties but by one party or even by none of the parties but by a special organ, the public prosecutor. The functions of tribunals were originally restricted to deciding whether or not the law had been violated and who had been responsible for the violation. They could recommend an agreement concerning compensation for an illegally caused damage. However, they did not have the authority to order and make binding the execution of the sanction in case no such agreement could be reached, and they had no means of enforcing the law at their disposal. This function was left to the party injured by the delict ascertained by the tribunal. Its centralization was the last step in the development of that system of collective security which is the law of the modern state.

As long as only the judicial function but not the execution of the sanction is centralized, in other words, as long as the means for the enforcement of the law are not concentrated in the hands of a special organ strong enough to overpower any delinquent—that is, to render successful resistance against the executive force of the community impossible in principle—cases where the law remains unenforced because the delinquent is more powerful than his opponent may be quite frequent. Hence, only a relatively low degree of security is reached. Nevertheless, the importance of a centralization restricted to the establishment of tribunals without the centralization of the execution of the sanction should not be underestimated. There is an essential difference between a situation in which the question as to which party in a conflict between two parties is right and which is wrong cannot be decided in an objective and impartial way and a situation in which it can. The chance of the law being obeyed is much greater in the second situation than in the first even if the law cannot be enforced by a central organ of the community. If a party is declared to be wrong by decision of an impartial tribunal, it will be much less inclined to enforce its illegal claim against a party declared to be right by the tribunal or to refuse to comply with the legal claim of this party. Where courts competent to decide this question exist, the readiness of the parties to a conflict to settle this question by agreement is much greater than it is under a social order which authorizes each party to decide this question for itself, thus enabling it to justify any enforcement action taken for the realization of its interests. The moral power of courts has played a decisive part in the evolution of the law, and it remains greatly important for the efficacy of a legal order and thus for a collective security established by it. From the point of view of this security, the value of the centralization of the executive function remains problematical if this centralization is not preceded by the centralization of the judicial function. In other words, this value is problematical if the employment of force by the central organ of the community is not determined by the decisions of independent tribunals applying pre-established law, if this central organ can use its power not to maintain or restore this law but to realize political interests not necessarily in conformity with this law. In the field of internal relations there are indeed systems of collective security which correspond to this type of organization.[4]

3. THE PREVENTION OF THE ILLEGAL USE OF FORCE BY THE PEACEFUL SETTLEMENT OF CONFLICTS

The centralization of the first of the two functions of the application of the law—the ascertainment by special organs of the violation of the law and the determination of the party responsible for it—is the most effective means of bringing about the peaceful settlement of conflicts. The establishment of such organs is particularly effective in this respect if, as is usually the case, they are also competent to recommend, or even to order, the guilty party to repair the wrong by restoring the situation which existed before the delict was committed, or, if this is not possible, to compensate for the illegally caused damage. If the party concerned complies with this recommendation or order, the use of force both by the parties to the conflict and by the community (i. e., the use of force as a sanction) is actually prevented.

Prevention of the illegal use of force is usually distinguished from its repression by the legal use of force, i. e., the execution of sanctions. However, this distinction is only relative. The purpose of repressive measures taken in a concrete case as a reaction against an illegal use of force is to prevent, by deterrence, the illegal use of force in the future. If special organs for the peaceful settlement of conflicts are established, and if the legal use of force (i. e., the execution of a sanction) is permitted only after these organs have ascertained the existence of the delict (i. e., an illegal use of force) and determined the party responsible for it (i. e., the aggressor), and only after this party has refused to comply with their decision, does the function of these organs form a preparatory stage in the total procedure of applying the law. This is just the procedure established within a system of collective security as a reaction against an illegal use of force (i. e., an act of aggression). If there are no such organs established, a peaceful settlement of conflicts is possible only on the basis of a voluntary agreement by the parties involved in the conflict. However, for reasons already discussed, such an agreement can rarely be reached.

As has been pointed out, the organ competent to ascertain the existence of a delict and to determine the party responsible for it may or may not have the character of a tribunal. If it does not have this character, it may be authorized by the legal order to settle the conflicts brought before it by applying not only the existing law, pre-established by custom or legislation, but also other norms, especially principles of political convenience. Such a quasi-judicial organ may have the power only to make recommendations to the parties concerning the settlement of a conflict, so that a conflict can be settled finally only by an agreement of the parties which comply with the recommendations. However, if the decision of the quasi-judicial organ is legally binding upon the parties, it constitutes an individual legal norm, valid only for this particular case. If the organ has the character of a tribunal, it is usually authorized to apply only the existing, i. e., pre-established law. However, it is possible that a legal order may also authorize a tribunal to decide conflicts brought before it by applying norms other than those of the existing law. For example, a tribunal may be authorized to apply principles of justice or equity.[5] This means that the tribunal would be authorized by the existing law to create new law for the case at hand. This principle has the advantage of rendering the legal system more flexible, for it enables the tribunal to adapt the law in each case to those particular circumstances which were not, and often could not have been, foreseen by the legislator.

There can be no doubt of the fact that from the point of view of security it is preferable to have conflicts decided by judicial decisions legally binding upon the parties to the conflict. Furthermore, security is guaranteed to a higher degree if the individual norm, constituted by the judicial decision, is determined, as far as possible, by pre-established general norms of positive law rather than by principles of justice or equity. Since these principles—in contradistinction to the norms of positive law, especially those established by legislation—are not objectively discernible, the power to resolve conflicts of interest according to principles of justice or equity means that the conflict is decided according to the subjective opinion of a judge as to what is just or equitable. Hence, the advantage of flexibility is gained at the expense of security, for there is a higher degree of uncertainty concerning the content of the decision the tribunal will issue, and that means a lower degree of security, than there would be if the tribunal were bound by pre-established general norms of positive law. If these pre-established norms were applied, the decision could be foreseen, at least to a certain extent, by the parties concerned. This is the connection between the collective security guaranteed in general by a legal order and the above mentioned "legal security" (*Rechtssicherheit*) established by the so-called rule-of-law principle.

It should, however, be kept in mind that the difference between a judicial decision applying pre-established general norms of positive, i. e., customary or statutory law, and a judicial decision applying principles of justice or equity, is not as essential as it is usually assumed to be. The assumption that there exists an essential difference between the two kinds of judicial decision is based on the idea that the judicial application of positive law has a merely declaratory character, whereas the judicial application of principles of justice or equity has a constitutive character, insofar as by the latter a positive obligation and the corresponding right is created or abolished, whereas the former has no such effect. According to this view a judge in deciding a case by applying positive law does not create an obligation and the corresponding right which did not exist, nor does he abolish an obligation and the corresponding right which did exist prior to the decision. In a dispute, either the existence of the fact to which an undisputed rule of law is to be applied or the existence of a rule of law to be applied to an undisputed fact may be disputed. The judicial decision, according to this view, only ends the dispute by ascertaining in an authoritative way either the existence or non-existence of the disputed fact, which implies that the undisputed rule of law is or is not applicable in this case, or by ascertaining the existence or non-existence of the disputed rule of law. Thus the judicial decision transforms, so to speak, disputed law into undisputed and, finally, undisputable law. The fallacy of this doctrine is that the authoritative ascertainment of a disputed fact as well as the ascertainment of a disputed rule of law is not merely a declaratory but a highly constitutive act.

In case a fact is disputed, the judicial decision, ascertaining that the fact has occurred, legally "creates" the fact and consequently constitutes the applicability of the general rule of law referring to the fact. In the sphere of law the fact "exists," even if in the sphere of nature the fact has not occurred. If a court of last resort declares that an individual has concluded with another individual a contract and has not fulfilled it or that an individual has committed murder, the disputed nonfulfillment of the contract or the commission of murder are legal facts, even if in reality the defendant has not concluded a contract or the accused has not committed the murder. As a "legal" fact—that is, as a fact to which the law attaches certain consequences (duties, rights, sanctions)—the fact, and accordingly its consequences, are "created" by the judicial decision; and it is only as a legal fact that it counts. In case a general rule of law is disputed, because the existence or the meaning of the rule is doubtful, the decision of the court interpreting the legal order or a special rule of that order is not less creative than the authentic and definitive ascertainment of a fact as the essential condition of the application of a general legal rule. The application of a general norm to a concrete case is by its very nature an individualization of this norm. That the judicial decision is legally binding upon the parties means that it is a legal norm, an individual legal norm constituting an individual obligation and the corresponding individual right of the respective parties. This individual legal norm is created by the judicial act.

This becomes particularly evident when the meaning of a general rule of law is disputed. There are almost always two and sometimes even several different interpretations which, from a logical point of view, are equally possible. This means that the existing rule of law is a framework of several different rules. By choosing one of them the law-applying organ excludes the others and thus creates, for the concrete case, a new law. Prior to the decision, the question of law with respect to the dispute could be answered by referring to several rules equally applicable to the case, but after the decision the question can be answered only by referring to one of them, the one chosen by the law-applying organ.

There is, to be sure, a certain difference between a judicial decision by which one of several different interpretations of a pre-existing rule of positive law is chosen and a judicial decision by which a principle of justice or equity—that is, a norm—is applied which cannot be presented as one of several possible interpretations of a pre-existing rule of positive law. However, this difference is not as strongly marked as it seems to be. It is an undeniable fact that under the pretext of interpreting the pre-existing law courts have applied new principles and thus considerably changed the positive law. There is, indeed, only a difference of degree between a judicial decision applying a general norm of pre-established positive law and a judicial decision applying a new principle, whether this new principle is called justice or equity or something else. Even if a tribunal is not expressly authorized to decide cases according to principles of justice or equity, it is hardly possible to restrict its power completely to the application of the existing law, to prevent the tribunal from creating new law, especially if the tribunal is the supreme judicial organ and its decisions are endowed with the force of law—that is, if its decisions are final. The application of the law necessarily presupposes an interpretation of the law to be applied, and even remarkable changes in an existing law may be, and often are, presented merely as interpretations of the law.

4. LEGAL (JUSTICIABLE) AND POLITICAL (NON-JUSTICIABLE) CONFLICTS (DISPUTES)

The difference between settling a conflict by applying a general norm of pre-established law and settling it by having the organ competent to settle a conflict establish a new law has led to the distinction between two kinds of conflicts: legal conflicts and non-legal or political conflicts. "Legal" conflicts are considered to be those conflicts capable of being settled by the application of a general norm of pre-established law, and consequently capable of being settled by tribunals which normally are competent to settle conflicts only by the application of the existing law. "Political" conflicts, on the other hand, are considered to be those conflicts not capable of being settled in this way and consequently, if not settled by the use of force or by voluntary agreement of the parties, capable of being settled by the decision of an organ competent to create a new legal norm valid for the particular case. With respect to the capacity or incapacity of a conflict to be settled by applying pre-established law, legal conflicts are considered justiciable and political conflicts non-justiciable.

This distinction between legal or justiciable and political or non-justiciable conflicts presupposes the view that there are conflicts which cannot be settled by the application of a general norm of pre-established law because this law does not contain a norm referring to the subject concerned—that is, to the interest with respect to which the parties are in conflict. Hence, according to this view, in this respect there is a gap in the law. If there is a gap—that is, if there is no general legal norm capable of regulating a definite subject—a conflict concerning this subject cannot be settled by the application of the existing law. Consequently, if it cannot be settled by agreement of the parties, it can be settled peacefully only by a new legal norm to be created expressly by the judicial or quasi-judicial organ to cover this subject.

The view that there are conflicts which cannot be settled by applying the law which exists at the time a conflict arises because this law does not contain a general norm referring to the subject of the conflict is erroneous. Whatever the content of a positive legal order, there are only two possibilities with respect to applying it to a conflict. A so-called dispute, i. e., a conflict which does not yet imply the use of force and hence which can still be settled peacefully, consists of one party, the plaintiff, claiming that another party should behave in a certain way, while this other party, the defendant, refuses to so behave. One possibility is that the existing law does contain a norm imposing an obligation upon the defendant to behave in the way the plaintiff claims. In applying the existing law, then, the conflict would be decided in favor of the plaintiff. The other possibility is that the existing legal order does not contain a norm imposing an obligation upon the defendant to behave in the way the plaintiff claims. This would mean that the defendant would be legally free to behave as he pleases, the plaintiff's claim would have no legal basis, and, in applying the existing law to this case, the conflict would be decided in favor of the defendant, since the claim of the plaintiff would be rejected. There is no third possibility. This is the consequence of the fundamental principle of a positive law that what is not legally forbidden is legally permitted, or—formulated in a positive way—if a subject is not legally obliged to behave in a certain way, he is legally free to behave as he pleases, and this freedom is a legal freedom, a freedom guaranteed by the law. This means that the subject matter of a dispute is regulated by the existing legal order not only if this order contains a general norm obligating one party to behave in a certain way towards the other party with respect to this subject, but also if the legal order does not contain such a norm. If the legal order does not regulate a subject in a positive way, it regulates it in a negative way. Hence, there is no subject which is not regulated—either positively or negatively—by a positive legal order. There are no "gaps" in a positive legal order, or, what amounts to the same, there are no cases where the law-applying organ is forced to declare a *non liquet*, that is to say, refuse to decide a dispute because there is no general norm applicable to it.[5a] Under a positive legal order there are no conflicts which, on account of this subject, cannot be decided by the application of existing law and which, in this sense, are not legal or justiciable but political conflicts. The assumption that a positive legal order may not be applicable in a particular dispute because of a gap in this legal order is not correct. What is possible is that the application of the existing law to a concrete case is considered—from one point of view or another—to be not satisfactory, i. e., inequitable or unjust. The basic fact in the distinction between justiciable and non-justiciable conflicts, which is usually presented as a "gap" in the existing law, is really the difference between the positive law as it actually is established and a law as it should be established if it is to conform with equity or justice.[6] What is presented as a logical impossibility is in truth a moral-political insufficiency. Yet the judgment that the positive law, or its application in a concrete case, is inequitable or unjust is a subjective value judgment by which any application of the law may be disapproved. From the point of view of socialism, the entire legal order based on the capitalist principle of private property is unsatisfactory, inequitable and unjust. The application of the existing law is always unsatisfactory from the point of view of the party whose claim is not confirmed by the decision which applies the law and satisfactory from the point of view of the party in whose favor the dispute is decided. Since, under the law of modern states, tribunals have compulsory jurisdiction and consequently are competent to decide a dispute even if only one party submits the case to the tribunal, and since normally at least one party to a dispute may expect a favorable decision from an application of the existing law, a distinction between justiciable and non-justiciable disputes is of no practical importance.

The situation is different in the case of a primitive legal order under which tribunals are established by agreement of the parties to an existing dispute or, when already established prior to the coming into existence of a dispute, under which tribunals have no compulsory jurisdiction. Under these conditions, it is quite possible that one party, by an agreement with the other party, would be willing to establish a tribunal competent to settle their dispute, or, again by agreement, to submit the dispute to an already established tribunal, but only if this tribunal were authorized by the agreement to settle the dispute not in conformity with the existing law but by a decision in which principles of equity or justice would be applied. In this case, a distinction between disputes the parties want settled in conformity with existing law and disputes the parties want settled in another way would be justified. If it is this difference which is meant by the terms "legal" (justiciable) disputes and "political" (non-justiciable) disputes, the distinction is acceptable.

When a legislator, aware of the fact that he cannot foresee all possible circumstances and that consequently the application of the general norms he has established may not be appropriate in some cases, wants to authorize the tribunals not to apply these norms in these cases but to decide them by creating a new and more appropriate norm, he faces the problem of how to formulate the conditions under which the judge should be authorized to act, exceptionally, as a legislator. It is understandable that a legislator would not want to use the formula: if the application of the existing law is not satisfactory. This would be authorization for the judge to set aside the existing law whenever he does not consider this law to be satisfactory. On the other hand, this authorization cannot be restricted to cases in which the legislator considers the application of the existing law not to be satisfactory. Such a restriction would be possible only if the legislator could specify these cases, and if he could specify these cases he would not need to substitute the judge for the legislator. Hence the legislator has no choice but to allow the judge to decide for himself the question as to whether or not the application of the existing law to a concrete case is satisfactory. In effect, this means that the judge has the power to set aside the existing law and decide a case as legislator whenever he does not consider the application of the existing law to be appropriate, for there are always circumstances which may justify the opinion that the application of the existing law is not appropriate and hence which may lead to the assumption that the legislator had not foreseen them. In order to avoid a formula which expressly confers such an extraordinary power upon a judge, the fiction of gaps in the law is used. The legislator authorizes the judge to act as legislator if the existing law cannot be applied to a concrete case because this law does not contain a general norm applicable to the case. Psychologically, this fiction may have the intended effect of restricting the authority of the judge, for if the judge believes that he is allowed to act as legislator when the law *cannot* be applied, he will make use of this authorization only in very rare cases.[7]

That there are gaps in the existing law because there are elements in cases which the lawmaker has not foreseen is a juristic fiction. Its purpose is to justify the fact that legislative power is expressly conferred upon, or actually exercised by, judicial organs. This justification applies particularly within a legal and political system based on the principle of the separation of powers in general and on the principle of the rule-of-law in particular. The power of the judge to act as legislator constitutes a remarkable restriction of these principles. On the other hand, it is the nearest approach to the ideal of a perfectly flexible law. If the judge makes use of this power, his decisions cannot be foreseen. As previously noted, this means that the degree of security afforded by the law is reduced.

5. REMOVAL OF THE CAUSES OF THE ILLEGAL USE OF FORCE

A more effective method of preventing an illegal use of force and thus of guaranteeing collective security than the establishment of organs for the peaceful settlement of conflicts is the removal of circumstances which are the causes of these breaches of the peace. This point is stressed particularly in the political doctrine of socialism. Starting from the assumption that the main causes of the disturbance of a social order, the breach of internal peace, are of an economic nature, this doctrine arrives at the conclusion that only a social order which guarantees its subjects the complete satisfaction of their economic needs is able to guarantee peace and that collective security is thus essentially economic security. Since only a socialist economic system can afford this guarantee, only under socialism can collective security be achieved, and achieved to such a degree that no coercion is necessary to maintain the order. When the causes of a violation of the order are removed, there is no reason for using force as a reaction against such violations. The social order of perfect socialism, which is called communism, is not a coercive order which means that it is not a legal order. A communist society of the future would be a stateless and lawless society. The collective security of communism would not be legal security.

This is a utopian scheme because its presupposition that violations of a social order are caused only or mainly by its economic insufficiency is contrary to all our social experiences. Even in a capitalist society, ambition and sexual desire are motives of violence which are no less effective than hunger, and it is more than likely that they would play an even greater part in a society in which economic motives for illegal conduct were removed. It is therefore an illusion to believe that, even if it could secure the satisfaction of all economic needs, a social order could prevent all its violations (i. e., every possible breach of peace by an illegal use of force) and thus make the legal use of force, as a sanction, superfluous. Hence, this concept of absolute security is an illusion, the illusion of a social order without force. It is necessary to be aware of this illusion because in the theory of international security there is a strong tendency to consider economic circumstances as the main causes of war and hence to assume that preventing war by removing its economic causes is more important than attempting to prevent war by providing for repressive sanctions to be imposed by internationally organized enforcement actions. If the development of collective security under national law can teach us anything with respect to the development of collective security under international law—and there is good reason to assume that the latter will not be essentially different from the former—it is that there is a danger implied in overestimating the economic factors of social life and in underestimating the necessity for a coercive order, that is, in underestimating the necessity for repressive enforcement measures for the maintenance of peace, which means underestimating the necessity for a legal system of collective security.

6. THE CENTRALIZATION OF THE USE OF FORCE AS A SANCTION

As has been noted, the centralization of the second stage of the procedure by which the law is applied to a concrete violation, the execution of the sanction (i. e., the use of force as a reaction against the delict) either may or may not be preceded by the centralization of the first stage, the ascertainment of the delict and the determination of the party or parties responsible for it. Furthermore, the second stage may be carried out in different ways each constituting a different degree of centralization. Even without instituting special judicial or quasi-judicial organs for the first stage of the procedure, the legal order may authorize not only the subject directly injured by a delict but also the other members of the community to execute the sanctions—that is, to apply the enforcement measures provided for by the law. This means that in case the legal order is violated, all the members of the community have the right to assist the victim in his legitimate reaction against the violation of his rights—that is, against the illegal use of force which, in the narrower sense of the term, means only the illegal use of physical force, or, in the wider sense, means any violation of legally protected interests. Even the most primitive legal order must be interpreted as establishing this right. Under such a legal order, several subjects may enter an agreement for the purpose of mutual assistance. This agreement may impose an obligation upon the parties to the agreement to assist each other against an illegal use of force either on the part of subjects not parties to the agreement or on the part of members of the particular community constituted by the agreement. However, the legal order constituting the total community may impose such an obligation upon all its members, and even the most primitive legal orders do so, to protect the community against aggression from outside the community, especially against warlike enforcement action taken by a hostile community. Defense of an entire community against external aggression by another community requires organization, and organization means centralization, for example, the establishment of a special organ to direct defense, the appointment of a military leader, etc. Military leaders were probably the first central organs and military organizations for either defensive or aggressive purposes the first attempts at centralization in the process of social evolution. In the past, the centralization of the use of force by one community in its war against another community undertaken to guarantee external security preceded the centralization of the use of force within the community guaranteeing internal security.

The extent of the obligation imposed upon the members of a total or partial community to come to the assistance of the victim of an illegal use of force committed within this community may differ. The members of the community may be obliged to assist the victim only by means short of the use of physical force, or they may be obliged to give assistance by employing all appropriate means including the use of physical force. Whether the members of the community are only authorized or whether they are obliged to participate in the defense of the immediate victim, and whether their assistance is or is not limited to certain measures, the defense has a collective character. It is collective and no longer merely individual or self-defense. To speak of collective self-defense, a term used in Article 51 of the Charter of the United Nations, is misleading. The member of a community who, without being injured himself, comes to the assistance of the victim of an illegal use of force (in either the narrower or wider sense of the term) does not defend himself, he defends another. Only if the individual is identified with the other members of the group to which he belongs can the defense of one member by the others be called collective self-defense. However, such identification, if admissible at all, is justified only within a group in which the members are so closely connected that their thinking and feeling have a thoroughly collectivistic character. This is the case within a primitive family or tribe but not within an international community like the United Nations. Collective defense against an illegal use of force constitutes collective security. However, it is a very low degree of security as long as neither the first nor the second stage of the application of the law is centralized—that is, as long as neither special organs for the peaceful settlement of conflicts nor special organs for the legal use of force provided for as sanctions are established—and the principle of self-help prevails.

The establishment of a judicial or quasi-judicial organ for the peaceful settlement of conflicts is a first attempt to overcome this. However, the decisive step in eliminating the principle of self-help is the institution of a central organ whose competence refers to the execution of the sanctions as reactions against violations of the legal order, or, what amounts to the same, against an illegal use of force in the widest sense of the term. This executive organ may or may not be a government, or it may or may not be subordinated to a government—that is, the community may or may not be so centralized that it has the character of a state. Even if the executive organ does not have the character of a government or is not placed under a government, it may be bound in the exercise of its function by the decisions of an independent tribunal, so that it may be able to take action only in case the tribunal has ascertained the existence of an illegal use of force, and only against a party which the tribunal has found responsible. However, an executive organ may have the power to decide these questions for itself, not in conformity with the existing law as a tribunal is supposed to decide, but by applying principles of political convenience. The organ may be competent only to make recommendations to the members of the community concerning the exercise of their right, or the fulfillment of their obligation, to assist the victim of an illegal use of force. At a higher stage in the development of collective security, its decisions are binding upon the members of the community. As long as the executive organ does not have its own means to perform enforcement actions at its direct disposal, it can only direct the actions which the members of the community take to assist the victim of an illegal use of force either by making recommendations to the members of the community or by making decisions binding on the members of the community. In this case, the difference between this stage of collective security and the stage in which the principle of self-help still prevails is not very great. This is particularly true because the members of the community must remain armed in order to be able to exercise their right, or fulfill their obligation, to assist the victim of an illegal use of force. However, the executive organ may have a police force at its direct disposal. A police force is a body of armed individuals professionally trained and organized for the purpose of applying the enforcement measures provided for by the law as reactions against an illegal use of force by a member of the community. If the executive organ has such a force at its disposal, it can effect the disarmament of the members of the community, one of the most important conditions for an effective system of collective security. Only then is the complete centralization of the force monopoly of the community, and thus the highest degree of collective security, achieved. This stage has been reached only within the modern state.

It is important to note that the disarmament of the members of a national legal community is effected by the establishment of a police force rather than by express prohibitions concerning the possession of arms. Besides, such prohibitions are never absolute. Under the law of modern states, the legal possession of arms, or at least of certain arms, by private persons is normally possible if an individual obtains a special license granted by the administration. In certain military organizations, for example in the militia system of Switzerland, persons belonging to the reserve are obliged to keep their guns in their possession even during the period they are not in active service.

7. SELF-DEFENSE

With the establishment of a police force at the disposal of a central organ accompanied by the disarmament or effective control of the armament of the members of a community, the centralization of the force monopoly of a community approaches its culmination. Nevertheless even at this stage the principle of self-help is not completely eliminated. It is preserved in the right of self-defense which individuals have even under the law of the modern state, the order guaranteeing the highest possible degree of collective security. The right of self-defense is considered to be an application of the principle of self-preservation which is an inherent or innate right of man. According to the natural-law doctrine, the right of self-defense authorizes an individual to protect his life, person and sometimes his property by the use of physical force against an attempt by another individual to inflict injury on him by an illegal use of physical force. This right may include the use of physical force for the purpose of defending not only one's own life, person and property but also the life, person and property of each of the members of one's own family. It may be exercised not only in case of an actual but also in case of an imminent illegal use of physical force. However, it may be exercised only in case of necessity—that is, only if there is no other possibility of defending one's legitimate interest.

The right of self-defense presupposes that, in principle, the use of physical force is legally forbidden. Hence, the use of physical force in the exercise of self-defense constitutes an exception to this prohibition. Under a social order which does not contain such a prohibition, no right of self-defense, as the right to react by the use of physical force against an illegal use of physical force, can exist. Under a primitive legal order which does not centralize the employment of force, the right of self-defense is implied in the principle of self-help which is the reaction of an individual against any violation of his rights. Even under a legal order which establishes a centralized force monopoly, self-defense is the indispensable minimum of self-help. It is indispensable because a centralized security organization cannot function at the same time that an illegal use of force is attempted. Since self-defense is permitted only as a reaction against an illegal use of force, its exercise involves a certain risk if a legal authority must eventually confirm its lawfulness. If it is lawful, its exercise may be interpreted as a decentralized function of the legal community acting through the individual who enforces the law of the community by using force in defending himself.

There is a certain relationship between the right of self-defense and the delict of aggression. If the right of self-defense is the right to react by the use of physical force against an act of aggression as an illegal use of physical force, the right of self-defense and the delict of aggression are complementary: where there is an act of aggression there is a right of self-defense; and there is a right of self-defense only where there is an act of aggression. But within a system of col-

370624—57——3

lective security the right of self-defense may be restricted to the reaction against an illegal use of physical force, whereas the legal order constituting the security organization may prohibit as acts of aggression not only the illegal use of physical force but other violations of protected interests. Then there may be acts of aggression without a corresponding right of self-defense.[8]

8. THE CENTRALIZATION OF THE LAW-CREATING FUNCTION (THE PEACEFUL CHANGE OF ESTABLISHED LEGAL RELATIONS)

The development of national law is characterized by the fact that the centralization of the law-creating function has been preceded by the centralization of the law-applying function. Long after tribunals and central executive organs had come into existence, the law of states was created, in a completely decentralized way, by custom. The establishment of legislative organs was the last step in the process of centralization which led to the law of the modern state. Even when parliamentary bodies assumed the power to create general legal norms, great and important parts of the legal order preserved the character of customary law, e. g., the common law in the Anglo-Saxon countries. This is evidence of the fact that from the point of view of collective security the centralization of the law-creating function by establishing legislative organs is of minor importance. However, in the theory of international security, it is still argued, and the argument is considered to be of great weight, that the establishment of courts and the organization of collective enforcement actions are useless as long as there are no international legislative organs to afford the possibility for a peaceful change of established legal relations which have become unbearable for one party for one reason or another. It is a widespread view that centralizing the law-applying function without centralizing the law-creating function results in conserving the *status quo*, and that the attempt to maintain existing legal relations in spite of changing power relations inevitably constitutes a serious threat to the peace, which means a serious threat to security. This argument is not confirmed by the development of national law which has actually led to the relatively highest degree of collective security. Those who apply this argument underestimate the decisive influence tribunals exercise on the formation of the law, especially when these tribunals have compulsory jurisdiction. The development of customary law stems mainly from the practice of courts; nor is statutory law immune from being changed in the judicial process. Threats to the internal peace of a community arise from concrete situations, especially those established by contracts, rather than from the insufficient content of general norms. In order to remove the danger implied in a concrete situation, as a rule it is not necessary to change these general norms by a legislative act. The danger may be removed by creating an individual norm providing a single exception valid only for the concrete case. This is the proper task of a tribunal. It is not the proper task of a legislative organ whose function is to create general legal norms. If such a judicial decision creating an individual norm constitutes a precedent followed in other judicial decisions of similar cases, a law-creating custom is established, and the general norm referring to these cases is abolished and replaced by a new general norm adapted to the circumstances which caused the precedent. The change of a general norm is not justified if its application proves to be unsatisfactory in only one case. It is justified if the circumstances which make its application unsatisfactory exist in several cases. It is difficult to decide whether the adaptation of the existing law to changing circumstances is better achieved by the function of the legislative organ within a system of statutory law or by the practice of courts within a system of customary law. However, there is no question that the necessary adaptation, and hence peaceful change, of legal relations which have become a threat to the peace is possible without the establishment of a legislative organ. The adaptation can be made by the courts, provided that the courts have sufficient jurisdiction to exercise this function.

9. UNIVERSAL AND REGIONAL SECURITY ORGANIZATIONS

A security organization whose members are individual human beings is universal if it comprises the whole of mankind; it is regional if it comprises only a part of mankind. In this sense the difference between a universal and a regional security organization is that of a total and a partial organization. However, by "regional" security organization may be meant not only a partial organization but also an organization of individuals living on definite territory, or an organization whose security functions are limited to a certain geographical area. As long as no world state exists, security organizations whose members are individual human beings must have a regional character. The states which exist today and which are constituted by national legal orders are regional security organizations in the sense that they are organizations of only parts of humanity and that their members are living on a definite territory. The security organization of a state guarantees not only internal security, that is, protection against internal aggression, the use of force by one subject directed against another subject of the state, but also external security, that is, protection against external aggression: use of force by another state. The internal security guaranteed by a state organization is evidently of a much higher degree than the external security it can insure; the latter reaches its highest degree only within a world state where, as a result of the universality of the organization, external aggression is excluded. Even if the world state had the character of a federal state within which the member states were not completely disarmed, so that the use of armed force by one member state against another were not absolutely excluded, this act of aggression would be, from the viewpoint of the world state, an act of internal aggression. Such an act of aggression, however, would risk an effective reaction by the police force of the world state and hence probably would be prevented by the organization. Hence the tendency toward the universality of the security organization, the demand for a world state.

The international community constituted by general international law is indeed a universal security organization, but its subjects are states. This does not mean that individual human beings are not its members, but it does mean that individual human beings are only indirectly (as subjects of states) members of the international security organization. As has been pointed out, collective security is always the security of individual human beings, and the acts of states regulated by an international security system are always acts performed by individual human beings. However, these individual acts are not determined directly by the legal order constituting the security system, as is the case within the national security organization of the state, but indirectly as the international legal order constituting the international security system determines these individual acts through the intermediary of the national legal orders.

The universal security organization constituted by general international law, because of its high degree of decentralization, guarantees only the lowest possible degree of collective security (provided the *bellum justum* principle is positive law).[9] Where there exists a higher degree of centralization and hence a higher degree of collective security in the relations between states, it is established by particular international law, that is, by treaties to which not all of the states are contracting parties, such as the Covenant of the League of Nations and the Charter of the United Nations. Insofar as the one did not and the other does not comprise all the states of the world, the one was and the other is only a regional, not a universal, security organization. But since the overwhelming majority of the states of the world were members of the League and are members of the United Nations, and since both organizations were established with a tendency toward universality and the purpose to guarantee world peace, they may be considered as quasi-universal security organizations. The question as to whether and in what sense within such quasi-universal international security organizations so-called regional security organizations are possible, shall be discussed later.[10]

NOTES

1. *Cf.* pp. 66 ff.

2. L. Ehrlich (*Collective Security*, p. 154) said: "Security, in the legal sense of the term, means the actual protection of the interests which are safeguarded by the existing legal system." This is a tautological definition. If interests are safeguarded by the law, they are protected by the law. Security, in the legal sense of the term (and there is no other sense in which this term may be considered), means simply the protection of certain interests by the law.

3. As we shall see later, the question of the narrower or broader meaning of the term "force" is also important in defining the right of self-defense—that is, the right to use force against some kind of aggression—and in interpreting the prohibition against the "threat or use of force" stipulated by the Charter of the United Nations. *Cf.* p. 57.

4. *Cf.* pp. 120 ff.

5. It is usual to distinguish between justice and equity; but there is hardly any difference between them insofar as equity is supposed to be—like justice—a system of norms different from positive law, conceived of as pre-established general norms created by custom, legislation or international agreement. In a study on "Justice and Equity in International Relations" (*Justice and Equity in the International Sphere.* The New Commonwealth Institute Monographs, Series B, No. 1, 1936, pp. 1–13), Gustav Radbruch, one of the leading legal philosophers, admits that the principles of justice and equity are identical (p. 5) but tries to differentiate two normative systems by the method of acquiring the knowledge of the principles concerned. The specific method by which the principles of justice called "equity" are established is the case method of the Anglo-American legal systems. This method does not consist, as Radbruch asserts, in the general principle of justice, applied by the tribunal, being derived from the nature of the concrete case—that is, by an inference from that what actually is to that what ought to be, or—what amounts to the same—from a fact to a norm or from social reality to a social value. Such an inference is based on a logical fallacy; nor can such a result be achieved by "intuition." Intuition is a highly subjective, uncontrollable faculty of the human mind. Two different judges, starting from the same case, by their intuition arrive at wholly different and even contradictory principles of justice or equity. To leave the decision of a case to the intuition of the judge means to leave it to his unlimited discretion, and this is indeed what the case method, at least to a certain extent, amounts to. It is characterized by the fact that the first case is decided by the application of a principle which the judge, within his subjective discretion, considers as just. This decision becomes a precedent and, in this way, finally a rule of customary law. It is the specific function of the case method to transform justice (or equity), and that means a principle which in the first case of its application is considered by the judge as a principle of justice or equity, into a rule of positive, namely customary, law which determines the decision of the following cases. However, in deciding the first case the judge is not determined by a pre-established general rule of positive law. The position of the

judge is the same as that of a legislator who, too, transforms a principle which he considers just into positive law. It is in this respect that the case method, as the specific method of customary law, differs from the method of statutory law according to which no judicial decision is possible without a pre-established general rule of positive law. Within this legal system, the rule-of-law principle has no exception, whereas within a system of customary law there are necessarily cases, the precedential cases, which are to be decided without a pre-established general rule of positive law being applied.

It is of the greatest importance to be aware that the principle of justice or equity applied in these cases is not—as it is usually assumed to be as a matter of course—an objectively ascertainable value, a norm the cognition of which can be acquired independently of the subjective preferences of the judging subject in the same way that the knowledge of the rules of positive law is obtained. These rules are objectively ascertainable because they are established by legislation, custom or treaties—that is, by facts perceptible by our senses under the control of our reason. However, principles of justice or equity, applied in a first case, before being transformed into a rule of customary law, are not established by objectively ascertainable facts but are, in the last analysis, based on highly subjective, emotional elements of the human mind. Consequently, there is not one justice or equity as there is only one positive law—one French, one American, one international law—but many different and contradictory systems of justice or equity, each of them claiming validity for the same territorial and personal sphere. The idea that there exists only one justice or equity is one of the most misleading illusions, and to speak of justice or equity—as most writers do—as if there were only one system of norms properly called justice or equity is either an intellectual insincerity or a naive, but unpardonable, ignorance. Hence, to establish a tribunal of equity means: to establish a tribunal endowed with the power of deciding—at least first cases—according to its free discretion. The objection that even such a tribunal should be directed by considerations of general welfare, commonweal, interest of the community, and the like, does not hold. All these terms designate values which are no less subjective than justice or equity.

5a. It has been objected that the denial of the possibility of gaps in the law and hence of a *non liquet* is limited to decisions of disputes; that if the parties without asserting any right in the matter of their conflicting interests ask a court to decide the case, it may be that the court is not able to do so. Such a case may arise, *e. g.*, when the frontier between two estates or two state territories is in question, insofar as there is between those parts of the two estates or state territories which are not in question a piece of land the legal status of which is uncertain. In these cases, too, there are only two possibilities. Either the court can ascertain facts which according to the existing law constiute property or sovereignty and consequently can, in applying the existing law, draw a definite line between the two estates or state territories. Or the court cannot ascertain such facts because none of the parties can prove that it has with respect to the piece of land in question performed acts which constitute property or sovereignty. Then the legal status of the piece of land in question is that of *res nullius* or of stateless territory, both statuses regulated by national and international law respectively. The court, in applying this law, has to make a decision to this effect. There is no gap in the law, but there may be a gap in the knowledge of facts. But facts which are not known to the law-applying organ and hence cannot be ascertained by it, *legally* do not exist.

6. Sometimes the term "gap" in law is used to characterize merely technical defects in the drafting of a statute, e. g., if a statute provides that an assembly must elect its chairman, and that it must be convoked by its chairman, but contains no provision concerning the convocation of the first meeting of the assembly. However, such technical "gaps" are not decisive as far as the above mentioned doctrine is concerned.

7. The above mentioned fiction is used in the famous paragraph 1 of the Swiss Civil Code which provides that in default of a provision of statutory law applicable (to the case at hand) the judge shall decide in accordance with customary law; and in default of a rule of customary law in accordance with the rules he would establish if he had to legislate.

8. *Cf.* pp. 59 ff.

9. *Cf.* pp. 34 eff.

10. *Cf.* pp. 258 ff.

III. INTERNATIONAL SECURITY

1. COLLECTIVE SECURITY UNDER GENERAL INTERNATIONAL LAW

(a) The *Bellum Justum* Principle

As pointed out in the first part of this study, international security is the collective security which states enjoy within the international community constituted by international law. As it is an essential function of any legal order to afford security to the persons subjected to it, general international law, i. e., the system of norms binding upon all the states of the world, must also fulfill this function, provided that it is law in the specific sense, which means law in the same sense as national law, the law of an individual state.

The nature of the normative order called "international law" may be, and actually is, described in different ways. From the considerations in the first part of this study, it follows that this description depends mainly on the answers to two preliminary questions: (1) does this order have a coercive character—that is, do its norms provide for the use of force as a sanction, as a reaction against a violation of certain interests of the states, the persons subjected to this order; and (2) is the use of physical force, which in international relations means armed force, permitted only as a sanction? In other words, is any use of armed force resorted to by one state against another to be considered as illegal, i. e., as a delict, if it does not have the character of a sanction?

As far as the first question is concerned, there is no doubt that there are enforcement measures provided for by general international law to protect certain interests of the states. General international law authorizes the states to react against a violation of these interests by acts called reprisals. Reprisals are usually defined as measures which are normally illegal but are permitted exceptionally as a reaction by one state against a violation of its rights by another state. A reprisal constitutes an interference by one state in the otherwise protected sphere of interests of another. A reprisal is a forcible interference, insofar as it is undertaken against the will of the state against which the action is directed, and in this sense, it is an enforcement measure, the term "force" used in its wider sense. A reprisal may even involve the use of physical, i. e., armed, force, as, for example, in case of a so-called pacific blockade. However, this forcible interference in the sphere of interests of another state must be limited to the violation of certain interests, in contradistinction to that unlimited interference undertaken by the armed force of a state against another state which is called war. A reprisal may be interpreted as being a sanction, because a reprisal is provided for by general international law as a reaction against a violation of the law. Hence, general international law may be considered to be a coercive order—that is, a system of norms providing for coercive measures as sanctions.

As far as the second question is concerned, the answer is rather doubtful. It is true that the limited use of force is considered to be illegal, i. e., a delict, if it is not a reaction against a violation of the law—that is, if it is not a sanction. However, as far as the unlimited use of armed force, war, is concerned, two diametrically opposed opinions are advocated in the theory of international law. According to one, war is never a delict under general international law. As a consequence of its sovereignty, every state may resort to war against another state for any reason whatsoever without violating international law, unless a state has assumed an obligation in a treaty which restricts its freedom of action in this respect. Furthermore, war is not a sanction, for general international law does not provide for war, as it does provide for reprisals as specific reactions against the illegal conduct of a state. According to this opinion, only a limited use of force, but not an unlimited use of armed force, is a delict if it is not a sanction. Hence, under general international law there is no force monopoly of the community constituted by this law, not even a decentralized one, analogous to the force monopoly established by national law, constituting a community of individuals. A state which resorts to war against another state, even if it does so in defense against an attack, cannot be considered to act as an organ of the international community enforcing the law against a violator. In a war between two states, whatever the motive or purpose of either enforcement action, there is no legal difference between the use of force by one state and the use of force by the other—both are equally legal. The question of which of the belligerents is the "aggressor" is irrelevant. Consequently, under a general international law which does not prohibit the resort to war, in case of war there can be no right of self-defense in the specific sense of this term, which means no right to use armed force against an illegal use of armed force. Since a war of aggression is not illegal, a counterwar is not a reaction against an illegal use of armed force. Only a reprisal taken against an illegal action involving the use of limited force may be considered to be an exercise of the right of self-defense.

Reprisals are not possible against an aggressive war because in this case they are not directed against an illegal use of force. If international law does not prohibit the resort to war, it is hardly possible to maintain that it imposes upon the states the mutual obligation to respect their territorial integrity and political independence. The fact that war, as an unlimited use of armed force for the purpose of overpowering the opponent and enforcing upon him the conditions of peace, is not illegal, is incompatible with such an obligation. It is even doubtful whether it can be assumed that under general international law states have any rights—that is, any legally protected interests—if general international law does not prohibit that unlimited interference in the sphere of interests of a state which is called war.

If general international law does not stipulate the obligation that states must refrain from resorting to war except as a reaction against violation of the law, the mutual relations of states under this normative order are not very different from their mutual relations in a state of international anarchy. However, it must be admitted that only if war is not prohibited, which means only if there is no difference between a legal and an illegal war and all belligerents have the same legal status, is the usual interpretation of the status of neutrality consistent. According to this interpretation, neutral states, the states not involved in a war, have equal obligations and equal rights in relation to both belligerents. Strict impartiality of the neutral towards the belligerents is the essential element of the institution of neutrality. Furthermore, it must be admitted that only if all the belligerents are legally on an equal footing is it appropriate to terminate a war by a treaty, a so-called peace treaty concluded between two partners enjoying equality of rights.[1]

The opinion that under general international law war is neither a delict nor a sanction is advocated by the majority of writers on international law. If this view is correct, general international law is not law in the specific sense of the term as defined in the first part of this study. Since it is far from realizing the tendency toward a force monopoly of the community, since it does not forbide that use of armed force which is called war, this normative order does not guarantee any degree of security to the states subjected to it. International security can be established only within particular international organizations on the basis of treaties imposing upon the contracting parties—at least—the obligation not to resort to war, i. e., the use of armed force, in their mutual relations except as a reaction against a state which has resorted to war in violation of the constituent treaty—that is, except as a reaction against an aggressor.

According to the opposite opinion, such an obligation is already established by general international law which forbids the resort to war in principle and permits it only as a reaction against a violation of the law—that is, only against a definite conduct of states determined by international law. Like the limited use of force, which is called a reprisal, the unlimited use of force, which is called war, is legal only as a sanction. If it is not a sanction, it is a delict. This is the doctrine of *bellum justum* or just war, the term "just" meaning legal or in conformity with positive law.

Only if this doctrine is accepted, can general international law be conceived of as law in the specific sense of the term. By prohibiting war and by permitting this unlimited use of force as well as the limited use of force, reprisals, only as sanctions, general international law establishes a force monopoly of the international community, although it is only a decentralized force monopoly. A state resorting to reprisals or war in conformity with international law may be conceived of as enforcing the law, acting as an organ of the community constituted by this law. In a war between two states, only one of the two enforcement actions can be considered to be legal. The other is illegal. Hence, if the *bellum justum* principle is recognized, it is necessary to distinguish between these two actions which may be termed war and counterwar. Consequently, the problem of "aggression," as the illegal use of armed or any other kind of force, is of the greatest importance. If it is necessary to distinguish between a legal and an illegal war, it is impossible to maintain the usual definition of war as a contest between two or more states by their armed forces—that is, as a bilateral action. Only one of the two actions constituting the contest is legal or illegal. Hence, war must be defined as an enforcement action involving the unlimited use of armed force, and the unlimited use of armed force has to be considered to be war even if it is not opposed by a counterwar.[2] War must be considered to be an employment of force directed by one state against another without regard to the counteraction of the latter, not only when war is a delict, but also when war is a sanction.[3] This is of particular importance in case war is a collective enforcement action involving the use of armed force taken by an international security organization as a reaction against a violation of international law. By calling such an action a "police action," we cannot deprive it of the character of war. If there is no legal equality in the relations between the two belligerents, the legal consequence of the status of neutrality may not be the strict impartiality of the nonbelligerents in relation to the belligerents. Hence, the possibility of terminating a war by concluding a treaty between a state which is trying to enforce the law and a state which is the lawbreaker becomes problematical.[4]

According to the *bellum justum* principle, not only is the immediate victim of an international delict permitted to make war against a delinquent state but the other states who are members of the international community are authorized to assist the victim in its legitimate reaction against a violation of the law. If the *bellum justum* principle is part of general international law, this legal order guarantees a certain degree of security to the states as members of the international community. However, it is a very low degree of security, for the international legal order is completely decentralized. It does not institute special organs for the legal functions of creating and applying the law. There are no courts, no executive and no legislative organs under general international law. All the legal functions are left to the individual states. If there is a conflict between them, the states involved must decide whether or not the law has been violated and which state is responsible for the violation. If agreement cannot resolve these questions, each state may act in conformity with its own answer—that is, it may or may not resort to either reprisals or war. Even if the law is on its side, a state will not initiate such an enforcement action if its opponent is more powerful. However, if an enforcement action taken by one state meets with resistance in the form of an enforcement action by another state, the question as to which of these two actions is a sanction and which a delict remains open. For these reasons, many writers consider the *bellum justum* principle useless as long as a certain minimum of centralization, at least the establishment of a tribunal competent to decide in an objective and impartial way which of the parties to a conflict is right and which is wrong, is not yet achieved. They further argue that even in this case the value of reprisals and war as sanctions remains highly problematical if their execution is left to the victim and to the voluntary assistance the victim may get from other states. Hence, the *bellum justum* doctrine advocated by the followers of the natural-law theory during the 17th and 18th centuries was almost completely abandoned during the 19th century and was reassumed only after the first World War, and then only by a relatively few scholars.

This doctrine then lost its importance because, as a result of this war, the use of armed force was forbidden by two treaties to which almost all of the states of the world were contracting parties: the Covenant of the League of Nations, 1919, (the first part of the peace treaties with Germany, Austria, Hungary and Bulgaria) and the

Treaty for the Renunciation of War, 1928, (the Pact of Paris or Kellogg-Briand Pact). If—in conformity with the opinion of the majority of writers on international law—the *bellum justum* principle is not considered to be part of general international law, the Covenant of the League of Nations together with the Kellogg-Briand Pact constitutes the first attempt in the field of international relations to establish a relatively universal system of collective security. As a matter of fact, it was only after the two treaties had come into force that the problem of collective security began to attract the attention of scholars and politicians and that the term became commonly used in the literature of international law.[5]

However, as an effect of the second World War, the Covenant of the League of Nations ceased to be valid. The second World War led to the conclusion by the majority of the states of the world of the Charter of the United Nations, by which not only war as the use of armed force but also the threat of force was forbidden and a system of international security established which displayed the highest degree of centralization reached until that time in the history of international law.

(b) Alliances and the Balance of Power

The idea of a universal international organization for collective security is directed against the policy of alliances in general and the so-called balance of power in particular. Though intended as a means of guaranteeing a kind of security to the states adhering to them, these policies have ultimately led to war.

Alliance treaties are usually concluded for the purpose of preserving the *status quo* in the relationships between allied states and other states by preventing the latter from expanding their power at the expense of the former. In this sense, they have a defensive character as they are directed mainly against an aggression on the part of states not parties to the alliance treaty. However, states may unite in an alliance not for the purpose of preserving but for the purpose of changing the *status quo* in their favor. The alliance then has an aggressive character. In a concrete case, it is hardly possible to distinguish a defensive alliance from an aggressive one, because the purpose of an alliance depends on the intention of the allied governments, and an aggressive intention is never admitted. The official purpose of an alliance is always defensive, although under general international law, if the *bellum justum* principle is excluded, a war of aggression is not illegal. This is a fact which seems to prove that the principle concerned is at least recognized as a rule of international morality.

If alliances really have a defensive character, there is a certain similarity between them and regional organizations for collective security. An alliance treaty either expressly stipulates that the contracting parties are obliged to refrain from resorting to war in their mutual relations, which, in this respect, makes it a non-aggression pact, or it tacitly presupposes such an obligation, at least in the moral sense of the term. An alliance treaty always imposes upon the contracting parties the obligation to assist each other in case of aggression. Hence, in this respect, it is a mutual assistance agreement. Prohibition of war and mutual assistance against aggression are essential elements of a collective security arrangement. However, it must be noted that a treaty of alliance, in the specific sense of the term, provides for mutual assistance only in case of external aggression, whereas universal collective security organizations are directed only, and certain regional security organizations to some extent, against an illegal use of force within the organization. In case one of the contracting parties to a mutual assistance alliance violates the express or tacit obligation of non-aggression and attacks another contracting party, no obligation of assistance applies. It is precisely because alliances are directed against third states that they create an atmosphere of suspicion, lead to counter-alliances and, in many cases, have led to war. This is the reason why merely regional agreements for mutual assistance have been stigmatized as "camouflaged alliances."[6] It has been suggested that the obligation of mutual assistance should be restricted to aggression originating within an organization in order to avoid the possibility that a mutual assistance agreement will degenerate into a mere "alliance."[7] This demonstrates an important aspect of regional arrangements. An agreement for mutual assistance can be an "alliance" only if it is regional—that is, only if it is restricted to a relatively small group of states on the basis of a common interest uniting them against another state or other states. If it is universal, it cannot be directed against a state outside the organization. If it is almost universal—that is, if it unites an overwhelming majority of the states of the world including all or the majority of the great powers—aggression by a state outside the organization is so unlikely that the relationship of the organization to non-member states is of secondary importance. Only regional organizations for mutual assistance and not universal or quasi-universal organizations may be conceived of as "alliances."

Regional arrangements for international security also differ from alliances in that the former provide for mutual assistance only in case of an illegal use of force whereas in alliance treaties concluded under general international law, as it is usually interpreted, the legal or illegal character of the use of armed force is irrelevant, for aggression as an illegal use of armed force does not exist under a general international law which does not prohibit the resort to war. This means that a regional organization for international security can be established only within the framework of a universal or quasi-universal organization whose constituent treaty prohibits, in principle, the use of armed force, so that under this legal order particular agreements of regional character providing for collective action against aggression as the illegal use of armed force are possible. Under general international law, a treaty binding only upon the contracting parties may oblige these parties to assist each other in case of the use of force by a third state directed against one of them, but it cannot make the use of armed force by a third state an illegal act. Consequently, there can be no regional organization for international security without a universal or quasi-universal organization for collective security in the field of international relations, provided the principle of *bellum justum* is not part of general international law.

What has been said about alliances also applies to the so-called balance of power policy which is almost always realized by alliances and counter-alliances.[8] By "balance of power," that political principle is meant which maintains or brings about by all means considered appropriate by the policy-making state or alliance of states a situation in which power is distributed with approximate equality between this state or alliance of states and other states or another alliance of states. Insofar as this policy aims at preserving the *status quo* and tries to prevent the states against which it is directed from changing the existing distribution of power by the use of armed force at the expense of the states parties to the balance of power alliance, this type of alliance seems to pursue the same purposes as any other organization for collective security. This purpose is to protect the states who are parties to the alliance against the use of armed force on the part of other states and thus to guarantee to the former their territorial integrity and political independence. In addition, the collective measures provided for by the treaty which constitutes a collective security organization are supposed to outweigh the power of any state or group of states as a potential aggressor. Hence, the idea of a certain balance of power seems to be implied in the principle of collective security. However, if a collective security organization is universal, or even almost universal, it differs from a balance of power alliance in that the latter is always directed against states outside this alliance. Furthermore, even if a collective security organization is only a regional arrangement within a universal or quasi-universal collective security system, it still differs from a balance of power alliance as the latter pursues its purpose by all means, legal or illegal, without regard to the question of whether the action undertaken or intended by its adversary is legal or illegal, whereas a regional organization of collective security is supposed to react only in a legal way against an illegal use of force.[8a] By its very nature, collective security is a legal principle, while the balance of power is a principle of political convenience.[9]

(c) The Opposition to International Security

A universal or quasi-universal international organization for collective security is not a generally accepted ideal. There is a remarkable opposition to establishing such an organization, or if the organization has been established as in the cases of the League of Nations and later the United Nations, there is opposition to consolidating it by making it more centralized and thus more effective. The main arguments set forth by representatives of governments at international conferences and by writers of texts and monographs on international law and international politics will be discussed in this section.

The first argument is that an international organization for collective security is neither desirable nor useful unless it is of limited competence, because, by its very nature, it tends to preserve the existing distribution of power; in reality it constitutes only a legal ideology the purpose of which is to justify a *status quo* policy in general and a balance of power policy in particular. The second argument holds that because this ideology is in conflict with the nature of the state as a sovereign power and particularly with its egotistic interests, an international security organization cannot work in conformity with its principles. The third argument is that not only is an international security organization unable to prevent the use of force in international relations, it also makes the use of force, especially war, inevitable. Furthermore, it prevents the localization of war and hence leads to universal war.[10]

As to the argument that an international security organization tries to preserve the *status quo* as it exists at a particular moment and hence tries to prevent any change of this status, it must be remembered that a collective security organization, whether national or international, is a legal order. By its very nature, every legal order has a conservative tendency which manifests itself in the principle that relations between the subjects, constituting a certain distribution of possessions (as under national law) or of power (as under international law), shall be established and consequently shall also be changed only in conformity with the general norms of the legal order which prohibit the use of force. Hence, the argument referring to the preservation of the *status quo* is directed not only against collective security but also against a legal regulation of inter-individual or inter-state relations, and is based on an exaggeration of the conservative function of the law in general and of a collective security system in particular. That a legal order tries to preserve the *status quo* does not mean that it tries to prevent every change but only that it prohibits a forcible change of existing legal relations, a change brought about by an illegal use of force. This also applies to an international organization for collective security. Such an organization preserves as much or as little of the *status quo* in the relations among states as a legal order regulating the conduct of individual human beings preserves in the relations among its subjects. Even under the law of the most primitive society of human beings, just as under an international organization which guarantees the lowest possible degree of collective security, there is always a possibility for a peaceful change of the legal relations established among the members of the community. It is true that this possibility varies according to the stage in the development of the legal order. The more decentralized the legal order, the less chance there is of adapting an established legal relation to changing circumstance. The legal system guaranteeing collective security is less flexible if there is no central legislative organ and no court with compulsory jurisdiction. Peaceful change of an established legal relation can be brought about only by agreement of the parties concerned, as is the case under general international law. However, despite this, international law is not a static force, for nothing in the nature of this law, just as nothing in the nature of national law, and consequently nothing in the nature of a national or international system of collective security, can prevent the establishment of institutions which promote the possibility for a peaceful change of established legal relations. It is highly significant that the opposition to the establishment of these institutions, especially legislative or quasi-legislative organs, and particularly to the establishment of courts with compulsory jurisdiction which are the most effective instruments to bring about peaceful change, emanates from just those politicians and writers who are opposed to collective security because of its alleged tendency to preserve the *status quo*. If an international organization for collective security, such as the League of Nations or the United Nations, does not work, failure is due not to its allegedly necessary tendency to preserve the *status quo*, erroneously supposed to be inherent in such organization, but to the lack of willingness to provide for effective institutions for the peaceful change of legal relations within the organization. To a great extent, this lack of willingness is the

370624—57——4

result of the same ideology which disparages collective security as a utopian scheme.

The conservative attitude which any legal order has in regard to any change of established legal relations is quite understandable if one takes into consideration the fact that preserving the *status quo* is not justifiable only if this status is not satisfactory or is even injurious. However, this is a highly subjective and relative value judgment. An established legal relation which is satisfactory to one party and hence considered to be just by this party may be unsatisfactory to the other party and hence considered to be unjust by this party. A change of this relation in favor of the latter may be very unsatisfactory to the former. It is a utopian illusion to believe that any change could be made which would result in a distribution of possessions or power satisfactory to all parties concerned. Rightly or wrongly, a legal order presupposes the idea that a change of established relations by the use of force is more unsatisfactory than a situation in which a peaceful change is difficult, though not impossible. An international legal organization for collective security presupposes the value of peace to be a higher value than the value of justice. Hence, it allows a change of established legal relations only by either agreement of the parties concerned or decisions by more or less objective central organs of the community. The opposition to collective security based on the argument that it preserves the *status quo* is the consequence of an anti-legal, which means an anti-pacific, ideology, which, consciously or unconsciously, directly or indirectly, advocates power policy.

If the preservation of the *status quo* which, to be correctly understood, should be stated as the prohibition of a forcible change of established legal relations, is an essential function of every legal order, and consequently also of an international organization for collective security, there is no reason to disparage such an organization by characterizing it as an "ideology" aimed at justifying the preservation of the *status quo*. "Ideology" is a specific concept of Marxian sociology. It designates an incorrect, illusive reflexion of social reality in the consciousness of man. By presenting a distorted picture of reality, it tries either to justify or, on the contrary, to disqualify this reality. According to Marx, bourgeois law is an ideology (or ideological superstructure set up above social reality) because it presents itself as a norm and thus tries to justify the actually established social relations which constitute the economic exploitation of one class by another. However, in truth the law neither justifies nor disparages; it regulates social relations, and insofar as it is effective, the law is itself a part of the social reality. It is always only a specific theory which serves as an ideology by distorting the legal reality for the purpose of justifying or rejecting it. A legal order establishing a system of international security really preserves the *status quo* only insofar as it prohibits changing established relations by the use of force. If there is an "ideology" at work, it is that theory of collective security which describes the legal reality as an attempt to prevent a change of the *status quo* without insisting upon the fact that it is only the forcible change which a system of collective security tries to prevent. An international security organization may not be effective and a state or a group of states may pretend to apply the norms of the constituent treaty, although in reality they practice a balance of power policy directed against other states. However, this does not mean that the legal order constituting the organization is an ideology either justifying or disparaging the reality of the balance of power policy. It means only that a false interpretation of this legal order is used as an ideology to justify a reality not in conformity with this order.

The view that a universal international security organization is impossible because it would be incompatible with the sovereignty of the state and with international law as an order regulating the mutual relations of sovereign states, is the consequence of a doctrine which prevailed prior to the first World War. According to this doctrine, international law is binding only upon states and not, as national law, upon individual human beings. There is an essential difference between a state and an individual human being as the subject of a legal order. Therefore, there is an essential difference between national and international law. Consequently, what is possible under national law, namely collective security achieved by a general prohibition of the use of force and collective reaction against an illegal use of force, is impossible under international law. To cite only one characteristic example, on the basis of this doctrine the Spanish jurist, Professor Antonio de Luna y Garcia, declared in an address delivered at the International Studies Conference on Collective Security at London in 1935: [11]

> "The idea of sovereignty is not obsolete. . . . But since sovereignty is not obsolete, there arises a truly dramatic situation in the international legal order, made up as it is of territorial units each of which is sole master of its own decisions and actions: namely, the impossibility in such an order, of ever realizing . . . a security of the international society; only an increase of national security is possible. If international law wishes to perfect itself, it must begin by committing suicide."

This means that the centralization of the international legal functions is impossible because it would be contrary to the nature of international law. Professor de Luna's conclusion was: "Peace by law is, then, a mirage."[12] Since it is easy to prove and indeed was proved prior to the first World War, that the doctrine at the basis of this opposition to international security is erroneous, it may be assumed that the true reason for this opposition is not a theoretical consideration but a political tendency hidden by an incorrect doctrine. This was an essential element of fascist ideology.

A characteristic document showing the attitude of this ideology towards collective security was the memorandum "The Idea of Collective Security"[13] presented by Professor Francesco Coppola to the above mentioned conference. The author asserted that a state could establish only its own security and that it could achieve this security by a military policy, by a policy of special alliances, or by pursuing both policies together. He spoke of the "myth of security," which he characterized as a "nightmare," and said that it "has disturbed and distorted political intelligence throughout the world and especially in Europe," and has acted as "a paralyzing burden on European politics," constituting "one of the greatest obstacles to the establishment in the world, and especially in Europe, of a veritable peace." It must be recalled that the main objection to collective security is that it tries to preserve the *status quo* and thus immobilize history at a given moment in its perpetual development. Consequently, Professor Coppola postulated another system "giving elasticity and flexibility to the legal equilibrium set up by the treaties" which follow a major war. However, he did not answer the question of how to achieve this " flexibility." He also suggested that instead of organizing the repression of war, the causes of war should be eliminated. However, he did not say how this could be done. Although he tried to avoid the impression of defending war as a legitimate instrument of national policy, his attack on collective security could hardly be otherwise interpreted. He even tried to justify such a national policy by a kind of natural-law doctrine saying that it was quite "natural" that a state undertake war "on behalf of its special interests, i. e., on behalf of its national interest." However, it was his opinion that according to the principle of collective security:

> ". . . nations would be forbidden to make war on behalf of their national interests, which are the only motives capable of arousing their passions to the point of braving this terrible danger and enduring suffering and death, while at the same time they would be obliged, on the contrary, to be always ready to engage in the terrible war of our time for reasons which do not concern them, which they do not understand, which do not by any means arouse their passions; sometimes, even, they would be obliged to fight for interests contrary to their own historic interests, that is to say, they would be

> forbidden to make war *according to nature;* and they would be ordered to make war *against nature.* This is evidently anti-historic and anti-human, and—since the nations are made up of men and not of machines—impossible."

In addition "a particular war would be transformed, always and necessarily, into a world war."

These arguments against collective security were set forth at a time when the international organization which had been established for the realization of this idea, the League of Nations, was obviously on the decline. However, similar arguments are advanced today by distinguished and influential writers ten years after the establishment of the United Nations, a security organization intended to be more effective than its predecessor organization, the League of Nations. The similar argument that is particularly proposed is that collective security is incompatible with the national policy of a state—the policy on the part of a state to cultivate its own national interest and only that interest—and that, from a realistic point of view, only this national policy should be taken into consideration. It is asserted that any system of international security is doomed to failure because it demands that an individual nation forsake national policy which serves its own national interest, and because, by imposing upon individual nations the obligation of mutual assistance, it expects them to act in a spirit of self-sacrifice. However, this is impossible, for it is contrary to the only motive of national policy: national egotism.[14]

This argument is fundamentally wrong. For purely egotistic reasons, a state may conclude with other states a treaty establishing collective security and comply with all its provisions, just as an individual, for purely egotistic reasons, may comply with the norms of national law, either because he wants to avoid the evil of the sanctions or because he is aware of the fact that the effectiveness of the system which protects his own interests depends on the obedience of those subjected to it. An international legal order establishing the collective security of the states is neither more nor less a system for preserving the *status quo* than a legal order which regulates the mutual relations of individuals and thus guarantees their security. Similarly, the former is neither more nor less incompatible with the egotism of states than the latter is with the egotism of individual human beings.

"Egotism" is a concept so broad that it comprises all possible motives of action. No attitude of human beings, and consequently no policy of government, is, by its very nature, necessarily incompatible with "egotism." Every attitude is actually motivated by "egotism"—in other words, the actions of an individual are motivated by his intention to realize what he considers to be his own interest. Hence, the argument that something is incompatible with egotism has no weight at all. No matter how a state acts, its action is motivated by egotism. A state may fulfill its obligation to come to the assistance of another state, of *any* other state, by resorting to war against an aggressor because its government is convinced that only in this way can the state secure its own national interest. On the other hand, a state may refuse to fulfill this obligation because its government feels that this fulfillment would not be in its interest. In both cases, the state acts motivated by its egotism, its "sacro egoismo," to use the terminology of Italian nationalism. That all actions of a state are motivated by its egotism is an undeniable fact and the ascertainment of this fact is a truism. However, the answer to the question of what is in the interest of a state is the result of a highly subjective value judgment. In the opinion of one government of a state a policy may be in the interest of the state, while in the opinion of another government of the same state under another political party, this same policy may not be in the interest of the state.

The view that an international security organization is doomed to failure because sooner or later it must come into conflict with the interests of some of its members, could be accepted as an argument against the principle of international security only if the "own interest of the state" were ascertainable by an objective value judgment. However, this is evidently not the case. The opposite view that an international security organization always furthers interests of all the states which are members of the organization cannot be excluded by a scientific—that is, objectively verifiable—consideration, nor is it correct to argue that a treaty for collective security is impossible or unnatural because by imposing the obligation of mutual assistance upon nations it expects them to act in a spirit of self-sacrifice.[15] The fulfillment of this obligation motivates a state to risk self-sacrifice only if those who violate the constituent treaty, the aggressor or aggressors, are more powerful than those who comply with it—that is, only if the legal order constituting the security organization has lost its effectiveness to the extent that it may no longer be considered to be valid. A certain degree of effectiveness is the condition for the validity of any legal order, and its validity is its specific existence. As long as a collective security organization exists as a valid legal order, the risk of a state's being destroyed by fulfilling its obligations as a member of this organization is certainly less than its risk of being destroyed if no such organization exists. It is just for the purpose of diminishing this risk as far as possible—in other words, of preserving their existence—that states join a security organization.

Hence, this argument does not militate against the idea of an international security organization but against the attitude of its members which deprives this organization of its effectiveness.

The last argument—which holds that an attempt to organize international security under contemporary conditions cannot prevent war but, on the contrary, makes war inevitable and, by preventing the localization of war, leads to a universal war—is the same exaggeration of an ideology which is hostile to the idea of international security as the argument that this idea necessarily implies a tendency to preserve the *status quo*. The only statement which can be made from the point of view of an unbiased analysis of international relations is that up to date the international organizations which have been established for the purpose of collective security have not been effective enough to prevent war, but, on the other hand, they certainly have not made, nor will such organizations ever make, war inevitable. Besides, the statement that an international system of collective security makes war universal contradicts the statement that such a system cannot prevent war, falsely presented by the exaggerated assertion that it makes war inevitable. It cannot prevent war because it cannot force the members of the security organization to fulfill their obligations. A security organization makes only that war inevitable which is resorted to by a state in fulfillment of the obligation imposed upon it by the organization. If a war between two states should become universal, this universal war could be attributed to a security organization only if this organization were so effective that it could force the overwhelming majority of its members, including some of the great powers, to fulfill their obligations to resort to war against an aggressor. However, if it were so effective, a local war would come to an end immediately, as soon as all the member states only showed their readiness to come to the assistance of the victim of aggression. Thus a war would not only be localized but even prevented. A universal war cannot be the effect of an international organization for collective security. It can take place only if this organization is not effective.[16]

NOTES

1. *Cf.* pp. 152 ff.

2. Even under general international law, when it is interpreted as not containing the *bellum justum* principle, it is admitted that a unilateral enforcement action involving the use of armed force constitutes "war" if it is preceded by a declaration of war by the state performing the enforcement action, or if the state against which the action is directed declares that it considers the action to be an act of war. The question as to whether or not war is essentially a bilateral action should not be confused with the question as to whether or not it is necessary to determine that war exists and to ascertain who is competent to make

this determination. Like any fact to which international law attaches certain consequences, the fact of "war" must be ascertained by competent authorities. As long as no objective authority is established, the states concerned must determine the existence of the fact of "war" in a concrete case. Hence, these states must decide whether there is or is not war in their mutual relations. However, a state attacked by another state may declare itself to be at war with an aggressor without resorting to a counterwar and without the aggressor formally declaring war. Consequently, the existence of a war does not depend on the existence of a counterwar.

In the case of *The Nyade* (Great Britain, High Court of Admiralty, 1802, 165 The English Reports 602–603), the question arose as to whether or not Portugal, an ally of Great Britain, was at war with France. The Court stated that "there was a wish on the part of Portugal not to consider herself as being at war with France," but declared that "it is by no means necessary that both countries should declare war. Whatever might be the prostration and submissive demeanour on one side, if France was unwilling to accept that submission and persisted in attacking Portugal, it was sufficient."

In *The Eliza Ann* (Great Britain, High Court of Admiralty, 1813, 1 Dodson 244), the Court stated: "A declaration of war by one country only is not, as has been represented, a mere challenge, to be accepted or refused at pleasure by the other. It proves the existence of actual hostilities on one side at least, and puts the other party also into a state of war, though he may, perhaps, think proper to act on the defensive only."

Article 16 of the Covenant of the Leage of Nations provided for sanctions in case a member should "resort to war in disregard of its covenants" against another member. A delict conditioning a sanction was committed even if an attacked member did not resort to a counterwar. It might omit doing so and rely on action by the other members obliged by the Covenant to take enforcement measures against a delinquent state.

The Kellogg-Briand Pact forbade war as an instrument of national policy. However, only the employment of force by a state violating the pact and not a counteraction against this state could be characterized as an instrument of national policy.

It is highly significant that in the provision of the Charter of the United Nations in which war is prohibited (Article 2, Paragraph 4), the term "war" does not appear. The Charter imposes upon the members the obligation to refrain from the use of force in their international relations. War, as the use of force by one state against another state, is forbidden, regardless of the attitude of the state against which force is used.

3. Julius Stone, *Legal Controls of International Conflict*, New York 1954, pp. 304 f.: "The essentials of war under customary international law are two. International war is a relation of one or more governments to at least one other government, in which at least one of such governments no longer permits its relations with the other or others to be governed by the laws of peace. It is involved in this statement, as has been wittily observed, that, while it takes two to make a quarrel, it takes only one government to make a war."

If the definition of war as a bilateral action is maintained, then within a system of collective security where war is permitted only as a sanction, the concept of war has no place. *Cf.* C. A. Pompe, *Aggressive War an International Crime,* The Hague 1953, pp. 35 ff.: "The traditional concept of war was bilateral;

the same juridical concept cannot be used to indicate simultaneously a lawful and an illegal proceeding. Today 'war' is either a sanction or a crime and therefore 'war' does no more exist." *Cf.* also Hans Kelsen, *Principles of International Law*, New York 1952, pp. 25 ff.

4. *Cf.* pp. 152 ff.

5. *Cf. Collective Security*, p. 162.

6. *Cf.* Bourquin, *op. cit.*, p. 522.

7. Bourquin, *op. cit.*, pp. 522–23. He referred to the Treaty of Locarno (1925) as a model of such regional agreements for mutual assistance.

8. *Cf.* Hans J. Morgenthau, *Politics Among Nations*, 2nd ed., New York 1954, pp. 155 ff., 169 ff.

8a. Quincy Wright, "The Prevention of Aggression," *American Journal of International Law*, Vol. 50 (1956), p. 517: "collective security seeks stability through general observance of law, while balance-of-power politics seeks it through the curbing of excessive power."

9. Ernest B. Haas, "Types of Collective Security: An Examination of Operational Concepts." *The American Political Science Review*, Vol. XLIX (1955), pp. 40 ff., examines the question as to whether it is possible to maintain collective security by "balancing of influence and power." By this formula he understands the question whether it is possible to induce "the two chief antagonists to accept compromise solutions to tension-laden problems." (*Loc. cit.*, pp. 54 f.) This is a political question, which may be raised from the point of view of that "deliberately non-normative approach to the issue of peace," which Haas applies in his essay. It has nothing to do with the problem of collective security.

10. *Cf.* Morgenthau, *op. cit.*, pp. 84, 175, 388 ff. *Cf.* also Kenneth W. Thompson, "Collective Security Reexamined," *The American Political Science Review*, Vol. XLVII (1953), pp. 770 ff.

11. *Collective Security*, p. 178.

12. *Op. cit.*, p. 179.

13. *Op. cit.*, pp. 144 ff.

14. *Cf.* Morgenthau, *op. cit.*, p. 391. *Cf.* also Howard C. Johnson and Gerhart Niemeyer, "Collective Security: The Validity of an Ideal," *International Organization*, Vol. VIII (1954), p. 35: "The following findings, therefore, seem to be justified: (*a*) In the present international order of armed states great powers, according to their pattern of behavior, cannot be expected to accept clearly defined legal commitments of universal collective security. (*b*) Judging from the actual behavior of states in response to general principles of collective security the policies of states cannot be expected to measure up to what, according to the concept, would be necessary if universal collective security were to become a working reality. (*c*) As far as our present experience goes, there do not appear to be habit-forming effects from attempts to invoke collective security or permanent advances in the attitudes and policies of governments toward the ideal standards of collective security. (*d*) Collective security, conceived in universal terms, is not actually considered by the great powers as a remedy for the basic insecurity of the present international system.

From these findings, we would venture to draw these conclusions: It is (and has been) a mistake to work for an improvement of international relations by starting from universal concepts and seeking to impose them, intellectually or otherwise, on national policies. Collective security, in the definition here employed, is such a concept; its elements (world-wide obligation, a global common interest, a community of nations, world law, world security, aggression conceived as a universal crime, indivisibility of peace, world solidarity against aggression) represent universal standards and fail to allow for the particular situations that make up the reality of international politics. Collective security has actually been possible in certain historical instances when those universal concepts and standards happened so to coincide with configurations of the political forces that some concrete action required in the interests of a number of nations could be taken in the name of the universal principle. We should in soberness be aware of the concrete conditions that govern the use and action of national power; we should continue to employ national power, in the concrete setting of political forces, for the promotion of those human values for the sake of which governments enjoy allegiance. Any further contribution that international organization may make to the problem of security on a global scale will have to stem from new and deeper insights into the problem of causation in international politics, and the ways in which common values and interests relevant to the use of force could actually take global shape. This would suggest the importance of providing the United Nations with a new conceptual foundation if it is to develop its greatest potential under present conditions as well as under more auspicious circumstances which it is hoped history will provide in the future." The authors do not define this "new conceptual foundation."

15. This is the essence of Walter Lippmann's objection against the idea of collective security. He wrote in his column of January 15, 1951 (quoted in: Frederick L. Schuman, *The Commonwealth of Man*, New York 1952, p. 406): "The trouble with collective security is . . . that when the issue is less than the survival of the *great* nations, the method of collective security will not be used because it is just as terrifying to the policeman as it is to the lawbreaker. It punishes the law-enforcing states, at least until they have paid the awful price of victory, as much as the law-breaking states. Therefore it cannot be used as a method of ordinary and continuing enforcement. . . ."

16. Frederick L. Schuman, *op. cit.*, p. 345, says that the formula of collective security "is based on false premises and has never worked in practice;" it "cannot conceivably work in the very nature of our system of states." "That this formula is futile and indeed productive of more, rather than less anarchy and violence has been experimentally demonstrated beyond reasonable doubt in the mind of reasonable men" (p. 369). The starting point of this pessimistic evaluation of collective security is the identification of this concept with the "now long familiar notion that peace among sovereignties can best be preserved by having all sovereigns solemnly compact to wage war against any sovereign who might take the sword" (p. 345). This, however, is not a definition of collective security, but only of a very low degree of it. Schuman does not deny the possibility of establishing by international agreement permanent peace, the very goal of collective security. He says: " 'Permanent' peace is possible only through a permanent termination of the game of power among rival sovereignties. . . . This goal is attainable only through the subjugation of all sovereignties by one, with a World-State emerging out of victory—or through the voluntary merging of sovereignties in a global policy, with a World-State emerging out of agreement. The first solution . . . is unattainable in our own [time] . . . The second solution has never been attained. Yet it deserves to be regarded (unlike 'collective security') as within the realm of the humanly possible" (pp. 419 f.). This second solution must not be opposed to collective security, for it is only a higher degree of this very principle.

2. COLLECTIVE SECURITY UNDER PARTICULAR INTERNATIONAL LAW

(a) Defining the Use of Force To Be Prohibited

Since collective security in international relations means primarily protection against that use of armed force which is called war, and since general international law does not prohibit war, if the *bellum justum* principle is not considered to be part of it, international security can be established only by treaties imposing upon the contracting states the obligation to refrain from resorting to war. In an ideal case, war would be prohibited under all conditions with the exception of war as a sanction—that is, with the exception of war as a reaction against a violation of the law in general and the treaty constituting the international security organization in particular. If war is exceptionally permitted as a sanction, it is also permitted in the exercise of self-defense, for self-defense is a reaction against an illegal use of armed force. However, a constituent treaty may permit war not only as a sanction (including its use in self-defense) but also for other purposes, or, what amounts to the same thing, a constituent treaty may prohibit war only under definite conditions. For example, the contracting parties may assume only the obligation not to resort to war against each other without having previously submitted their conflict to a special agency competent to make recommendations for a peaceful settlement and not before a certain period of time after the decision of this agency has expired. If these conditions are fulfilled, a war resorted to by one of the parties is not illegal.[1]

Even if war is prohibited under all conditions (with the exception of war as a sanction against an illegal resort to war), international security is not satisfactorily established. Acts involving the use of armed force but not having the character of acts of war—as, for example, so-called pacific blockades—are left outside the system of collective security—that is, they are not under the specific sanctions provided for by the treaty constituting this system as reactions against the use of force prohibited by it. If a member of the security organization is a victim of the use of armed force short of war, the treaty constituting the security system does not apply. Only general international law applies, under which the use of armed force short of war is permitted only as a reprisal—that is, only as a reaction against a violation of the law. However, reprisals are the only sanctions which may be taken by the members of a security organization against such an illegal use of force short of war if a resort to war is permitted only as a reaction against an illegal resort to war. Moreover, the use of armed force is an objectively ascertainable fact. However, there is no objective criterion by which an act of war can be distinguished from an act involving the use of armed force which is not to be considered as an act of war. An act is an act of war if the state performing the act does not intend to restrict its action against the other state to this act, if its intention is an unlimited interference by the use of armed force in the sphere of interests of the other state. If only acts of war are prohibited, the application of the specific sanctions, and this means the operation of the security system, depends on the answer to the question concerning the intentions of the state concerned. In many cases, it is impossible to answer this question immediately after the act has been performed but only after this act is followed by other acts of armed force which have done irreparable damage to the victim.[2] There can be no doubt that if a security organization is intended to be effective, at least to a certain extent, not only the resort to war but every use of armed force must be prohibited by the constituent treaty—that is, the specific sanctions of the security system must apply not only in case of a resort to war but in case of any use of armed force. Any use of armed force may be considered to be a breach of the peace, and the very purpose of a system of international security is to guarantee peace.

However, there is a certain tendency not to agree with such a far-going prohibition of any use of armed force. This tendency is based on the opinion that an unconditional renunciation of the use of armed force by an individual state in its relations with other states is not an essential element of a system of international security and that preventive measures, such as procedures for the peaceful settlement of conflicts and measures for the removal of the causes of war, are more important.[3] This opinion is not very different from that advocated by those who are opposed in principle to the idea of international security. As we shall see later, an obligation imposed upon states to settle their conflicts by peaceful means is, so to speak, like a blank cartridge, if it is not combined with an obligation to refrain from the use of any kind of armed force. Furthermore, as has been noted, if they are applicable at all, measures for removing the causes of war have a rather limited effect.

If a treaty constituting a system of collective security prohibits not only the resort to war but also the use of armed force short of war, it parallels general international law as far as the second prohibition is concerned. In this respect, the only difference between the situation under the security treaty and that under general international law is that the special sanctions provided for by the treaty as reactions against an enforcement action short of war are more effective than those provided for by general international law. In addition, a security treaty may also place under its specific sanctions violations of general international law other than the use of armed force short of war, e. g., the violation of the rules concerning the treatment of aliens or of the rule *pacta sunt servanda.* It may attach its specific sanctions to all violations of international law, as it exists at the moment the treaty enters into force, committed by members of the security organization, and even to a conduct which was not a delict under general international law as it existed prior to the treaty, e. g., to conduct which constitutes a mere threat to the peace, such as a concentration of troops or an armament exceeding the limits prescribed by the treaty. In other words, in addition to the obligation not to resort to war and the obligation to participate in the execution of sanctions, a security treaty may impose other obligations not established by general international law upon the members of a security organization. This means that under such a security system a greater sphere of interests of the state may be legally protected than under general international law. It stands to reason that the further a system of international security goes in this direction, the more restricted the freedom of action of the member states, and the greater the resistance of all those who insist on the sovereignty of the state. As has been noted,[4] an extension of a security system from the protection of interests only against their violation by the use of armed force to the protection of interests against their violation in any way including a way other than by the use of armed force, goes hand in hand with an extension of the concept of force. "Force" is meant to include not only armed force, but any illegal action of one state which violates the legally protected interests of another and which is undertaken against the will of this other state. Hence, enforcement actions involving the use of armed force are distinguished from enforcement actions not involving the use of armed force.[5] This change in the meaning of the concept of force implies a change in the meaning of the concept of aggression. This latter concept is an essential element of a system of international security insofar as the purpose of such a system is protection against aggression.

NOTES

1. This was the case under the Covenant of the League of Nations which declared in its preamble that a purpose of the organization was: . . . "international peace and security by the acceptance of obligations not to resort to war . . ." It imposed upon the members not an unconditional obligation not to resort to war but only the obligation not to resort to war under the particular conditions set forth in the following Articles of the Covenant:

ARTICLE 12.—1. The Members of the League agree that, if there should arise between them any dispute likely to lead to a rupture, they will submit the matter either to arbitration *or judicial settlement* or to inquiry by the Council, and they agree in no case to resort to war until three months after the award by the arbitrators *or the judicial decision*, or the report by the Council. 2. In any case under this Article the award of the arbitrators *or the judicial decision* shall be made within a reasonable time, and the report of the Council shall be made within six months after the submission of the dispute.

Article 13.—1. The Members of the League agree that, whenever any dispute shall arise between them which they recognize to be suitable for submission to arbitration *or judicial settlement*, and which can not be satisfactorily settled by diplomacy, they will submit the whole subject-matter to arbitration *or judicial settlement*." . . . 4. The Members of the League agree that they will carry out in full good faith any award *or decision* that may be rendered, and that they will not resort to war against a Member of the League which complies therewith. In the event of any failure to carry out such an award *or decision*, the Council shall propose what steps should be taken to give effect thereto.

Article 15.—1. If there should arise between Members of the League any dispute likely to lead to a rupture, which is not submitted to arbitration *or judicial settlement* in accordance with Article 13, the Members of the League agree that they will submit the matter to the Council. Any party to the dispute may effect such submission by giving notice of the existence of the dispute to the Secretary-General, who will make all necessary arrangements for a full investigation and consideration thereof. 2. For this purpose the parties to the dispute will communicate to the Secretary-General, as promptly as possible, statements of their case with all the relevant facts and papers, and the Council may forthwith direct the publication thereof. 3. The Council shall endeavour to effect a settlement of the dispute, and, if such efforts are successful, a statement shall be made public giving such facts and explanations regarding the dispute and the terms of settlement thereof as the Council may deem appropriate. 4. If the dispute is not thus settled, the Council either unanimously or by a majority vote shall make and publish a report containing a statement of the facts of the dispute and the recommenations which are deemed just and proper in regard thereto. 5. Any Member of the League represented on the Council may make public a statement of the facts of the dispute and of its conclusions regarding the same. 6. If a report by the Council is unanimously agreed to by the Members thereof other than the Representatives of one or more of the parties to the dispute, the Members of the League agree that they will not go to war with any party to the dispute which complies with the recommendations of the report. 7. If the Council fails to reach a report which is unanimously agreed to by the Members thereof, other than the Representatives of one or more of the parties to the dispute, the Members of the League reserve to themselves the right to take such action as they shall consider necessary for the maintenance of right and justice. 8. If the dispute between the parties is claimed by one of them, and is found by the Council, to arise out of a matter which by international law is solely within the domestic jurisdiction of that party, the Council shall so report, and shall make no recommendation as to its settlement. 9. The Council may in any case under this Article refer the dispute to the Assembly. The dispute shall be so referred at the request of either party to the dispute, provided that such request be made within 14 days after the submission of the dispute to the Council. 10. In any case referred to the Assembly, all the provisions of this Article and of Article 12 relating to the action and powers of the Council shall apply to the action and powers of the Assembly, provided that a report made by the Assembly, if concurred in by the Representatives of those

Members of the League represented on the Council and of a majority of the other Members of the League, exclusive in each case of the Representatives of the parties to the dispute, shall have the same force as a report by the Council concurred in by all Members thereof other than the Representatives of one or more of the parties to the dispute."

2. Professor Bourquin, *op. cit.*, p. 481, correctly asserted that if the differentiation between acts of war and acts involving the use of armed force not having the character of acts of war, so-called "pacific measures of coercion," were introduced in a system of collective security, it would endanger the fundamental principle of this system which he defined as the prohibition of violence exerted for the purpose of imposing one's own will on others. He referred to the fact that "actually there is no external difference between an act of armed force and an act of war. The materiality of the facts is exactly the same in both cases; it is only the intention of the Parties which makes the difference. In order to remain within the limits of pacific measures of coercion the two states concerned must have the willingness not to allow a state of war to be born among them." He went on to say: "To authorize armed coercive measures means to permit the states to apply certain forms of coercion which may or may not be war according to circumstances not yet ascertained at the moment the event takes place."

Professor Bourquin seems to ignore the fact that even if enforcement actions short of war are not prohibited by the treaty constituting a system of collective security, they are prohibited by general international law and are permitted only exceptionally as reprisals.

3. *Cf. Collective Security*, p. 10.

4. *Cf.* p. 11.

5. Article 2, paragraph 4 of the Charter of the United Nations imposes upon the members the obligation to "refrain in their international relations from the threat or use of force against the territorial integrity or political independence of any state, or in any other manner inconsistent with the Purposes of the United Nations." The wording of this Article can be interpreted to mean that members are obliged to refrain from not only the use of armed force but the use of any kind of force. A distinction between armed force and other kinds of force necessarily follows from the provisions of Articles 39, 41, 42 and 50, concerning the measures to be taken by the Security Council for the maintenance of international peace and security. According to the provisions of Articles 41 and 42, two kinds of measures are to be distinguished, and according to Article 50 both are to be considered as "enforcement measures": measures "not involving the use of armed force" (Article 41), and measures involving the use of armed force (Article 42). If there are "enforcement" measures involving the use of armed force and "enforcement" measures not involving the use of armed force, armed force—that is, force exercised by the use of arms—must be distinguished from force exercised in another way—that is, force not exercised by the use of arms. There are two kinds of force not exercised by the use of arms: (1) an action of a state directed against another state which constitutes a violation of international law but which is not performed by the use of arms; (2) a reprisal which does not involve the use of armed force. Article 2, paragraph 4, refers to the "use of force." It therefore prohibits both kinds of force. Hence, not only is the use of armed force prohibited but any action of a member state illegal under general international law which is directed against another state is prohibited by the Charter, and the member states are forbidden to resort not only to war but also to reprisals.

The application of sanctions is reserved to the Organization. However, the provisions of the Charter concerning sanctions are not very clear. The definition of an action against which the Security Council may take enforcement measures is not quite consistent with the provision of Article 2, paragraph 4. According to Article 39, the Security Council may take the enforcement measures referred to in Articles 41 and 42 in case of a "threat to the peace, breach of the peace, or act of aggression," whereas Article 2, paragraph 4, prohibits "the threat or use of force." The use of non-armed force may be considered by the Security Council to be a "threat to the peace" and may then constitute the condition of an enforcement measure to be taken by this organ as a sanction. However, if the violation of international law is not committed by the use of armed force and hence is not a breach of the peace or an act of aggression, and if it is not considered by the Security Council to be a "threat to the peace," a sanction as an enforcement action in conformity with Articles 39, 41 or 42 cannot be taken. It is true that the sanction stipulated in Article 6, the expulsion from the Organization of a member who has violated the Principles of the Charter, is applicable in case of a use of force as referred to in Article 2, paragraph 4, the term force used in the wider sense comprising the use not only of armed force but of any kind of force. However, Article 6 applies only if the Principles of the Charter are "persistently" violated by a member, not if a member violates international law in a single case. If, as the wording of Article 2, paragraph 4, seems to indicate, the Charter prohibits any violation of international law on the part of the members and reserves the application of sanctions to the Organization, the Charter should have provided for sanctions to be applied by the Organization in case of any violation of international law. Since this is not the case, in contradiction to its wording, Article 2, paragraph 4, may be interpreted as prohibiting only the use of armed force and not as forbidding reprisals to be taken by member states.

(b) The Problem of Aggression

(aa) *The military concept of aggression and the legal concept.*

The term "aggression" was originally a military-technical concept. It means a first attack. A state which is the first to perform an act of war against another state is an aggressor. The war to which this first state resorts is an aggressive war, or war of aggression, whereas, in resorting to a counterwar to defend itself, the other state wages a defensive war or war of defense. This distinction assumes legal importance only when the resort to war is prohibited either conditionally or unconditionally. The concept of aggression and the concept of illegal war are not identical. From a military-technical point of view, a war may be aggressive because it constitutes a first attack. However, this does not necessarily make it illegal. For example, the law prohibits the resort to war only under definite conditions. In conformity with these conditions, a war against a state which refuses to comply with the decision of an international tribunal is not forbidden. In this case the state which, in order to enforce the decision which the tribunal has issued in its favor, is the first to use armed force against the recalcitrant state is, from a military-technical point of view, the aggressor but the war to which it resorts is perfectly legal, while the counterwar to which the other state resorts, is a defensive war but must be regarded as illegal. The same is true with respect to a war which the members of an international security organization are obliged to wage against a member state which has resorted to war against another member state in violation of the constituent treaty. The war which the states who are not being attacked themselves wage against the delinquent state is an aggressive war but is legal, while the counterwar to which the delinquent resorts is a defensive war but is illegal.

However, in legal terminology, there is an outspoken tendency to identify the concept of aggression with that of an illegal war or even an illegal use of force, a tendency to substitute a specifically legal concept of aggression for the original military-technical concept. The tendency is to designate as "aggression" that conduct of a state which a treaty constituting an international security system prohibits by attaching to it the specific sanctions of this system. Consequently, the meaning of the term "aggression" changes with the scope of the types of conduct against which an international security organization tries to protect its members. Hence, if the constituent treaty prohibits war under definite conditions, only a war resorted to under these conditions is considered to be aggression, while, even if it constitutes a first attack, a war resorted to under other conditions is not so stigmatized. Following the extent of the prohibition stipulated in the constituent treaty, any resort to war is regarded as aggression if the war is waged for a purpose other than that permitted by the constituent treaty, especially for a purpose other than the participation in the execution of the specific sanctions of the security system or the exercise of self-defense.[1]

(bb) *Aggression and self-defense as a restriction of the prohibition of the use of armed force.*

As pointed out in a previous chapter, self-defense means the use of force by the victim of an act of aggression as a reaction against this aggression, i. e., as a reaction against an illegal use of force. Hence, the right of self-defense presupposes a legal order prohibiting in principle the use of force by the subjects of the order, so that the right of a subject to use force represents a restriction of this principle. If general international law does not prohibit the resort to war as the use of armed force, in other words if the *bellum justum* principle is not part of general international law, there can be no right of self-defense under this law because there can be no use of armed force as a reaction against an illegal use of armed force. There is no need to justify the use of armed force as self-defense, as a restriction of or

370624—57——5

exception to a general prohibition of the use of armed force, if no such prohibition exists. If the use of armed force by an aggressor is as legal as the use of armed force by a defender, self-defense is a legally irrelevant concept. Just as under general international law, if it does not contain the *bellum justum* principle, there is no collective security, there is no right of self-defense. There is a definite connection between the two legal phenomena. If general international law does not prohibit the use of armed force, an international right of self-defense—that is, the right of a state to use armed force as a reaction against an illegal use of armed force—can be recognized only under a treaty prohibiting the use of armed force and thus establishing a system of international security.

Since the right of self-defense represents a restriction of the prohibition of the use of force, and since this restriction may be of wide or narrow scope, the right of self-defense should always be expressly defined in the legal order establishing the system of collective security in general and in the treaty constituting the system of international security in particular. From the point of view of legal positivism, the widespread idea that the international right of self-defense, as a consequence of the natural right of self-preservation, is always presupposed and hence does not need express stipulation, is without foundation and is the source of serious difficulty in interpreting the treaties prohibiting the use of armed force.[1a]

Within a system of international security, self-defense may be permitted only as a reaction against an illegal use of armed force, against an "attack" which has actually begun. Hence, self-defense would be "defense" and the illegal use of armed force would be "aggression" in the military-technical sense of these terms. However, self-defense may also be recognized as a reaction against an attack which has not yet actually begun but which may reasonably be expected imminently. In this case, from a military-technical point of view, the use of armed force in the exercise of self-defense is an act of aggression, while from a legal point of view, the state against which self-defense is exercised is the aggressor. If an attack is not considered to be imminent but only to be probable in the near future, a war resorted to in order to forestall the attack is a preventive war. As a rule, a preventive war is prohibited within a system of international security and hence must be regarded as aggression.[1b] Within a security organization, the use of physical force by the individual members is permitted to a certain extent because the coercive machinery of the organization cannot function at the same moment the attack starts or appears imminent and hence the procedure of putting into operation the special sanctions of the system requires time. However, if the attack has not yet started or is not imminent but is only considered probable in the near future, and consequently if there is time to prepare the operation of the coercive machinery of the security organization, there is no reason to permit the exercise of self-defense. Since it is difficult, if not impossible, to distinguish an international situation in which an attack on one state by another is imminent from a situation in which such an attack is only probable in the near future, the exercise of the right of self-defense within a system of international security may be properly restricted to the case of an armed attack which has already begun.

In conformity with the terminology of the Charter of the United Nations, a distinction must be made between individual and collective self-defense. Individual self-defense is the action exercised by a state which is the immediate victim of an armed attack. Collective self-defense is the action by other members of the security organization which, without being attacked themselves, come to the assistance of the victim. Hence, collective self-defense is not "self"-defense but the defense of another, and if it consists of the use of armed force, it is defense and not aggression only from a legal point of view and not from a military-technical standpoint.

So-called collective self-defense—that is, the right to come to the assistance of the victim of an illegal use of armed force—may be restricted to the case in which a state—member or non-member of the organization—uses its own armed forces against a state which is a contracting party to the treaty constituting the security organization. However, the treaty may authorize or oblige the members to come to the assistance not only of another member but also of any other state, and not only in case the state is the victim of an illegal use of armed force by another state but also in case another state directly or indirectly supports revolutionary forces within the former, or even in case of a revolution not supported by a foreign state. This means that the security organization may protect its members not only against external and direct aggression but also against internal and indirect aggression.[2]

Since within a more or less centralized system of international security the exercise of the right of individual and collective self-defense must be permitted because the central organ of the organization cannot interfere immediately after an illegal use of armed force has taken place, the question of whether or not the use of armed force which has actually taken place is illegal must be decided by the state which claims to be exercising the right of individual or collective self-defense. However, this is true only as long as the central organ of the security organization does not interfere. As soon as it does, this central organ must decide that question, and it may decide that question in another way than the state which claims to be exercising its right of self-defense. The central organ may decide that no armed attack has taken place which would justify the exercise of the right of self-defense, and that consequently the state claiming to be a defender is, in truth, an aggressor. Consequently, a state can exercise the right of self-defense only at its own risk.[3]

(cc) *Other exceptions to the prohibition of the use of armed force.*

The prohibition of the use of armed force may be restricted not only by permitting the use of armed force in executing the specific sanctions provided by the constituent treaty and in exercising self-defense, but also in case a state comes to the assistance of its own nationals abroad whose lives or property are seriously endangered.

The use of armed force may be prohibited by the constituent treaty and may thus constitute aggression only if it has the definite purpose of imposing the will of the state exercising the armed force on the state against which this action is directed. A state may resort to war against another state not in order to force this state to accept a change of their relations which could be brought about legally only with the voluntary consent of this state, but, on the contrary, in order to prevent the latter from forcing its will upon the former. This is the case of a preventive war which has already been discussed. Without resorting to war, a state may also perform a single act of armed force, e. g., it may occupy a definite place in the territory of a more powerful state only for the purpose of securing its defense against an attack by this state expected immediately or in the near future. This case differs from the case of a preventive war, but the difference is irrelevant within a system of international security. Whatever its purpose, unless it is an act of self-defense against an armed attack or an act of participation in the execution of the specific sanctions of the system, any use of armed force is a breach of the peace. Hence, without regard to its purpose, the use of armed force should be prohibited by a treaty constituting an effective system of international security. However, security treaties frequently prohibit the use of armed force only insofar is it may be directed against the territorial integrity or political independence (i. e., the sovereignty) of another state,[4] which means only if the purpose of the enforcement action is to violate the territorial integrity or political independence of another state. Since it is hardly possible to use armed force against another state without violating its territorial integrity or political independence, this restriction does not really impair the effectiveness of the security system.

The purpose of an act of armed force performed by a state—to impose its will upon another state—is sometimes designated as the "aggressive intention."[5] The question as to whether or not an act of armed force is performed with such an intention or for this purpose must be distinguished from the question as to whether or not an act of armed force is performed deliberately, or because of negligence, error or accident. Whether or not a treaty constituting an international security organization should prohibit, and thus qualify as aggression, only acts of armed force deliberately performed, is not a particular problem of collective security but a general problem of the legal technique of international law. It is really the problem of the responsibility of the states, the question of whether responsibility based on fault or whether absolute responsibility should be established by international agreements. There is a general tendency in favor of restricting the responsibility of a state to cases of deliberate violations of international law, although other cases establishing the absolute responsibility of a state are not completely excluded.

Another general problem which is not particular to collective security but which may be considered to be relevant to it is the question of whether a state should be made responsible only for acts violating international law performed by the government, or by subordinate organs at the command, or with the authorization of the government, or also for acts performed by subordinate organs without the command or authorization of the government. If the principle is accepted that a state is to be made responsible for violations of international law committed by subordinate organs without command or authorization by the government if the act constituting the violation is performed in connection with the normal function of this organ, then such acts may also be regarded as aggression if they consist of an illegal use of armed force. A typical case is the invasion of the territory of a state by a part of the armed forces of another state undertaken by a comanding officer on his own initiative.

(dd) *Aggression as conduct not including the use of armed force; indirect aggression.*

International security is not satisfactorily guaranteed if the treaty constituting the security system provides its specific sanctions as a reaction only against an actual use of armed force—that is, if it protects the members of the security organization against violations of their interests only by the use of armed force, or, what amounts to the same thing, if aggression is constituted only by the actual use of armed force. Hence, there is a tendency to extend the security system so that it protects its members against a violation of interests committed in a way other than by the actual use of armed force, and to qualify also a conduct not constituting the actual use of armed force as aggression. The constituent treaty may prohibit as acts of aggression not only the use but also the threat of armed force—its preparation by military or economic mobilization, or even its planning or initiating. The extension of the prohibition, stipulated in the constituent treaty, to an indirect use of armed force, which is the basis of the concept of indirect aggression,[6] is of the greatest importance. In indirect aggression a state does not use its own armed forces but operates through armed persons performing hostile acts against another state, seemingly on their own initiative. The following actions are examples of indirect aggression: the supporting by a state of the revolutionary forces fighting against the legitimate government of another state, the arming by a state of organized bands for offensive purposes against another state, the sending by a state of so-called "volunteers" to engage in hostilities against another state, the non-prevention by a neutral state of its own nationals from participating as volunteers in a civil or international war against another state (an action not forbidden by general international law), the undertaking or encouragement by a state of terrorist activities in another state or the toleration by a state of organized activities calculated to result in terrorist acts in another state.[6a]

An international security system may even protect the governments of the contracting states against internal aggression by providing for repressive measures to be taken either by the individual states who are members of the security organization or by a central organ against revolutionary movements within a member state not supported, directly or indirectly, by external forces. Such a system guarantees the political and economic regimes of the members of the security organization which exist at the time the security treaty is concluded. Hence, this system goes far beyond general international law which does not guarantee the internal organization of states. If the enforcement measures taken by the organs of the security organization against the insurgents are considered to be sanctions, revolution against the legitimate government constitutes not only a violation of national law but also an international delict.

Revolution understood to be internal aggression involves the use of armed force. However, an undertaking of a state may be prohibited as aggression even if the use of arms is not involved at all, as, for example, in poisoning a stream rising in a state's territory but flowing through a neighboring country, or in altering its course and thus depriving the inhabitants of the neighboring state of a vital means of subsistence, or in using life-destroying rays against the population of another state.[7]

If the security treaty imposes upon the contracting parties the obligation to settle their disputes by peaceful procedures, the refusal to submit a dispute to such procedures or to comply with the decision of an organ competent to bring about its peaceful settlement or with a provisional measure, e. g., a call to discontinue military operations, may constitute a conduct against which the specific sanctions of the security system are directed. In that case, such conduct may be considered to be aggression.[7a]

One case of aggression in which the use of armed force is not involved is so-called ideological aggression. It consists of hostile propaganda organized or permitted by one state against another. It is supposed to be an appeal to the inhabitants of the other state. It may be disseminated by the press or by radio broadcasts, which may be controlled by the government, or be effected by the dispatch of pamphlets and the like. The propaganda may consist of imparting information or ideas or in discrediting a government. If it violates the honor of another state or if its evident purpose is to instigate a revolutionary movement, it is illegal under general international law.[8]

It has been suggested that any intervention in the internal or external affairs of another state should be prohibited as aggression in the treaty constituting an international security organization by having attached to it the specific sanctions of the security system. It has also been suggested that there is no reason why this security system should not be extended to include protection against all violations of international law, as it existed at the time the treaty constituting the security organization came into force. As has been pointed out, the security treaty may prohibit a conduct, which was not illegal under international law prior to its coming into force. Provided the *bellum justum* principle is not considered to be part of general international law, this is the case with respect to the most essential element of any security system: the prohibition of war. It is certainly the case if the international security organization tries to protect its members against so-called economic aggression.[9] Economic aggression has been defined as the conduct of a state which deprives another state of the economic resources derived from the fair practice of international trade or which endangers its basic economy. Such conduct does not involve the use of armed force and may be in complete conformity with international law as it existed prior to the treaty prohibiting it as aggression. There can be little doubt that such a security treaty establishes a remarkable restriction on the freedom of action of the contracting parties and confers extraordinary power on the organ competent to decide in a concrete case whether or not an act of economic aggression has been committed.

If the treaty constituting the international security system places under the specific sanctions of this system not only the violations of the particular obligations stipulated by this treaty but also all violations of general international law, the concept of aggression and the concept of international illegality may coincide.[9a] It may then be advisable to distinguish not only between direct and indirect, but also between major and minor aggression. A major aggression is a violation of international law constituted by an enforcement action involving the use of armed force, while a minor aggression means any other violation which may also be characterized as an enforcement action, in that it is taken against the will of the state which is the victim of the action, although this action does not involve the use of armed force.

(ee) *The defintion of aggression.*

It follows from the foregoing considerations, that the concept of aggression may be defined in different ways, and that the definition depends on what kind of conduct the treaty constituting an international security system does or should prohibit by attaching to it the specific sanctions of this system. Hence, it is quite understandable that the definition of aggression plays an important part in the discussion of the problem of international security, for defining aggression amounts to determining the scope of the security system *de lege lata* or *de lege ferenda*. *De lege lata*, from the point of view of an established law, that is a treaty concluded for the purpose of granting collective security to the contracting parties, it is a theoretical problem, the problem of describing by a general formula the acts which the treaty prohibits by attaching to them the specific sanctions of the security system. However, the treaty itself may contain such a formula which would then have the character of a legal definition, just as a penal code may contain a definition of theft. *De lege ferenda*, from the point of view of a law to be established—that is, of a treaty to be concluded—the definition of aggression is a practical-political, legislative problem, the problem of determining the conduct of states which should be prohibited, and especially of determining the conditions under which the use of armed force should be forbidden and under what exceptional conditions it should be permitted. However, strange as it may seem, the question concerned is usually formulated as whether or not aggression should be defined.[10] The representatives of many governments and some outstanding writers advocate the opinion that aggression should not be defined, that a definition is not desirable and is even dangerous, and that even if it should be defined the task is almost overwhelmingly difficult. There is also a school of thought which maintains that aggresion cannot be defined,[11] that it is a concept which by its very nature is not susceptible of definition. There is even a doctrine which holds that it is both possible and desirable to eliminate the problem of aggression from the organization of international security altogether. However, the opposite views have also been defended that the problem of aggression cannot be avoided, and that aggression can and should be defined. It has also been held that it can be defined but should not be because no politically satisfactory definition could be achieved, or that even if such a definition could be achieved it would be superfluous, or that aggression can and should be defined although the difficulties of defining it should not be ignored.

(ff) *The attempt to eliminate the problem of aggression.*

The view that it is both possible and desirable to eliminate the problem of aggression is advocated by those who suggest directing the collective measures to be provided by the treaty constituting an international security organization not against the state guilty of an act of aggression but against any state which has resorted, or is about to resort, to war or to the use of armed force, without deciding the question of which state is the actual or potential aggressor. They contend that a security system should react against the fact of war as such and not against a specific act of aggression committed by only one state. The advantage of such a method is that it would avoid the violation of national honor inevitably involved in stigmatizing a state as an aggressor.[12] This doctrine can easily be refuted. The problem of aggression cannot be avoided within a system of international security.

If the member states of an international security organization are obliged to apply only economic sanctions, as was the case under the Covenant of the League of Nations, the equal application of these sanctions to both states involved in a war may result in the defeat of the economically weaker state by the economically stronger state, which would be less affected by these sanctions. If one state is not economically superior to the other, and hence both are affected equally by economic sanctions, the militarily weaker state would be defeated. Hence, if an economically or militarily weaker state were the victim of an aggression, such a system is just the contrary of a security system. It affords no protection against aggression and does not have the effect of stopping or preventing war.

It may be that within a system of international security, for one reason or another, it is not possible to determine the aggressor. Then it may be inevitable to direct repressive measures against both states, the unidentified aggressor as well as the likewise unidentified defender.[13] However, such measures, especially those involving the use of armed force, can hardly be taken without a so-called provisional measure, a previous call to the belligerents to cease hostilities. In case only one state is ready to comply with this call, the application of military measures to this state would not only be considered as unjust, it would also be completely superfluous, and the state which refused to comply with the call to cease hostilities should be considered to be the aggressor. It is in just such a case that a definition of aggression which includes not only the use of armed force but also the non-compliance with a provisional measure is appropriate. Only if both belligerents refuse to comply with a call to cease hostilities is the application of military measures against both of them justified. However, in this case the actions of both fall within this definition of aggression.

Within an organization constituted by a treaty providing for economic and military sanctions to be directed against both states involved in a war, no right of self-defense is recognized, even though the coercive machinery of the organization, the main purpose of which is to stop the war, cannot go into effect immediately after the outbreak of war. This is highly objectionable, for if a state which is a victim of aggression does not offer resistance by the use of its armed force, in compliance with the prohibition not to resort to war, it will probably suffer irreparable damage. If in the case of a war between two states the question is not decided which of them is the aggressor, an obligation to repair the damage caused by the war can be imposed only upon both or upon none of the belligerents. In either case gross injustice is inflicted upon the state which is not the aggressor.

An effective system of international security must provide for sanctions not only in case of an actual breach of the peace by an act of aggression but also in case of a threat to the peace. If there is not an actual war between two states but only a danger of war because two states have started to mobilize or have concentrated troops on their frontiers, the central organ of the security organization must be able to apply preventive measures. It must therefore be able to call upon both states to stop their mobilization, or to withdraw their troops from their frontiers, and to submit their conflict to pacific procedures to be conducted by this organ or another organ of the security organization or an organ to be established for this purpose by the states in conflict. If one of the two states refuses to comply with the call, or if one of them refuses to comply with the decision of the organ competent to bring about a pacific settlement of the conflict, then repressive measures—that is, sanctions—would be directed against this state. It stands to reason that it would be foolish to direct repressive measures against the state which complies with the call of the organ of the security organization or the decision of the organ to which the conflict has been submitted. Such measures would not have the character of sanctions. They could reasonably be applied only to the state which refuses to comply with the call to stop mobilization, or to withdraw its troops from the frontier, or to submit the conflict to a pacific procedure, or to comply with the decision of the organ competent to bring about a pacific settlement of the conflict. However, this state would be an aggressor according to the definition of aggression referred to above. As far as repressive measures are concerned, and repressive measures are indispensable to an effective security system, such measures can reasonably be applied only as reactions against aggression. However, by aggression not only the use of armed force but also other illegal conduct, especially non-compliance with preventive measures taken by the (direct or indirect) agencies of a security organization, may be understood. Consequently, the problem of aggression must be included in a consideration of the organization of international security.[14]

(gg) *Is the concept of aggression not susceptible to definition?*

As to the doctrine that aggression is a concept which is not susceptible to definition,[15] it should be remembered that "definition" is a term which may designate different things. "Definition" may mean a statement determining the meaning of a *term*. Defining a *concept* consists of determining the qualities belonging to this concept. Insofar as a "concept" is the result of a definition, a concept which cannot be defined is a contradiction in terms. One of the purposes of a definition is to enable us to distinguish one object from another similar object. However, a definition may have to employ a term designating an object which exists in different degrees such as size, temperature, density, and the like. Then it is inevitable that there are concrete cases in which it is not certain whether the definition applies to concrete objects of which it is doubted whether they fall under the definition, as, for instance, whether or not a man is a giant, this concept being defined as a man of extraordinary size. To maintain that such a definition is not a definition, is as much a fallacy as to maintain that there is no difference when there is only a difference in degree and not in kind, or, what amounts to the same thing, only a relative but not an absolute difference (the so-called black or white fallacy). This is the fallacy implied in the statement that aggression cannot be defined, if this statement is based on the fact that there is no absolute difference but only a relative one between a conduct which may and a conduct which may not be regarded as aggression and that there are intermediate states between these two kinds of conduct. However, aggression is not this kind of a concept, and it can be defined in a way that never makes it doubtful whether a concrete conduct, provided it is known, does or does not constitute aggression.[15] If aggression could not be defined, it would be impossible in a concrete case to apply the general norm attaching a sanction to an act of aggression. Hence, it would be impossible to determine an aggressor. The law-applying organ, whether it be the government of an individual state or an international agency such as a council or a court, can apply this norm to a concrete case and thus determine the aggressor only if it is able to ascertain that a concrete conduct of a state constitutes aggression, which means that this conduct must exhibit all the essential qualities of the concept concerned. This presupposes that the law-applying organ has a definition of aggression in mind. If this organ does not find the definition included within the general norm to be applied, it must construct this definition itself. Furthermore, if the general norm does not contain a definition of aggression, it must authorize the law-applying organ to define that conduct which the general norm prohibits by attaching to it a specific sanction, just as a penal law prohibiting murder by attaching capital punishment to this conduct must define it or leave the definition to the court competent to apply the law in a concrete case of murder. If this were not done, the court would be unable to ascertain the fact that a definite individual had committed murder and to inflict the prescribed punishment on the murderer.

(hh) *The two methods of defining aggression.*

In regard to defining aggression, the only legitimate question is whether the definition of aggression should be inserted into the general norm attaching a specific sanction to aggression or whether this definition should be left to the organ competent to apply this norm in a concrete case of aggression and thus competent to determine the aggressor. It is essential to a system of international security that it contain such a general norm. The question of defining aggression is not a question of the possibility and advisability of defining it, as the question is usually presented, but rather of determining at what stage of the legal process the definition should be established. The question is whether within a system of international security the organ competent to ascertain that a concrete act of aggression has occurred and thus to determine an aggressor should be bound by a pre-established definition of aggression or whether it should be authorized to construct this definition itself. The question of defining aggression is implied in the general problem of the rule-of-law principle within a system of international security. As has been noted, this is the principle which, as far as possible binds the law-applying organs to pre-established general norms, and leaves these organs as little discretion as possible in exercising their functions in order to render their decisions calculable and thus reduce the uncertainty with respect to these decisions and increase the so-called legal security as far as possible. It is evident that if the definition of aggression is left to the organs competent to apply the treaty constituting an international security system, the definition adopted in one case may differ from that adopted in another. Consequently, the states which are members of an international security organization cannot foresee what conduct will be regarded by the competent organ as aggression and thus as illegal. As has been pointed out, this situation certainly does not correspond to the ideal of international security. Of course, this does not mean that an attempt to maintain the rule-of-law principle within a system of international security does not encounter certain difficulties or that the realization of this principle does not have certain disadvantages. In addition, it is understandable that there should be some doubt as to which of the two methods is preferable: to bind the law-applying organs to the definition of aggression pre-established in the constituent treaty, or to leave this definition to the law-applying organs. The choice between these two methods is a difficult one, and it is quite possible and understandable that the government of a state would favor one method under certain political circumstances and another under other circumstances. In the Sixth Committee of the United Nations General Assembly, in explaining his country's past and present position with regard to the question of defining aggression, the representative of the United States declared:

> "A number of delegations had said the United States had in 1945 argued the view which was now that of the Soviet Union. That was quite true, and the United States did not in any way pretend that it was not. In 1945, the United States had been in favour of a definition of aggression because at that time there had been every reason to believe that the term 'international co-operation' would have a real connotation. Unfortunately, the state of international relations had become such as to convince the United States that a definition of aggression had become not only undesirable but even dangerous. The United States delegation had not obeyed a whim; it had adopted a position which was diametrically opposed to the stand it had taken in 1945 and had done so in view of international developments." [16]

There are good reasons for preferring one or the other method. However, in order to make a reasonable choice, it is necessary to formulate the two methods correctly. Hence, it is not the choice between defining and not defining aggression that must be made, because aggression must be defined anyway; nor is the choice to be made the choice between a method of defining aggression and a method of determining an aggressor, as it is sometimes formulated,[17] for an aggressor can be determined only on the basis of a definition of aggression, whether the definition is pre-established or left to the organ competent to determine an aggressor.[18] No matter how important it may be, the difference between these two methods is only relative and not absolute. Even if the constituent treaty contains a very detailed definition of the prohibited aggression, the law-applying organ is not completely bound in determining an aggressor, for no definition can determine its object, and no general norm can bind the law-applying organ completely. Every definition contains elements, i. e., employs terms, which themselves require definition. It is therefore not justifiable to object to a definition of aggression if it employs such terms. For example, if in a penal law, murder is defined as bringing about the death of another human being intentionally, each term of this definition is open to interpretation. This means that each term has to be defined by the court in each concrete case. Every application of a general norm in a concrete case requires interpretation and so do the definitions of the terms used in the general norm. Consequently, a certain degree of discretion is always left to the law-applying organ.

On the other hand, if the constituent treaty prohibits aggression without defining this concept, the discretion of the law-applying organ in defining the concept is not unlimited. If a word like "aggression" has any meaning at all, there is always a minimum of general understanding, and it is only to achieve a maximum of understanding that a determination of the meaning by definition is required. The meaning of a word is a sphere with a relatively solid center, like the stone of a fruit, and a more or less liquid, i. e., vague, periphery. Hence, even if "aggression" is prohibited without being defined in advance, not every conduct of a state can be regarded by the law-applying organ as aggression. The difference between the two methods consists only of the fact that much less discretion is left to the law-applying organ in the case where aggression is defined in advance than in the case where aggression must be defined together with the determination of the aggressor. The difference is sometimes assumed incorrectly to be that the former method is "automatic,"[19] while the latter is not, which means that if aggression is defined in advance, the determination of the aggressor is, so to speak, self-acting because it does not depend on the will of the organ determining the aggressor, while in case there is no pre-established definition, the determination of the aggressor cannot be performed without a conscious and deliberate action of a competent organ morally responsible for this action. Such action is necessary in both cases.

No general norm can be applied automatically in a concrete case, because such an application always requires the creative function of a law-applying organ. The procedure by which a general norm prohibiting aggression by attaching a sanction to this conduct is applied in a concrete case can never be the automatic consequence of this norm, even if the norm contains the most detailed definition of aggression. The execution of a sanction prescribed in the general norm is not possible without the ascertainment of a fact that occurs only after the general norm has been established: an act of aggression performed by a definite state at a definite time and at a definite place. This ascertainment, as a function of the law-applying organ, is necessary whether the general norm does or does not contain a definition of aggression, and it requires a conscious and deliberate action constituting the responsibility of the acting organ, whether its liberty of action in determining an aggressor is more or less limited. It is true that it is always limited, but only to a certain extent, since a certain degree of discretion is always left to the law-applying organ.[20] However, it must be admitted that the moral responsibility of the organ determining the aggressor is much greater if this organ must define aggression itself than if the definition is pre-established and the discretion the organ may exercise in determining the aggressor is very limited.

(ii) *The arguments against a pre-established definition of aggression.*

Among the arguments set forth against a pre-established definition of aggression are some which can easily be refuted. One is that no definition of aggression will discourage "major" aggressors whose motives are military and political.[21] While this may be true, it is not an argument against a particular method of organizing international security but a pessimistic evaluation of the possible effectiveness of any international security organization. The other argument was presented in the famous statement made on 26 November 1927 by Sir Austen Chamberlain in the House of Commons in which he said that a definition of aggression (especially by enumerating the acts of aggression) "will be a trap for the innocent and a sign-post for the guilty." The possibility that a state may accomplish a plan most harmful to another state and yet evade the most carefully formulated definition of aggression can certainly not be denied. However, neither can it be denied that this possibility may be restricted to a certain extent if potential aggressors are informed in advance which of their acts will probably lead to a most undesirable reaction on the part of the security organization. Consequently, potential aggressors may make some effort to alter their aggressive actions in order to avoid these reactions. There is no legal prohibition which cannot be eluded in some way, but this is certainly not sufficent reason to renounce a legal regulation of human relations. During the discussion of the Report of the Special Committee on the question of defining aggression in the Sixth Committee, the representative of the United Kingdom justified his rejection of a pre-established definition also by the statement: "The real safeguard against aggression lay not in definition, but in disarmament." [22] It stands to reason that a definition in itself has no effect. The effect is expected from the application of a legal rule attaching a sanction to an act which, in accordance with a definition contained in this rule, has been declared by the law-applying organ to be an act of aggression. It cannot be denied that a legal rule which precisely determines the act prohibited by it, may have a greater effect than a rule which does not answer the question as to what exactly is prohibited.

The arguments which may reasonably be set forth for or against a pre-established definition of aggression are, in principle, the same as those which may be advanced for or against the rule-of-law principle. The most important argument in favor of inserting into the treaty constituting an international security organization a definition of aggression, provided that this term is used in the treaty, or what amounts to the same thing, the main reason why the constituent treaty should determine as precisely as feasible the conduct of states against which the sanctions stipulated by the treaty are to be directed, is that all the members of a security organization have a legitimate right to know in advance what conduct is prohibited. It cannot be denied that a legal order is most unsatisfactory if it leaves its subjects in complete uncertainty about the content of their obligations.[23] This is especially true if the sanctions provided for by a legal order have the character of punishment, if the law is penal law, if the constituent treaty establishes individual criminal responsibility for all or even some of its violations.[24] If such a treaty does not define the crimes which constitute aggression, for the commission of which individuals may be punished, but leaves the definition of these crimes to the law-applying organ, such crimes may very well be regarded, if not formally at least substantially, as so-called *crimen sine lege*, and the punishment inflicted by the organ upon a person found guilty of such a crime may very well be considered to be *poena sine lege*. This means that establishing individual criminal responsibility for crimes constituting aggression without defining these crimes in advance implies the violation of a fundamental principle generally recognized in the field of criminal law: *nullum crimen et nulla poena sine lege*, no crime and no punishment without a pre-established general norm defining, as precisely as possible, the crime as well as the punishment. This is the application of the rule-of-law principle to criminal law.[25]

If the opposite principle of leaving the definition of aggression to the law-applying organ is adopted in a security system, it is usually justified by the argument that it guarantees the flexibility of the legal order.[26] There can be no doubt that lawmakers in general, and those who on behalf of their states conclude a treaty constituting an international security system in particular, cannot foresee all the possible circumstances under which a pre-established general norm has to be applied and cannot provide for unforeseen circumstances in which an application of the norm may lead to unsatisfactory results. However, this problem is not particular to a system of international security, but applies to any legal order. The disadvantage involved is a consequence of the rule-of-law principle and may be considered to be outweighed or at least compensated for by the advantages of this principle. In regard to this rule-of-law principle, it may be added that the greater the discretion left to the law-applying organ, the greater the possibility of its decisions being influenced by motives other than the sincere intention of realizing the main purpose of a security system which is to react against an aggressor, or, as it is usually formulated, the greater the possibility of being influenced by political considerations. An organ competent to determine the aggressor, especially if this function is left to the individual states, will hesitate to apply the constituent treaty in conformity with its spirit if the state against which the sanctions provided for by the treaty are to be directed is very powerful or is united with the state competent to determine the aggressor by a common interest other than an interest in the collective security for which the international organization is established. If the answer to the question of which state is the aggressor depends on a definition of aggression by the law-applying organ, the state acting as an organ of the security organization will naturally find justification for an attitude determined by its political interests.

(jj) *Is aggression a political concept and not a legal one?*

It is because of this possibility that the method of defining aggression in advance is sometimes opposed. This opposition is frequently justified by a doctrine which holds that aggression is not a legal concept, or not an exclusively legal concept, but a political concept or a partially political concept. The conclusion this doctrine reaches is

370624—57——6

that only legal, and not political, concepts can or should be defined in advance; or, that as far as the problem of collective security in general or the concept of aggression in particular are concerned, legal functions cannot be separated from political considerations; or, assuming that juridical considerations cannot be divorced from political factors,[27] that the treaty constituting an international security organization is not a legal but a political instrument and consequently has to be formulated and interpreted in a political way and not from a strictly juridical standpoint.

In the opinion of the author these views are theoretically untenable. A concept is legal if its object is a set of legal norms or social relationships constituted by legal norms, and a concept is political if its object is a set of norms other than legal norms or the social relationships constituted by such norms. There is no reason to assume that political concepts are less definable than legal concepts or that only legal concepts must be more or less precisely defined. The question of whether or not a concept is definable and if it is, to what extent it is definable, is a logical question which has nothing to do with the legal or political character of a concept. It cannot be maintained that concepts employed in political norms, in contradistinction to concepts employed in legal norms, should not be defined in advance in order to allow the organ applying the political norms the greatest possible liberty of action, because a pre-established definition of a legal concept may be rejected for the same reason. It is a peculiarity of the law that it regulates its own creation and application. However, the creation and application of the law are always determined not only by legal norms but also by non-legal, political norms, or, as it is usually formulated, by political considerations. This is not particular to a legal system of international security. The establishment of the historically first constitution of a legal community, a state, for example, is determined exclusively by political norms. The creation of statutes under a constitution is determined by the legal norms of the constitution but usually only insofar as the legislative procedure in which the statutes are to be created is concerned. The content of statutes is determined only by non-legal, i. e., political norms. The application of statutes by courts and other law-applying organs is determined to a much greater extent by legal norms (by the statutes themselves) and to a much lesser extent by non-legal, political norms than the creation of statutes. If discretion is left to an organ competent to create or to apply the law, in fulfilling its function the organ may be influenced by other than legal norms—that is, by political norms or, as it is usually formulated, by political considerations. However, the influence of political norms or political considerations must take place only within the framework of the legal norms determining the function of the organ. Since the function of either a law-creating or a law-applying organ can never be determined completely by legal norms, the legal function really cannot be separated from political considerations, except in the sense that political considerations cannot be eliminated in that area of an organ's function that is not determined by legal norms. In this sense, political considerations cannot be divorced from the function of a law-applying organ within a system of international security, whether the constituent treaty prohibiting aggression does or does not contain a definition of this concept. However, there is more room for political considerations if the treaty does not contain such a definition. Since the treaty is a legal instrument, stipulating legal obligations and legal rights of the contracting parties on the basis of general international law, the concept of aggression employed in the treaty is a legal concept. However, in defining the concept of aggression, the lawmakers—that is, the contracting parties—are directed not by general international law, if this law does not prohibit aggression, but by political principles. Insofar as the concept of aggression is both a legal and a political concept, just as the treaty itself is both a legal and a political instrument, the same is true if the definition of aggression is left to the law-applying organ. This is a consequence of the fact that the legal functions of creating and applying the law are always determined not only by legal but also by non-legal, political norms.

As far as the interpretation of the constituent treaty, or the interpretation of any legal instrument, is concerned, it is neither legal nor political because no interpretation is specifically legal or specifically political; all possible methods of interpretation are applicable to all possible objects of interpretation. A constitution, a treaty, or a political agreement which has no legal character at all can be interpreted in the same way as the Bible or Shakespeare's Hamlet.

It follows from this analysis that the above mentioned view which rejects a pre-established definition of aggression by referring to the political character of the concept, or of the constituent treaty employing this concept, is open to argument. However, it does not follow that a pre-established definition of aggression cannot be rejected. What does follow is that such a rejection must be justified in another way and can best be justified by arguments in favor of a high degree of flexibility of a security system which, as pointed out, can be achieved only at the expense of the degree of security. However, a reasonable degree of flexibility of this system can be established without abandoning the attempt to define aggression in the treaty constituting the international security organization.

(kk) *General or enumerative definition of aggression.*

Aggression may be defined in a constitutent treaty either by a general formula (a so-called general definition), by specifying the particular actions which constitute aggression (a so-called enumerative definition), or by a general formula illustrated by the specifications of certain actions which fall within the scope of the general definition (mixed definition).[28]

A typical example of a general formula defining aggression is the statement: aggression is any use of armed force by one state against another for purposes other than self-defense or the execution of a sanction stipulated by the treaty constituting a security organization.[29] It makes no difference whether the treaty contains an express statement defining aggression in this way, or whether it simply prohibits any use of armed force by attaching specific sanctions including enforcement measures involving the use of armed force to it, excluding the application of these sanctions in the case of self-defense. It stands to reason that if a constituent treaty includes a general norm of this content, it need not employ the term "aggression" at all, and it would be superfluous to insert an express statement defining this term into the treaty. The definition of aggression is implied in the general norm and may be deduced from it by interpretation. Hence, the fact that a definition is superfluous in this case cannot be used, as it actually has been used, as an argument against a pre-established definition of aggression; nor can such an argument be based on the fact that a general definition, which is either implied in the general norm or is expressly formulated, could not achieve the main object of indicating precisely the cases in which aggression could be said to have occurred, and that in spite of such a definition it would be impossible to say in advance whether or not a given act was an aggressive act.[30] The main object of a general definition is not to enable one to indicate precisely and in advance all possible acts of aggression. At any rate, such a prediction is impossible. However, without doubt, there is a greater probability of foreseeing which acts will be declared acts of aggression by law-applying organs if there is a general definition of aggression inserted in the constituent treaty than if the treaty forbids aggression without any express or implied definition of this concept.[31]

Because the general norm formulated above or an express definition corresponding to such a norm does not allow a precise indication of all possible acts which are to be recognized as acts of aggression, a security system of this type has a relatively high degree of flexibility. It is flexible although it is not the definition of aggression, but the definition of a term used in the definition of aggression, the term "armed force," which is left to the law-applying organ. There is no doubt that this term can be defined in very different ways and that a remarkable amount of discretion in defining the term is conferred upon the law-applying organ competent to decide whether a concrete act does or does not constitute a use of armed force.

A characteristic example of a so-called enumerative definition is the definition of agression contained in the proposal of the USSR Delegation submitted to the General Commission of the Disarmament Conference (1932–1933) on 6 February 1933. The proposal did not present a definition of aggression but a definition of the aggressor which ran as follows (Doc. 1933. IX., 10, p. 237):

> "1. The aggressor in an international conflict shall be considered that State which is the first to take any of the following actions:
>
> (a) Declaration of war against another State;
>
> (b) The invasion by its armed forces of the territory of another State without declaration of war;
>
> (c) Bombarding the territory of another State by its land, naval or air forces or knowingly attacking the naval or air forces of another State;
>
> (d) The landing in, or introduction within the frontiers of, another State of land, naval or air forces without the permission of the Government of such a State, or the infringement of the conditions of such permission, particularly as regards the duration of sojourn or extension of area;
>
> (e) The establishment of a naval blockade of the coast or ports of another State."

To this enumeration of acts of aggression, intended to be considered as exhaustive, the following provision was added:

> "No considerations whatsoever of a political, strategical, or economic nature, including the desire to exploit natural riches or to obtain any sort of advantages or privileges on the territory of another State, no references to considerable capital investments or other special interests in a given State, or to the alleged absence of certain attributes of State organization in the case of a given country, shall be accepted as justification of aggression as defined in Clause 1."

There followed an enumeration of particular facts on which a justification for attack could not be based. Since the enumeration of the acts of aggression in Clause 1 was exhaustive, the provision of Clause 2 as well as the enumeration of facts on which a justification of attack could not be based, was superfluous from the point of view of correct legal technique.[32]

The USSR proposal was discussed by the General Commission and after discussion submitted to the Committee on Security Questions, which presented to the General Commission a report containing the following Articles (Doc. 1935. IX. 4, p. 683):

"ARTICLE 1.—The aggressor in an international conflict shall, subject to the agreements in force between the parties to the dispute, be considered to be that State which is the first to commit any of the following actions:

(1) Declaration of war upon another State;

(2) Invasion by its armed forces, with or without a declaration of war, of the territory of another State;

(3) Attack by its land, naval or air forces, with or without a declaration of war, on the territory, vessels or aircraft of another State;

(4) Naval blockade of the coasts or ports of another State;

(5) Provision of support to armed bands formed in its territory which have invaded the territory of another State, or refusal, notwithstanding the request of the invaded State, to take in its own territory all the measures in its power to deprive those bands of all assistance or protection.

ARTICLE 2.—No political, military, economic or other considerations may serve as an excuse or justification for the aggression referred to in Article 1."

The most important difference between the USSR definition and the definition by the Committee on Security Questions is found in the latter's point 5 which added acts of indirect aggression.[32a]

In 1953 the USSR submitted to the Special Committee on the Question of Defining Aggression the following draft resolution (A/AC.-66/L.2/Rev.1):

> The General Assembly, considering it necessary to formulate directives with a view to determining which party is guilty of aggression, declares that:
>
> 1. In an international conflict that State shall be declared the attacker which first commits one of the following acts: (a) declaration of war against another State; (b) invasion by its armed forces, even without a declaration of war, of the territory of another State; (c) bombardment by its land, sea or air forces of the territory of another State or the carrying out of a deliberate attack on the ships or aircraft of the latter; (d) the landing or leading of its land, sea or air forces inside the boundaries of another State without the permission of the government of the latter, or the violation of the conditions of such permission, particularly as regards the length of their stay or the extent of the area in which they may stay; (e) naval blockade of the coasts or ports of another State; (f)

support of armed bands organized in its own territory which invade the territory of another State, or refusal, on being requested by the invaded State, to take in its own territory any action within its power to deny such bands any aid or protection.

2. That State shall be declared to have committed an act of indirect aggression which: (a) encourages subversive activity against another State (acts of terrorism, diversion, etc.); (b) promotes the outbreak of civil war within another State; (c) promotes an internal upheaval in another State or a reversal of policy in favour of the aggressor.

3. That State shall be declared to have committed an act of economic aggression which first commits one of the following acts: (a) takes against another State measures of economic pressure violating its sovereignty and economic independence and threatening the bases of its economic life; (b) takes against another State measures preventing it from exploiting or nationalizing its own natural riches; (c) subjects another State to an economic blockade.

4. That State shall be declared to have committed an act of ideological aggression which: (a) encourages war propaganda; (b) encourages propaganda in favour of using atomic, bacterial, chemical and other weapons of mass destruction; (c) promotes the propagation of fascist-nazi views of racial and national exclusiveness, and of hatred and contempt for other peoples.

5. An act other than those listed in the preceding paragraphs may when committed by a State be deemed to constitute aggression if declared by resolution of the Security Council in a particular case to be an attack or an act of economic, ideological or indirect aggression.

6. Attacks such as those referred to in paragraph 1 and acts of economic, ideological and indirect aggression such as those referred to in paragraphs 2, 3, and 4 may not be justified by any arguments of a political, strategic or economic nature, or by the desire to exploit natural riches in the territory of the State attacked or to derive any other kind of advantages or privileges, or by reference to the amount of capital invested in the State attacked or to any other particular interests in its territory, or by the affirmation that the State attacked lacks the distinguishing marks of statehood.—In particular, the following may not be used as justifications:

A. The internal position of any State, as for example: (a) the backwardness of any nation politically, economically or culturally; (b) alleged shortcomings of its administration; (c) any danger which may threaten the life or property of aliens; (d) any revolutionary or counter-revolutionary movement, civil war, disorders, or strikes; (e) the establishment or maintenance in any State of any political, economic or social system.

B. Any acts, legislation or orders of any State, as for example: (a) the violation of international treaties; (b) the

> violation of rights and interests in the sphere of trade, concessions or any other kind of economic activity acquired by another State or its citizens; (c) the rupture of diplomatic or economic relations; (d) measures in connexion with an economic or financial boycott; (e) repudiation of debts; (f) prohibition or restriction of immigration or modification of the status of foreigners; (g) the violation of privileges granted to the official representatives of another State; (h) refusal to allow the passage of armed forces proceeding to the territory of a third State; (i) measures of a religious or anti-religious nature; (j) frontier incidents.
>
> 7. In the event of the mobilization or concentration by another State of considerable armed forces near its frontier, the State which is threatened by such action shall have the right of recourse to diplomatic or other means of securing a peaceful settlement of international disputes. It may also in the meantime adopt requisite measures of a military nature similar to those described above, without, however, crossing the frontier.

The enumerative definition formulated in this draft resolution is characterized by the fact that it includes not only acts of indirect but also of economic and ideological aggression.[33]

It is evident that an enumerative definition of aggression (or the aggressor) such as the one quoted above, restricts the freedom of action of the organ competent to apply the treaty containing such a definition to a much greater extent, and thus renders the security system less flexible, than the general definition mentioned above. However, neither a general nor an enumerative definition of aggression inserted into the constituent treaty attaching specific sanctions to acts of aggression necessarily leads to an application of these sanctions in all cases which, in the opinion of the law-applying organ, fall within the scope of the definition, or, as it is usually but incorrectly formulated, to the "automatic" operation of the coercive machinery of the security system. The law laid down in the constituent treaty may authorize the law-applying organ not to proceed immediately to the determination of the aggressor but first to call upon the parties to the conflict to cease hostilities and conform to certain measures of conservation, such as the withdrawal of troops beyond a certain line, or the acceptance of an investigation on the spot by impartial authorities. The law may also authorize the law-applying organ, once it has ascertained the existence of an act of aggression, to apply peaceful measures to settle the conflict before applying sanctions. The law-applying organ may even be authorized to abstain altogether from applying sanctions under particular circumstances to be determined by this organ. However, in this latter case the fact must be considered that, if a definite conduct is not made the condition of a sanction, it is not illegal, and hence it is not "aggression" in the sense of an action prohibited by the security treaty.

A mixed definition of aggression is the one proposed by the representative of Panama at the 406th meeting of the Sixth Committee on 20 October 1954 [34], which runs as follows:

> 1. Aggression means any use of armed force by one State against another State for any purpose other than individual or collective self-defence, or in pursuance of a decision or recommendation of a competent organ of the United Nations;
>
> 2. In addition to any other acts that the competent organs of the United Nations may declare to constitute aggression, the acts enumerated below are specific acts of aggression if committed for purposes other than those stated in the preceding paragraph: (a) invasion of the territory of a State by the armed forces of another State; (b) armed attack against the territory, population or land, naval or air forces of one State by the land, naval or air forces of another State; (c) blockade of the coast, ports, or any other part of the territory of a State by the land or naval forces of another State; (d) the organization, or the encouragement of the organization, by the authorities of a State, of armed bands within its territory or any other territory for incursions into the territory of another State, or the toleration of the organization of such bands in its own territory, or the toleration of the use by such armed bands of its territory as a base of operations or as a point of departure for incursions into the territory of another State, as well as direct participation in or support of such incursions; (e) the annexation by the authorities of one State or territory belonging to another State by means of acts contrary to international law.
>
> 3. It shall rest with the General Assembly in the exercise of its general powers or with the Security Council in the exercise of the special power vested in it by Article 39 of the United Nations Charter to declare, at such time as it may deem appropriate, that the State that has directly or indirectly employed force in any of the ways set forth in paragraphs 1 and 2 of this resolution is guilty of aggression.

(11) *The difficulties in defining aggression and in determining the aggressor.*

It can certainly not be denied that defining aggression is difficult. However, to overcome the difficulties concerned, it is necessary to have a clear idea of their nature. First of all, it is necessary to avoid a confusion which almost always affects the discussion of the definition of aggression: the confusion between the difficulties which exist in defining "aggression" and those which exist in ascertaining that a concrete act is an act of aggression or, what amounts to the same thing, in determining the aggressor in a concrete case in conformity with the definition of aggression. That this confusion actually occurs may be explained by the fact that if, and to the extent that, a definition of aggression is not pre-established in a constituent treaty but left to the law-applying organ, this function and that of determining the aggressor are both performed by the same individual or individuals, and hence the distinction between the two functions is not very clear in their minds. As a result, the difficulties involved in determining a concrete aggressor are mistaken for the difficulties involved in defining aggression, and vice versa.

From the foregoing it follows that the main difficulties which every attempt to define aggression encounters are caused by the decision concerning the scope of the definition—that is, by the answer to the question of how far the security system should go in prohibiting a definite conduct of states by attaching specific sanctions to it. As far as a pre-established definition is concerned, the difficulty consists of the fact that under particular circumstances which are not and cannot be foreseen, a certain action which does not fall under the definition may be, and an action which does fall under the definition may not be, an appropriate condition for a sanction. In other words, the difficulty is that the definition may prove to be too narrow or too broad. We have dealt with this problem which, as has been pointed out, is a problem of all legislation, as the formulation of general norms. The difficulty in an enumerative definition of aggression is that no exhaustive enumeration can be complete, especially in view of the modern technique of warfare, and if an enumeration is not exhaustive but only illustrative, the acts enumerated being only examples of aggression, the enumeration is not a definition at all.

Totally different from the difficulties in defining aggression are the difficulties in ascertaining that an act is an act of aggression, or, what amounts to the same thing, in determining the aggressor, in conformity with a definition, whether the definition is established in advance or is to be established by the law-applying organ competent to determine the aggressor. These difficulties are exactly the same as those encountered in any legal procedure for the ascertainment of a fact to which the law attaches certain consequences. They are the typical difficulties involved in gathering, examining and evaluating evidence whether the question is which of the states involved in a conflict was the first to use force, whether it is the intention of this state, or whether it is any other question to be answered in connection with the application of the general norm of the security system prohibiting aggression in a concrete case.

In the procedure by which the treaty constituting the security organization is to be applied, there are, as in any law-applying procedure, two different methods of regulating the procedure for ascertaining the legally relevant facts: one consists of leaving the law-applying organ completely free in this respect, the other of establishing definite rules concerning the means of evidence and their evaluation. To adopt the first method within a system of international security means to confer an extraordinary power upon the organ competent to determine an aggressor. In this case, the position of this organ is not very different from that which results from leaving the definition of aggression to this organ. The restrictions imposed upon the law-applying organ by a pre-established definition may be outweighed by the organ's liberty in adjudging evidence. Attempts may be made to restrict this liberty or, to look at the problem from another angle, to facilitate the function of the organ. For this purpose, certain actions, indicated in the constituent treaty, may allow the presumption that aggression has taken place, e. g., the invasion of the territory of one state by the troops of another, or an attack on a considerable scale launched by one state against the frontier of another. It is especially difficult to ascertain that an act is an act of aggression if a definite intention of the state, which is to be stigmatized an aggressor, is an element of this concept. Hence, it may be considered advisable to insert into the constituent treaty an enumeration of certain objective facts as symptoms of such an intention, e. g., economic or military mobilization, presence of the armed forces of one state in the territory of another, or the refusal to submit the conflict to a pacific procedure. These facts would allow the law-applying organ to presume that the intention exists. The presumption may or may not be conclusive—that is, the inference as to the existence of aggression or aggressive intention may or may not be made peremptory by the existence of the indicated facts. If the presumption is conclusive, it cannot be reversed by any proof to the contrary, however strong the proof may be. It is irrebuttable, a *presumptio juris et de jure*. The enumeration of facts as irrebuttable evidence of the existence of aggression is equivalent to an enumerative definition of aggression.[35] If the presumption is not irrebuttable, (a *presumptio juris* but not *de jure*), it can be rejected by a decision of the law-applying organ. The Geneva Protocol, a draft treaty adopted by the Assembly of the League of Nations on 2 October 1924 but abandoned the following year, contains a series of presumptions by which an aggressor may be determined "in the event hostilities having broken out," but provides that these presumptions may be rejected by a unanimous decision of the Council.[36]

(mm) *The problem of provocation.*

Finally, it should be mentioned that there is a certain tendency to restrict the prohibition of the use of armed force and hence the concept of aggression to an unprovoked attack, so that a provoked use of armed force would be permitted and could be justified as self-defense. Provocation may consist of the use of armed force, or of the violation of international law not involving the use of armed force, or of an unfriendly attitude of a state towards another state which does not constitute any violation of international law. If a system of international security is to eliminate the principle of self-help as far as possible, only a provocation which consists of the use of armed force by one state against another can justify the use of armed force by the state attacked—that is, only if provoked by the use of armed force by another state, would a state be justified in using armed force itself. In this case, self-defense would be permitted only as a reaction against the use of armed force, and any use of armed force which is not self-defense (or the execution of a specific sanction of the security system) would be aggression. If any violation of international law, and not only the use of armed force, is recognized as a provocation justifying the use of armed force by a single state—that is, if the states are authorized to resort to the use of armed force as a reaction against any violation of their rights—the principle of self-help prevails together with the *bellum justum* principle. This means that the lowest possible degree of international security exists. In this case, the concept of self-defense—that is, the use of armed force as a reaction against an illegal use of armed force—is of little importance, since the use of armed force is legal as a reaction against any violation of the law. Hence, the concept of self-defense may be extended to include the reaction of a state against any violation of its rights, and the concept of aggression may be restricted to the use of armed force which is not a reaction against a violation of the law. If even the unfriendly attitude of a state, which does not constitute a violation of the law, is recognized as a provocation which justifies the use of armed force, and if a state may thus resort to the use of armed force as a reaction against the conduct of another state which is not illegal, even the principle of *bellum justum* does not prevail, and no international security whatsoever exists. In this case, the concept of aggression is not applicable at all, since the use of armed force is not illegal, and the concept of self-defense has no legal meaning.

NOTES

1. The International Law Commission, established in pursuance of General Assembly Resolution 174 (II) of 21 November, 1947, adopted in its third session (16 May–27 July 1951) as a basis of discussion the following definition of aggression: "Aggression is the threat or use of force by a State or government against another State, in any manner, whatever the weapons employed and whether openly or otherwise, for any reason or for any purpose other than individual or collective self-defence or in pursuance of a decision or recommendation by a competent organ of the United Nations." However, when submitted to the final vote the definition was rejected. Report of the International Law Commission covering the work of its third session 16 May–27 July 1951. *General Assembly, Official Records:* Sixth Session, Suppl. No. 9 (A/1858), pp. 9, 10.

1a. Because the Kellogg-Briand Pact did not contain an express clause stipulating the right of self-defense, the contracting parties had to make reservations concerning their right to resort to war in the exercise of self-defense. It was generally assumed that the right of self-defense was presupposed by the Pact. However, the extent to which this right could be exercised under the Pact remained an open question which was answered in different ways by the various signatories. Thus in a note of June 23, 1928, the United States Government declared that the proposed treaty did not restrict or impair the right of self-defense; but it justified this reservation by the doctrine that the right of self-defense is established by natural law and hence does not need positive stipulation. "That right is inherent in every sovereign state and is implicit in every treaty. Every nation is free at all times and regardless of treaty provisions to defend its territory from attack or invasion and it alone is competent to decide whether circumstances require recourse to war in self-defense." *Treaty for the Renunciation of War*, Department of State Publication No. 468 (1933), p. 57. *Cf.* Philip C. Jessup, *A Modern Law of Nations*, New York 1948, p. 163. The statement that every nation "alone is competent to decide whether circumstances require recourse to war in self-defense" is hardly compatible with Articles 51 and 39 of the Charter of the United Nations. *Cf. infra*, note 3.

1b. Article 51 of the Charter runs as follows: "Nothing in the present Charter shall impair the inherent right of individual or collective self-defense if an armed attack occurs against a Member of the United Nations, until the Security Council has taken the measures necessary to maintain international peace and security. Measures taken by Members in the exercise of this right of self-defense shall be immediately reported to the Security Council and shall not in any way affect the authority and responsibility of the Security Council under the present Charter to take at any time such action as it deems necessary in order to maintain or restore international peace and security."

The wording of this provision presupposes a natural right of self-defense existing independently of the Charter and declares only that it is not in conflict with this right: "Nothing in the present Charter shall impair the inherent right of individual and collective self-defense if an armed attack occurs against a Member of the United Nations . . ." (In the French text the term "droit naturel de légitime défense" is used.) However, in truth, the Charter does not merely respect an already existing right but establishes a right and must establish it as an express restriction to the provision of Article 2, paragraph 4, which imposes upon the members the obligation to refrain in their international relations from the use of force. Since under Article 51 of the Charter the right of self-defense may be exercised only "if an armed attack occurs," that means: if such an attack actually takes place, a preventive war on the part of a member state is illegal.

2. According to the wording of Article 51, the exercise of the right of self-defense is justified only in case of an armed attack "against a Member of the United Nations." However, according to an almost generally accepted interpretation of Article 51, the right of collective self-defense may also be exercised in case of an armed attack against a non-member state. *Cf. supra*, p. 61. Since the Charter of the United Nations does not define the term "armed attack" used in Article 51, the members of the United Nations in exercising their right of individual or collective self-defense may interpret "armed attack" to mean not only an action in which a state uses its own armed force but also a revolutionary movement which takes place in one state but which is initiated or supported by another state. In this case, the members could come to the assistance of the legitimate government against which the revolutionary movement is directed.

Such an interpretation would be consistent with the fact that, according to the wording of Article 39, in case the Security Council considers such a revolutionary movement to be a threat to or breach of the peace, it may take enforcement measures against the revolutionary forces as well as against the state which has initiated or supported this movement, to assist the attacked government. Article 39 authorizes the Security Council to take measures "to maintain or restore international peace and security." It says nothing about the party against which these measures are to be taken.

3. According to Article 51 of the Charter of the United Nations, the right of individual or collective self-defense may be exercised only "until the Security Council has taken the measures necessary to maintain international peace and security." According to Article 39, the Security Council "shall determine the existence of any threat to the peace, breach of the peace, or act of aggression." Hence as soon as the Security Council intervenes, it must decide which state is the aggressor and which is the defender. However, according to the wording of Articles 39 and 51, the Security Council is not bound to take enforcement measures only against the state which it considers to be the aggressor—that is, only against the state it considers to be guilty of an "armed attack." The Council may take any measures which it considers necessary to restore peace.

4. For instance, Article 10 of the Covenant of the League of Nations stipulated: "The Members of the League undertake to respect and preserve as against external aggression the territorial integrity and existing political independence of all Members of the League. In case of any such aggression or in case of any threat or danger of such aggression the Council shall advise upon the means by which this obligation shall be fulfilled." *Cf.* Article 2, paragraph 4, of the Charter of the United Nations.

5. The question as to whether aggressive intent should be considered as an essential element of the concept of aggression has been discussed in the Special Committee on the Question of Defining Aggression, established by Resolution 688 (VII) adopted by the General Assembly in its 408th plenary meeting on 20 December 1952. *Cf.* the Report of this Committee: *General Assembly, Official Records:* Ninth Session, Supplement No. 11 (A/2638), p. 8.

6. *Cf.* the Report of the Secretary-General of the United Nations entitled: *Question of Defining Aggression. United Nations General Assembly.* Seventh Session. Document A/2211, 3 October 1952, p. 55 (hereafter referred to as: Doc. A/2211).

6a. The International Law Commission, in its Report Doc. A/1858, p. 9, declared itself in favor of including indirect aggression in the definition of aggression. The report speaks of "indirect forms of aggression such as the fomenting of civil strife by one State in another, the arming by a State of organized bands for offensive purposes directed against another State, and the sending of 'volunteers' to engage in hostilities against another State." The report refers to Resolution 380 (V) of 17 November 1950, in which the General Assembly "Solemnly reaffirms that, whatever the weapons used, any aggression, whether committed openly, or by fomenting civil strife in the interest of a foreign Power, or otherwise, is the gravest of all crimes against peace and security throughout the world."

7. *Cf.* Document A/2211, p. 48.

7a. The Draft Treaty of Disarmament and Security prepared by an American Group (Declaration outlawing Aggressive War) stipulated: "Article 1. The High Contracting Parties solemnly declare that aggressive war is an international crime. They severally undertake not to be guilty of its commission. Article 2. A State engaging in war for other than purposes of defence commits the international crime described in Article 1. Article 3. The Permanent Court of International Justice shall have jurisdiction, on the complaint of any Signatory, to make a judgment to the effect that the international crime described in Article 1 has or has not in any given case been committed. Article 4. The High Contracting Parties solemnly declare that acts of aggression, even when not amounting to a state of war, and preparations for such acts of aggression, are hereafter to be deemed forbidden by international law. Article 5. In the absence of a state of war, measures of force by land, by sea or in the air taken by one State against another and not taken for the purpose of defence against aggression or for the protection of human life shall be deemed to be acts of aggression. General or partial mobilization may be deemed to be preparation for an act of aggression. Any Signatory which claims that another Signatory has violated any of the terms of this Declaration shall submit its case to the Permanent Court of International Justice. A Signatory refusing to accept the jurisdiction of the Court in any such case shall be deemed an aggressor within the terms of this Declaration. Failure to accept the jurisdiction of the Court within four days after notification of submission of a claim of violation of this Declaration shall be deemed a refusal to accept the jurisdiction." *League of Nations. Official Journal.* Special Supplement No. 26 (1924), p. 169.

8. *Cf.* Doc. A/2211, p. 57. The International Convention concerning the Use of Broadcasting in the Cause of Peace, signed at Geneva on 23 September 1936, imposes upon the contracting parties the obligations to refrain from broadcasting within their respective territories matter of "such a character as to incite the population of any territory to acts incompatible with the internal order or the security of a territory of a High Contracting Party" (Article 1), and to ensure that transmissions "shall not constitute an incitement either to war against another High Contracting Party or to acts likely to lead thereto" (Article 2). In its Resolution 424 (V) adopted 14 December 1950, the General Assembly "invites all Governments to refrain from radio broadcasts that would mean unfair attacks or slanders against other peoples anywhere and in so doing to conform strictly to an ethical conduct in the interest of world peace by reporting facts truly and objectively." *Cf.* also *infra*, pp. 210 f.

In the Nuremberg Trial "aggressive acts" were proved to have been committed against Austria and Czechoslovakia, although the Nazi-Government had reached its goal without the use of armed force, by internal subversive actions and the threat of violence. *Cf.* Pompe, *op cit.*, p. 21.

9. *Cf.* Doc. A/2211, p. 58.

9a. Pompe, *op. cit.*, p. 53, distinguishes four categories of aggression "depending whether or not aggression is seen in direct conection with war and whether or not aggression is considered as an exclusively military action. The first, original concept indicates the military beginning of a war, the second includes an aggressive policy which causes a war. A further extension of 'aggression' comprises, in principle, every (illicit) use of armed force against another State, including the threat of armed force. And finally there is the last category, since at one time or another all sorts of either illegal, or merely unfriendly acts harmful to other States have in the course of the last years been named 'aggression.' "

10. *Cf.* Doc. A/2211, p. 36.

11. In his report on the *Project of a Treaty of Mutual Assistance* (Projet de Traité d'Assistance Mutuelle) presented at the Fourth Assembly of the League of Nations, Document A 111, 1923, IX (1st part), Mr. Benes declared: "Under the conditions of modern warfare it would seem impossible to decide even in theory what constitutes an act of aggression."

12. In a Memorandum on "The System of Sanctions of Article 16 of the Covenant and the Future Rôle of Neutrality," presented to the International Studies Conference on Collective Security (1934–1935), Dr. G. Cohn of the Danish Institute of History and Economics stated: "The system of sanctions should be directed against war as such, as a fact, without regard to its psychological basis. From this point of view defensive war must be included as well as offensive war, so that the states not involved in the conflict may not be obliged to make a choice which would at the same time necessitate the moral condemnation of one of the Powers, but may simply be confronted with the state of war as a fact which must be prevented and combated, in the common interest of all the nations. It is of little importance to determine who, from a purely formal standpoint, is playing the part of the aggressor. War is forbidden in all cases and for all parties, and it cannot provide any kind of advantage, whether economic, political or legal . . . The Council should decide when sanctions are to be applied and when they are to cease, so that the different Powers may not have on this point any individual responsibility, and so that it may thus be quite clear that they are not seeking an individual advantage and are not letting themselves be guided by selfish sympathies, but are acting solely in the general interest of the League of Nations as a whole. The decision of the Council should be binding on all, and should be reached by a modified majority—of three-fourths, for example—and under such conditions that the representatives on the Council of the belligerent States (both the aggressor and the State which has been attacked) would not have the right to vote. All dispositions, whether economic, political or military, should proceed from the League of Nations as such, and not from its individual members." *Collective Security*, pp. 402 f. In his book: *Neo-Neutrality*, New York, 1939, Dr. Cohn dealt with neutrality as a part of the system of war-prevention. As such, he asserted that it "is essentially different from traditional neutrality. The latter was based on an equal *evaluation* of the belligerents, with consequent impartiality toward both under detailed rules for war and neutrality. Traditional neutrality took a dependent and passive attitude toward war. It was oriented by war. Neo-neutrality, on the other hand, is based on an equal *devaluation* of the war in all cases; it does not seek its own *raison d'être* in reflections as to whether it has in one situation or another a moral or legal claim

to assert its nonparticipation as a right; it takes an exception in principle to participation in war in any form. It does not recognize the supremacy of the law of war; it replaces it instead with a system of combined sanctions and neutrality which centers about an effort to suppress and prevent war of every kind. The neo-neutral states are in reality those states which, without becoming a party to war, are participants in the system of sanctions designed to prevent war. They do not participate, and under no circumstances will participate, in war. Moreover, they do not recognize war as a legal situation, they recognize no obligation of impartiality, and they are willing to apply any means to prevent or to stop the war to the limit of their ability without themselves participating in it." *Op. cit.*, pp. 253–4. Consequently a security system must provide only for economic but not for military sanctions. Neo-neutrality asks in all cases of war "that the peaceful sanctions which are available to the League be extended and made sufficiently severe to compel cessation of the war." *Op. cit.*, pp. 29–30. However, it is very doubtful that economic sanctions can be made "sufficiently severe." Dr. Cohn did not go so far as to deny the right of self-defense within a system of neo-neutrality. He said: "To Neo-neutrality, it is of interest only to state the limits of what constitutes self-defense in international law. These limits are to be determined by a study of the analogous situation of the limits of the concept of self-defense in municipal penal law and have nothing to do with the traditional rules of war or neutrality." *Op. cit.*, p. 331. He thought that the right of self-defense under international law was totally different from the right of self-defense under national law. He asserted that self-defense under national law, i. e. "the right to use force for protection against an attack (*vim vi defendere*), is subject to quite definite legal restrictions (depending upon the purposes) for which there is no exact analogy nor application with respect to defensive war. The right of self-defense presumes the preexistence of a certain relation between the object of the attack and the means of defense which can be used. These limitations upon the right of self-defense naturally vary somewhat in different penal codes; nonetheless a common thought pervades them, which clearly indicates the distinct difference between this right and that of defensive war . . . But defensive war recognizes no limitations of this nature." *Op. cit.*, pp. 196–7.

The international right of self-defense may be limited within an international security system and thus be assimilated to the right of self-defense as established under national law, but it cannot be eliminated. If it exists, the distinction between a permitted defensive war and a prohibited aggressive war is inevitable, and then it is impossible to direct sanctions "against both belligerents," as the principle of neo-neutrality requires. *Op. cit.*, p. 282.

Cohn opposes his doctrine of neo-neutrality to the theory of aggression not only because he wants to avoid the politically undesirable moral condemnation of a state as an aggressor, but also because the theory of aggression makes concepts of criminal law such as "crime" and "guilt" the basis of a system of international security, and—as he assumes—there is no room for concepts of criminal law in international relations. He says: "The theory of aggression makes the penal concepts of private law the basis of an international system of war-prevention. Aggression is counted a crime, to be punished by the application of sanctions . . . It should be remarked, however, that no system of war-prevention can be founded upon the guilt of the individual leading statesmen in the aggressor state nor upon the collective guilt of an entire people. The conception of guilt between nations cannot be built upon analogies in municipal penal law. All the requisite conditions for a criminal arraignment of the aggressor as in municipal law, are lacking . . . Neo-neutrality, on the other hand, excludes in principle the question of guilt and of penal law concepts in the suppression of war." *Op. cit.*, pp. 332–3. The fundamental concept of criminal law is that of punishment; the concept of crime is of secondary nature, for a human conduct is a crime if it is the condition of a punishment. Punishment is—as pointed out—a reaction against a violation of the law, that is to say, it is a sanction. The characteristic of this sanction is that its purpose is prevention by deterrence, in contradistinction to a sanction the purpose of which is to repair the damage caused by the violation of the law. The concept of "guilt" (intention, negligence) is neither essential to nor specific of criminal law. There exists criminal responsibility not based on guilt, so-called absolute criminal responsibility; and there are rules of civil as well as international law which refer to intention or negligence as conditions of sanctions. Besides, Cohn admits "the fact that criminal blame or responsibility may be connected with the outbreak of war." (*Op. cit.*, p. 333.) Since the sanctions established by general international law as well as those stipulated in a system of international security are reactions against violations of the law with the purpose of prevention by deterrence, there is no essential difference between criminal and international law. Cohn defines neo-neutrality as a specific system of sanctions designed to prevent war as an illegal action. Hence his theory does not exclude penal law concepts in the suppression of war.

The term "neo-neutrality" is misleading, for it designates a system of collective security which tries to prevent war by means short of war and within which neutrality in the traditional sense—that is, implying the obligation of impartiality—is abandoned.

13. At the Eighth International Studies Conference, London, 1935, Professor Jessup suggested a way to terminate a war which has already broken out and to prevent future wars: ". . . a united neutral front against two unidentified aggressors or against two belligerents where judgment has not been reached as to which is the guilty party." *Collective Security*, p. 426. He sought of economic sanctions especially economic boycott of the belligerents by the neutral states. He referred to the action of the League of Nations in the Chaco affair where at least at the earlier stages an embargo was imposed upon both belligerents prior to a judgment as to which party was at fault, and to the Argentine anti-war pact of 1933 which provided for "a common and solidary attitude" of the neutrals towards the belligerents without imposing upon the former the obligation to take military measures against the latter. In his study *A Modern Law of Nations* (New York 1948), pp. 197 ff., Professor Jessup discusses a hypothetical situation, in which the Security Council in case of a military conflict between two states cannot get immediately the information necessary to determine the aggressor. He suggests that the Security Council in the meantime should announce the existence of a state of emergency and establish a blockade by land, sea and air, applied impartially to the area where the conflict is located and to both parties. He admits that this measure "would be hard on the state which is actually fighting in self-defense. But until there has been time for determination of the right and wrong of the case, no alternative is possible." Thus the purpose of the suggested procedure is not to avoid the determination of the aggressor.

14. In an article on "The Problem of Aggression and the Prevention of War," *American Journal of International Law*, vol. 31 (1937), pp. 244 ff., Mr. L. Kopelmanas came to the conclusion "that in case of war or threat of war, international society must possess an organ analogous to the internal police

for the purpose of acting against acts of war, without raising the question as to which of the belligerents is at fault. It should not be forgotten that the absence of discrimination between the aggressor and the victim would be of a nature to facilitate the action against war through avoiding the wounding of national susceptibilities." (p. 255). By "police" actions, Kopelmanas meant injunctions directed at both states involved in a war or both states whose attitudes constitute a threat of war. He also meant the enforcement of these injunctions against the state which does not comply with them. In this case, he said: "the aggressive intent of a state may be indicated by its refusal to obey the injunctions of the police, and the action can be directed against it alone. But it must be remembered that the problem of aggression, as it is construed in positive law, is not in question. The police acts against the eventual aggressor . . ."

If repressive measures are to be taken against a state responsible for a conduct which shows an intention to commit aggression, the problem of aggression is indeed involved. If the law provides for repressive measures to be directed against a state which does not comply with the injunction of a competent organ, the conduct of this state is a violation of the law and the repressive measures are sanctions, whether or not the organ is called the "police" and its action a "police" action. To regard illegal conduct as evidence of "aggressive intent" amounts to the same thing as regarding one's conduct as an act of aggression, the concept of aggression used in the wider sense as it is actually used in the theory and practice of international law.

Kopelmanas' doctrine is based on the erroneous idea that there is an essential difference between the function of the police and the function of penal repression of disorder. He said: "The penal judge intervenes only after order has been re-established" by the police, whose task is "maintaining good order and security in a given society." (p. 253). However, the "good order" and security maintained by the police is exactly the same good order maintained by the penal judge, namely, the law and the security guaranteed by this law. Furthermore, the penal judge does not intervene until after order has been re-established by the police. Is order re-established before the murderer or thief is punished? Is order re-established after an individual has been arrested by the police as a suspected murderer or thief but has later been acquitted by the judge as innocent? The preventive measures taken by a "police" organ may also be taken by a judge, especially by an international judge in case of war or threat of war, and the question as to whether or not in this case the judge acts as a "police" organ is simply a terminological question of minor importance. The repressive measures taken by the police are either reactions against non-compliance with its injunction and hence a sanction in exactly the same sense as a punishment inflicted in a judicial procedure on a person for having violated the penal law, or actions the purpose of which is to prepare and secure such judicial procedure.

15. The view that aggression is a concept not susceptible to definition has been advocated most characteristically in a report entitled: "The Possibility and Desirability of a Definition of Aggression," presented by Mr. Spiropoulos to the International Law Commission in its Third Session 16 May–27 July 1951. (Doc. *General Assembly, Official Records*, Sixth Session, Supplement No. 9, A/1858). In this report (Document A/CN. 4/44), the author came to the conclusion that the concept of aggression is a "notion *per se*" which "is not susceptible of definition." He seems to have had the idea that there are two kinds of concepts, those which are and those which are not definable. However, he did not maintain this view, for he evidently presupposed the possibility of

a definition when he stated that "whenever Governments are called upon to decide on the existence or non-existence of aggression under international law they base their judgment on criteria derived from the 'natural', so to speak, notion of aggression . . . and not on legal considerations."

This means that a government can decide whether aggression exists or does not exist only on the basis of definite criteria, and these criteria constitute the definition of the concept of aggression. In the first place, why can this determination be made only by a government. Why not by any law-applying organ, e. g., an international agency, a court, and the like? Secondly, how can this concept be a "natural" concept. It can be only a legal concept, the concept of aggression referred to in the law to be applied, the definition of which has been left to the government, or, more exactly, to the law-applying organ.

The author of the report then proceeded to an analysis of this allegedly "natural" concept of aggression—that is, he tried to construct a definition of this undefinable concept. He said that the notion of aggression is composed of both objective and subjective elements, namely, the fact that a state commits an act of violence and is the first to do so, and the fact that this violence is committed with aggressive intent (*animus aggressionis*). Hence, his definition of aggression is: an act of violence performed by the state which is the first to do so with aggressive intent.

This is a logically objectionable definition, because in part it constituted a so-called *idem per idem*—the element to be defined, aggression, appears in the definition. However, this defect could easily be avoided by restating the definition as follows: agression is an act of violence performed by one state with the intention of imposing its own will on another state. The author went on to state that the kind of violence, direct or indirect, or the degree of violence which constitutes aggression cannot be determined *a priori* but depends on the circumstances of the particular case. This means that he added two other elements to his definition: (1) the violence must have certain degrees, and (2) it may be direct or indirect. The definition which he tacitly presupposed then runs as follows: aggression is a direct or indirect act of violence, of a certain degree, performed by the state which is the first to do so with aggressive intent (meaning with the intention of imposing its will on the other state). That the kind of violence and its degree cannot be determined *a priori* does not mean that it cannot be determined at all. If it could not be determined, the government could not decide that aggression does or does not exist. What is meant is only that the determination of these elements is left to the law-applying organ.

16. *Official Records of the General Assembly*, Sixth Session, Sixth Committee, 286th meeting, paragraph 36.

17. Cf. Doc. A/2211, p. 12.

18. At its 408th plenary meeting on 20 December 1952, the General Assembly adopted Resolution 688 (VII) which reads as follows:

> The General Assembly, having regard to its resolution 599 (VI) of 31 January 1952, considering that the discussion of the question of defining aggression at the sixth and and seventh sessions of the General Assembly and in the International Law Commission has revealed the complexity of this question and the need for a detailed study of: (a) the various forms of aggression, (b) the connexion between a definition of aggression and the maintenance of international peace and security, (c) the problems raised by the inclusion of a definition of aggression in the Code of Offences against the Peace and Security of

Mankind and by its application within the framework of international criminal jurisdiction, (d) the effect of a definition of aggression on the exercise of the jurisdiction of the various organs of the United Nations, (e) any other problem which might be raised by a definition of aggression, considering that continued and joint efforts shall be made to formulate a generally acceptable definition of aggression, with a view to promoting international peace and security and to developing international law,

1. Decides to establish a Special Committee of fifteen members, each representing one of the following Member States: Bolivia, Brazil, China, Dominican Republic, France, Iran, Mexico, Netherlands, Norway, Pakistan, Poland, Syria, Union of Soviet Socialist Republics, United Kingdom of Great Britain and Northern Ireland, United States of America, to meet at the Headquarters of the United Nations in 1953;

2. Requests the said Special Committee: (a) to submit to the General Assembly at its ninth session draft definitions of aggression or draft statements of the notion of aggression; (b) to study all the problems referred to above on the assumption of a definition being adopted by a resolution of the General Assembly;

3. Requests the Secretary-General to communicate the Special Committee's report to Member States for their comments and to place the question on the provisional agenda of the ninth session of the General Assembly.

This resolution seems, in the author's opinion, to presuppose the view that a pre-established definition of aggression is possible and desirable. This was also the opinion of many members of the Special Committee established by the Resolution, but others held that the resolution "did not compel the Committee necessarily to adopt one or more specific draft definitions of aggression or one or more draft statements of the notion of aggression, but left it entirely free to choose between several courses." *Report of the Special Committee on the Question of Defining Aggression* (A/2638), pp. 2 f. During the discussion of this Report in the Sixth Committee, the representative of the United States declared at the 404th meeting, on 15 October 1954, after having referred to the fact that previous attempts to define aggression have failed: "the failure of the various attempts made in the past showed that it was impossible to reach agreement on an *a priori* definition of aggression. That had also been the conclusion of the authors of the Charter. There were obvious dangers in *a priori* definitions. A general definition would leave important concepts, like self-defence, unelaborated, while a list of examples, even if it did not claim to be all-inclusive, would have the disadvantage of singling out certain kinds of aggression for special emphasis. A combination of the two types of definition would run the risk of suffering from the defects of both.—The United States delegation also had a certain distrust of establishing *a priori* categories for future situations. Rather, the law should develop empirically out of actual cases. Aggression was not simply a combination of predefined elements; in fact, in order to determine whether aggression had occurred, it was necessary to weigh a whole set of complex facts and circumstances. That was why paper definitions had been avoided and the organs of the United Nations, particularly the Security Council, by virtue of Article 39 of the Charter, and also the General Assembly, under the Charter—as indicated by Resolution 377 (V) entitled 'Uniting for peace' had been given responsibilities for deciding what constituted an act of aggression or a threat to peace . . . . . to adopt a paper definition might jeopardize the efforts of the General Assembly and the Security Council to maintain international peace and security. In the absence of a definition, there could be no doubt, as the General Assembly had noted at its sixth session, that the existence of the crime of aggression might be inferred from the circumstances peculiar to each particular case. . . . The United States believed that the history of efforts to define aggression and the various considerations already referred to pointed to the conclusion that no constructive purpose would be served at this time by the preparation of a formula. The General Assembly should now consider that it had explored to the limits of usefulness the possibilities of defining aggression by a word formula prepared today for possible applications in the future." United Nations. *General Assembly.* Ninth Session. *Official Records,* Sixth Committee (A/C.6/SR. 404) p. 37.

The Special Committee did not suggest a definition of aggression; and the Sixth Committee in its Report of 2 December 1954 (Doc. A/2806) recommended to the General Assembly to establish a new special committee. Following the suggestion, the General Assembly adopted on 4 December 1954 Resolution 895 (IX), in which it established a Special Committee comprising representatives of 19 states, and requested the Committee "to submit to the General Assembly at its eleventh session a detailed report followed by a draft definition of aggression . . ." This report is not yet published.

The Charter of the United Nations does not contain a definition of aggression. Article 1, paragraph 1 declares as a Purpose of the Organization "to take effective collective measures for the suppression of acts of aggression"; and Article 39 authorizes the Security Council to "determine the existence of any . . . act of aggression" and then to make recommendations, or decide what measures shall be taken as a reaction against such acts. That means that the Charter leaves it to the Security Council to define in each case the concept of aggression. Only by an amendment could a definition be inserted into the text of the Charter. Such definition would certainly restrict the freedom of action of the Security Council. This was the reason why some members of the Sixth Committee were against a definition of aggression. *Cf.* the *Official Records,* especially of the 408th meeting on 25 October 1954, p. 58.

19. *Cf.* Doc. A/2211, p. 37.

20. In a memorandum presented to the International Studies Conference (1934–1935), Mr. Arnold Forster (of the British Coordinating Committee for International Studies) declared: "A definition [of aggression] . . . is of value, but should not be regarded either as an all-inclusive formula or as an automatic test which can always be relied upon to cut with precision through a tangled political situation. It may be of very substantial value as a means of crystallising and extending the new social ethic as to the use of national force, and it should help in the process of curtailing the anarchic liberties too often claimed by imperial Powers; but it will not work by itself automatically. It must be used by an international authority; it must be treated as a guide—normally a decisive guide—but not as an immutable law; and in case of doubt, the international authority should be empowered to impose obligatory peace-conserving measures, including an armistice." *Collective Security,* p. 308.

21. *Cf.* Doc. A/2211, p. 40.

22. Sixth Committee, 406th meeting (A/C.6/SR. 406) p. 47.

23. This is the case under the Charter of the United Nations. Article 39 authorizes the Security Council to take enforcement measures in case of a "threat to the peace, breach of the peace or act of aggression," but does not

define these concepts, so that the Security Council has discretion in deciding in each concrete case whether or not the conduct of a state constitutes a threat to the peace, breach of the peace or act of aggression. This regulation is particularly objectionable with respect to what the Charter calls a "threat to the peace." A state cannot foresee what the Security Council may consider to be a "threat to the peace," and consequently cannot adapt its conduct to the norm, implied in Article 39, of refraining from acts which constitute a threat to the peace.

24. *Cf.* infra pp. 122 ff.

25. *Cf.* the statement of the representative of Cuba at the 403rd meeting of the Sixth Committee on 14 October 1954 (A/C.6/SR. 403, p. 35) and of the representative of the Netherlands at the 410th meeting on 28 October 1954 (A/C.6/SR. 410) p. 72.

26. The principle of flexibility is sometimes opposed to the principle of law. In his *History of the Peace Conference of Paris* (London 1920, Vol. VI, p. 441), H. W. V. Temperley says with respect to the antagonism between the French and the Anglo-American view of international security: "The real divergence lay between the adherents of the rigid, the definite, the logical, in other words the juridical point of view, and those who preferred the flexible, the indefinite, the experimental, the diplomatic; between those who feared human nature and wished to bind the future, and those who believed in human nature and were content to trust the future; between those who desired written guarantees, and those who desire moral obligations only; to be cynical, between those who expected to receive under the Covenant, and those who expected to give; in a word, betweeen the continental point of view and the Anglo-Saxon." There is, however, no opposition between the juridical and the flexible point of view, for the antagonism between rigidity and flexibility exists within the law. They are two different methods of formulating a legal order; nor is the identification of the logical with the juridical point of view correct. A "flexible" legal order must not be illogical. It has to be as logical as a rigid one. Besides, the application of a general legal norm—whether formulated in a flexible or in a rigid way—to a concrete case is not a purely logical operation. Moral-political considerations are always more or less involved.

27. *Cf.* Doc. A/2211, p. 38.

28. *Cf. Ibid.* pp. 43 ff., and the *Report of the Special Committee on the Question of Defining Aggression* (A/2638), pp. 4 f.

29. In the Draft Convention on Rights and Duties of States in Case of Aggression, published by the Harvard Research in International Law, *American Journal of International Law*, Vol. 33 (1939) Supplement, pp. 823 ff., aggression is defined as "a resort to armed force by a State when such resort has been duly determined, by a means which that State is bound to accept, to constitute a violation of an obligation."

In its observations on the Draft Code of Offences against the Peace and Security of Mankind and on the Question of Defining Aggression, the Netherlands Government proposed that the concept of aggression should be defined as follows: "Aggression is the threat or use of force by a State or government against the territorial integrity or political independence of another State or against a territory under international regime in any manner, whatever the weapons employed and whether openly or otherwise, for any reason or for any purpose other than individual or collective self-defence against such a threat or use of force or in pursuance of a decision or recommendation by a competent organ of the United Nations." *Official Records of the General Assembly.* Seventh Session,

Annexes, agenda item 54, documents A/2162 and Add. 1. *Cf.* also *Report of the Special Committee on the Question of Defining Aggression* (A/2638), p. 12.

30. *Cf.* Doc. A/2211, p. 40.

31. In the Special Committee on the Question of Defining Aggression a general definition was criticized by some members. The representative of Poland maintained "that such a definition would serve no purpose as it would not refer to the elements constituting the crime. Its vagueness would open the way for dangerous polemics on the nature of a given act; the aggressor could challenge the description given of his act and take advantage of the necessarily lengthy discussions arising out of a definition which was lacking in clarity and precision to continue his aggressive activity. Moreover, that type of definition could not help effectively to combat the many types of aggression." The representative of the USSR stated "that a so-called general definition of aggression was inadequate, as could be seen from the specific proposals for such a definition. For example, aggression had been defined as an international crime, which, in effect, was rather like saying that aggression was aggression. Naturally, such an approach would not help that Committee to carry out the task before it." *Report of the Special Committee on the Question of Defining Aggression* (A/2638), p. 4.

32. In his criticism of the USSR definition, Professor Bourquin, *op. cit.*, p. 510, said: "Should the social reaction which ensues from the determination of the aggressor be possible if public opinion, without the support of which such reaction could not be understood, turned against the result of the operation, refusing to associate itself with the injustice involved in it? Within a realm of this kind [i. e., international relations] the algebra of formulas, even if passed by a convention, has little chance of offering resistance to the feeling of the people."

To which people does Professor Bourquin refer? Does he mean the people of the state against which the sanctions are directed? There will always be feeling against an action which imposes suffering on people, even if the action involves no injustice at all. The feeling of the people who are to be protected by the reaction of a security organization will certainly not turn against this reaction if it is directed against an aggressor in conformity with the USSR definition. The argument of public opinion is highly problematical, because it presupposes only one public opinion, whereas in reality there are almost always at least two public opinions, often in opposition to one another. Professor Bourquin's criticism of the USSR proposal could be used against any system of collective security which prohibits aggression by attaching sanctions to it.

32a. The definition of the Committee on Security Questions was followed in the Convention Defining Aggression between the Soviet Union and Afghanistan, Estonia, Latvia, Persia, Poland, Rumania, Turkey, signed at London on 3 July 1933. The territorial element plays a decisive part in this definition. *Cf.* W. Komarnicki, *La Définition de l'Agresseur dans le Droit International Moderne.* Académie de Droit International. Recueil des Cours. 1949, II., Vol. 75, p. 50.

33. In the Special Committee on the Question of Defining Aggression the representative of Poland stated that "an enumerative definition had the advantages of setting forth the elements which constituted the crime, indicating unequivocally the type of acts to be condemned, and placing the burden of proof upon the aggressor instead of requiring the victim to prove that the action complained of was aggression. In his opinion, the Soviet draft, from this point of view, was a perfect solution of the problem. In the opinion of other representatives, such a definition would be dangerous. It would necessarily be incomplete and would thereby inevitably imply that acts not enumerated did not constitute aggression. That in turn would enable a State to commit aggression by circumventing the defi-

nition. The decisions of international organs would be rendered automatic and the re-establishment of peace would thus be made more difficult." The representative of China "expressed the opinion that an enumeration could not be regarded as a true definition. It would not be sufficiently scientific and could not serve as guidance either for the organs of the United Nations responsible for the maintenance of peace and security, nor for the courts which might be set up to judge the perpetrators of crimes against humanity. The generally accepted sense of the word 'define' showed that enumeration could not achieve the purpose sought which was to make clear the essential nature of a concept. From a purely practical standpoint, an enumeration of crimes could only cause criminals to change their methods. Moreover, on the one hand, the competent political or legal organs would tend to study the methods of aggression rather than the act itself, and on the other, they would not have the proper perspective for judging each individual case, and that was absolutely necessary to prevent the act or to punish the author."

The representative of the United Kingdom emphasized that enumerative definitions "were the most deceiving. They were not so much definitions as incomplete catalogues of acts constituting aggression. Thus paragraphs 2, 3 and 4 not to mention the all-embracing provision of paragraph 5 had had to be added to the original text of the USSR proposal (A/AC.66/L.2/Rev.1). He questioned the value of a definition which, after listing various acts constituting aggression, stated that any other act declared to be aggression by the Security Council would also come into that category. Either the matter should be left to the Council, in which case there was no need for a catalogue, or the catalogue was effective in itself, in which case a list such as that proposed by the USSR delegation (A/AC.66/L.2/Rev.1) went too far. If applied literally, it would result in acts being wrongly declared as constituting aggression, and governments might argue that any act not covered in the text did not constitute aggression notwithstanding any decision to the contrary by the Security Council."

"Some members of the Committee had been in favour of a mixed definition that would start with a text in very general terms describing the characteristics of aggressive activity. This general text would be followed by an enumeration of specific acts, but the enumeration would be neither limitative nor exhaustive. It would not be obligatory but would simply be a series of examples. The advantage of a mixed definition was that it combined the merits and the positive aspects of the general and enumerative definitions. A mixed definition should therefore start with a generic concept including elements specific in their significance and be followed by an enumeration of the types of acts of aggression..." This type of definition had been criticized by other members of the Committee as embodying the defects of the two other types. The representative of the United States said "that instead of trying to establish a general formula which would probably be incomplete, it would be better to offer the competent organs of the United Nations, and in the first place the Security Council, a list of factors to be taken into account in deciding a given case. Some other members of the Committee thought this idea constructive and worth examining." *Report of the Special Committee on the Question of Defining Aggression* (A/2638), pp. 4 f.

Some members of the Committee decidedly rejected the inclusion of indirect and especially of economic and ideological aggression in the definition of aggression. *Cf. op. cit.*, pp. 8 ff.

34. *United Nations. General Assembly.* Ninth Session. *Official Records,* Sixth Committee, 406th meeting (A/C.6/SR. 406), pp. 45 f.

35. In his memorandum presented to the Committee on Arbitration and Security, established on 30 November 1924, by the Preparatory Commission for the Disarmament Conference, Mr. Rutgers (Netherlands) rejected the principle of defining the concept of aggression in advance. However, he considered that "it would be . . . practical to enumerate some of the facts which, according to circumstances, may serve as evidence that aggression has taken place." He distinguished between acts which "constitute acts of aggression," such as the invasion of the territory of one state by the troops of another or an attack on a considerable scale launched by one state on the frontiers of another, and "factors which may serve as basis in determining the aggressor: (a) Actual industrial and economic mobilization carried out by a State either in its own territory or by persons or societies on foreign territory. (b) Secret military mobilization by the formation and employment of irregular troops or by a declaration of a state of danger of war which would serve as a pretext for commencing hostilities. (c) Air, chemical, or naval attack carried out by one party against another. (d) The presence of the armed forces of one party in the territory of another. (e) Refusal of either of the parties to withdraw its armed forces behind a line or lines indicated by the Council. (f) A definitely aggressive policy by one of the parties towards the other, and the consequent refusal of that party to submit the subject in dispute to the recommendations of the Council or to the decision of the Permanent Court of International Justice and to accept the recommendation or decision when given." *Series of League of Nations Publications* IX. Disarmament 1928. IX, 6, pp. 142 ff.

36. League of Nations. Records of the Fifth Assembly, Minutes of the First Committee (*Official Journal*, Special Supplement No. 24), p. 138 ff. Article 10 of the Protocol ran as follows:

"Every State which resorts to war in violation of the undertakings contained in the Covenant or in the present Protocol is an aggressor. Violation of the rules laid down for a demilitarized zone shall be held equivalent to resort to war. In the event of hostilities having broken out, any State shall be presumed to be an aggressor, unless a decision of the Council, which must be taken unanimously, shall otherwise declare:

1. If it has refused to submit the dispute to the procedure of pacific settlement provided by Articles 13 and 15 of the Covenant as amplified by the present Protocol, or to comply with a judicial sentence or arbitral award or with a unanimous recommendation of the Council, or has disregarded a unanimous report of the Council, a judicial sentence or an arbitral award recognizing that the dispute between it and the other belligerent States arises out of a matter which by international law is solely within the domestic jurisdiction of the latter State; nevertheless, in the last case the State shall only be presumed to be an aggressor if it has not previously submitted the question to the Council or the Assembly, in accordance with Article 11 of the Covenant.

2. If it has violated provisional measures enjoined by the Council for the period while the proceedings are in progress as contemplated by Article 7 of the present Protocol.

Apart from the cases dealt with in paragraphs 1 and 2 of the present Article, if the Council does not at once succeed in determining the aggressor, it shall be bound to enjoin upon the belligerents an armistice, and shall fix the terms, acting, if need be, by a two-thirds majority and shall supervise its execution.

Any belligerent which has refused to accept the armistice or has violated its terms shall be deemed an aggressor.

The Council shall call upon the signatory States to apply forthwith against the aggressor the sanctions provided by Article 11 of the present Protocol and any signatory State thus called upon shall thereupon be entitled to exercise the rights of a belligerent."

(c) Sanctions

(aa) *The concept of sanctions.*

As pointed out in a previous chapter, a social order guaranteeing collective security is by its very nature a legal order, and a legal order is a system of norms providing for sanctions. Hence, the organization of sanctions is one of the most important problems, if not the most important problem, of collective security.

The term "sanction" can have different meanings. In its widest sense, it means any measure taken in support of a social order regulating human behavior. The purpose of a sanction is to bring about that behavior which, according to the opinion of the social authority, is useful to society and hence is considered to be in conformity with the social order; and to prevent that behavior which, according to the opinion of the social authority, is harmful to society and hence is considered to be contrary to the social order. This purpose may be achieved in two different ways: with the use of force or without it. It is the essence of a legal order that it tries to bring about lawful and to prevent unlawful behavior by coercive measures—that is, by the forcible deprivation of life, freedom, property or other values as a reaction against a violation of the order. The coercive character of the measures concerned is established by the fact that they are applied without or even against the will of the person against whom they are directed and that physical force may be used in case of resistance. In this sense, legal sanctions are coercive reactions against a violation of the law. A violation or a delict may be already committed and ascertained in a legal procedure, as in the case of a punishment which is inflicted upon a criminal by a penal court. Alternatively, a delict may be only suspected, and coercive actions taken as provisional measures in order to prepare and secure the procedure for the ascertainment of a violation of the law and the execution of a sanction, as, for instance, in the case of arrest of a person by the police. A coercive measure may even be taken in order to prevent a violation of the law which, with a certain degree of probability, is expected in the future by the person against whom the measure is directed, e. g., the confinement of insane persons in an asylum, or the forcible internment of citizens of an enemy state in time of war in order to prevent them from committing delicts against the state at war with their home state. In the widest sense, legal sanctions are coercive reactions against an actual violation of the law or against a possible violation, "possible" meaning suspected or expected.

The coercive reaction against a violation of the law may have no other purpose than to inflict an evil on the delinquent in order to deter him and others from committing similar delicts in the future. Such a sanction is called a punishment. The usual punishments of national law are capital punishment, imprisonment and fine, but the punishment may also consist of the forfeiture of political rights, discharge from office, and the like. It may even be restricted to the ascertainment of the fact that a person has violated the law. In this case one speaks of a "moral" sanction because its immediate purpose is to bring about moral disapprobation of the delinquent in the opinion of the public, although this measure may be a reaction provided for by the law and hence a legal sanction. It may not be the primary purpose, or even the purpose at all, of a coercive reaction against a violation of the law to deter others from similar violations of the law. The purpose may be to restore the situation which existed prior to a violation of the law, especially to repair the damage caused by the violation of the law. This is characteristic of the specific sanction of civil law, the so-called civil execution, which consists of forcibly depriving the violator of the law of part of his property, and which differs from the fine as a punishment of penal law in that the seized property or the result of its forced sale does not go to the public treasury, as a fine would, but to the damaged person. However, although this is not its main purpose, civil execution, the forcible deprivation of property, is aimed at deterring persons from similar violations of the law. Hence, it has a certain punitive character. The distinction between punishment and other sanctions is only relative. Sanctions, as evils forcibly inflicted upon men, always have the function of preventing further violations of the law and hence have a punitive character. However, this character may be more or less emphasized.

There are also coercive measures provided by the law which have no relation to an actual or possible violation of the law, such as the forcible destruction of buildings or other property in order to prevent the extension of a fire, or the forcible internment of persons inflicted by a contagious disease in order to prevent or restrict an epidemic. These coercive measures are not sanctions because they are not reactions against an actual or potential violation of the law. However, they are applied only under conditions and by persons precisely determined by the law. In this sense, the use of force constituted by these measures, like the use of force constituted by sanctions, is reserved to the legal community.

Like the sanctions of national law, the specific sanctions of international law, reprisals and war, consist of forcibly depriving the individuals who are subjects of the state against which a sanction is directed of life, freedom, property or other values. The sanctions of international law differ from the sanctions of national law in their collective character. They are not directed against a definite individual, like the sanctions of national law, but against a group of individuals, the individuals belonging to a state, who are subjected to the legal order constituting this state. This means that, in contradistinction to national law which establishes individual responsibility, international law, as a rule, establishes collective responsibility for its violations. However, in exceptional cases, individual responsibility for violations of international law is established by general as well as by particular international law which provides for punishment or civil execution of definite individuals as a reaction against acts constituting a violation of international law. Although the term "reprisals" in its specific and original sense means only enforcement actions directed against states—that is, actions constituting collective responsibility—it is sometimes used in a wider sense to cover also sanctions constituting individual responsibility.

A disputed question which plays a certain part in the discussion of international security is whether reprisals and war, as international sanctions, do or do not have a punitive character. The answer depends on the definition of punishment, and punishment can hardly be characterized by any other criterion than by its function of deterrence. Punishment is that reaction against a violation of the law which consists of forcibly depriving a person of certain values for the purpose of deterring him and other persons from similar violations of the law. If this definition is accepted, it cannot be denied that reprisals and war, as sanctions of international law, have a punitive character. The punitive character, which means the deterrent function, of a war waged as a sanction is obvious. The same is true with respect to reprisals taken in time of war. If a belligerent reacts against the illegal use of poison gas on the part of another belligerent by applying the same measure, he does so in order to prevent his opponent from using this illegal weapon again. Only in regard to reprisals taken in time of peace as a reaction against a violation of international law, is the purpose of inducing a violator of the law to repair the damage caused by a violation primary, as in the case of the civil execution of national law. However, the function of preventing future violations of the law by deterrence is not excluded.

The rejection of the punitive character of international sanctions in general and of the sanctions provided for in a system of international security in particular may be explained by the fact that under national law punishment has a certain defamatory connotation and some penalties are actually combined with defamatory consequences such as the forfeiture of political rights. However, neither this connotation nor these consequences are essential to the concept of punishment. Consequently, the view that the sanctions of international law do not have, or that the sanctions of an international security system should not have, a punitive character is without foundation. Nor is the requirement that the sanctions of an international security system must not be vindictive of any practical importance. They are vindictive if they are taken by the victim of aggression with the intention of taking revenge on an aggressor. As an objectively ascertainable action, revenge is a reaction against a wrong suffered and hence is not distinguishable from a sanction. As a subjective motive, revenge may be characterized by a feeling of resentment or hatred, but such a feeling is legally irrelevant as long as its expression in an enforcement action directed against an aggressor remains within the limits of a sanction. It is not the uncontrollable motive of a reaction against an aggressor but the objectively ascertainable reaction and its conformity or non-conformity with the law which counts.

If within a system of international security not only war but any use of armed force is prohibited in principle and exceptionally permitted only as a sanction, the two types of international sanctions must be designated as enforcement measures involving the use of armed force and those not involving it, or as military and non-military sanctions, but not as war and reprisals. By non-military sanctions, economic, financial and diplomatic sanctions are usually meant. However, sometimes the term "economic" sanctions covers all non-military sanctions and includes financial and diplomatic sanctions.[1]

(bb) *The execution of sanctions within an international security system.*

The execution of the sanctions may be left to the individual members of the international organization and these members may—just as under general international law—be only authorized to fulfill this function. However, within a system of international security which prohibits the use of armed force, at least the execution of the non-military, or so-called economic sanctions, should be obligatory.[2] A higher degree of security is achieved if a central organ endowed with a certain competence regarding the execution of sanctions is established.[3] This organ may be composed of representatives of all the members of the organization, usually called an assembly, or of only some of them, elected by the assembly for a certain period of time, usually called a council.[4] Some members, especially the great powers, may have a permanent seat in the council, so that only the other members of the council are elected. The central organ may adopt its decisions either by a unanimous vote or by a majority vote. The majority may have to include the affirmative votes of all the permanent members of the council so that each of the permanent members could have a so-called veto right. The decisions of the organ may have the character of mere recommendations or they may be legally binding upon the members of the organization. The central organ may be a committee of ambassadors, so that political considerations may prevail in adopting its recommendations or decisions, or the decision to apply sanctions may be conferred upon an independent court and only the execution of these decisions left to the assembly or council. The possible relationships between such a court and the executive organ will be discussed later. It stands to reason that international security is guaranteed to a higher degree if the central organ is composed only of some and not of all the members of the organization, if it may adopt its decisions by a majority vote and not unanimously, if there is no veto right of permanent members, and if its decisions are not mere recommendations but are legally binding upon the members.

It makes an important difference whether the central organ does or does not have the means by which sanctions are to be executed at its direct disposal. If these means are not at the direct disposal of the central organ, sanctions can be executed only by the member states of the security organization in conformity with the recommendations or binding decisions of the central organ. Then there is no essential difference between an enforcement action taken as a sanction by the security organization and the exercise of individual or collective self-defense, especially if the question as to whether or not an illegal act of aggression has been committed and if so which state is the aggressor, is to be decided by the members executing the sanctions. The difference consists only in the fact that in case of self-defense no central organ of the security organization interferes; and even this difference is reduced to a minimum if the central organ has only the power to make recommendations. On the other hand, the exercise of individual and, especially, of collective self-defense itself has the character of a sanction, insofar as it is a legally authorized reaction against a violation of the law. It is, as pointed out, a decentralized execution of sanctions, the states exercising self-defense acting as organs of the security organization. This is particularly evident if collective self-defense is, under the treaty constituting the security organization, not merely a right but an obligation of the members, that is to say, if the member states are obliged to come to the assistance of the victim of an illegal aggression.[5]

If the central organ of the security organization has not at its direct disposal the means by which the sanctions are to be executed, the execution of the sanctions—and this means the operation of the security system—depends in the last analysis on the good will of the member states. Hence, the execution of the sanctions may be seriously endangered by the political considerations of the various governments, especially the governments of great powers, if—rightly or wrongly—they consider that the interests of their own state are not compatible with their obligations under the security system. The situation is different if the means by which the sanctions are to be executed are at the direct disposal of the central organ and the execution of the sanctions independent of the will of the individual members.

In this respect there is a certain difference between military and non-military sanctions. Armed forces, the specific means by which military sanctions are executed, may very well be placed at the direct disposal of the central organ, without depriving the members of the security organization of their character as sovereign states. However, non-military, especially financial and economic sanctions, can be directly applied only by the government of a state, because only a state government controls the means by which these sanctions may be executed, and if such control is conferred on the central organ of a security organization, this organization comes near to that of a super-state. This is a consequence of the nature of non-military, especially financial and economic, sanctions.

If the international security organization is not universal and, consequently, there are states which are not members of the organization and hence are not bound by the provisions of the treaty constituting the organization concerning the application of sanctions, these states may support the organization without joining it by assuming the obligation or expressing the willingness to refrain from any action tending to defeat the execution of a sanction taken by or on behalf of the organization.[6]

(cc) *Non-military sanctions.*

As far as so-called diplomatic sanctions are concerned, it may appear that an international organization may apply these measures directly, that is to say, not through the governments of the member states, without losing its international character. The diplomatic means which may be employed are: a protest against an illegal conduct of a state, the withdrawal of the head of the embassy, the severing of all diplomatic relations, and also of all consular relations; the non-recognition of a situation established by an illegal action.[7] With the exception of cutting off consular representation, all these diplomatic means may be applied by an international organization which exchanges diplomatic representatives both with states which are members of the organization and states which are not. However, these diplomatic means have no effect if they are not applied also by the member states in conformity with a recommendation or binding decision of the central organ of the security organization.

Financial sanctions consist of denying all financial assistance to a state guilty of aggression and its nationals, cutting off long-term loans, suspending short-term banking credits, and the like. Only an authority which is competent to impose legal obligations upon public and private banking institutions, which therefore can exercise legislative and executive power directly over individuals, can apply such measures. To confer such powers upon a security organization would hardly be compatible with its international character.[8] Financial sanctions are less effective than other economic sanctions and consequently should be combined with them. These sanctions also presuppose legislative and executive powers which are characteristic of a state government.

Economic sanctions may be applied in different degrees. The most important economic sanction consists of prohibiting the commerce in arms, ammunition and the raw materials essential to the production of arms and ammunition and to the prosecution of hostilities between the member states of the security organization and the aggressor. Among these prohibitions an oil embargo is of particular importance. The refusal to accept exports from a state is an economic sanction which may have a remarkable effect on the state against which it is applied. The highest possible degree of an economic sanction is achieved by prohibiting all commerce, which includes prohibiting the nationals of the member states from entering the territory of the aggressor, prohibiting the nationals of the aggressor state from entering the territory of the member states, controlling all transport and international exchanges of goods, and interrupting the diplomatic and consular relations between the member states and the aggressor. This is a complete international boycott of the aggressor.[9] It stands to reason that the economic measures taken against the aggressor should be accompanied by economic measures, especially those of a financial nature, taken in favor of the victim, and that in this respect every possible assistance should be given to the state which is the victim of the aggression.

370624—57——8

There can be little doubt that economic sanctions are not very effective if the boycotted state has strong economic resources, if it is more or less self-sufficient, and especially if it is in possession of the raw materials essential to the production of arms and ammunition and has a prosperous armament-producing industry. A serious difficulty in executing economic, and especially financial, sanctions is the possibility of retaliatory economic measures which may be taken by the boycotted state against a boycotting state. Economically weak states may be affected seriously by such measures. Consequently, economic sanctions directed against an aggressor should be complemented by mutual economic assistance to boycotting states.[10] States which are the immediate neighbors of the boycotted state are particularly exposed to retaliatory measures by the latter, and the economic sanctions taken against a state may have undesirable effects on its neighbors. Hence it may be necessary to exempt these neighboring states from the obligation of participating in the execution of economic sanctions, which consequently cannot be universal. However, if economic sanctions are not applied by all states, or at least by all the members of a security organization comprising the overwhelming majority of states, their value becomes highly problematical. Furthermore, even if the organization is universal, it is hardly possible to guarantee the effective cooperation of all members in the execution of economic sanctions. From what has been said before, it appears that the effective execution of a sanction depends on the centralization of this function. Within an international security organization, economic sanctions can be centralized only to a very limited extent. Since the organization must remain "international," it cannot have the means by which economic sanctions are applied at its direct disposal. Hence, the execution of economic sanctions must be left to the individual members of the organization. They may be obliged to execute the economic sanction decided upon by the central organ under the direction of this organ. However, as has been pointed out, this organ cannot rely on the strict fulfillment of these obligations.

Another insufficiency of economic sanctions is that they cannot have an immediate effect on the aggressor, and consequently this state may inflict irreparable damage on its victim before economic sanctions force it to stop its aggression. There can be little doubt that economic sanctions alone cannot guarantee international security in a way which could be considered satisfactory, even from the point of view of a very modest expectation. Within the League of Nations, the stubborn resistance to the establishment and application of military sanctions and the attempt to realize the purpose of the security organization by the application of economic sanctions only led to the breakdown of this organization. Besides, in order to be effective, economic sanctions cannot be isolated from military enforcement measures. A complete economic boycott of an aggressor who has a seacoast is hardly possible without a blockade which has to be established by men-of-war and which consequently constitutes a use of armed force.

As has been pointed out in a previous chapter,[11] the treaty constituting an international security organization may protect the members not only against aggression (in the wider sense of the term) on the part of a member state but also against aggression by a non-member state by providing that the sanctions stipulated in the treaty are to be directed against any state which commits an act of aggression against a member state.[12] In this respect, there is a difference between sanctions which constitute enforcement measures short of war and enforcement measures which have the character of war. Under general international law, enforcement measures short of war are permissible only as reprisals. That is, if they constitute the violation of a right of the state against which they are directed, they are legal only as a reaction against a violation of the law committed by this state. If under a security treaty all members of the organization are obliged to take enforcement measures short of war against a non-member state which has committed an act of aggression against only one of them without violating a right of the others, the action of the members whose rights are not violated by this act of aggression of the non-member state is illegal under general international law if their action constitutes a violation of a right of the non-member state. Some of the non-military sanctions provided for by a security treaty, for instance diplomatic sanctions, may not violate any right of the non-member state against which they are directed. However, economic sanctions may do so if, for example, they can be applied only in violation of a treaty concluded between the non-member state and a member state which is not a victim of the aggression. The blockade of the coasts of a non-member state is certainly illegal under general international law if it is not a reaction against a violation by the blockaded state of a right of the blockading state not a victim of the aggression. If an act of aggression, against which a security treaty provides for enforcement measures short of war, does not constitute a violation of general international law, for example, if military mobilization or the refusal to submit a conflict to peaceful settlement is considered to be an act of aggression, and if the members of the security organization are obliged to take enforcement measures short of war against a non-member state which has committed such an act of aggression, the enforcement measures taken by the members are illegal under general international law if they constitute the violation of a right of the non-member state. In both cases, an opposite opinion can be maintained only under the problematic presupposition that the security treaty is also binding upon states which are not contracting parties to it.

On the other hand, if they have the character of war, military sanctions stipulated by a security treaty may be directed against a non-member state without constituting a violation of general international law by members which are not victims of the aggression and by all members if the act of aggression for which the non-member state is made responsible is illegal only under the security treaty to which this state is not a contracting party. This is the paradoxical consequence of the view that the *bellum justum* principle is not part of general international law, and hence that any state may resort to war against any other state for any reason whatsoever.

(dd) *Military sanctions.*

(A) THE OPPOSITION TO MILITARY SANCTIONS

Any use of armed force as a reaction against a violation of international law is a military sanction, and if armed force is used for this purpose to an extent characteristic of war, a military sanction has the character of war. The fact that armed force is used as a sanction does not deprive this use of armed force of its legal character of war. Hence the rules of international law regulating the conduct of war apply to it.[12a]

The opposition to providing military sanctions in a treaty constituting an international security organization is based on two kinds of reasons: political and moral. Governments are averse to imposing the sacrifices involved in a military action upon their subjects if this action cannot be justified as necessary for self-defense, and they are disinclined to resort to or participate in a war which, from a purely military point of view, is aggressive, if its outcome is doubtful. However, as we shall see, a reasonable degree of certainty that a military sanction will achieve its purpose and that those who execute this sanction will be able to impose their will on the delinquent state, exists only in case this sanction is highly centralized, and, for political reasons, it is just this centralization which encounters the strongest resistance on the part of governments defending the so-called sovereignty of their states.

The moral arguments against military sanctions are partly the same as those set forth against capital punishment: human life should never be destroyed, not even as a sanction. However, capital punishment can be replaced by a sanction which is only a little less effective, namely, imprisonment and especially imprisonment for life, whereas the only sanctions which can be substituted for military sanctions are economic sanctions which are far less effective. The most impressive argument against military sanctions is the undeniable fact that, even if their destructive effect is restricted to the members of the armed forces of an aggressor and even more if such restriction is impossible as in the case of aerial bombardment, military sanctions bring about the death and suffering of many individual human beings who by their own voluntary acts did not commit the violation of the law against which the sanction is a reaction. However, this is an inevitable consequence of the collective responsibility which exists not only in the military but also in the economic sanctions of international law. This consequence cannot be avoided by renouncing military sanctions and by restricting the reaction of the security organization against aggression to economic sanctions. In order to avoid the morally undesirable consequences of collective responsibility, military and economic sanctions both must be abandoned, and only those sanctions provided for which can be imposed upon the individual persons who by their own voluntarily performed acts committed the international delicts which impaired international security. These sanctions will be discussed later.[13]

(B) THE ORGANIZATION OF MILITARY SANCTIONS

Different ways of organizing military sanctions may be distinguished according to the degree of centralization. Military action against an aggressor may be left completely to the individual member states which may not be obliged but only authorized to take such action through their own armed forces without any interference on the part of a central organ of the security organization. However, a treaty constituting the security organization may establish a central organ competent to make recommendations concerning the military action of the member states [14] or to oblige them to execute the military sanction decided upon by the central organ in conformity with its directions.[15]

If the constituent treaty stipulates such an obligation, the central organ may entrust the execution of the sanction to one single state or to some states, the territories of which are nearer to that of the aggressor than the territories of the other members, or which have a particular interest in maintaining and restoring peace within the area where the aggression has taken place. In all these cases there is no armed force at the direct disposal of the central organ of the security organization.

The armed forces through which the military sanction is to be executed remain under the command of their national governments, and consequently the coordination of their operations is very difficult, if not impossible, to achieve. As in the case of the analogous organization of economic sanctions, the working of the coercive machinery of the security system depends, in the last analysis, on the readiness of the respective governments to exercise their rights or to fulfill their obligations to take military action against the aggressor.

In order to place an armed force at the direct disposal of the security organization the members may be obliged to make contingents or "quotas" of their armed forces available to the central organ, and in case it decides to take military action, this organ would be authorized to call upon members to provide the armed forces in conformity with their obligations and to use these forces in the military action against the aggressor. The numerical strength, composition, armament and location of the contingents may be determined in advance by the constituent treaty or by special agreements to be concluded between the individual members on the one hand and the organization on the other. As long as they are not made available to the central organ for the purpose of a military action of the organization, the contingents of the armed forces of the member states remain under the exclusive control of their national governments. Only if they are actually placed at the disposal of the central organ are they unified under the military command of the central organ or of a commander in chief appointed by this organ, and assisted by a military staff as an auxiliary organ.[16] The financial problems of this system are relatively simple. Each member state has to bear the costs of its contingent in time of peace and possibly also in case of a military action of the organization in which its contingent takes part. However, the expenses for this action may be paid out of the funds at the disposal of the organization established by the financial contributions of the member states.[17]

The difference between the contingent or quota system and a system in which there is no armed force at the direct disposal of the international organization is not as great as it may first seem. It is true that, if placed within a unified command, the cooperation of the different contingents would be much easier to achieve than if the armed forces of the member states each operated under its own national command.[18] However, it should not be ignored that, even if superior in numerical strength and armament, an armed force composed of contingents of the armed forces of different nations is always handicapped in a fight against a homogeneous armed force of an aggressor state. Although legally parts of an international force, the contingents would retain their national spirit. Their readiness to fight an opponent which is not a particular enemy of their country could leave much to be desired.[19] Since a many-headed international agency cannot satisfactorily fulfill the functions of military command, the appointment of a commander in chief is indispensable. For understandable reasons, this appointment is a very difficult task especially if the commander in chief is not appointed only for a particular military action but as a permanent organ of the international community.

A still greater difficulty consists in concluding the agreements concerning the strength and composition of the contingent each member state has to place at the disposal of the organization.[20] Even if this difficulty is surmounted, the operation of the quota system would depend on the willingness of the member states to fulfill their main obligation: to respond to the call of the central organ by placing their contingents at its disposal. The same political considerations which could prevent the government of a member state from resorting to war against a state which has attacked another state, could prevent a government from placing the contingent of its armed forces at the disposal of the security organization. Hence, the central organ might never know in advance which armed forces would be at its disposal, and consequently the organ would not be in a position to base its military operations on a prearranged plan which is an essential condition of quick and effective action.[21]

Since the armed forces at the disposal of the organization must be superior in numerical strength and armament to the armed forces of any potential aggressor, universality or at least quasi-universality of the organization is an essential condition of the effectiveness of the quota system. In addition, the treaty constituting the security organization must not stipulate expulsion from the organization as a sanction and not allow withdrawal from the organization. However, even if the treaty does not contain a clause authorizing the members to withdraw under certain conditions, or even if it does contain a prohibition expressly forbidding a member state to denounce the treaty by a unilateral act, actual withdrawal of a member state and hence loss of its contingent can hardly be prevented.[22]

(C) THE INTERNATIONAL POLICE FORCE ORGANIZED AS A PERMANENT AND SEPARATE ARMED FORCE AT THE DIRECT DISPOSAL OF THE SECURITY ORGANIZATION

Most of the difficulties and insufficiencies involved in the organization of military sanctions discussed in the previous sections could be avoided by placing at the direct disposal of the security organization an international armed force which is not established on an *ad hoc* basis, as under the quota system. In other words, the international armed force would not be available only in case of a particular military action of the organization, but would be permanent and completely separate from and independent of the national armed forces of the member states, a separate armed force belonging exclusively to the security organization and not an armed force composed of parts of the armed forces of the member states.

It is usual to designate such a permanent and separate armed force at the direct disposal of a security organization as a true "international" armed force in contradistinction to the merely "joint" or "collective" force which exists under the quota system. This terminology is not quite correct. An armed force composed of contingents of the armed forces of member states is as "international" as a permanent and separate armed force of a security organization. There is even an international armed force under a constituent treaty which does not provide for contingents of the armed forces of member states but only obliges or simply authorizes member states to take military action through their own armed forces against the aggressor. In the first place, the international character of an armed force depends on the law under which the force is used. If this law is international law, the armed force is an international force. Hence, if used in the execution of a sanction provided for by international law, even the national armed force of a state would have an international character. In the second place, this character depends on the international character of the authority under the control of which the armed force is operated, and this authority is "international" if it is established on the basis of international law or if its functions are determined by international law. Hence an armed force composed of the armed forces of member states, but operated by the organ of a security organization constituted by a treaty, is certainly an international force, and, if in exercising a right conferred upon it or in fulfilling an obligation imposed upon it by international law, a state uses its armed force to execute a sanction provided for by international law, this state may very well be considered to be an international organ. Hence the armed forces which execute sanctions provided for by any system of international security, however organized, may be considered to be international forces.

Another terminology, the correctness of which is doubtful, is to designate as an international "police" force only a permanent and separate armed force at the direct disposal of the central organ of an international security community. A police force is an armed force used in the performance of a police action. A police action is any enforcement action performed by an organ of a community for the welfare of its members, their health, morals, prosperity and, especially, their security. However, it is not a sanitary police force or a police force for the purpose of morals or economics, but a security police force with which an international security organization is concerned. The specific functions of a security police force are to prepare and secure by enforcement actions the judicial or quasi-judicial procedure for ascertaining a violation of the law, and to execute the sanction ordered by the judicial or quasi-judicial organ. There is a difference between the so-called police force of a state and its "armed force," the term designating its army, navy and air force. The former is used to maintain order within the state, whereas the purpose of the latter is to defend the state against external aggression. Hence the armament of the two forces is not the same. Neither artillery nor bombers are necessary to maintain order within a state as long as the disturbance of the internal order does not assume the character of a revolutionary movement. If it does, however, the army, navy, and air force may be used, and if used for the maintenance of internal order their function is a police function. The difference between a "police force" for the maintenance of internal order and an "armed force" for defense against external aggression is irrelevant within an international security organization. The aggression against which the armed force of this organization is used is always external aggression from the point of view of the state which is its victim and internal aggression from the point of view of the international community, if this community is universal. If it is not universal, the aggression is external aggression also from the point of view of the security organization if the aggressor is a non-member state and if the constituent treaty also provides for enforcement action in this case. It is true that the constituent treaty may also provide for enforcement action in case an internal aggression takes place within a member state—that is, in case a revolution is directed against the legitimate government. However, as has been pointed out, in this case the attacked government must use its armed forces itself, and if it is assisted by the armed forces of the security organization, both actions are police actions, insofar as they are taken to maintain or restore the internal order of the state, although they are taken by forces which are "armed forces" with respect to their armament. Consequently, any enforcement action taken in conformity with the legal order constituting an international security system is a police action, whether it is performed by the armed force of an individual state, or by an armed force composed of contingents of the armed forces of the member states, or by a permanent and separate armed force under the direct control of a security organization. There is no cogent reason why the term "police force" should be restricted to an armed force of this latter type.

There are some characteristic problems involved in organizing a permanent and separate armed force at the direct disposal of a security organization. First of all, there is the question of recruitment.[23]

In regard to recruitment, there are two possibilities. A security organization may have the right to recruit directly with its own organs in the territories of member states. Such a right requires the corresponding obligation imposed on the member states by the constituent treaty to allow, and if necessary to support with their own organs, the recruitment procedure. Of the two methods of recruitment, compulsory conscription and voluntary enlistment on the basis of free contract, only the latter is a practical consideration. The former is not excluded, but direct recruitment presupposes the power of the security organization to impose by legislative acts the obligation upon the citizens of the member states to do military service in the armed force of the organization. Hence, this direct recruitment is not compatible with the international character of a security organization. Legislative power exercised directly over individuals brings a security organization very near to being a super-state.

The other possibility is indirect recruitment. The recruitment of the members of the international armed force may be left to the governments of the member states acting on behalf of the security organization and obliged to place at the disposal of the organization a certain number of recruits, determined by agreement or by a binding decision of the central organ of the organization. In the case of indirect recruitment, compulsory conscription is more feasible and practical than it is in the case of direct recruitment. If a state has the power to impose by national law upon its subjects the obligation to do military service in its own armed force, it also has the power to impose in this way upon its subjects the obligation to do military service in the armed force of an international organization of which this state is a member. However, voluntary enlistment on the basis of free contract is in both cases preferable to compulsory conscription, for the length of time of military service in a separate and independent armed force of an international security organization must be much longer than that of military service in a national armed force. In contradistinction to the latter, the former can hardly have effective reserves at its disposal. If a member of a separate and independent armed force of an international security organization returns to civil life, he ceases to be under the control of the international organization and hence is not liable to call, unless this function is also performed by the governments of the member states on behalf of the international organization.[24] For the same reason, in order to make the terms of enlistment sufficiently attractive, the wages paid to the members of the armed force of an international security organization must be much higher than the small pay to which the enlisted men below the rank of commissioned and non-commissioned officers are entitled in a national armed force. If an international security organization is so centralized that it assumes the character of a federal state, its armed force may be recruited in the same way as that of a national state.

Another problem of a permanent and separate armed force of an international security organization is the personal legal status of its members. Since they owe allegiance only to an international organization, they should not be citizens of a particular state. They should be released from their nationality during the time of their service in the armed forces of the organization,[25] and their status of belonging legally to the international community constituted by the security treaty, a legal status analogous to that of national citizenship, should be recognized by the member states and certified by appropriate documents, such as passports. This problem is not particular to the organization of a permanent and separate armed force but applies to all organs of an international security organization.[26] In order to guarantee complete independence of the governments of the member states, the members of the armed forces should be exempt from the jurisdiction of the member states and should be subject to the exclusive jurisdiction of the international organization which should be endowed with special organs competent to exercise this jurisdiction.[27]

A most delicate problem is the location of the armed forces. The inconvenience of stationing the armed force of an international security organization in the territory of a member state is obvious, and stationing the force in the territory of a non-member, even if permanently neutralized, like Switzerland, is out of the question. Besides, as we shall see later, the institution of neutrality and especially of permanent neutralization is not compatible with a universal or quasi-universal security organization. The only satisfactory solution of this problem is to locate the armed forces and the main organs of the security organization in a territory which is under the direct sovereignty of the organization and not under the sovereignty of an individual state. This internationalized territory may be of relatively small size, like that placed under the sovereignty of the Pope, the territory of the state of the Vatican City. However, for purely strategic reasons, military bases at different points all over the surface of the earth would be needed. Hence, it would be necessary to have not one but several internationalized territories. Such territories could be acquired only with the agreement of the states in possession of them.

This, of course, implies an almost insurmountable difficulty.

The independence of the armed force of the international security organization may be seriously endangered by the fact that both the manufacturing of armaments and the raw material necessary for the execution of a military action would remain under the control of the national governments. The transfer of this control to the international organization would imply a restriction of the sovereignty of member states and consequently constitutes another difficulty.

The question of the composition of the international armed force—that is, whether it should comprehend all three arms of the service, land, sea and air forces, or whether there should be a preponderance of one, especially of the air force, over the others—is a purely military-technical problem. More important from the point of view of this study is the financial question. There can be no doubt that the cost of a permanent and separate armed force is very high. This cost must be covered by contributions from member states as long as an organization does not have the power of direct taxation, a power incompatible with its international character. However, the contribution of a state would not be larger than the cost to a state of its own armament, and the establishment of a permanent and separate armed force of a security organization allows, and even imperatively requires, a radical reduction of the armament of the member states. This is an advantage which this method of organizing military sanctions shares with no other. Because they are not exposed to the danger of being weakened by the withdrawal of a member state and its armed forces from the organization, enforcement measures taken by a separate and permanent armed force may really achieve the ideal purpose of a sanction: to prevent the violation of the law against which it is provided. As the danger of aggression is reduced, to the extent that this is possible at all, the right of self-defense can be restricted to a degree which makes its misuse very difficult. Only individual and not collective self-defense may be permitted, and permitted only against external aggression actually carried out by the armed forces of another state.

If the international security organization has a permanent and separate armed force at its disposal far superior to the armed forces of the member states which are reduced to the minimum necessary to maintain internal order and to offer initial resistance to external aggression, the danger of intervention by the organization in the domestic affairs of the members must not be underestimated. Certain institutions protecting the member states against such intervention should be established in the constituent treaty, e. g., the opportunity of invoking an international court competent to decide the question of whether or not an action of the organization constitutes such intervention and to order the organization to cancel it if the action is declared illegal. However, it must be admitted that within such a system there is no absolutely effective guarantee for maintaining the distribution of competence between the organization and its members laid down in the constituent treaty. As has been said before, this system appears to imply a strong tendency of becoming transformed into a super-state. The central organ which is in control of the permanent and separate armed force has a character not very different from that of a state government, for the concentration of the means of force in the hands of a central organ has, more than anything else, the effect of conferring on this organ the power of a government in the specific sense of the term.

If the central organ of a security organization has the character of a government or quasi-government, the question of the form of government, the dilemma: democracy or autocracy, becomes paramount. This question is of little or no importance as long as the central organ of a security organization has no real governmental power. If an international community is supposed to be organized on a democratic basis, the problem of the representation of the member states in the organs and especially in the main organ of the security organization arises. The democratic principle of equal representation can be applied in two quite different ways: on the basis of the equality of states, or on the basis of the equality of the individuals who are subjects of the states. If the equality of states is accepted as the basic principle, the vote of each state, regardless of the number of its subjects, must have the same weight as that of any other state. If the equality of the individual subjects is accepted as the basic principle, the vote of each state must be in proportion to the number of its subjects. The application of both principles implies grave inconveniences, and the choice as well as the attempt to find an acceptable compromise between them involves difficulties which seem to be insurmountable in view of the circumstances that exist at present and probably will exist in the foreseeable future.

It is therefore understandable that even the most enthusiastic defenders of an international police force do not dare to suggest a radically centralized armed-force monopoly of the security organization, which means that a permanent and separate armed force be at the direct disposal of the organization and that there be complete disarmament of the member states. What can be suggested as a politically possible scheme is combining the quota system with a relatively small permanent and separate armed force of a security organization. The main function of the latter would be to come to the immediate assistance of a victim of aggression. In the course of military operations the armed force of the security organization would be supported by the contingents of the armed forces of the member states which had been placed at the disposal of the security organization.[28]

It stands to reason that under such a system no complete disarmament of the member states and not even a considerable reduction of national armament, could be achieved. However, it has been suggested that this scheme be based on the principle of differentiation of armament.[29] The most destructive and most mobile arms would be reserved for the use of the permanent and separate armed force of the security organization, the less destructive and less mobile arms left to the armed forces of the member states. The most destructive and, at the same time, most mobile weapons are those used by the air force. Hence, an air-force monopoly of the security organization becomes a consideration. In view of the fact that civil aircraft can easily be adapted to military purposes, such a monopoly is hardly possible without the internationalization of civil aviation.[30] It is more than doubtful that this internationalization of civil aviation is politically feasible on a universal basis. If restricted to a regional security organization, a combination of the quota system and a permanent and separate armed force of the organization may be nearer to political reality than a completely centralized armed-force monopoly of a universal or even regional security organization. However, it must be admitted that this combination combines the difficulties of both with the disadvantages of the quota system.[31]

(D) THE PROCEDURE PRECEDING THE EXECUTION OF SANCTIONS

The execution of a sanction must be preceded by a procedure to ascertain the delict, i. e., to ascertain the violation of the law against which a sanction is provided as a reaction. This is especially true if the delict is an act of aggression. The procedure is then referred to as determining the aggressor. The execution of a sanction to be directeed against the aggressor may also be preceded by a procedure to put into operation certain provisional measures to prevent the aggravation of the situation created by the delict, especially if this delict is an act of aggression, actually committed or expected.

Under a relatively primitive system of international security, the ascertainment of the act of aggression and hence the determination of the aggressor is left to the states who are members of the security organization and who are authorized or obliged to apply the nonmilitary or military sanctions provided for by the constituent treaty without any interference on the part of a central organ.[32] The disadvantages of such a decentralization of the legal function have been discussed in a previous chapter of this study.[33]

One of the fundamental conditions of an effective system of international security consists of conferring upon a central organ the ascertainment of the act of aggression against which a sanction in the constituent treaty is provided. This may be the same executive organ as that competent to apply the sanctions, an organ composed of representatives of some or all of the states who are members of the organization, whereby these representatives are bound by the instructions of their respective governments.[34] However, this central organ may also be an international court composed of individuals who are not representatives of any state but are independent judges. In view of the fact that the ascertainment of the delict is a specifically legal function, the fulfillment of which in strict conformity with the law established by the constituent treaty is essential to the security to be achieved by the international organization, an independent court would seem to be the most appropriate organ. If the ascertainment of the delict, and especially of the act of aggression, is conferred upon a court, in applying sanctions the executive organ must conform to the decisions of the court.

This solution of the problem is strongly opposed by governments as well as by writers on international law, especially with respect to the determination of the aggressor. In the main, their arguments are that the political interests involved in this function do not allow decisions to be based only on legal considerations, and that a judicial procedure is too slow if, as in case of an act of aggression, immediate action is necessary. The first argument may be rejected by referring to the fact that, as pointed out in another connection, political considerations are not excluded from the procedure in which an international court decides that an act of aggression has taken place. Of course, this is not so as far as the finding of facts is concerned. In this respect the truth and nothing but the truth must be disclosed, and it can hardly be denied that in this respect an independent and impartial court is more reliable than an agency which is exclusively influenced by political motives. However, in qualifying the facts as aggression, in deciding that the facts constitute aggression as determined by the law to be applied, the discretion left to a court by the law may be very wide, and within the limits of this discretion political considerations may legitimately be introduced and actually are introduced in all judicial decisions. Hence, it is probably not the possibility of introducing political considerations in general which is behind the argument against a court as the organ competent to determine the aggressor, but the wish to protect definite political interests of particular governments having decisive influence within the international organization. Indeed, these interests can be defended only by the representatives of these governments as members of the organ competent to determine the aggressor and not by independent judges. However, this is not a legitimate argument as far as an organization is concerned which has to guarantee security equally for all its members.

The second argument concerning the slowness of the judicial procedure is more serious. However, it is possible to solve this problem by authorizing the executive organ to act without waiting for a judicial decision in case of a *prima facie* aggression and at the same time obliging this organ to submit the case to the court immediately after action has been taken and to cancel the action if the court so decides. This is the only way to guarantee the legality of the execution of sanctions.

Provisional measures, as, for instance, a call to cease hostilities, may be taken prior to or after the determination of the aggressor, and they may be taken by a court as well as by an executive organ. If the act of the central organ has the character of a decision legally binding on the parties, non-compliance with this decision constitutes a delict entailing a reaction on the part of the security organization.[35]

(E) SANCTIONS CONSTITUTING INDIVIDUAL RESPONSIBILITY FOR VIOLATIONS OF INTERNATIONAL LAW

As pointed out in a previous chapter, the economic and military sanctions usually established within an international security system are directed against a state as such and thus constitute collective responsibility. This means that the forcible deprivation of life, freedom, property and other values, implied in these sanctions, in the last instance affects individual human beings who by their own voluntary acts have not committed the delicts against which the sanctions are directed. This is one of the main objections to military sanctions in general. However, as has been pointed out, this objection could also be raised against economic sanctions. The only way to avoid the injustice of making individuals responsible for a delict which they have not committed is to provide for sanctions which, unlike economic and military sanctions, are not directed against a certain group of individuals, namely, individuals belonging to the state the organ of which has committed the delict, but only and exclusively against a definite individual, especially against that individual who in his capacity as the organ of a state or as a private person has committed the delict. Such sanctions, capital punishment, imprisonment and fine, for example, are usually provided for in national law, especially in the penal law of modern states. If the sanction provided for as a reaction against a delict is punishment, the delict may be called a crime. The crimes which an international security organization tries to prevent are crimes against international peace, or, what amounts to the same thing, crimes against international security. There can be no doubt that the main crime against security, the illegal use of armed force by one state against another, can be committed only at the order or with the authorization of the supreme organs of the state, the head of the state or other members of the government, for only these individuals have the legal power to make use of the armed forces of the state. If individual responsibility for a crime against international security is to be established, the treaty constituting the international security organization must provide for punishment of the individuals who, in their capacity as organs of a state and in violation of the treaty, have ordered or authorized the armed forces of a state to take action against another state, or have ordered or authorized or personally performed any act which must be considered as aggression, especially the act of threatening with the use of armed force. For this purpose, the constituent treaty must confer upon an international court the power to try the individuals accused of a crime against security and, if they are found guilty, to inflict a definite punishment on them. This means a considerable deviation from the principle of traditional international law which holds that only states and not individuals can be parties to a case before an international court.[36] To comply with the generally recognized principle of penal law that no crime should be punished unless the punishment is determined by a pre-established law, the constituent treaty should specify the penalties which the court is authorized to inflict upon guilty individuals.

Acts performed, ordered or authorized by the government are acts of state. According to a principle of general international law, a state can exercise jurisdiction over another state through its courts, and this means jurisdiction over acts of another state, and thus make the organ of another state individually responsible for a violation of international law, only with the consent of this state. Insofar as an international court is a common court of the states which are contracting parties to the treaty by which a court or its jurisdiction is established, an international court can try individuals for having violated international law by acts of state, and this means in their capacity as organs of a state, only with the consent of this state. In other words, the state, over whose acts an international court exercises jurisdiction by inflicting punishment upon the individuals who have performed these acts, must be a contracting party to the treaty establishing the jurisdiction of the court or must express its consent to

370624—57——9

this jurisdiction in some other way. If such a court is established only after aggression has taken place, it stands to reason that only the government of a state defeated in the war which was the consequence of the aggression, will consent to the prosecution of former members of its government.[37] Hence, individual criminal responsibility for crimes against international security should be pre-established in the treaty constituting the security organization. If the organization is universal, there is no difficulty in applying the provision concerned. However, if the organization is not universal and a non-member state is the aggressor, the prosecution of organs of this state for having committed the act of aggression is legally possibly only if the government of the non-member state consents. It should be noted, however, that according to an opinion advocated by some authorities, the rule of general international law requiring the consent of a state to the prosecution of an individual who in his capacity as an organ of this state has violated international law by committing a crime against international security, has been abrogated by the practice of states, especially by the Agreement signed on 8 August 1945 in London for the prosecution of the major war criminals of the European Axis.[38]

Whether individual criminal responsibility for violations of international law, and especially for crimes against international security, should be extended to acts performed at superior order, is a delicate question. If this question is answered in the affirmative, not only the member or members of the government who ordered the illegal use of armed force, but all members of the armed force who executed the order, would be punishable. This, of course, is absurd. Hence, the principle of excluding the plea of superior order should be restricted with respect to the crimes to which it may be applied, as well as with respect to the conditions under which a crime committed at superior order should be considered punishable.[39]

Although individual criminal responsibility for violations of international law by acts of state is certainly a very effective means of preventing these violations and especially of preventing the illegal use of armed force, it is evident that the sanctions constituting this responsibility do not suffice if, in spite of such responsibility established by the constituent treaty, an act of aggression has actually taken place and a military action is necessary to stop the aggression and save the victim, to the extent that this is possible.

Individual criminal responsibility for violations of international law by acts of state is not a consideration in case of internal aggression constituted by a revolutionary movement within a member state, for revolutionary acts are not acts of state and violate only national law and not international law. The situation is different if a security treaty provides for enforcement action against a revolutionary movement within a member state and if the insurgents are recognized as a belligerent power. The internal aggression constituted by the revolutionary movement is then analogous to aggression by a non-member state against a member state, for the government of the insurgents cannot be considered to be a contracting party to the security treaty. Consequently, the provisions of the treaty concerning individual criminal responsibility for acts of aggression are not applicable to the members of the revolutionary government. Only the collective responsibility implied in the enforcement action taken against the revolutionary movement applies. It should not be ignored that even within the national law of modern states the principle of collective responsibility cannot be completely replaced by that of individual responsibility. There are cases where only the former is applicable.

(F) SANCTIONS CONSISTING OF THE FORFEITURE OF RIGHTS

As pointed out in a previous chapter, sanctions may consist of the forcible deprivation of rights. The expulsion of a member state from a security organization is such a sanction. It implies the forfeiture of all the rights a state has in its capacity as a member of the organization. However, the consequence of expulsion is that the state concerned is also released from the obligations imposed upon it by the constituent treaty.[40] For this reason, expulsion is not an appropriate sanction within a security organization which intends to be universal. More appropriate is a forefeiture of rights not accompanied by a release from obligations, especially the forfeiture of specific rights, e. g., the right to participate in the voting of a collegiate organ in which the state is represented.[41]

NOTES

1. *Cf.* the excellent study: *International Sanctions.* A Report of a Group of Members of the Royal Institute of International Affairs. Oxford University Press, London, New York, Toronto, 1938. Quoted in the following as: *International Sanctions.*

2. This was the case under the Covenant of the League of Nations which in Article 16, paragraph 1 (*cf. infra*, p. 134) imposed upon the members only an obligation to take economic sanctions. As far as military sanctions were concerned, the members were under no obligation; they were only authorized to take such action.

3. According to Article 16, paragraph 2, of the Covenant of the League of Nations, the Council had the power to make recommendations concerning the execution of the military sanctions. Under this Article the Council had no competence with respect to the execution of the economic sanctions by the members. However, Article 10 provided: "The Members of the League undertake to respect and preserve against external aggression the territorial integrity and existing political independence of all Members of the League. In case of

any such aggression or in case of any threat or danger of such aggression the Council shall advise upon the means by which this obligation shall be fulfilled." In so far as the "means" referred to in this Article had the character of economic sanctions in the sense of Article 16, paragraph 1, the Council was competent to make recommendations also concerning the execution of these measures. Under the Charter of the United Nations the execution of the sanctions—military as well as non-military—is reserved to the Security Council, and the members are obliged to carry out the decisions of the Council. Article 39 provides: "The Security Council shall determine the existence of any threat to the peace, breach of the peace, or act of aggression and shall make recommendations, or decide what measures shall be taken in accordance with Articles 41 and 42, to maintain or restore international peace and security." Article 25 stipulates: "The Members of the United Nations agree to accept and carry out the decisions of the Security Council in accordance with the present Charter." In addition, Article 48 provides: "1. The action required to carry out the decisions of the Security Council for the maintenance of international peace and security shall be taken by all the Members of the United Nations or by some of them, as the Security Council may determine. 2. Such decisions shall be carried out by the Members of the United Nations directly and through their action in the appropriate international agencies of which they are members." Decisions of the Security Council concerning enforcement measures involving or not involving the use of armed force as sanctions are to be taken according to Article 27, paragraph 3, by an affirmative vote of seven members including the concurring votes of the five permanent members. If, however, the Security Council, because of lack of unanimity of the permanent members, fails to exercise its responsibility with respect to execution of sanctions, the General Assembly is authorized by the Resolution "Uniting for Peace" (*cf.* p. 139) to recommend to the members collective measures including, in the case of a breach of the peace or act of aggression, the use of armed force.

4. Article 4 of the Covenant of the League of Nations provided: "1. The Council shall consist of representatives of the Principal Allied and Associated Powers (United States of America, the British Empire, France, Italy and Japan), together with Representatives of four other Members of the League. These four Members of the League shall be selected by the Assembly from time to time in its discretion. Until the appointment of the Representatives of the four Members of the League first selected by the Assembly, Representatives of Belgium, Brazil, Greece and Spain shall be Members of the Council. 2. With the approval of the majority of the Assembly, the Council may name additional Members of the League, whose Representatives shall always be Members of the Council; the Council with like approval may increase the number of Members of the League to be selected by the Assembly for representation on the Council. 3. *bis. The Assembly shall fix by a two-thirds' majority the rules dealing with the election of the non-permanent Members of the Council, and particularly such regulations as relate to their term of office and the conditions of reeligibility.*"

Article 23 of the Charter of the United Nations reads as follows: "1. The Security Council shall consist of eleven Members of the United Nations. The Republic of China, France, the Union of Soviet Socialist Republics, the United Kingdom of Great Britain and Northern Ireland and the United States of America shall be permanent members of the Security Council. The General Assembly shall elect six other Members of the United Nations to be non-permanent members of the Security Council, due regard being specially paid, in the first instance to the contribution of Members of the United Nations to the maintenance of international peace and security and to the other purposes of the Organization, and also to equitable geographical distribution. 2. The non-permanent members of the Security Council shall be elected for a term of two years. In the first election of the non-permanent members, however, three shall be chosen for a term of one year. A retiring member shall not be eligible for immediate re-election. 3. Each member of the Security Council shall have one representative."

5. It is significant that the Covenant of the League of Nations—in contradistinction to the Charter of the United Nations—does not contain an express provision concerning self-defense. This right is presupposed as self-evident. The provisions of Article 16, paragraph 1, of the Covenant concerning economic sanctions only transform the right of so-called collective self-defense into an obligation, (the economic sanctions considered as a use of force not involving armed force); and the provisions of Article 16, paragraph 2, confer upon the Council only the power to make recommendations with respect to the exercise of the right of collective self-defense by military measures.

The exercise of the right of individual and collective self-defense, expressly stipulated in Article 51 in the Charter of the United Nations, differs clearly from the execution of sanctions taken as enforcement measures by the central organ of the United Nations, the Security Council, under Articles 39–50. The right of individual and collective self-defense may be exercised only as long as the central organ of the United Nations, the Security Council, does not intervene ("until the Security Council has taken the measures necessary to maintain international peace and security").

Under Article 51 so-called collective self-defense is a right of the members. By an agreement of the members, this right may be transformed into an obligation. In this way regional security organizations may be established within the framework of the relatively universal security organization of the United Nations. (As to the question of whether or not these organizations are "regional arrangements" within the meaning of Chapter VIII of the Charter, *cf. infra*, p. 252). They constitute important implementations of Article 51 of the Charter. Such an agreement is the Inter-American Treaty of Reciprocal Assistance signed at the Inter-American Conference for the Maintenance of Continental Peace and Security at Rio de Janeiro on 2 September 1947. Article 3, paragraph 1, of this treaty stipulates: "The High Contracting Parties agree that an armed attack by any state against an American State shall be considered as an attack against all the American States and, consequently, each one of the said Contracting Parties undertakes to assist in meeting the attack in the exercise of the inherent right of individual or collective self-defense recognized by Article 51 of the Charter of the United Nations." Another agreement implementing Article 51 of the Charter is the treaty signed by Belgium, France, Luxembourg, the Netherlands and Great Britain at Brussels on 17 March 1948. Article 4 of this treaty provides: "If any of the High Contracting Parties should be the object of an armed attack in Europe, the other High Contracting Parties will, in accordance with the provisions of Article 51 of the Charter of the United Nations, afford the Party so attacked all the military and other aid and assistance in their power." The most important treaty for the organization of collective self-defense is the so-called North Atlantic Treaty signed at Washington on 4 April 1949 by Belgium, Canada, Denmark, France, Iceland, Italy, Luxembourg, Netherlands, Norway, Portugal, United Kingdom, United States of America, and adhered to by Greece and Turkey. Article 3 of the Treaty stipulates: "In order more effectively to achieve the objectives of this Treaty, the Parties, separately and jointly, by means of continuous and effective self-help and mutual aid, will maintain and develop their individual and collective capacity to resist armed attack." Article 5 of the treaty runs as follows: "The Parties agree that an armed attack against one or more of them in Europe or North America shall be considered an attack against them all; and consequently they agree that, if such an armed attack occurs, each of them, in exercise of the right of individual or collective self-defence recognized by Article 51 of the Charter of the United Nations, will assist the Party or Parties so attacked by taking forthwith, individually and in concert with the other Parties, such action as it deems necessary, including the use of armed force, to restore and maintain the Security of the North Atlantic area. Any such armed attack and all measures taken as a result thereof shall immediately be reported to the Security Council. Such measures shall be terminated when the Security Council has taken the measures necessary to restore and maintain international peace and security." Article 9 provides: "The Parties hereby establish a council, on which each of them shall be represented, to consider matters concerning the implementation of this Treaty. The council shall be so organized as to be able to meet promptly at any time. The council shall set up such subsidiary bodies as may be necessary; in particular it shall establish immediately a defense committee which shall recommend measures for the implementation of Articles 3 and 5." It is important to note that some of the contracting parties were, at the time the treay was concluded, not members of the United Nations: Italy and Portugal.

In conformity with Article 3 of the North Atlantic Treaty, the United States of America concluded on the basis of the Mutual Defense Assistance Act of 1949 various Defense Assistance Agreements. The Agrement concluded with France on 27 January 1950 contains in its Preamble the following statements: "The Governments of the United States of America and the Republic of France . . . . Taking into consideration the support that the Government of the United States of America has brought to these principles by enacting the Mutual Defense Assistance Act of 1949 which provides for the furnishing of military assistance to nations which have joined with it in collective security arrangements; desiring to set forth the understandings which will govern the transfer of such assistance; have agreed as follows: Article I. 1. Each Government, consistently with the principle that economic recovery is essential to international peace and security and must be given clear priority, will make or continue to make available to the other, and to such other governments as the parties hereto may in each case agree upon, such equipment, materials, services, or other military assistance as the government furnishing such assistance may authorize and in accordance with such terms and conditions as may be agreed. The furnishing of any such assistance as may be authorized by either party hereto shall be consistent with the Charter of the United Nations and with the obligations under Article 3 of the North Atlantic Treaty. Such assistance shall be so designed as to promote an integrated defense of the North Atlantic area and to facilitate the development of, or be in accordance with, defense plans under Article 9 of the North Atlantic Treaty approved by each Government. . . . . Article II. In conformity with the principle of mutual aid, the Goverment of the Republic of France agrees to facilitate the production and transfer to the Government of the United States of America, for such period of time, in such quantities and upon such terms and conditions as may be agreed upon, of raw and semiprocessed materials required by the United States as a result of deficiencies or potential deficiencies in its own resources, and which may be available in France or dependent territories under its administration. Arrangements for such transfers shall give due regard to requirements for domestic use and commercial export of France." "Article VI. 1. The two Governments will, upon the request of either of them, consult regarding any matter relating to the application of this Agreement or to operations or arrangements carried out pursuant to this Agreement. 2. Each Government agrees to receive personnel of the other Government who will discharge in its territory the responsibilities of the other Government under this Agreement and who will be accorded facilities to observe the progress of assistance furnished pursuant to this Agreement. Such personnel who are nationals of that other country, including personnel temporarily assigned, will, in their relations with the Government of the country to which they are assigned, operate as a part of the Embassy under the direction and control of the Chief of the Diplomatic Mission of the Government of such country."

On the basis of the Mutual Defense Assistance Act of 1949, as amended, and the Mutual Security Act of 1951, the United States concluded with Yugoslavia an Agreement, signed at Belgrade on 14 November 1951, which contains among others the following provisions: "The Governments of the United States of America and the Federal People's Republic of Yugoslavia ; Desiring the foster international peace and security within the framework of the Charter of the United Nations through measures which will further the ability of nations dedicated to the purposes and principles of the Charter to participate effectively in arrangements for individual and collective self-defense in support of those purposes and principles . . . . have agreed as follows: Article I. 1. The Government of the United States of America will make or continue to make available to the Government of the Federal People's Republic of Yugoslavia equipment, materials, services or other assistance in accordance with such terms and conditions as may be agreed. The furnishing of such assistance shall be consistent with the Charter of the United Nations. Such assistance will be furnished under the provisions, and subject to all of the terms, conditions and termination provisions, of the Mutual Defense Assistance Act of 1949 and the Mutual Security Act of 1951, acts amendatory and supplementary thereto and appropriation acts thereunder. The two Governments will, from time to time, negotiate detailed arrangements necessary to carry out the provisions of this paragraph. 2. The Government of the Federal People's Republic of Yugoslavia will use the assistance exclusively in furtherance of the purposes of the Charter of the United Nations for the promotion of international peace and security and for strengthening the defenses of the Federal People's Republic of Yugoslavia against aggression. 3. The Government of the Federal People's Republic of Yugoslavia undertakes not to transfer to any person not an officer or agent of that Government, or to any other nation, title to or possession of any equipment, materials, information, or services, received on a grant basis, without the prior consent of the Government of the United States of America. 4. The Government of the Federal People's Republic of Yugoslavia will provide the United States of America with reciprocal assistance by continuing to facilitate the production and transfer to the United States of America in such quantities and upon such terms and conditions as may be agreed on, of raw and semiprocessed materials required by the United States of America as a result of deficiencies or potential deficiencies in its own resources, and which may be available in Yugoslavia. Arrangements for such transfers shall give due regards to requirements of Yugoslavia for domestic use and commercial export. . . . . Article V. The Government of the Federal People's Republic of Yugoslavia agrees to receive personnel of the Government of the United States of America who will discharge in its territory the responsibilities of the Government of the

United States of America under this Agreement and who will be accorded facilities to observe the progress of the assistance furnished pursuant to this Agreement. It is understood between the two Governments that the number of such personnel will be kept as low as possible. Such personnel who are United States nationals, including personnel temporarily assigned, will, in their relations with the Government of the Federal People's Republic of Yugoslavia, operate as a part of the Embassy of the United States of America under the direction and control of the Chief of the Diplomatic Mission, and will have the same status as that of other personnel with corresponding rank of the Embassy of the United States of America who are United States nationals. Upon appropriate notification by the Government of the United States of America full diplomatic status will be granted to an agreed number of the personnel assigned thereto."

Mutual defense treaties analogous to the North Atlantic Treaty were concluded between the United States and Far Eastern countries, as, for instance, the Treaty concluded on 2 December 1954 with the so-called nationalist government of the Republic of China (having its seat on Formosa) whose Article V provides: "Each Party recognizes that an armed attack in the West Pacific Area directed against the territories of either of the Parties would be dangerous to its own peace and safety and declares that it would act to meet the common danger in accordance with its constitutional processes. Any such armed attack and all measures taken as a result thereof shall be immediately reported to the Security Council of the United Nations. Such measures shall be terminated when the Security Council has taken the measures necessary to restore and maintain international peace and security."

Another treaty concluded for the purpose of collective defense is the Southeast Asia Collective Defense Treaty, signed on 8 September 1954 by France, New Zealand, Pakistan, the Republic of the Philippines, the Kingdom of Thailand, the United Kingdom of Great Britain and Northern Ireland, and the United States. (Text in: *Disarmament and Security. A Collection of Documents 1919–1955.* Subcommittee on Disarmament. Pursuant to Senate Resolution 93, and continued by Senate Resolution 185, Eighty-fourth Congress. United States Government Printing Office, Washington 1956 [thereafter quoted: *Disarmament and Security,*] pp. 611 ff).

On 24 February 1955, at Baghdad, a Pact of Mutual Cooperation was concluded between Iraq and Turkey, to which Pakistan on 23 September 1955, the United Kingdom on 5 April 1955, and Iran on 3 November 1955 adhered. The Pact refers in its Preamble to the responsibilities borne by the contracting parties "in their capacity as members of the United Nations concerned with the maintenance of peace and security in the Middle East region. . . ." It contains among others the following provisions: "Article I. Consistent with Article 51 of the United Nations Charter the High Contracting Parties will cooperate for their security and defence. Such measures as they agree to take to give effect to this cooperation may form the subject of special agreements with each other." "Article II. In order to ensure the realization and effect application of the cooperation provided for in Article I above, the competent authorities of the High Contracting Parties will determine the measures to be taken as soon as the present Pact enters into force. These measures will become operative as soon as they have been approved by the Governments of the High Contracting Parties." "Article V. This Pact shall be open for accession to any member of the Arab League or any other state actively concerned with the security and peace in this region and which is fully recognized by both of the High Contracting Parties. . . ." "Article VI. A Permanent Council at Ministerial level will be set up to function within the framework of the purposes of this Pact when at least four Powers become parties to the Pact. The Council will draw up its own rules of procedure."

On 14 May 1955, at Warsaw, a Treaty of Friendship, Cooperation and Mutual Assistance was concluded between the Soviet Union and Albania, Bulgaria, Hungarian People's Republic, German Democratic Republic, Polish People's Republic, Rumanian People's Republic, Czechoslovak Republic. In the Preamble the contracting parties express "their desire for the establishment of European collective security based on the participation of all European states irrespective of their social and political systems, which would make it possible to unite their efforts in safeguarding the peace of Europe"; and declare to be "guided by the objects and principles of the Charter of the United Nations Organization." Article 1 stipulates: "The Contracting Parties undertake, in accordance with the Charter of the United Nations Organization, to refrain in their international relations from the threat or use of force, and to settle their international disputes peacefully and in such manner as will not jeopardize international peace and security." Article 4: "In the event of armed attack in Europe on one or more of the Parties to the Treaty by any state or group of states, each of the Parties to the Treaty, in the exercise of its right to individual or collective self-defence in accordance with Article 51 of the Charter of the United Nations Organization, shall immediately, either individually or in agreement with other Parties to the Treaty, come to the assistance of the state or states attacked with all such means as it deems necessary, including armed force. The Parties to the Treaty shall immediately consult concerning the necessary measures to be taken by them jointly in order to restore and maintain international peace and security. Measures taken on the basis of this Article shall be reported to the Security Council in conformity with the provisions of the Charter of the United Nations Organization. These measures shall be discontinued immediately the Security Council adopts the necessary measures to restore and maintain international peace and security." Article 5: "The Contracting Parties have agreed to establish a Joint Command of the armed forces that by agreement among the Parties shall be assigned to the Command, which shall function on the basis of jointly established principles. They shall likewise adopt other agreed measures necessary to strengthen their defensive power, in order to protcet the peaceful labours of their peoples, guarantee the inviolability of their frontiers and territories, and provide defence against possible aggression."

Prior to the coming into force of the United Nations Charter, on 22 March 1945, a pact between the Syrian Republic, Transjordan, Iraq, Saudi Arabia, the Lebanese Republic, Egypt, and Yemen, constituting the Arab League, was concluded. It provides for a Council composed of the representatives of the member states (Article 3) and stipulates in Article 5: "Any resort to force in order to resolve disputes arising between two or more member states of the League is prohibited. If there should arise among them a difference which does not concern a state's independence, sovereignty, or territorial integrity, and if the parties to the dispute have recourse to the Council for the settlement of this difference, the decision of the Council shall then be enforceable and obligatory. In such a case, the states between whom the difference has arisen shall not participate in the deliberations and decisions of the Council. The Council shall mediate in all differences which threaten to lead to war between two member states, or a member state and a third state, with a view to bringing about their reconciliation. Decisions of arbitration and mediation shall be taken by majority vote." Article 6 runs as follows: "In case of aggression or threat of aggression by one state against a member state, the state which has been attacked or threatened with aggression may demand the immediate convocation of the Council. The Council shall, by unanimous decision, determine the measures necessary to repulse the aggression. If the aggressor is a member state, his vote shall not be counted in determining unanimity. If, as a result of the attack, the government of the state attacked finds itself unable to communicate with the Council, that state's representative in the Council shall have the right to request the convocation of the Council for the purpose indicated in the foregoing paragraph. In the event that this representative is unable to communicate with the Council, any member state of the League shall have the right to request the convocation of the Council."

On 13 April 1950 the members of the Arab League signed a Joint Defense and Economic Cooperation Treaty, which provides in Article 2: "The contracting States consider any (act of) armed aggression made against any one or more of them or their armed forces, to be directed against them all. Therefore, in accordance with the right of self-defense, individually and collectively they undertake to go without delay to the aid of the State or States against which such an act of aggression is made, and immediately to take, individually and collectively, all steps available, including the use of armed force, to repel the aggression and restore security and peace. In conformity with Article 6 of the Arab League Pact and Article 51 of the United Nations Charter, the Arab League Council and U. N. Security Council shall be notified of such act of aggression and the means and procedure taken to check it." (Full text in *Disarmament and Security*, pp. 622 ff.)

Article 51 of the Charter has been implemented also by Resolution 378 (V): Duties of States in the Event of the Outbreak of Hostilities, adopted by the General Assembly on 17 November 1950, recommending: "(a) That if a State becomes engaged in armed conflict with another State or States, it takes all steps practicable in the circumstances and compatible with the right of self-defence to bring the armed conflict to an end at the earliest possible moment; (b) In particular, that such State shall immediately, and in any case not later than twenty-four hours after the outbreak of the hostilities, make a public statement wherein it will proclaim its readiness, provided that the States with which it is in conflict will do the same, to discontinue all military operations and withdraw all its military forces which have invaded the territory or territorial water of another State or crosses a demarcation line, either on terms agreed by the parties to the conflict or under conditions to be indicated to the parties by the appropriate organs of the United Nations; (c) That such State immediately notify the Secretary-General, for communication to the Security Council and to the Members of the United Nations, of the statement made in accordance with the preceding subparagraph and of the circumstances in which the conflict has arisen; (d) That such State, in its notification to the Secretary-General, invite the appropriate organs of the United Nations to dispatch the Peace Observation Commission to the area in which the conflict has arisen, if the Commission is not already functioning there; (e) That the conduct of the States concerned in relation to the matters covered by the foregoing recommendations be taken into account in any determination of responsibility for the breach of the peace or act of aggression in the case under consideration and in all other relevant proceedings before the appropriate organs of the United Nations."

6. *Cf.* the declaration made by the representative of the United States of America on 22 May 1933, at the League of Nations Disarmament Conference, *infra*, p. 175.

7. The principle of not recognizing an illegally established situation is known as the Stimson Doctrine, named after the U. S. Secretary of State Stimson and formulated in an identical note to Japan and China of January 7, 1932 in which the Government of the United States declared that it ". . . cannot admit the legality of any situation *de facto* nor does it intend to recognize any treaty or agreement entered into between those Governments, or agents thereof, which may impair the treaty rights of the United States or its citizens in China, including those which relate to the sovereignty, the independence, or the territorial and administrative integrity of the Republic of China, or to the international policy relative to China, commonly known as the open-door policy; and that it does not intend to recognize any situation, treaty, or agreement, which may be brought about by means contrary to the covenants and obligations of the Pact of Paris of August 27, 1928, to which treaty both China and Japan, as well as the United States, are parties." The principle of non-recognition has been confirmed by a resolution of the Assembly of the League of Nations on 11 March 1932 which contained the following statement: "It is incumbent upon the Members of the League of Nations not to recognize any situation, treaty, or agreement, which may be brought about by means contrary to the Covenant of the League of Nations or to the Pact of Paris."

The Draft Convention on Rights and Duties of States in Case of Aggression, published by the Harvard Research in International Law, lays down the principle that an aggressor does not acquire rights or relieve itself of duties by becoming an aggressor (Article 2); Articles 3, 4, and 5 contain specific applications of this principle.

8. An interesting suggestion concerning the centralization of financial sanctions was made by M. Busch in two articles published on 22 and 23 September 1915 in the *Neue Züricher Zeitung*, later presented by Camille Gorgé, *Une nouvelle sanction du droit international. Le Projet Busch* (1926), and Schücking, Rühland, Böhmert, "Die Organisation der Völkerbundsexekution gegen den Angreifer." *Zeitschrift für Völkerrecht*, 1932, pp. 560 ff. The essential idea of the suggestion (as formulated in the last mentioned article) was that each member of a security organization would deposit a certain amount of gold, determined in proportion to the number of its inhabitants and its economic resources, at the disposal of the central organ of the organization. Each member state would then have the right to circulate bank notes which would have to be covered by this amount of gold on deposit. In case a state were declared to be an aggressor by the competent organ of the organization, its gold would be confiscated and, if necessary, transferred to the victim of the aggression. This confiscation of gold would then probably lead to the breakdown of the monetary system of the aggressor state. *Cf.* also F. N. Keen, *The World in Alliance*, p. 58 (quoted by John A. Hobson, *Towards International Government*, London 1915, pp. 94 f): "The States comprised in the international scheme might be required to keep deposited with, or under, the control of, the International Council sums of money, proportioned in some way to their relative populations or financial resources which might be made available to answer international obligations, and an international bank might be organized which would facilitate the giving of security by states to the International Council for the performance of their obligations and the enforcement of payments between one state and another (as well as probably assisting in the creation of an international currency and discharging other useful international functions)."

9. *Cf. International Sanctions*, pp. 24 ff., 60 ff., 76 ff., 91 ff., 106 ff. According to this study, a complete international boycott involves: "(a) the complete closing

of land frontiers, even to mails, in either direction; (b) the severance of telegraphic, telephonic, and radio communication; (c) exclusion of the shipping and aircraft of the boycotted state from the harbours and airports of all other states; (d) the prohibition and prevention of the shipping of all other states from entering the harbours of the boycotted state; (e) the prevention of all illicit communications, by land, sea, or air; (f) the internment or the repatriation of all nations of the boycotted state resident in other countries; (g) the withdrawal of all diplomatic and consular officers on both sides." *Op. cit.*, p. 109. The economic sanctions stipulated in Article 16, paragraph 1, of the Covenant of the League of Nations constituted a complete boycott. The provisions ran as follows: "Should any Member of the League resort to war in disregard of its covenants under Articles 12, 13 or 15, it shall *ipso facto* be deemed to have committed an act of war against all other Members of the League, which hereby undertake immediately to subject it to the severance of all trade or financial relations, the prohibition of all intercourse between their nationals and the nationals of the covenant-breaking State, and the prevention of all financial, commercial or personal intercourse between the nationals of the covenant-breaking State and the nationals of any other State, whether a Member of the League or not." An analogous provision is Article 41 of the Charter of the United Nations which runs as follows: "The Security Council may decide what measures not involving the use of armed force are to be employed to give effect to its decisions, and it may call upon the Members of the United Nations to apply such measures. These may include complete or partial interruption of economic relations and of rail, sea, air, postal, telegraphic, radio, and other means of communication, and the severance of diplomatic relations."

10. Article 16, paragraph 3, of the Covenant of the League of Nations provided: "The Members of the League agree, further, that they will mutually support one another in the financial and economic measures which are taken under this Article, in order to minimize the loss and inconvenience resulting from the above measures, and that they will mutually support one another in resisting any special measures aimed at one of their number by the covenant-breaking State . . ." Article 50 of the Charter of the United Nations stipulates: "If preventive or enforcement measures against any state are taken by the Security Council, any other state, whether a Member of the United Nations or not, which finds itself confronted with special economic problems arising from the carrying out of those measures shall have the right to consult the Security Council with regard to a solution of those problems."

11. *Cf.* p. 61.

12. According to Article 39 of the Charter of the United Nations, the enforcement measures to be taken by the Security Council in case of a threat to or breach of the peace may be directed not only against a member but also against a non-member state, and according to Article 51 the exercise of the right of individual and collective self-defense is justified not only in case of an armed attack launched by a member but also in case of an armed attack by a non-member state.

12a. Article 14 of the Draft Convention on Rights and Duties of States in Case of Aggression stipulates: "Nothing in this Convention shall be deemed to excuse any State for a violation of the humanitarian rules concerning the conduct of hostilities, prescribed by international law or by a treaty to which it is a party." This applies also to the conduct of hostilities against an aggressor.

13. *Cf.*, pp. 122 ff.

14. This system of military sanctions was adopted by the Covenant of the League of Nations, which in Article 16, paragraph 2, provided: "It shall be the duty of the Council in such case [if a Member of the League resorts to war in violation of the Covenant] to recommend to the several governments concerned what effective military, naval or air force the Members of the League shall severally contribute to the armed forces to be used to protect the covenants of the League." The words "to contribute to the armed forces to be used . . ." are misleading. There were no armed forces other than those of the members.

15. This is the case under the Charter of the United Nations. *Cf* Note 16.

16. The first attempt to organize military sanctions on the basis of the contingent system was made in a proposal submitted by the representative of France to the League of Nations Commission of the Peace Conference following the first World War. This proposal contained the following provisions:

"*III: MILITARY SANCTIONS*

(i.) *International Forces*

The execution of the military sanctions on land or at sea shall be entrusted either to an international force, or to one or more Powers members of the League of Nations, to whom a mandate in that behalf shall have been given.

The International Body shall have at its disposal a military force supplied by the various member States of sufficient strength:—

(1.) To secure the execution of its decisions and those of the International Tribunal;

(2.) to overcome, in case of need, any forces which may be opposed to the League of Nations in the event of armed conflict.

(ii.) *Strength of International Contingents*

The International Body shall determine the strength of the international force and fix the contingents which must be held at its disposal.

Each of the member States shall be free to settle as it deems best the conditions under which its contingent shall be recruited.

The question of the limitation of armaments in each of the member States will be dealt with elsewhere.

(iii.) *Permanent Staff*

A permanent international Staff shall investigate all military questions affecting the League of Nations. Each State shall appoint the officer or officers who shall represent it in a proportion to be determined later.

The Chief and Deputy Chiefs of Staff shall be appointed for a period of three years by the International Body, from a list submitted by the member States.

(iv.) *Functions of the Permanent Staff*

It shall be the duty of the permanent international Staff to deal, under the supervision of the International Body, with everything relating to the organisation of the joint forces and the eventual conduct of military operations. It will in particular be charged with the task of inspecting international forces and armaments in agreement with the military authorities of each State, and of proposing any improvements it may deem necessary, either in the international military organisation or in the constitution, composition, and methods of recruiting of the forces of each State.

The Staff shall report the result of its inspection, either as a matter of routine or at the request of the International Body. Military instruction shall be given in each member State in accordance with rules designed to procure, as far as possible, uniformity in the armaments and training of the troops destined to act in concert.

The International Body shall be entitled, at any time, to require that the member States introduce any alteration into their national system of recruiting which the Staff may report to be necessary.

(v.) *Commander-in-Chief and Chief of General Staff*

When circumstances shall so require, the International Body shall appoint, for the duration of the operations to be undertaken, a Commander-in-chief of the international forces.

Upon his appointment, the Commander-in-chief shall nominate his chief of General Staff and the officers who are to assist him.

The powers of the Commander-in-chief and his Chief of General Staff shall cease when circumstances become such that an armed conflict is no longer to be feared, or when the object of the military operations has been attained.

In either case, the date at which the powers of the Commander-in-chief and the General Staff shall cease shall be fixed by a decision of the International Body."

On 5 February 1932, at the Conference for the Reduction and Limitation of Armament, the French delegation submitted a set of proposals which contained a plan for the establishment of an international armed force organized according to the contingent system. The object of this plan was to set up on behalf of the League of Nations: "(1) an International police force to prevent war; (2) a first contingent of coercionary forces to repress war and to bring immediate assistance to any State victim of aggression. (a) The police force will be permanently available with complete freedom of passage to occupy in times of emergency areas where a threat of war has arisen, and to assist the action of commissioners of the League of Nations on the spot, and also to contribute to all conservatory measures within the scope of the Convention to improve the Means of Preventing War and of Article 11 of the League Covenant. This police force will be made up of contingents furnished by each of the contracting parties in a proportion to be determined. France is prepared to contribute a mixed brigade, a light naval division and a mixed group of reconnaissance and fighter aircraft. The League of Nations will arrange for the command of the international police force and will be entitled to inspect its component elements. (b) The first contingent of coercionary forces would in conformity with the undertakings to be assumed by contracting parties, be made up of elements of strength varying according to the regions concerned. These undertakings entered into by States towards the League of Nations would oblige them to come to the help of any State victim of aggression with forces of definite strength constantly available. The contracting parties would have the option of increasing this contribution on the recommendation of the Council of the League (Paragraph 2 of Article 16 of the Covenant) or, in the event of aggression, with a view to applying regional conventions of mutual assistance coming within the scope of the Covenant. The undertakings of the various States would differ according to the place of the conflict—a conflict concerning another continent from that to which the State belongs; a conflict concerning the continent to which the State belongs; a conflict in which the aggressor has a common frontier with the contracting State. France is prepared to undertake the following contributions: In the case of a conflict outside Europe, a mixed brigade, a light naval division, a mixed group of aircraft, material for land warfare without personnel, and munitions; for a conflict in Europe: a division of all arms, a naval division, a mixed group of aircraft, material for land warfare with personnel, and munitions; for a conflict in Europe in which the aggressor has a common frontier with France the contingents provided for in the preceding paragraph and, in addition, forces, the strength of which would be decided in each case in agreement with the League. As far as material for land warfare is concerned, the contracting parties which possess tanks or similar armoured implements, as well as heavy field artillery, undertake to contribute from them to the forces which will be placed at the disposal of the League under the conditions mentioned above. In these various eventualities the undertakings of each State would only become operative if the forces thus placed at any moment at the disposal of the League reached a minimum total to be determined, and if there were equitable proportion between the contributions of the principal States." *Series of League of Nations Publications*, IX. Disarmament, 1932. IX. 63; Vol. I, p. 115.

A special subcommittee on international organization, appointed in 1943 by Secretary of State Hull, prepared a Draft Constitution of International Organization which in its Article 10 contained the following provisions: "1. Any menace to the peace of nations, wherever it arises, is a matter of vital concern to all states. The International Organization through its Executive Committee [composed of representatives of the United States of America, the United Kingdom, the Union of Soviet Socialist Republics, and China] or Council [composed of eleven representatives, including one representative designated by the United States of America, one by the United Kingdom, one by the Union of Soviet Socialist Republics, one by China, two by the group of European states, two by the group of American states, one by the group of Far Eastern states, one by the states of the Near and Middle East, and one by the British Dominion] shall take any action necessary to safeguard or restore peace. 2. In the event of a breach, or imminently threatened breach, of the peace between nations, the Chairman of the Council, on consultation with such members of the Executive Committee as may be available, shall request the parties to desist from any action which would further aggravate the situation and shall forthwith summon a meeting of the Council. The Council shall request the parties to restore or maintain the position existing before the breach or threatened breach of the peace and to accept procedures of peaceful settlement. The state or states failing to comply with this request within the time specified shall be presumed to intend a violation of the peace of nations and the Executive Committee or the Council shall apply all the measures necessary to restore or maintain the peace. 3. Members of the International Organization undertake in no case to give a state, declared by the Council to be threatening or committing a violation of the peace, assistance of a character which in the opinion of the Council would aggravate the dispute. 4. Members of the International Organization agree to make available for action taken under paragraph 2 to restore or maintain peace such armaments, facilities, installations, strategic areas and contingents of armed forces, and to afford such freedom of passage through their territories, as the Council or the Executive Committee, advised by the General Security and Armaments Commission, may determine to be necessary for this purpose, having regard for the geographical position, regional or special obligations, and relative resources of member states. All national forces and facilities shall operate under their national authorities subject to the general control of the Executive Committee and the technical coordination of operations provided by the General Security and Armaments Commission. . . . 8. Any action by the Council under this Article shall require a two-thirds majority vote including three-fourths of the states members of the Executive Committee." *Postwar Foreign Policy Preparation 1939–1945.* Dept. of State Publication 3580. General Foreign Policy Series 15. Released February 1950. Washington, D. C., 1949, p. 478.

The contingent system is adopted by the Charter of the United Nations which provides: "ARTICLE 43. 1. All Members of the United Nations, in order to contribute to the maintenance of international peace and security, undertake to make available to the Security Council, on its call and in accordance with a special agreement or agreements, armed forces, assistance, and facilities, including rights of passage, necessary for the purpose of maintaining international peace and security. 2. Such agreement or agreements shall govern the numbers and types of forces, their degree of readiness and general location, and the nature of the facilities and assistance to be provided. 3. The agreement or agreements shall be negotiated as soon as possible on the initiative of the Security Council. They shall be concluded between the Security Council and Members or between the Security Council and groups of Members and shall be subject to ratification by the signatory states in accordance with their respective constitutional processes. ARTICLE 44. When the Security Council has decided to use force it shall, before calling upon a Member not represented on it to provide armed forces in fulfillment of the obligations assumed under Article 43, invite that Member, if the Member so desires, to participate in the decisions of the Security Council concerning the employment of contingents of that Member's armed forces. ARTICLE 45. In order to enable the United Nations to take urgent military measures, Members shall hold immediately available national air-force contingents for combined international enforcement action. The strength and degree of readiness of these contingents and plans for their combined action shall be determined, within the limits laid down in the special agreement or agreements referred to in Article 43, by the Security Council with the assistance of the Military Staff Committee. ARTICLE 46. Plans for the application of armed force shall be made by the Security Council with the assistance of the Military Staff Committee. ARTICLE 47. 1. There shall be established a Military Staff Committee to advise and assist the Security Council on all questions relating to the Security Council's military requirements for the maintenance of international peace and security, the employment and command of forces placed at its disposal, the regulation of armaments, and possible disarmament. 2. The Military Staff Committee shall consist of the Chiefs of Staff of the permanent members of the Security Council or their representatives. Any Member of the United Nations not permanently represented on the Committee shall be invited by the Committee to be associated with it when the efficient discharge of the Committee's responsibilities requires the participation of that Member in its work. 3. The Military Staff Committee shall be responsible under the Security Council for the strategic direction of any armed forces placed at the disposal of the Security Council. Questions relating to the command of such forces shall be worked out subsequently. 4. The Military Staff Committee, with the authorization of the Security Council and after consultation with appropriate regional agencies, may establish regional subcommittees. ARTICLE 48. 1. The action required to carry out the decisions of the Security Council for the maintenance of international peace and security shall be taken by all the Members of the United Nations or by some of them, as the Security Council may determine. 2. Such decisions shall be carried out by the Members of the United Nations directly and through their action in the appropriate international agencies of which they are members. ARTICLE 49. The Members of the United Nations shall join in affording mutual assistance in carrying out the measures decided upon by the Security Council."

The Resolution 377 (V) A, entitled "Uniting for Peace," adopted by the General Assembly on 3 November 1950, provides "that if the Security Council, because of lack of unanimity of the permanent members, fails to exercise its primary responsibility for the maintenance of international peace and security in any case where there appears to be a threat to the peace, breach of the peace, or act of aggression, the General Assembly shall consider the matter immediately with a view to making appropriate recommendations to Members for collective measures, including in the case of a breach of the peace or act of aggression the use of armed force when necessary, to maintain or restore international peace and security. If not in session at the time, the General Assembly may meet in emergency special session within twenty-four hours of the request therefor. Such emergency special session shall be called if requested by the Security Council on the vote of any seven members, or by a majority of the Members of the United Nations." The Resolution provides for the establishment by the General Assembly of a Peace Observation Commission composed of 14 member states "which could observe and report on the situation in any area where there exists international tension the continuance of which is likely to endanger the maintenance of international peace and security"; and of a Collective Measures Committee consisting of 14 member states. This committee is directed to study and make a report "in consultation with the Secretary-General and with such Member States as the Committee finds appropriate" on methods "which might be used to maintain and strengthen international peace and security in accordance with the Purposes and Principles of the Charter, taking account of collective self-defence and regional arrangements (Articles 51 and 52 of the Charter)." The Resolution "invites each Member of the United Nations to survey its resources in order to determine the nature and scope of the assistance it may be in a position to render in support of any recommendations of the Security Council or of the General Assembly for the restoration of international peace and security"; and "recommends to the States Members of the United Nations that each Member maintain within its national armed forces elements so trained, organized and equipped that they could promptly be made available, in accordance with its constitutional processes, for service as a United Nations unit or units, upon recommendation by the Security Council or the General Assembly, without prejudice to the use of such elements in exercise of the rights of individual or collective self-defence recognized in Article 51 of the Charter."

Prior to the adoption of the Resolution "Uniting for Peace" by the General Assembly of the United Nations, a resolution (the Thomas-Douglas Resolution S. Con. Res. 52, 81st Cong., 1st sess.) was submitted, on July 8, 1949, to the U. S. Senate. It contained the provisions: ". . . be it *Resolved by the Senate (the House of Representatives concurring)*, (I) That the Congress reaffirm its faith in the United Nations as the cornerstone of the international policy of the United States and as an institution which can progressively be made more adequate to assure the security of its members; (II) That to this end the Congress pledges its support to a supplementary agreement under Article 51 of the Charter open to all members of the United Nations, by which the signatories agree, if the Security Council is prevented from fulfilling its duties, to come to the aid of the victim of attack if requested to do so by a two-thirds vote of the General Assembly, including three of the permanent members of the Security Council; (III) That such an agreement should specify the forces that each signatory agrees to maintain, under the spirit of paragraphs 1 and 2 of Article 43, for immediate use of the United Nations—(a) upon call of the Security Council, or (b) upon call of the General Assembly by a two-thirds vote, including at least three of the permanent members of the Security Council, and (IV) That such an agreement should specify that if a matter pertaining to a threat to or breach of the peace, or act of aggression, is on the agenda of the Security Council, and the Security Council is prevented from fulfilling its duties, the signatories who are members of the Security Council will take such steps as may be required to remove it from the agenda of the Security Council; and (V) That such an agreement should come into force when ratified by a majority of the United Nations including three of the permanent members of the Security Council. Sec. 2. Such an agreement shall not in any way impair the inherent right of the parties to engage in self-defense under Article 51 of the United Nations Charter, individually or through other collective arrangements consistent with their obligations under the United Nations Charter, or the North Atlantic Security Pact, or the Pact of Rio de Janeiro."

The Collective Measures Committee suggested in its first report (*General Assembly. Official Records:* Sixth Session. Supple. No. 13 [A/1891,] New York, 1951) that the United Nations, "whenever it determines upon the use of collective force," should appoint an "executive military authority" responsible for the direction and control of its military operations. This agency "should be empowered to coordinate the efforts of individual States and to organize contributions of forces, assistance and facilities in order to initiate effective military operations against the aggressor in the shortest possible time. Accordingly, upon the determination to adopt measures involving the use of United Nations armed force, the Organization should authorize a State or group of States to act on its behalf as executive military authority, within the framework of its policies and objectives as expressed through such resolutions as it may adopt at any stage of the collective action." As to the relationship between the executive military authority and the state victim of an aggression, the Report states: "In some cases, the victim State might itself be designated as the executive military authority, particularly when it is in a position to conduct its own defence with only limited assistance from the United Nations. More often, however, it might be appropriate for the executive military authority to consist of a group of States, of which the victim State would be one. Finally, the executive military authority might be a State or a group of States which would not include the victim State. Special consideration should also be given to the inclusion in the executive military authority of States situated in, or contiguous to, the area of hostilities, particularly when those States are participating in the United Nations action with their full military potential." "In the theatre of operations the executive military authority should have full responsibility for the coordination and strategic direction and control of the United Nations forces, within the framework of the policies and objectives as expressed through such resolutions as the United Nations may adopt at any stage of the collective action. . . . In accordance with its responsibility, the executive military authority should be authorized to designate the Commander-in-Chief of the United Nations forces and to replace him. Where the executive military authority consists of a group of States, the Commander-in-Chief should be designated by mutual agreement. The Commander-in-Chief's authority should be defined by the executive military authority, and he should receive instructions from that authority." As to the identification of the United Nations character of operations, the Report states: "In identifying military measures with the United Nations, the Security Council or the General Assembly and the executive military authority should take action of several types. First, the body deciding upon or recommending military measures should provide that the forces serving under the executive military authority will be known as the United Nations Forces. The Commander-in-Chief should initiate and conduct all operations as Commander of the United Nations Forces, and should issue all orders, reports and instructions, and carry on all relationships, in the name of the United Nations Command. The Security Council or the General Assembly should authorize the use of the United Nations flag in the field, and the Commander-in-Chief should ensure that that flag, in addition to national flags, is used in United Nations operations. Arrangements should be made for the proper identification of personnel and property of the United Nations in the theatre of operations. Similarly, consideration should be given to providing a United Nations service medal for the forces engaged in future United Nations military action."

The Secretary-General of the United Nations submitted to the Collective Measures Committee the proposal to create a "United Nations Volunteer Reserve." In its second Report (*General Assembly. Official Records:* Seventh Session. Suppl. No. 17 [A/2215] New York 1952), the Collective Measures Committee states: "The Secretary-General proposed the creation of an international organizational framework through which, in his opinion, some States would be further enabled to contribute combatant or ancillary units. In addition, under these proposals, in his estimation at least fifty or sixty thousand volunteers willing to serve the principles of the United Nations might well become available through a United Nations Volunteer Reserve. Such a reserve would constitute additional supplementary strength to other forces provided to a United Nations Executive Military Authority at the time such an Authority was appointed to resist aggression." "Volunteers to a United Nations Volunteer Reserve would be recruited on behalf of the United Nations through the existing national military establishments of States willing to participate in the proposal." They would be "trained in advance on a part time voluntary basis."

17. The Charter of the United Nations provides in Article 17, paragraph 2, that "the expenses of the Organization shall be borne by the Members as apportioned by the General Assembly." It seems that the expenses of a military action taken by the Security Council are not to be considered as "expenses of the Organization." This may be inferred from Article 50: "If preventive or enforcement measures against any state are taken by the Security Council, any other state, whether a Member of the United Nations or not, which finds itself confronted with special economic problems arising from the carrying out of those measures shall have the right to consult the Security Council with regard to a solution of those problems." This provision presupposes that each state must bear the expenses of its own armed force which carry out the measures taken by the Security Council. From Article 49, which stipulates that the members of the United Nations "shall join in affording mutual assistance in carrying out the measures decided upon by the Security Council," may follow the principle of an

equitable sharing of the burdens involved in collective measures. *Cf.* the Second Report of the Collective Measures Committee, p. 6.

18. It is assumed that the difficulty of cordination in naval operations is not as pronounced as in land operations. *International Sanctions* contained the following statement: "Division of effort between navies is more easily organized than between armies, particularly in the type of operations that are likely to be needed in common action against an aggressor state. Sea power is not the instrument of an aggressor; of itself it can do little against any Great Power. It is only when sea power is allied to land power that it has any strength for conquest; intrinsically, it is rather the weapon of collective defence against aggression. Such naval operations as an aggressor undertakes are likely to be strictly local, in support of, or ancillary to, his main effort by land, whereas the naval action taken against him may be widespread, and therefore easily apportioned between various Powers without such close contact as is likely to involve the difficulties of jealousy or divided command." *Loc. cit.*, p. 119.

19. *Cf. International Sanctions*, p. 119.

20. As a matter of fact, the special agreements which, according to Article 43 of the Charter of the United Nations, are to be concluded between the United Nations, represented by the Security Council, and the member states for the purpose of determining the numbers and types of forces to be placed at the disposal of the Council, their degree of readiness and general location, and the nature of facilities and assistance to be provided, have not yet been concluded, nor is it very likely that they will ever be concluded.

Under Article 39 of the Charter, the Security Council, after having determined the existence of a threat to the peace, breach of the peace, or act of aggression, may make "recommendations" or "decide" upon enforcement measures involving or not involving the use of armed force (Articles 42 and 41). The armed forces referred to in Article 42 are the armed forces to be placed at the disposal of the Security Council according to Article 43. As long as the special agreements referred to in Article 43 are not concluded, the Security Council is not in a position to "decide" to take enforcement measures involving the use of armed force. Consequently, when, on 25 June 1950, North Korean forces invaded South Korea and the Security Council in its Resolution of 25 June 1950 (UN Doc. S/1501) determined the existence of a breach of the peace, the Council did not adopt a decision legally binding upon the members of the United Nations but, in its Resolution of 27 June 1950 (UN Doc. S/1511), *recommended* "that the Members of the United Nations furnish such assistance to the Republic of Korea as may be necessary to repel the armed attack and to restore international peace and security in the area." Seventeen states actually contributed armed forces to the action recommended by the Security Council. On 7 July 1950, the Security Council adopted a Resolution (UN Doc. S/1588) in which the Council "1. Welcomes the prompt and vigorous support which governments and peoples of the United Nations have given to its Resolutions of June 25 and 27, 1950, to assist the Republic of Korea in defending itself against armed attack and thus to restore international peace and security in the area; 2. Notes that Members of the United Nations have transmitted to the United Nations offers of assistance for the Republic of Korea; 3. Recommends that all Members providing military forces and other assistance pursuant to the aforesaid Security Council resolutions make such forces and other assistance available to a unified command under the United States; 4. Requests the United States to designate the commander of such forces; 5. Authorizes the unified command at its discretion to use the United Nations flag in the course of operations against North Korean forces concurrently with the flags of the various nations participating; 6. Requests the United States to provide the Security Council with reports as appropriate on the course of action taken under the unified command."

In spite of the fact that Article 42 of the Charter could not be applied, the action in Korea was a police action of the United Nations, the execution of a military sanction within the system of collective security established by the Charter of the United Nations. As to the legal standing of the action, *cf.* Hans Kelsen, *The Law of the United Nations*, London 1951, pp. 927 ff., and Stone, *op cit.*, pp. 228 ff.

21. *Cf.* the Observations on the Draft Treaty of Mutual Assistance submitted to the League of Nations by the British Government. League Document A. 35, 1924, IX, p. 16, quoted in *International Sanctions*, p. 116.

22. In this respect the Charter of the United Nations differs from the Covenant of the League of Nations. The latter provided in Article 1, paragraph 3: "Any Member of the League may, after two years' notice of its intention so to do, withdraw from the League, provided that all its international obligations and all its obligations under this Covenant shall have been fulfilled at the time of its withdrawal," and in Article 26: "1. Amendments to this Covenant will take effect when ratified by the Members of the League whose Representatives compose the Council and by a majority of the Members of the League whose Representatives compose the Assembly. 2. No such amendment shall bind any Member of the League which signifies its dissent therefrom, but in that case it shall cease to be a Member of the League." The Charter of the United Nations does not contain a provision concerning withdrawal from the organization. However, the Report of Commission I to the plenary session of the San Francisco Conference at which the Charter was signed contained the following commentary adopted by Committee I/2 of the Conference: "The Committee adopts the view that the Charter should not make express provision either to permit or to prohibit withdrawal from the Organization. The Committee deems that the highest duty of the nations which will become Members is to continue their cooperation within the Organization for the preservation of international peace and security. If, however, a Member because of exceptional circumstances feels constrained to withdraw, and leave the burden of maintaining international peace and security on the other Members, it is not the purpose of the Organization to compel that Member to continue its cooperation in the Organization. It is obvious, particularly, that withdrawals or some other forms of dissolution of the Organization would become inevitable if, deceiving the hopes of humanity, the Organization was revealed to be unable to maintain peace or could do so only at the expense of law and justice. Nor would a Member be bound to remain in the Organization if its rights and obligations as such were changed by Charter amendment in which it has not concurred and which it finds itself unable to accept, or if an amendment duly accepted by the necessary majority in the Assembly or in a general conference fails to secure the ratification necessary to bring such amendment into effect. It is for these considerations that the Committee has decided to abstain from recommending insertion in the Charter of a formal clause specifically forbidding or permitting withdrawal."

23. *Cf.* Lord Davies, *The Problem of the Twentieth Century*, 1930, Second Ed., 1934, pp. 425 ff., 441 ff., and *International Sanctions*, p. 121 ff.

24. *Cf. International Sanctions*, p. 127. However, Davies, *op. cit.*, pp. 446 f. suggested four categories of reserve formations. Recruits should be enlisted ". . . at the age of seventeen for a minimum term of five years. At the end of this period a proportion of, let us say, three-quarters of the total force would be eligible

for reenlistment for a further term of five years. Their eligibility would be determined by their conduct, achievements and the results of examinations during the preceding period. The retiring contingent, representing twenty-five per cent of the total force, would be relegated to a distinct category of reserves. Similarly, another group would retire at the end of the second period of enlistment, a third and fourth at the conclusion of fifteen and twenty years' service. The minimum period would, therefore, be five years and the maximum period twenty years, whilst the ages of retirement would be twenty-two, twenty-seven, thirty-two and thirty-seven years respectively." However, Davies did not discuss the question of how the international organization might force the reservists to reenter the military service in the international armed force.

25. Davies, *op. cit.*, p. 441, suggested that each member of the international armed force ". . . swear his oath of allegiance to the international authority. From that moment until he is demobilized he becomes de-nationalized in the sense that his services belong exclusively to the authority and that he recognizes no other official claims upon his loyalty."

26. The Charter of the United Nations does not provide for a denationalization of the members of the Secretariat. Article 100 stipulates only: "1. In the performance of their duties, the Secretary-General and the staff shall not seek or receive instructions from any government or from any other authority external to the Organization. They shall refrain from any action which might reflect on their position as international officials responsible only to the Organization. 2. Each Member of the United Nations undertakes to respect the exclusively international character of the responsibilities of the Secretary-General and the staff and not to seek to influence them in the discharge of their responsibilities." This provision is implemented by Article I, Rules of the Staff Regulations, which runs as follows: "1.1. Members of the Secretariat are international civil servants. Their responsibilities are not national but exclusively international. By accepting appointment, they pledge themselves to discharge their functions and to regulate their conduct with the interests of the United Nations only in view. 1.2. Staff members are subject to the authority of the Secretary-General and to assignment by him to any of the activities or offices of the United Nations. They are responsible to him in the exercise of their functions. The whole time of staff members shall be at the disposal of the Secretary-General. The Secretary-General shall establish a normal working week. 1.3. In the performance of their duties members of the Secretariat shall neither seek nor accept instructions from any government or from any other authority external to the Organization. 1.4. Members of the Secretariat shall conduct themselves at all times in a manner befitting their status as international civil servants. They shall not engage in any activity that is incompatible with the proper discharge of their duties with the United Nations. They shall avoid any action and in particular any kind of public pronouncement which may adversely reflect on their status. While they are not expected to give up their national sentiments or their political and religious convictions, they shall at all times bear in mind the reserve and tact incumbent upon them by reason of their international status. 1.5. Staff members shall exercise the utmost discretion in regard to all matters of official business. They shall not communicate to any person any information known to them by reason of their official position which has not been made public, except in the course of their duties or by authorization of the Secretary-General. Nor shall they at any time use such information to private advantage. These obligations do not cease upon separation from the Secretariat. 1.6. No member of the Secretariat shall accept any honour, decoration, favour, gift or

fee from any government or from any other source external to the Organization during the period of his appointment, except for war service. 1.7. Any member of the Secretariat who becomes a candidate for a public office of a political character shall resign from the Secretariat. 1.8. The immunities and privileges attached to the United Nations by virtue of Article 105 of the Charter are conferred in the interests of the Organization. These privileges and immunities furnish no excuse to the staff members who enjoy them for non-performance of their private obligations or failure to observe laws and police regulations. In any case where these privileges and immunities arise, the staff member shall immediately report to the Secretary-General, with whom alone it rests to decide whether they shall be waived. 1.9. Members of the Secretariat shall subscribe to the following oath or declaration: 'I solemnly swear (undertake, affirm, promise) to exercise in all loyalty, discretion and conscience the functions entrusted to me as an international civil servant of the United Nations, to discharge these functions and regulate my conduct with the interests of the United Nations only in view, and not to seek or accept instructions in regard to the performance of my duties from any government or other authority external to the Organization.' 1.10. The oath or declaration shall be made orally by the Secretary-General and Assistant Secretaries-General at a public meeting of the General Assembly and by all other members of the Secretariat before the Secretary-General or his authorized deputy."

27. The Charter of the United Nations does not impose upon the member states the obligation to grant complete exemption from their jurisdiction to the individuals who are organs of the organization. It provides only: "ARTICLE 104. The Organization shall enjoy in the territory of each of its Members such legal capacity as may be necessary for the exercise of its functions and the fulfillment of its purposes. ARTICLE 105. 1. The Organization shall enjoy in the territory of each of its Members such privileges and immunities as are necessary for the fulfillment of its purposes. 2. Representatives of the Members of the United Nations and officials of the Organization shall similarly enjoy such privileges and immunities as are necessary for the independent exercise of their functions in connection with the Organization. 3. The General Assembly may make recommendations with a view to determining the details of the application of paragraphs 1 and 2 of this Article or may propose conventions to the Members of the United Nations for this purpose." These provisions are implemented by a convention on privileges and immunities of the United Nations, prepared by the General Assembly in its Resolution of 13 February 1946 and the Headquarters Agreement between the United Nations and the United States of America (on the territory of which the Headquarters of the United Nations is established) of 26 June 1947 approved by the General Assembly in its Resolution of 31 October 1947.

28. *Cf. International Sanctions*, pp. 123 f., and Davies, *op. cit.*, p. 376 ff.

29. Davies, *op. cit.*, pp. 376 ff.

30. The Internationalization of European civil and military aviation together with the establishment of an international air-police for Europe was suggested by Rear Admiral R. N. Lawson in his pamphlet, *A Plan for the Organization of a European Air Service.* The New Commonwealth Institute Monographs. Series C, No. 2, 1936.

31. The "United Nations Guard," proposed by the Secretary-General in his report to the General Assembly of 28 September 1948 (A/656), was originally intended to be a miniature police force organized to protect United Nations missions in the field in troubled areas without incurring the suspicion of partiality which the use of local police or national militia might engender. The

guard was to consist of 800 men. The nucleus of 300 men was to be located and trained either at United Nations Headquarters or at an appropriate place in Europe, and a volunteer reserve cadre of up to 500 men was to be recruited multinationally and held in reserve in their home states at the call of the Secretary-General as and when required. The General Assembly did not accept this proposal, but, in conformity with a revised suggestion of the Secretary-General, adopted a Resolution on 22 November 1949 (297 IV, A, B) in which it confirmed the power of the Secretary-General to establish the "United Nations Field Service" and authorized him to establish a "Panel of Field Observers." According to the revised suggestion of the Secretary-General, the Field Service was to consist of 300 persons who were to be part of the Secretariat and who were to provide the following services: providing land transport for missions and such incidental air transport as might be required; maintaining radio communications for missions; maintaining the security of United Nations premises and members of missions, safe custody of supplies, records and archives; maintaining order during meetings, hearings and investigations; performing guard duties at Headquarters. The members of the Field Service were not to be regularly supplied with arms of any kind. The Field Reserve Panel was to be simply a list of names of qualified persons available for service only in response to a specific decision of the General Assembly, the Security Council or an organ authorized by them. Their task was to be to assist United Nations missions in the functions of observation and supervision. The two services were not designed to act as a military force or to enforce Security Council decisions. *Cf.* Yearbook of the U. N., 1948/49, pp. 419 ff.

32. This was the situation under the Covenant of the League of Nations.

33. *Cf.* pp. 12 ff.

34. This is the solution of the problem by the Charter of the United Nations which provides in Article 39: "The Security Council shall determine the existence of any threat to the peace, breach of the peace, or act of aggression and shall make recommendations, or decide what measures shall be taken in accordance with Articles 41 and 42, to maintain or restore international peace and security." The Security Council, not the individual members of the United Nations, must ascertain the facts against which the Charter provides for enforcement measures. Only as long as the Security Council does not interfere, are the member states, exercising the right of individual or collective self-defense in accordance with Article 51, authorized to determine the existence of an "armed attack." According to the Resolution of the General Assembly "Uniting for Peace" (*cf. supra*, p. 139), the General Assembly, too, is authorized to make, under certain conditions, determined in this resolution, recommendations to members for collective measures. In order to make these recommendations the General Assembly must determine the existence of a threat to the peace, breach of the peace, or act of aggression.

35. The Charter of the United Nations provides in Article 40: "In order to prevent an aggravation of the situation, the Security Council may, before making the recommendations or deciding upon the measures provided for in Article 39, call upon the parties concerned to comply with such provisional measures as it deems necessary or desirable. Such provisional measures shall be without prejudice to the rights, claims or position of the parties concerned. The Security Council shall duly take account of failure to comply with such provisional measures." The provisional measures referred to in this Article may be taken before or after the Security Council has determined the existence of a threat to, or breach of, the peace, but before it has taken the enforcement

measures referred to in Article 39, which have the character of sanctions. However, after the Security Council has determined the existence of a threat to, or breach of, the peace, it may not take these enforcement measures immediately but may make "recommendations," which probably means recommendations for a peaceful settlement of the conflict. These recommendations may also be considered as provisional measures.

36. This principle is maintained in the statute of the International Court of Justice, the principal judicial organ of the United Nations. Article 34, paragraph 1, of the Statute of the Court expressly stipulates: "Only states may be parties in cases before the Court."

37. The Peace Treaty with Germany terminating the first World War contained the following provision in Article 231: "The Allied and Associated Governments affirm and Germany accepts the responsibility of Germany and her allies for causing all the loss and damage to which the Allied and Associated Governments and their nationals have been subjected as a consequence of the war imposed upon them by the aggression of Germany and her allies." In ratifying this treaty, the Government of defeated Germany admitted that Germany had been the aggressor. Article 227 of the Peace Treaty established the individual criminal responsibility of the former head of the German state. It stipulated that the ex-Emperor, William II, should be brought before an international criminal court "for a supreme offence against international morality and the sanctity of treaties." The "offence" referred mainly to the act of aggression committed by Germany in violating her obligation to respect the neutrality of Belgium and Luxembourg which she had guaranteed. Article 227 stipulated further that it will be the duty of this tribunal "to fix the punishment which it considers should be imposed." Article 227 of the Peace Treaty was never applied.

38. *Cf.* the following note.

39. The principle of individual criminal responsibility for violations of international law by acts of state was applied in the Agreement signed on 8 August 1945, at London, which was the legal basis for the so-called Nuremberg trial. As stated in its Preamble, this treaty was concluded by the Government of the United Kingdom of Great Britain and Northern Ireland, the Government of the United States of America, the Provisional Government of the French Republic, and the Government of the Union of Soviet Socialist Republics and had as its purpose the prosecution and punishment of the major war criminals of the European Axis. The contracting parties were the states occupying the territory of Germany after its defeat in the second World War. They concluded the agreement not in their capacity as the joint government of Germany, but, as declared in the Preamble to the Agreement, "in the interest of all the United Nations." As a matter of fact, some of the United Nations adhered to the Agreement in conformity with Article 5 which provided that "any Government of the United Nations may adhere to this Agreement." (By "United Nations," those states which had signed the Declaration by United Nations of 1 January 1942 were meant). Neither of the European Axis Powers, Germany and Italy, signed or adhered to the Agreement.

Article 1 of the London Agreement instituted "an International Military Tribunal for the trial of war criminals whose offenses have no particular geographical location, whether they be accused individually or in their capacity as members of organizations or groups or in both capacities." According to Article 2, "The constitution, jurisdiction and functions of the International Military Tribunal shall be those set out in the Charter annexed to this Agreement, which Charter shall form an integral part of this Agreement." According to Article 2 of the Charter, the International Military Tribunal was to consist of four members, each with an alternate. One member and one alternate were to be appointed by each of the signatories. According to Article 14, each signatory was to appoint a chief prosecutor for the investigation of the charges against and the prosecution of major war criminals.

Article 6 of the Charter stipulated: "The Tribunal established by the agreement referred to in Article 1 hereof for the trial and punishment of the major war criminals of the European Axis countries shall have the power to try and punish persons who, acting in the interests of the European Axis countries, whether as individuals or as members of organizations, committed any of the following crimes. The following acts, or any of them, are crimes coming within the jurisdiction of the Tribunal for which there shall be individual responsibility:

(A) Crimes against peace: namely, planning, preparation, initiation or waging of a war of aggression, or a war in violation of international treaties, agreements or assurances, or participation in a common plan or conspiracy for the accomplishment of any of the foregoing;

(B) War Crimes: namely, violations of the laws or customs of war. Such violations shall include, but not be limited to, murder, ill-treatment or deportation to slave labor or for any other purpose of civilian population of, or in, occupied territory, murder or ill-treatment of prisoners of war or persons on the seas, killing of hostages, plunder of public or private property, wanton destruction of cities, towns, or villages, or devastation not justified by military necessity;

(C) Crimes against humanity: namely, murder, extermination, enslavement, deportation, and other inhumane acts committed against any civilian population, before or during the war; or persecutions on political, racial or religious grounds in execution of, or in connection with, any crime within the jurisdiction of the Tribunal, whether or not in violation of the domestic law of the country where perpetrated. Leaders, organizers, instigators and accomplices participating in the formulation or execution of a common plan or conspiracy to commit any of the foregoing crimes are responsible for all acts performed by any persons in execution of such plan."

Article 7 established individual responsibility for acts of state. It provided: "The official position of defendants, whether as Heads of State or responsible officials in Government Departments, shall not be considered as freeing them from responsibility or mitigating punishment." Article 8 excluded the plea of superior order: "The fact that the defendant acted pursuant to order of his Government, or of a superior shall not free him from responsibility, but may be considered in mitigation of punishment if the Tribunal determines that justice so requires."

On the basis of the London Agreement, the International Military Tribunal established by this Agreement declared in its judgment: "The principle of international law, which under certain circumstances, protects the representatives of a State, cannot be applied to acts which are condemned as criminal by international law. The authors of these acts cannot shelter themselves behind their official position in order to be freed from punishment." As to the question of under what conditions a violation of international law was to be considered a punishable crime constituting individual responsibility, the International Military Trbunal assumed that a violation of international law might be considered such a crime even if international law did not impose a penalty for an act constituting a violation of international law. This meant that the question of whether or not an individual might be punished for having violated international law by an act performed in his capacity as an organ of a state, was to be decided within the discretion of the authority competent to apply the international law in this case. According to the London Agreement, as interpreted by the International Military Tribunal, this authority might be a national court of one of the belligerents, or an international court established without the participation of the state whose organ had violated international law and was to be punished therefor. The principle that a state has jurisdiction over acts of another state only with the consent of the latter was no longer recognized as a rule of general international law.

In the trials of war criminals conducted by the military tribunals of the Allied and Associated Powers in connection with the second World War, the plea of superior order was raised by the defense more frequently than any other. (*Cf. Law Reports of Trials of War Criminals*, Selected and prepared by the United Nations War Crimes Commission [1949] XV, 157 ff.) In the practice of these tribunals the test was "whether an order, illegal under international law, on which an accused had acted was or must be presumed to have been known to him to be so illegal, or was obviously so illegal ('illegal on its face' to use the term employed by the Tribunal in the *High Command Trial*) or should have been recognized by him as being so illegal. The general upshot of a large number of decisions, and of the advice of Judge Advocates to British or Commonwealth courts, is that, if the order comes within one or more of these categories, then the accused cannot rely upon the plea of superior orders."

In its Resolution of 21 November 1947 (177/II), the General Assembly of the United Nations directed the International Law Commission to "formulate the principles of international law recognized in the Charter of the Nuremberg Tribunal and in the judgment of the Tribunal." The International Law Commission formulated these principles as follows: "I. Any person who commits an act which constitutes a crime under international law is responsible therefor and liable to punishment. II. The fact that internal law does not impose a penalty for an act which constitutes a crime under international law does not relieve the person who committed the act from responsibility under international law. III. The fact that a person who committed an act which constitutes a crime under international law acted as Head of State or responsible Government official does not relieve him from responsibility under international law. IV. The fact that a person acted pursuant to order of his Government or of a superior does not relieve him from responsibility under international law, provided a moral choice was in fact possible to him. V. Any person charged with a crime under international law has the right to a fair trial on the facts and law. VI. The crimes hereinafter set out are punishable as crimes under international law: a. Crimes against peace: (i) Planning, preparation, initiation or waging of a war of aggression or a war in violation of international treaties, agreements or assurances; (ii) Participation in a common plan or conspiracy for the accomplishment of any of the acts mentioned under (i). b. War crimes: Violations of the laws or customs of war which include, but are not limited to, murder, ill-treatment or deportation to slave labour or for any other purpose of civilian population of or in occupied territory, murder or ill-treatment of prisoners of war or persons on the seas, killing of hostages, plunder of public or private property, wanton destruction of cities, towns, or villages, or devastation not justified by military necessity. c. Crimes against humanity: Murder, extermination, enslavement, deportation and other inhuman acts done against any civilian population, or persecutions on political, racial or religious grounds, when such acts are done or such persecutions are carried on in execution of or in connection with any crime against peace or any war crime. VII. Complicity in the commission of a crime against peace, a war crime, or a crime against humanity, as set forth in Principle VI is a crime under international law." *General Assembly Official Records.* Fifth Session, Supplement No. 12 (A/1316)

In its sixth session the International Law Commission adopted the following Draft Code of Offences against the Peace and Security of Mankind, in which the principle of individual criminal responsibility for violations of international law is applied: (*General Assembly Official Records:* Ninth Session. Supplement No. 9 [A/2693] New York, 1954) :

Article 1

Offences against the peace and security of mankind, as defined in this code, are crimes under international law, for which the responsible individuals shall be punished.

Article 2

The following acts are offences against the peace and security of mankind:

(1) Any act of aggression, including the employment by the authorities of a State of armed force against another State for any purpose other than national or collective self-defence or in pursuance of a decision or recommendation of a competent organ of the United Nations.

(2) Any threat by the authorities of a State to resort to an act of aggression against another State.

(3) The preparation by the authorities of a State of the employment of armed force against another State for any purpose other than national or collective self-defence or in pursuance of a decision or recommendation of a competent organ of the United Nations.

(4) The organization, or the encouragement of the organization, by the authorities of a State, of armed bands within its territory or any other territory for incursions into the territory of another State, or the toleration of the organization of such bands in its own territory, or the toleration of the use by such armed bands of its territory as a base of operations or as a point of departure for incursions into the territory of another State, as well as direct participation in or support of such incursions.

(5) The undertaking or encouragement by the authorities of a State of activities calculated to foment civil strife in another State, or the toleration by the authorities of a State of organized activities calculated to foment civil strife in another State.

(6) The undertaking or encouragement by the authorities of a State of terrorist activities in another State, or the toleration by the authorities of a State of organized activities calculated to carry out terrorist acts in another State.

(7) Acts by the authorities of a State in violation of its obligations under a treaty which is designed to ensure international peace and security by means of restrictions or limitations on armaments, or on military training, or on fortifications, or of other restrictions of the same character.

(8) The annexation by the authorities of a State of territory belonging to another State, by means of acts contrary to international law.

(9) The intervention by the authorities of a State in the internal or external affairs of another State, by means of coercive measures of an economic or politi-

cal character in order to force its will and thereby obtain advantages of any kind.

(10) Acts by the authorities of a State or by private individuals committed with intent to destroy, in whole or in part, a national, ethnic, racial or religious group as such, including:

(i) Killing members of the group;

(ii) Causing serious bodily or mental harm to members of the group;

(iii) Deliberately inflicting on the group conditions of life calculated to bring about its physical destruction in whole or in part;

(iv) Imposing measures intended to prevent births within the group;

(v) Forcibly transferring children of the group to another group.

(11) Inhuman acts such as murder, extermination, enslavement, deportation or persecutions, committed against any civilian population on social, political, racial, religious or cultural grounds by the authorities of a State or by private individuals acting at the instigation or with the toleration of such authorities.

(12) Acts in violation of the laws or customs of war.

(13) Acts which constitute:

(i) Conspiracy to commit any of the offences defined in the preceding paragraphs of this article; or

(ii) Direct incitement to commit any of the offences defined in the preceding paragraphs of this article; or

(iii) Complicity in the commission of any of the offences defined in the preceding paragraphs of this article; or

(iv) Attempts to commit any of the offences defined in the preceding paragraphs of this article.

Article 3

The fact that a person acted as Head of State or as responsible government official does not relieve him from responsibility for committing any of the offences defined in this code.

Article 4

The fact that a person charged with an offence defined in this code acted pursuant to an order of his Government or of a superior does not relieve him of responsibility in international law if, in the circumstances at the time, it was possible for him not to comply with that order.

40. Article 16, paragraph 4, of the Covenant of the League of Nations stipulated: "Any Member of the League which has violated any covenant of the League may be declared to be no longer a Member of the League by a vote of the Council concurred in by the Representatives of all the other Members of the League represented thereon." Article 6 of the Charter of the United Nations provides: "A Member of the United Nations which has persistently violated the Principles contained in the present Charter may be expelled from the Organization by the General Assembly upon the recommendation of the Security Council."

41. The Charter of the United Nations stipulates in Article 5: "A Member of the United Nations against which preventive or enforcement action has been taken by the Security Council may be suspended from the exercise of the rights and privileges of membership by the General Assembly upon the recommendation of the Security Council. The exercise of these rights and privileges may be restored by the Security Council." Suspension from the rights and privileges of membership is an additional sanction, insofar as the "preventive or enforcement action" taken against a member state already has the character of a sanction. Article 19 stipulates a special sanction for a special violation of the Charter. It runs as follows: "A Member of the United Nations which is in arrears in the payment of its financial contributions to the Organization

shall have no vote in the General Assembly if the amount of its arrears equals or exceeds the amount of the contributions due from it for the preceding two full years. The General Assembly may, nevertheless, permit such a Member to vote if it is satisfied that the failure to pay is due to conditions beyond the control of the Member."

(d) Peace Treaties and Neutrality

(aa) *Peace treaties within a system of international security.*

The fact that within a system of international security the use of armed force, especially war, is, in principle, forbidden and is permitted only as a sanction, has important consequences with respect to the termination of this action and the obligations and rights of the states not involved in it.

It is usual to terminate a war by a peace treaty concluded by the belligerents. The purpose of this treaty is expressed in a clause declaring that there shall be peace, or that the state of peace is established, or that the state of war is terminated between the belligerents. This clause implies that the contracting parties assume the obligation to abstain from further acts of war. Sometimes this obligation is expressly stipulated. A peace treaty usually also contains other provisions, but the termination of the war by the stipulation of the obligation just mentioned is its essential function. If, in violation of a peace treaty, a belligerent continues hostilities, a war is not terminated. Hence it is not quite correct to assume that a war is terminated by a peace treaty. It is terminated by the fact that the belligerents definitively cease hostilities with the intention of terminating the war. This intention is usually, but not necessarily, expressed in the conclusion of a peace treaty. There are cases where no peace treaty can be concluded, for instance when, as an effect of a war, one of the belligerents ceases to exist as a subject of international law because its territory is annexed by the victorious belligerent or because it is dismembered and new states are established in its place. Treaties may be concluded regulating the relationships between these new states on the one hand and the state which was the opponent of the state succeeded by the new states established in its territory, on the other. However, these treaties are not really peace treaties, although they may be so termed. They are concluded after the war has been terminated. In these and in other cases the termination of a war may be ascertained by a unilateral declaration on the part of a belligerent. Without a peace treaty having been concluded, the Congress of the United States passed a resolution, approved by the President on 2 July 1921, to the effect that "the state of war declared to exist between the Imperial German Government and the United States of America by the joint resolution of Congress approved

April 6, 1917, is hereby declared at an end." This was an ascertainment of the fact that the war between the two states was terminated. The treaty between the United States and Germany signed afterward, on 25 August 1921, was not a peace treaty in the specific sense of the term—that is, it was not a treaty concluded for the purpose of terminating a war but a treaty concluded "to restore friendly relations existing between the two nations prior to the outbreak of war." On 31 December 1946, the President of the United States proclaimed "the cessation of hostilities of World War II," and in a statement explaining the proclamation said that the action did not have "the effect of terminating the state of war iself." However, by a joint resolution of Congress, approved by the President on 19 October 1951, "the state of war" which had been declared to exist between the United States and Germany by the joint resolution of Congress approved on 11 December 1941 was declared terminated.

The practice of terminating a war, or, more exactly formulated, of expressing an intention to terminate a war by concluding a peace treaty—that is, a treaty imposing upon the belligerents the obligation to abstain from further acts of war—evidently presupposes that without assuming such an obligation the states concerned have the right to wage war against each other. Such a presupposition is possible under general international law if the *bellum justum* principle is not part of it. If this principle is recognized as a part of international law or if war is prohibited by a multilateral treaty, the conclusion of a peace treaty for the purpose of terminating a war which has broken out in violation of the *bellum justum* principle or in violation of the treaty, may still be justified. The conclusion of a peace treaty is justified if the question as to which of the belligerents has violated its obligation not to resort to war—that is, the question as to which of the belligerents is the aggressor and which the defender—is not decided by an objective and impartial authority and consequently if both belligerents may claim to be exercising the right of self-defense. However, the situation is different under a treaty constituting an international security organization, which not only imposes upon the members the obligation not to resort to war against each other and which permits war only as a sanction to be directed against a member violating the treaty, but also confers upon a special organ the power to ascertain the fact that the treaty has been violated, or, to term it differently, gives the special organ the power to determine the aggressor. Within such an organization, a member state which has resorted to war in violation of the constituent treaty, as ascertained by the competent organ, cannot assume the obligation to abstain from further acts of war in a special treaty because this obligation is already implied in the general obligation imposed upon it in the constituent treaty. Furthermore, a state engaged in a war waged as a sanction against a legally determined aggressor cannot assume an obligation to abstain from acts of war against a delinquent state in a treaty concluded with the other state if it is its obligation to perform these acts. However, even if this state is not obliged, but only authorized, to resort to war against the legally ascertained violator of the constituent treaty, a peace treaty concluded between the state executing a sanction and the delinquent state is quite inappropriate because, unlike the same situation under general international law, the two belligerents are not on an equal legal footing, since the war of one is illegal and the counter war of the other legal, or vice versa. Such a peace treaty is particularly problematical in case the war against the delinquent state is the action of an international police force under the direction of the central organ of a security organization. To terminate such a war by concluding a peace treaty between the international organization enforcing the law and the delinquent state is just as absurd as terminating a punitive action taken by a court against a criminal by an agreement between the court and the criminal. If war is a sanction, it can properly be terminated only when it has achieved its purpose, and this may be ascertained by a unilateral declaration of the authority executing the sanction.

(bb) *Neutrality within a system of international security.*

The question of to what extent, if at all, the legal institution of neutrality is compatible with a system of international security can be answered in an unambiguous manner only after the concept of neutrality has been clearly defined. The considerable confusion usually found in a discussion of this question is due to the fact that the term "neutrality" is used to mean different things. In the main, it indicates the status of a state which is not involved in a war between other states. However, at the same time it is employed to denote the consequences which international law attaches to this status, the duties and rights a non-belligerent state has in relation to the belligerent states and especially the duty of the non-belligerent to observe an attitude of impartiality toward the belligerents, impartiality meaning the principle that a state not involved in a war between other states shall fulfill its obligations and exercise its rights toward all belligerents in an equal way. Sometimes neutrality means non-belligerency accompanied by impartiality, and there are writers who even identify neutrality with impartiality. An example of the different possible meanings of neutrality is the treatment of that concept in the two Hague Conventions which deal with neutrality. The term "neutral" in the expression "neutral Powers" (Articles 5, 6 and others of Convention V) refers to the status of Powers not involved in a war, "neutral Powers" as opposed to "belligerent" Powers (Preamble of Convention XIII). The term "neutral" in this sense is expressly defined in Article 16 of Convention V: "The nationals of a State which is not taking part in the war are considered as neutrals." However, in Article 10 of Convention V neutrality evidently means the rights of a non-belligerent state and the corresponding duties of belligerents: "The fact of a neutral Power resisting even by force attempts to violate its neutrality cannot be regarded as a hostile act." Neutrality can be "violated" only if it is an obligation or a right. The status of not being involved in a war can be adopted or abandoned by a state but it cannot be violated. The two Conventions distinguish between neutrality and impartiality. Article 9 of Convention V provides: "Every measure of restriction or prohibition taken by a neutral Power in regard to the matters referred to in Articles 7 and 8 (that is: to prevent the export or transport of arms, munitions of war, or anything which can be of use to an army or fleet, and to forbid or restrict the use of telegraph or telephone cables or of wireless telegraphy apparatus) must be impartially applied by it to both belligerents." Here impartiality is not at all identical with neutrality but is the manner in which a neutral state must exercise its right to take certain measures of restriction and prohibition. This term is used in the same sense in Article 9 of Convention XIII, and the Preamble of this Convention states: "that it is, for neutral Powers, an admitted duty to apply these rules [regulating the relations between neutral Powers and belligerent Powers] impartially to the several belligerents." Here impartiality characterizes the way in which a neutral Power must fulfill all its duties and exercise all its rights in relation to belligerent Powers. In accordance with this terminology, a neutral state may violate its duty to treat belligerents impartially without losing its status of neutrality. To quote a leading writer, Oppenheim [1] defined the concept of neutrality as follows: "Such states as do not take part in a war between other states are neutrals." This means that neutrality is the status of non-belligerency, i. e., the status of a state which does not take part in a war between other states. Such a status may or may not be accompanied by an attitude of impartiality on the part of a neutral state toward belligerents. In his preceding chapters, Oppenheim analyzed the different types of neutrality which do not imply the impartiality of the neutral states or imply only a restricted impartiality. He mentioned the fact that the impartiality demanded by the theory and practice of the eighteenth century was not at all strict, and that a state was considered not to have violated its obligations as a neutral if it furnished one of the belligerents with such limited

370624—57——11

assistance as it had previously promised by treaty or if it allowed one of the belligerents to levy troops in its territory.[2] He referred to Grotius' concept of neutrality [3] which was not at all identical with his concept of impartiality. Grotius formulated two principles concerning neutrality. The first was that neutrals shall do nothing which may strengthen a belligerent whose cause is unjust or hinder the movement of a belligerent whose cause is just. This concept is certainly contrary to impartiality. Grotius' second principle concerning neutrality was that neutrals shall treat both belligerents alike only if there is doubt as to whose cause is just. However, immediately after defining neutrality as non-belligerency, Oppenheim said: "Neutrality may be defined as the attitude of impartiality adopted by third states towards belligerents and recognized by belligerents, such attitude creating rights and duties between the impartial states and the belligerents." [4] Hence, neutrality is now identified with impartiality, but in discussing the end of neutrality Oppenheim stated: "Neutrality ends with the cessation of war, or through a hitherto neutral state beginning war against one of the belligerents, or through one of the belligerents commencing war against a hitherto neutral State." Neutrality which ends in this way can be only the status of not taking part in a war. It cannot be the attitude of impartiality. Oppenheim then emphasized that "the ending of neutrality must not be confounded with mere violation of neutrality. A mere violation of neutrality does not *ipso facto* bring neutrality to an end." [5] In this statement, the term "neutrality" is used in both senses, as the "duty of impartiality" and as the "status of not taking part in a war." What this statement means is that the status of not taking part in a war must not be confused with the duty of impartiality. A mere violation of the duty does not *ipso facto* end the status. Under the heading "Violation of Neutrality," [6] Oppenheim distinguished between violations of neutrality in the narrower and in the wider sense of the term. He stated: "It is necessary for obvious reasons to discuss, not only violations of the duty of impartiality of neutrals, but violations of all duties deriving from neutrality, whether they are incumbent upon neutrals or upon belligerents." Here neutrality is far from being "the attitude of impartiality" for impartiality is only one of the duties which derive from neutrality.

Another writer has stated that "the notion of neutrality as merely non-involvement in direct hostilities is inconsistent with the traditional concept and if it should come to have this meaning, the concept would have been strikingly narrowed." [7] Nevertheless, the only way to avoid the confusion just illustrated is to understand neutrality as nothing else but the status of a state which is not involved in a war between other states, and impartiality as the principle according to which a neutral state shall fulfill the obligation and exercise the rights, which a neutral state has under general international law, equally towards all belligerents. Of course, the theoretical suggestion that neutrality should be defined as the status of non-belligerency does not imply any political preference with respect to the desirable consequences of such a status for the neutral state. The question as to whether or not the status of neutrality entails the obligation of the neutral state to treat the belligerents impartially is a question of positive law and can be answered only by an analysis of this law.

In regard to the general international law of our time, the answer is certainly in the affirmative. Under this law, a state is under no obligation to remain neutral in a war between other states, but if a state is neutral, the relationships between this state and the belligerents are regulated by definite rules of general international law. The main obligations a neutral state has in relation to belligerents are:[8] the obligation to refrain from giving assistance to one of the belligerents which may be detrimental to the other; the obligation to refrain from inflicting injuries on one of the belligerents which may benefit the other; the obligation to refrain from granting any facilities whatsoever for military operations of the belligerents (however, the neutral state is not obliged to prohibit its own nationals from supplying belligerents with such facilities); the obligation to prevent the fitting out or arming of any vessel within its jurisdiction which it has reason to believe is intended to cruise or engage in hostile operations against either belligerent; the obligation to prevent the departure from its jurisdiction of any vessel intended to cruise or engage in hostile operations which has been adapted entirely or partly within its jurisdiction for use in war; the obligation to prevent belligerents from making use of its neutral territory and its resources for military purposes during the war. The most important obligations of the belligerent are the obligation to refrain from making use of neutral territory for military purposes and from interfering with the legitimate intercourse of the neutral states with the other belligerents, and the obligation to refrain from appropriating neutral goods on enemy ships with the exception of contraband. Belligerents have the right to appropriate neutral merchant ships for breach of blockade and to appropriate contraband on a neutral vessel.

It is evident that the legal institution of neutrality—that is, the duties and rights which general international law imposes or confers upon the states not involved in a war between other states in relation to the belligerents and upon the belligerents in relation to the neutral states, especially the principle of impartiality—presupposes that the *bellum justum* principle is not part of general international law; that each state has the right to resort to war against any other state for any reason whatsoever; and, consequently, that if there is a war between two states there is no legal question as to which of the belligerents is wrong in using its armed force and which is right or which is an aggressor and which a defender. Even if two states have submitted their dispute to an international tribunal by a treaty and even if, in violation of the treaty, one state refuses to comply with the decision of the tribunal, and the other state consequently resorts to war against the former, the counterwar is not illegal. Only the non-compliance with the judicial decision is illegal. The rules of general international law concerning neutrality, and especially concerning the principle of impartiality, are justifiable only if in a war between two states both belligerents are equally right as far as the use of their armed forces is concerned. It is significant that Grotius who recognized the *bellum justum* principle did not consider impartiality as an unconditional obligation of neutral states.[9]

General international law which, according to the traditional doctrine, does not contain the *bellum justum* principle, may be abrogated by treaties imposing upon the contracting parties the conditional or unconditional obligation not to resort to war. As treaties are in principle binding only upon the contracting states, a bilateral treaty in which the parties assume the obligation not to resort to war against each other, a so-called non-aggression pact, has no effect on third states which means it has no effect on neutral states. If, in violation of the treaty, one contracting party resorts to war against the other, and thus commits an act of aggression, and if the other party resorts to a counterwar, a war of defense, the relations between the neutral states and the belligerents remain under general international law. However, if the treaty imposing upon the contracting parties the obligation not to resort to war has a multilateral character and if in violation of its treaty obligation one party resorts to war against another contracting party and this latter party consequently resorts to a counterwar, the legal situation of the other contracting parties not involved in this war, which means the legal situation of the neutral contracting parties, is different from that of neutral states under general international law. By resorting to war in violation of the treaty, a contracting party not only infringes upon the right of that contracting party against which it uses its armed force, but also infringes upon the rights of all other contracting parties. Each contracting party assumes the obligation not to resort to war against any of the contracting parties in relation to all other contracting parties. According to general international law, a state whose right is violated by another state is authorized to resort to reprisals—that is, to enforcement measures short of war—against the state which has violated its right, but these reprisals may be taken only against this state. Hence the obligation of the neutral states, who are contracting parties to the treaty prohibiting the resort to war, to adopt an attitude of impartiality toward the belligerent contracting parties, is superseded by the right they have under general international law to resort to enforcement measures short of war against the violator of the treaty, the aggressor, and thus to assist the victim of the aggression. This means that without violating international law, the neutral states, contracting parties to the treaty, may take measures against an aggressor constituting violations of the rights this state has as a belligerent in relation to neutral states. Since these measures are taken as reprisals and hence are legal, the aggressor state is not entitled to react by retaliatory measures constituting violations of the obligations it has as a belligerent in relation to the neutral state. However, if a state violates its obligation not to resort to war, it will probably take retaliatory measures against neutral states, even if these measures are illegal.

The abrogation of the principle of impartiality is a legal effect which a multilateral treaty prohibiting the resort to war has under general international law. The right to take enforcement measures short of war as reprisals against a violator of the treaty is derived directly from general international law and exists even if not expressly stipulated by the treaty. If the treaty stipulates an obligation of the contracting parties to come to the assistance of the victim of an aggression with measures short of war, the contracting parties not involved in the war resulting from the aggression are not only entitled but are obliged to adopt an attitude which is not impartial towards the belligerents. The treaty may expressly stipulate that the prohibition of resorting to war does not apply to a war resorted to against a state which has resorted to war in violation of the treaty—that is, to a war resorted to against an aggressor. However, in this respect the situation of the neutral states contracting parties to the treaty does not differ from the situation of a neutral state under general international law which does not impose the obligation to remain neutral upon states.[10] It must be noted that the abrogation of the obligation of neutral states to adopt an attitude of impartiality towards the belligerents applies only to the relations among the states contracting parties to the multilateral treaty prohibiting the resort to war and not to the relation between neutral states which are not, and belligerents which are, contracting parties to the treaty. If a treaty prohibits the resort to war only under particular conditions, an abrogation of the obligation also does not apply to a war the resort to which does not constitute a violation of the treaty. In all these cases, the rules of general international law concerning the obligations and rights of neutral states are not affected.

A multilateral treaty may impose upon the contracting states not only the obligation not to resort to war against each other, but also the obligation not to resort to war against any other state except in the exercise of self-defense. This is a treaty in favor of third states. In case of an illegal resort to war by a contracting party against a non-contracting party, the legal situation of the neutral states which are contracting parties is the same as in the case of an illegal resort to war by a contracting party against another contracting party. The resort to war by a contracting party against a state not a contracting party is, like a resort to war by a contracting party against another contracting party, a violation of the rights of all other contracting parties. However, the obligation of neutral states which are not contracting parties to remain impartial is not affected by the treaty, since no right of these states is violated by a violation of the treaty to which they are not contracting parties. A multilateral treaty prohibiting the resort to war against any state may also claim to be binding upon states not contracting parties to the treaty.[11]

From the preceding analysis it follows that a system of international security constituted by a multilateral treaty which imposes upon the contracting states the obligation not to resort to war or to any use of armed force in their mutual relations and the further obligation to take enforcement measures short of war, especially economic (but not military) sanctions against the aggressor, is incompatible with the principle of impartiality to be applied according to international law in the relations between neutral states and belligerents. The members of the security organization not involved in the war against the aggressor may remain neutral, but they cannot adopt an attitude of strict impartiality toward the belligerents. If the constituent treaty imposes upon the contracting states the obligation to resort to war against the aggressor or to participate with their armed forces in a military action of the security organization which has the character of war, the international organization is incompatible even with a neutrality which does not imply the principle of impartiality.

The extent to which the neutrality or impartiality of neutrals in relation to the belligerents is excluded from, or is compatible with, a system of international security, is different according to the nature of the system.

1. Neutrality of the members of a security organization and their strict impartiality towards the belligerents in case of a war between other members or between a member and non-members can be maintained under any security organization as long as the aggressor has not been determined in accordance with the constituent treaty. If the determination of the aggressor is left to the individual members of the organization, even if obliged to resort to war against the aggressor, each member may remain neutral until the moment it decides which of the belligerents is the aggressor and which the defender, and during this time the neutral member has all the duties and rights of a neutral state under general international law. However, it may surrender its status of neutrality by resorting to war. It may give up its attitude of impartiality, even if it remains neutral, if it takes measures short of war against that state which it considers to be the aggressor. Within such a system, the neutrality of member states and their obligation to adopt an attitude of impartiality towards belligerents may still play an important part.[12] The situation is different if the function of determining the aggressor is conferred upon a central organ of the security organization; but under such a security system it might take some time for this organ to fulfill its function and there may even be circumstances which prevent its fulfillment altogether.[13] If the constituent treaty establishes not an obligation but a right of collective self-defense which may be exercised in case of an act of aggression, especially in case of an armed attack, as long as the central organ does not intervene, the members of the organization not involved in a war between other members or between members and non-members may remain neutral as long as they please, and during this time they are under the rules of general international law concerning neutrality. However, they may surrender their neutrality by resorting to war or give up their attitude of impartiality by taking measures short of war only against the state which they consider to be an aggressor.[14] If the constituent treaty establishes an obligation of collective self-defense,[15] the legal situation of the members of the organization not involved in the war following the act of aggression is not very different, for this obligation comes into actual existence for each member only if it arrives at the opinion that an act of aggression has taken place and decides the question as to which state is the aggressor. Hence, the answer to the question as to whether or not in a concrete case the obligation concerned exists depends on the very subject of this obligation. There is a real difference between the status of having an obligation to behave in a certain way and that of having a right to

behave in this way only if the answer to the above mentioned question does not depend on the subject of the obligation but on the decision of an objective authority (which is not the case when collective self-defense is exercised).

2. Neutrality of the members of a security organization and their strict impartiality towards the belligerents in case of a war between other members or between members and non-members can also be maintained under a security system constituted by a multilateral treaty in which the general prohibition of war is restricted not only insofar as war as a sanction is concerned (including war in self-defense), but also insofar as war under other circumstances, determined by the treaty, is permitted. Under such a security system there are cases in which a war between members or between members and non-members is not illegal on the part of both belligerents. Consequently, the other members are under no obligation to resort to war or to take measures short of war against one of the belligerents. Their relation to the belligerents is regulated by the unaltered rules of general international law concerning neutrality.[16]

3. The neutrality of the members of a security organization not involved in a war between other members or between members and non-members, but not their obligation to adopt an attitude of strict impartiality, can be maintained under a security system constituted by a multilateral treaty which does not impose upon the members an obligation to resort to war or to participate in a military action of the organization but imposes only the obligation to apply measures short of war, especially economic sanctions, against the aggressor.[17] Under such a system, the members of the organization not involved in the war may remain neutral, but they are not allowed to observe an attitude of strict impartiality towards the belligerent. However, not all the members not involved in the war may be obliged to take measures short of war against the aggressor. For specific reasons or under definite circumstances certain members may be exempt from this obligation and hence may observe strict impartiality toward belligerents.[18] Besides, the incompatibility of the security system and the principle of impartiality may be moderated by the fact that the constituent treaty may only restrict and not abrogate completely the principle of impartiality. With respect to the measures a neutral state must take under general international law to the equal disadvantage or to the equal advantage of both belligerents, a distinction may be made between military and non-military measures—that is, between measures which may and those which may not be advantageous or disadvantageous to the military operations of the belligerents as, for instance, preventing belligerents

from using the territory of a neutral state as a base for military operations, or prohibiting the export and transport of arms and munitions to belligerents, and measures which do not affect, at least not directly, the military operations of belligerents, like merely economic measures. The constituent treaty may impose upon the neutral members of the organization or upon some of them no obligation which would prevent them from adopting an attitude of impartiality with respect to military measures, but would impose upon them only obligations to take non-military, especially economic, measures disadvantageous to the aggressor and advantageous to its victim. It has even been maintained that the obligation imposed by general international law upon neutral states to adopt an attitude of impartiality toward the belligerents refers only to military matters.[19] However, the validity of this doctrine is doubtful, and it is rather difficult to distinguish between measures taken by neutral states which affect the military operations of the belligerents and measures which do not. If the treaty constituting the security organization does not abrogate neutrality but only restricts or abolishes the obligation of impartiality neutral members would have under general international law, one may speak of their neutrality as qualified, imperfect, partial, or differential neutrality.[20] This terminology shows clearly that neutrality and impartiality are not identical, although it may be admitted that if a state not involved in a war between other states is called neutral even though it is not obliged to treat both belligerents impartially in every respect, the term "neutrality" is of little value.

4. The status of neutrality and the obligation of neutral states to adopt an attitude of impartiality toward the belligerents are compatible to a very restricted extent in the case of a security system constituted by a treaty prohibiting war under all circumstances (with the exception of war as a sanction, which includes war in the exercise of self-defense) and imposing upon the members of the security organization the obligation to apply not only non-military but also military sanctions to the aggressor in conformity with the decisions of a central organ. In addition to the case mentioned under paragraph 1, the status of so-called qualified neutrality of all members not involved in a war between other members or between members and non-members can be maintained if the central organ orders them to apply only non-military sanctions to the aggressor and to come to the assistance of the victim only with economic and financial measures. If the central organ orders only some of the members, but not all of them, to take such action, the others are not excluded from preserving a neutrality which may even be a perfect neutrality. Since it is not very likely

that the central organ will order some of the members not involved in the war to apply military sanctions without ordering all of the members to take non-military sanctions, only a qualified neutrality of the members not participating in the military sanctions is possible. It should be noted that if a member participates in the execution of military sanctions, even if only with those contingents of its armed forces which are at the disposal of the central organ of the security organization, it cannot be considered to be neutral. Although the execution of the military sanction is an action of the organization, it is at the same time also an action of the member state whose contingents are involved.[21] Only if the security organization has a separate and permanent armed force at its disposal can military sanctions be executed without the status of neutrality of the member states being abolished. However, it will be only a status of so-called qualified neutrality if the members are obliged to take non-military measures to the disadvantage of the aggressor and the advantage of its victim.

NOTES

1. *Cf.* Oppenheim, *International Law,* 7th Ed. Edited by H. Lauterpacht. Vol. II (1952), p. 653.

2. *Op. cit.*, p. 627.

3. *Op. cit.*, pp. 625–6.

4. *Op. cit.*, p. 653.

5. *Op. cit.*, pp. 671–2.

6. *Op. cit.*, pp. 751 f.

7. Robert R. Wilson, "'Non-belligerency' in Relation to the Terminology of Neutrality." *The American Journal of International Law,* Vol. 35 (1941), pp. 122–3.

8. *Cf.* Oppenheim, *op. cit.*, pp. 653 ff.

9. Grotius, *De Jure Belli ac Pacis,* Book III, Chap. XVII, III: "It is the duty of those who keep out of a war to do nothing whereby he who supports a wicked cause may be rendered more powerful, or whereby the movements of him who wages a just war may be hampered. . . . In a doubtful matter, however, those at peace should show themselves impartial to either side in permitting transit, in furnishing supplies to troops, and in not assisting those under siege."

10. The General Treaty for the Renunciation of War, signed at Paris on 28 August 1928 (the so-called Kellogg-Briand Pact, or Pact of Paris) to which almost all the states of the world were parties provided: "Article 1. The High Contracting Parties solemnly declare in the names of their respective peoples that they condemn recourse to war for the solution of international controversies, and renounce it as an instrument of national policy in their relations with one another. Article 2. The High Contracting Parties agree that the settlement or solution of all disputes or conflicts of whatever nature or whatever origin they may be, which may arise among them, shall never be sought except by pacific means."

The Preamble stipulated that "any signatory Power which shall hereafter seek to promote its national interests by resort to war should be denied the benefits furnished by this treaty." This meant that the Treaty authorized the contracting parties to resort to war, as a sanction, against a violator of the treaty, an aggressor. However, as pointed out above, the states, contracting parties to the treaty, which did not resort to war against an aggressor, could resort to reprisals against this state—that is, they could take enforcement measures short of war. This meant that under the Kellogg-Briand Pact the principle of impartiality in the relations between neutral states and belligerents did not apply. This was also the interpretation of the Pact in the 38th Report adopted by the Conferences of the International Law Association at Budapest in 1934. Article 4 of this report ran as follows: "In the event of a violation of the Pact by a resort to armed force or war by one signatory State against another, the other State may, without thereby committing a breach of the Pact or of any rule of international law, do all or any of the following things:

(a) Refuse to admit the exercise by the State violating the Pact of belligerent rights, such as visit and search, blockade, etc.

(b) Decline to observe towards the State violating the Pact the duties prescribed by international law, apart from the Pact, for a neutral in relation to a belligerent.

(c) Supply the State attacked with financial or material assistance, including munitions of war.

(d) Assist with armed forces the State attacked."

Certain measures which the United States took during the second World War to the advantage of Great Britain and her allies and to the disadvantage of Germany might be justified as reprisals against the violation of the Kellogg-Briand Pact by Germany. The transfer of fifty over-age destroyers to Great Britain was such a measure. In a message to the Congress on 3 September 1940 the President declared: "I transmit herewith for the information of the Congress notes exchanged between the British Ambassador at Washington and the Secretary of State on September 2, 1940, under which this Government has acquired the right to lease naval and air bases in Newfoundland, and in the islands of Bermuda, the Bahamas, Jamaica, St. Lucia, Trinidad, and Antigua, and in British Guiana; also a copy of an opinion of the Attorney General dated August 27, 1940, regrding my authority to consummate this arrangement. The right to bases in Newfoundland and Bermuda are gifts—generously given and gladly received. The other bases mentioned have been acquired in exchange for fifty of our over-age destroyers. This is not inconsistent in any sense with our status of peace. Still less is it a threat against any nation. It is an epochal and far-reaching act of preparation for continental defense in the face of grave danger. Preparation for defense is an inalienable prerogative of a sovereign state. Under present circumstances this exercise of sovereign right is essential to the maintenance of our peace and safety. This is the most important action in the reinforcement of our national defense that has been taken since the Louisiana Purchase. Then as now, considerations of safety from overseas attack were fundamental. The value of the Western Hemisphere of these outposts of security is beyond calculation. Their need has long been recognized by our country, and especially by those primarily charged with the duty of charting and organizing our own naval and military defense. They are essential to the protection of the Panama Canal, Central America, the northern portion of South America, the Antilles, Canada, Mexico, and our own eastern and Gulf seaboards. Their consequent importance in hemispheric defense is obvious. For these reasons I have taken advantage of the present opportunity to acquire them." *The American Journal of International Law*, Vol. 34 (1940), Supplement, pp, 183 f.

Other measures of this kind were certain provisions of the Act to Promote the Defense of the United States, approved 11 March 1941. (*The American*

Journal of International Law, Vol. 35 (1941), Supplement, pp. 75 ff.) Section 3 of this Act stipulated:

"(a) Notwithstanding the provisions of any other law, the President may, from time to time, when he deems it in the interest of national defense, authorize the Secretary of War, the Secretary of the Navy, or the head of any other department or agency of the Government—

(1) To manufacture in arsenals, factories, and shipyards under their jurisdiction, or otherwise procure, to the extent to which funds are made available therefor, or contracts are authorized from time to time by the Congress, or both, any defense article for the government of any country whose defense the President deems vital to the defense of the United States. (2) To sell, transfer title to, exchange, lease, lend, or otherwise dispose of, to any such government any defense article . . . (3) To test, inspect, prove, repair, outfit, recondition, or otherwise to place in good working order, to the extent to which funds are made available therefor, or contracts are authorized from time to time by the Congress, or both, any defense article for any such government, or to procure any or all such services by private contract. (4) To communicate to any such government any defense information, pertaining to any defense article furnished to such government under paragraph (2) of this subsection. (5) to release for export any defense article disposed of in any way under this subsection to any such government."

Section 2 provided: "As used in this Act—

(a) The term 'defense article' means (1) Any weapon, munition, aircraft, vessel, or boat; (2) Any machinery, facility, tool, material, or supply necessary for the manufacture, production, processing, repair, servicing, or operation of any article described in this subsection; (3) Any component material or part of or equipment for any article described in this subsection; (4) Any agricultural, industrial or other commodity or article for defense. . . . (b) The term 'defense information' means any plan, specification, design, prototype, or information pertaining to any defenses article."

In an address delivered on 27 May 1941, the President announced:

"Our national policy today, therefore, is this: First, we shall actively resist wherever necessary, and with all our resources, every attempt by Hitler to extend his Nazi domination to the Western Hemisphere, or to threaten it. We shall actively resist his every attempt to gain control of the seas. We insist upon the vital importance of keeping Hitlerism away from any point in the world which could be used and would be used as a base of attack against the Americas. Second, from the point of view of strict naval and military necessity, we shall give every possible assistance to Britain and to all who, with Britain, are resisting Hitlerism or its equivalent with force of arms. Our patrols are helping now to insure delivery of the needed supplies to Britain. All additional measures necessary to deliver the goods will be taken. Any and all further methods or combination of methods, which can or should be utilized, are being devised by our military and naval technicians, who, with me, will work out and put into effect such new and additional safeguards as may be needed." *Documents on American Foreign Relations*, Vol. III, World Peace Foundation, 1941, p. 55.

In an address delivered on 11 September 1941, prompted by the attack on the United States destroyer *Greer*, the President stated:

"In the waters which we deem necessary for our defense American naval vessels and American planes will no longer wait until Axis submarines lurking under the water, or Axis raiders on the surface of the sea, strike their deadly blow—first. Upon our naval and air patrol—now operating in large numbers over a vast expanse of the Atlantic Ocean—falls the duty of maintaining the American policy of freedom of the seas—now. That means, very simply and clearly, that our patrolling vessels and planes will protect all merchant ships—not only American ships but ships of any flag—engaged in commerce in our defensive waters. They will protect them from submarines; they will protect them from surface raiders." *Documents on American Foreign Relations*, Vol. IV, 1942, p. 100.

11. In this way Article 2, paragraph 6 of the Charter of the United Nations may be interpreted.

12. This is one of the facts which justifies the view that neither the Kellogg-Briand Pact nor the Covenant of the League of Nations abolished entirely the legal institution of neutrality in the relations among the contracting parties, for under both treaties each contracting party was authorized to decide for itself whether or not a violation of the treaty had taken place.

13. This may be the case under the Charter of the United Nations which confers upon the Security Council the function of determining the existence of a threat to or breach of the peace (Article 39) but at the same time gives each of the five permanent members of the Council a veto right, by the exercise of which the Council may be prevented from fulfilling this function.

In this case, according to the resolution, "Uniting for Peace," the General Assembly, an organ of the United Nations within which no member state has a veto right, may assume the function not fulfilled by the Security Council and determine the existence of a threat to or breach of the peace. However, it is doubtful that a decision adopted by the General Assembly to this effect is binding upon the member states. The General Assembly can only make recommendations to the members to take enforcement measures against an aggressor. Since these recommendations are not legally binding, member states may remain neutral and then must adopt an attitude of impartiality towards belligerents.

14. This is the case if Article 51 of the Charter of the United Nations concerning collective self-defense applies. This Article sets forth the right of the members of the United Nations to come to the assistance of a victim of an armed attack by taking enforcement measures involving or not involving the use of armed force against a state responsible for an armed attack.

Since, according to Article 51, the right of collective self-defense exists "until the Security Council has taken the measures necessary to maintain international peace and security," the legal position of the members not involved in a war following an armed attack does not change if the General Assembly intervenes under the resolution "Uniting for Peace." The General Assembly can only make recommendations to the Members to take measures involving or not involving the use of armed force against a state which the General Assembly has determined to be an aggressor. These members may or may not comply with the recommendations and thus may or may not remain neutral, or, if they do remain neutral, they may give up their attitude of impartiality toward an aggressor by taking measures short of war against this state. It is even doubtful that the members not involved in a war following an armed attack are bound to share the opinion of the General Assembly that an armed attack has taken place and accept the finding of the General Assembly as to which state is the aggressor.

15. The right of collective self-defense established by Article 51 of the Charter is transformed into an obligation by certain treaties implementing Article 51. *Cf.* Note 5, page 127.

16. The Security System established by the Covenant of the League of Nations was of this type. The Covenant did not prohibit resort to war under all circumstances. It is significant that in the Preamble "the acceptance of *obligations* not to resort to war," not of the *obligation* not to resort to war was mentioned. According to Articles 12 and 15, the members were obliged to submit their disputes either to an international tribunal or to the Council. Submission to an international tribunal presupposed agreement of the parties to the dispute. The members were obliged to carry out the decision of the tribunal and not to resort to war against a member of the League which complied therewith. War against a state which, in violation of its obligation, did not comply with the decision of the tribunal was not excluded (Articles 12 and 13). In case agreement to submit a dispute to a tribunal could not be reached, each party was entitled to submit the case to the Council, which was authorized to proceed at the request of one party to the dispute. For this purpose no agreement was necessary. The Council was first to endeavor "to effect a settlement of the dispute" by bringing about an agreement between the parties. However, if a dispute could not be settled in this way, the Council was bound to settle a dispute by making a recommendation to the parties. Only a recommendation unanimously agreed to by those members of the Council who were not representatives of the parties to the dispute gave the recommendation of the Council a legal effect. This effect consisted of prohibiting war against a party which complied with the recommendation. War against a party which did not comply with the recommendation was not excluded, nor was war excluded in case none of the parties complied with the recommendation of the Council. In case a unanimous recommendation could not be reached by the Council, war was expressly permitted by the Covenant, but only "for the maintenance of right and justice" (Article 15, paragraph 7). Finally, war was not forbidden, or at least not expressly forbidden, in case a dispute arose from a matter of domestic jurisdiction. In all cases in which war was not forbidden, the parties were obliged not to resort to war until three months after a decision by an international tribunal or a report or recommendation of the Council (Article 12, paragraph 1).

17. As the Covenant of the League of Nations in Article 16.

18. According to an interpretation of Article 16 of the Covenant of the League of Nations adopted by resolution 9b of the Second Assembly of the League in 1921, the Council had the power to exempt a member state from participating in the sanctions taken against an aggressor, even if the member concerned shared with other members the view that an act of aggression had been committed by the state against which the sanctions were taken. *Cf.* Note 19.

19. *Cf.* Paul Guggenheim, "La securité collective et le problème de la neutralité." *Annuaire Suisse de droit international.* Vol. II (1945), pp. 9 ff, and J. F. Lalive, "International Organization and Neutrality." *The British Yearbook of International Law.* Vol. 24 (1947), p. 75. When Switzerland joined the League of Nations, the Council of the League declared in its resolution of 13 February 1920 that "the perpetual neutrality of Switzerland and the guarantee of the inviolability of her territory as incorporated in the law of nations, particularly in the treaties and in the Act of 1815, are justified by the interest of general peace, and as such are compatible with the Covenant." It was understood, however, that Switzerland, while refusing to participate in military action or to admit the passage of foreign troops, fully recognized the duties of the solidarity she was incurring as a member of the League, particularly the duty under Article 16 of participating in any economic action taken by

the League against a covenant-breaking state. However, by a resolution of the Council of the League of Nations adopted on 14 May 1938, Switzerland was freed of the obligation to take any sanctions, even economic sanctions, against the aggressor. To justify the attitude of Switzerland, Professor Schindler wrote in a memorandum presented to the International Studies Conference (*cf. supra*, p. 9) : "In entering the League of Nations, Switzerland did not abandon this political maxim, whose value has been proved to her satisfaction by an age-long experience. It is indispensable to her in both foreign and domestic policy. To participate in a war between other States means for Switzerland the almost certain prospect of seeing her entire territory turned into a battlefield. Surrounded by several very powerful States, Switzerland, if she were involved in a modern war, would risk, more than any other country in the world, complete annihilation. Even in the course of a long war, a large State can hardly be altogether destroyed." *Collective Security*, p. 420. The last argument is not quite correct. A great power, the Austrian-Hungarian Monarchy, was altogether destroyed in the course of a long war. In order to maintain its permanent neutrality, Switzerland did not join the United Nations.

20. *Cf. Collective Security*, p. 26.

21. The Charter of the United Nations forbids the use of armed force, and hence forbids war, under all circumstances with two exceptions—the exercise of self-defense and the execution of sanctions. In regard to members of the organization not involved in a war between other members or between members and non-members or between non-members only, the Charter imposes the obligation to resort to both military and non-military sanctions against the aggressor in accordance with the decisions of the Security Council (Article 39–50). Article 2, paragraph 5, provides: "All Members shall give the United Nations every assistance in any action it takes in accordance with the present Charter, and shall refrain from giving assistance to any state against which the United Nations is taking preventive or enforcement action." Article 25 stipulates: "The Members of the United Nations agree to accept and carry out the decisions of the Security Council in accordance with the present Charter." In view of these provisions, it follows that in case of a military action taken by the United Nations, constituting war between the Organization and a state, or in case of a war between two states in which the Organization intervenes by either a military or a non-military action, the status of neutrality, or the principle of impartiality, is excluded in principle. The Report of the Rapporteur of the Subcommittee to Committee I/1 of the San Francisco Conference contains the following statement in reference to paragraphs 5 and 6 of Chapter II of the Dumbarton Oaks Proposals which correspond to Article 2, paragraph 5, of the Charter: "The French Delegation proposed to add to Paragraph 5 of Chapter II the following phrase which was conceived in the French text as follows: '*Sans qu'un État puisse, pour s'y soustraire, invoquer un statut de neutralité.*' The French Delegate explained that what he meant by '*statut de neutralité*' was that of permanent neutrality. From the discussion that ensued, it was understood in the subcommittee that the status of permanent neutrality is incompatible with the principles declared in paragraphs 5 and 6 of Chapter II, in that no state can avail itself of the statute of permanent neutrality to be freed from the obligations of the Charter. The subcommittee, on that understanding, tacitly accepted that the vote taken on paragraphs 5 and 6 covers the French amendment." Although as a rule the status of neutrality, or if not the status of neutrality at least the principle of

impartiality, is excluded, there are nevertheless certain cases in which the one or the other may be maintained.

First of all, the fact must be considered that according to Article 48, paragraph 1, of the Charter, the action of the Organization may be carried out by all the members of the United Nations or by some of them, the determination as to which members must carry out the Organization's decision is made by the Security Council. Hence, the Security Council may call upon only some members to make available to the Organization contingents of their armed forces to be employed in a military action taken against a state at war with another state or guilty of an act of aggression which does not consist of resorting to war, as in the case of a threat of force. The members not involved in the war between the aggressor and its victim or in the war between the Organization and another state may then remain neutral and may even adopt an attitude of strict impartiality towards the belligerents, provided that the Security Council does not order them to apply non-military sanctions to the state against which the military action of the organization is directed. If they must apply non-military sanctions, they can observe only a qualified neutrality. In case of a war between states, if the Security Council decides to take only measures short of war, especially measures not involving the use of armed force, and if the Security Council calls upon only some members to execute these measures, the other members which are not involved in this war may observe a perfect neutrality, although the members called upon to execute the decisions of the Security Council may observe only a qualified neutrality. This interpretation of the Charter presupposes that Article 2, paragraph 5, means that the members are obliged to give the United Nations only that assistance which they are ordered to give by the competent organ of the United Nations, and that members are obliged to refrain from giving that state against which the United Nations action is directed only that assistance which they are prohibited from giving by the competent organ. However, the wording of Article 2, paragraph 5, certainly allows another interpretation, one not quite consistent with Article 48, paragraph 1. According to this interpretation, members not called upon by the Security Council to make available contingents of their armed forces or to take measures short of war are obliged to take military or non-military measures against the state against which the United Nations action is directed. In this case, the choice of the appropriate means is left to the discretion of the individual states. Consequently, while these states may remain neutral, they cannot adopt an attitude of impartiality, that is to say, they may observe a so-called qualified neutrality.

In view of the fact that the special agreements concerning the contingents of the armed forces which the members must place at the disposal of the Security Council have not yet been concluded, in case of a war the Security Council would not be in a position to take military measures by decisions binding upon the members. However, according to the wording of Article 39, it could recommend to members not involved in the war that they take such measures. Since these recommendations are not binding, the members concerned could choose whether they did or did not wish to remain neutral. If a military action taken by a member on the recommendation of the Security Council is considered to be an action of the United Nations, Article 2, paragraph 5, would apply. If it is interpreted as imposing on each member the obligation to give the United Nations every assistance in any action taken by the Organization even if the member is not under an order issued by the Security Council in conformity with Article 48, a member which does not comply with a recommendation to take military action made by the Security Council in conformity with Article 39 would be obliged to take such an action or enforcement measure not involving the use of armed force under Article 2, paragraph 5. This paradoxical consequence can be avoided if Article 2, paragraph 5, is interpreted to mean that the members are obliged to give the United Nations only that assistance which they are ordered to give by the Security Council in conformity with Article 48.

For one reason or another, especially because of the lack of unanimity of its permanent members, the Security Council may be prevented from making such recommendations or deciding upon non-military measures. In this event, Article 2, paragraph 5, would not apply. In case of a war, the members not involved in the war would be able to remain neutral and adopt an attitude of strict impartiality towards the belligerents. However, in case of an armed attack, they are under Article 51, in the exercise of the right of collective self-defense, entitled—but not obliged—to resort to war or to take measures short of war against the state which they consider to be the aggressor, that is to say, to give up neutrality or to observe a so-called qualified neutrality towards the belligerents. In case of a war, if under Article 39 the Security Council determined the existence of a breach of the peace or act of aggression, and thus determined the aggressor but did not take any measures against this aggressor state, the members not involved in the war which exercised their right of collective self-defense would be bound by the decision of the Security Council insofar as they could no longer decide for themselves which state was the aggressor.

Article 106 of the Charter stipulates: "Pending the coming into force of such special agreements referred to in Article 43 as in the opinion of the Security Council enable it to begin the exercise of its responsibilities under Article 42, the parties to the Four-Nation Declaration, signed at Moscow, October 30, 1943, and France, shall, in accordance with the provisions of paragraph 5 of that Declaration, consult with one another and as occasion requires with other Members of the United Nations with a view to such joint action on behalf of the Organization as may be necessary for the purpose of maintaining international peace and security." The states authorized to take joint action on behalf of the United Nations are the five permanent members of the Security Council. Consequently, it is not very likely that such action will ever be taken, since a "joint" action requires the unanimity of the five permanent members of the Security Council. However, if it should take place in case of a war, it would have to be considered a military action of the United Nations to which Article 2, paragraph 5, would apply. The question of the neutrality of the members of the United Nations not involved in the war would be answered according to which of the two interpretations of Article 2, paragraph 5, was accepted.

(e) Preventive Measures

(aa) *Consultation.*

As pointed out in a previous chapter of this study, the distinction between repressive and preventive measures is not an absolute one. As reactions against a violation of the law already committed, repressive measures, and especially sanctions, always also have a preventive effect, and some measures which, in principle, have a preventive character may be applied after the delict has been perpetrated. Consultation is such a measure.

370624—57——12

By consultation, any form of communication between governments may be understood. As a specific means to be applied within a system of international security, consultation is an exchange of views among governments for the purpose of preventing or terminating the use of armed force by one state against another.[1] Such consultation takes place among states which are not involved in the conflict, but the parties to the conflict may also participate in the discussion. The states concerned may consult each other in case of a mere threat to the peace in order to consider the means for its preservation. In this case, the consultation has a preventive character. On the other hand, consultation may take place in case of an actual breach of the peace. It then has a repressive character.[2]

Consultation may take place outside a security organization or within such an organization or between the organization and states not belonging to it. Consultation outside a security organization may be carried out either through the normal diplomatic channels or through the mechanism of an international conference.[3] Consultation within a security organization is an essential element of the procedure of the organs competent to apply preventive or repressive measures for the maintenance or restoration of peace. It necessarily precedes the decisions concerning the application of repressive measures, especially the application of sanctions. If not all the members are represented in the organ, the member not represented may be invited to participate in the discussion of the matter affecting the interest of that member.[4]

If the security organization is not universal, consultation is advisable between the organization on the one hand and the non-member involved in the conflict with which the organization is dealing on the other.[5] It is, however, not only consultation with a non-member involved in a conflict but also consultation with a disinterested, especially a neutral, non-member which is of importance, especially if the non-member is a great power, for the cooperation of all third parties is essential to the effectiveness of consultation.[6] As the United States was not a member of the League of Nations, consultation of the United States with the League was a paramount political problem. Since the United States is a member of the United Nations and a permanent member of the Security Council, consultation between this organization and the United States is no longer a problem.[7]

There can be no doubt that consultation through the mechanism of an international security organization is preferable to that through diplomatic channels and conferences. This is true, first, because the latter, as Cooper [8] correctly points out, rest upon no recognized authority and hence are "always open to the charge of being unwarranted and presumptuous." Another defect of consultation outside a security organization is the absence of an established procedure and the danger of conflicting with an action initiated by a security organization. "The ideal method of consultation," says Cooper, "is one which includes all neutrals, which has an established and recognized authority and organization, and which will not conflict with any other peace machinery." [9] It is evident that a universal or quasi-universal security organization, such as the League or the United Nations, is the most adequate instrument of consultation.[10]

It is an essential characteristic of consultation that it has no legal effect. Consultation does not imply any legal obligation whatsoever, especially no obligation to take a definite action for the maintenance or restoration of peace. Its purpose is political rather than legal. A treaty imposing upon the contracting parties an obligation to consult together is of the same nature as a treaty imposing upon the contracting parties the obligation to enter into negotiations. Just as negotiations may or may not result in an agreement of the parties, consultation may or may not lead to action for the maintenance or restoration of peace.

It was always with a reservation that no commitment to take action was implied, that the government of the United States accepted the obligation of consultation. Nevertheless, the opposition against consultative pacts was very strong among politicians and others of a more or less isolationist conviction. When at the London Naval Conference of 1930, in a press release of the United States delegation on 26 March 1930, the statement was made: ". . . that America had no objection to entering a consultative pact as such; on the contrary, the United States is already a party to a number of treaties involving the obligation of consulting with other powers. It will not, however, enter into any treaty, whether consultative or otherwise, where there is danger of its obligation being misunderstood as involving a promise to render military assistance or guaranteeing protection by military force to another nation," [11] Senator Borah, the Chairman of the Foreign Relations Committee, declared: "A consultative pact is a security pact in disguise. In a security pact you state in the pact what you are going to do after you have consulted. In a consultative pact you conceal what you are going to do after you have consulted, but you will be forced by the logic of the hour to do precisely what you expressly agreed to do in the security pact. A consultative pact in which the parties would not go forward and do whatever would be necessary to be done in accordance with the realities of the situation would be a pious fraud—and a fraud which under the exigencies of the hour would be rejected;" [12] and Senator Shipstead stated: "To agree to consult is to agree to decide. To agree to decide is to agree to act. To agree to act is to agree that we are going into the next war. They call this the road to peace. That is what they called the Triple Alliance, and the Triple Entente, and the Quadruple Alliance."[13] When at the Disarmament Conference in Geneva, 1933, the question of the commitment of the United States was discussed, Professor John Bassett Moore wrote: "The commitment of the United States to such a 'consultative pact' as is desired at Geneva would, I believe, constitute the gravest danger to which the country has ever been exposed, a danger involving our very independence. . . . It would destroy the last vestige of the power to control our own destiny that has heretofore been the most cherished part of our birthright. . . . Of all conceivable devices the 'consultative pact' is the most pernicious. It operates both as an incentive and as a lure. While it encourages the co-partner to do what he might otherwise refrain from doing, it fails, by reason of its indefiniteness, to deter the co-partner's antagonist from doing what he might not otherwise attempt. Numerous examples might be adduced to show this."[14]

Within a universal or quasi-universal security organization mere consultation implying no obligation of any action for the maintenance or restoration of peace may be useful if it is able to crystallize world public opinion concerning an actual or potential aggression and the state responsible for it. However there is seldom, and almost never in a world split into two ideologically hostile camps, only one public opinion. There are almost always at least two opposite ones, and thus, under actual circumstances, the value of this means for the establishment of international security remains problematical.

NOTES

1. *Cf.* Russell M. Cooper, *American Consultation in World Affairs for the Preservation of Peace*, with an Introduction by Dr. James T. Shotwell (New York: The Macmillan Company, 1934), pp. VII, 23; and Philip C. Jessup, *International Security. The American Rôle in Collective Action for Peace* (New York: Council on Foreign Relations, Inc., 1935), p. 64.

2. According to one interpretation, consultation was implied—although not expressly stipulated—in the Kellogg-Briand Pact. *Cf.* David Hunter Miller, *The Peace Pact of Paris*, 1928, pp. 130–1: "Inevitably the Government of the United States will be consulted, if not directly by Geneva, certainly by the Powers most influential at Geneva. Whether such consultation comes in the name of the League of Nations or whether it comes in the name of Members of the League of Nations as Parties with the United States to the Briand-Kellogg Treaty, is quite immaterial; it might take the form of discussions at Washington, or telegraphic exchanges, or a representative of the United States might sit with the Council; the consultation itself is certain and in any form it will be asked in fact by those Powers which are trying to preserve the peace. No Government of the United States could be indifferent to such an appeal; any threatened breach of a treaty

obligation made to the United States must be a matter of grave concern, above all when peace is at stake; of course there would be no legal duty on the part of the United States to intervene; still less would there be any obligation on the part of the United States to use threats; and I do not speak of sanctions because I am considering intervention before a breach and not afterwards; but no Government of the United States could refuse to use its influence in such a case in cooperation with the League of Nations to preserve peace and at the same time to preserve the sanctity of our own Treaty."

In June, 1932, both the Republican and the Democratic Parties required in their respective platforms the implementation of the Kellogg-Briand Pact by provisions for consultation in case of a threatened violation of the Treaty. On 8 August 1932 Secretary Stimson declared in an address before the Council on Foreign Relations: ". . . that consultation between the signatories of the Pact when faced with threat of its violation becomes inevitable. Any effective invocation of the power of world opinion postulates discussion and consultation. . . . That the Pact thus necessarily carries with it the implication of consultation has perhaps not been fully appreciated by its well-wishers who have been so anxious that it be implemented by a formal provision for consultation. But with the clarification which has been given to its significance by the developments of the last three years, and the vitality with which it has been imbued by the positive construction put upon it, the misgivings of those well-wishers should be put at rest. That the American people subscribe to this view is made clear by the fact that each of the platforms recently adopted by the two great party conventions at Chicago contains planks endorsing the principle of consultation." Henry L. Stimson, *The Pact of Paris: Three Years of Development*, Department of State, Publication No. 357, Washington, 1932, pp. 11–12.

On 11 August 1932 President Hoover, in accepting the Republican nomination, stated: ". . . we have given leadership in transforming the Kellogg-Briand Pact from an inspiring outlawry of war to an organized instrument for peaceful settlements backed by definite mobilized world public opinion against aggression. We shall, under the spirit of that pact, consult with other nations in times of emergency to promote world peace. We shall enter no agreements committing us to any future course of action or which call for use of force in order to preserve peace." *New York Times*, 12 August 1932.

And on 26 October, in a speech delivered at Pittsburgh, Secretary Stimson declared: "Whenever a breach of the treaty is threatened by approaching hostilities, it implies a duty of consultation among the other parties in order that public opinion may be mobilized against the impending disaster of war." Henry L. Stimson, *The Work of the United States Government in the Promotion of Peace During the Past Three Years*, Department of State, Publication No. 398, Washington, 1932, p. 11.

On 22 May 1933 Mr. Norman Davis, in his capacity as the chairman of the American Delegation to the Disarmament Conference in Geneva, accepted a British plan for disarmament which contained a provision to the effect that "in the event of a breach or threat of breach of the Pact of Paris, a conference between the High Contracting Parties shall at once meet at the request of any five of them, provided that at least one of the governments mentioned by name in Article 4 joins in that request." (*Series of League of Nations Publications.* IX Disarmament, 1933, IX, 2, Conference Document 157, p. 2.) He declared that the United States is: ". . . willing to consult with the other States in case of a threat to peace, with a view of averting conflict. Further than that, in the event that the States, in conference, determine that a State had been guilty of a breach of the peace in violation of its international obligations and take measures against the violator, then, if the U. S. concurred in the judgment rendered as to the responsible and guilty party, it would refrain from any action tending to defeat such collective effort which the States might thus make to restore peace." *Series of League of Nations Publications.* IX Disarmament, 1933, IX, 10, p. 475.

On 24 May the United Kingdom presented a revised text of its draft convention which contained the following provisions: "I. In the event of a breach or threat of breach of the Pact of Paris, either the Council or Assembly of the League of Nations or one of the parties to the present Convention who are not members of the League of Nations may propose immediate consultation between the Council or Assembly and any of the said parties to the present Convention. II. It shall be the object of such consultation, (a) in the event of a threat of a breach of the Pact to exchange views for the purpose of preserving the peace and averting a conflict; (b) in the event of a breach of the Pact to use good offices for the restoration of peace; and (c) in the event that it proves impossible thus to restore the peace, then to determine which party or parties to the dispute are to be held responsible. III. The provisions of the above article do not in any way prejudice the rights and obligations of the members of the League, nor conflict with nor limit the powers and duties of the Assembly and Council under the Covenant." Records of the Conference for the Reduction and Limitation of Armaments. Series B. Minutes of the General Commission, Vol. II. *Series of League of Nations Publications*, IX, Disarmament, 1933, IX, 10, p. 494.

Mr. Norman Davis also accepted the new British plan and declared on 24 May: "Recognizing that any breach or threat of breach of the Pact of Paris (the Briand-Kellogg Pact) is a matter of concern to all the signatories thereto, the Government of the United States of America declares that, in the event of a breach or threat of breach of this Pact, it will be prepared to confer with a view to the maintenance of peace in the event that consultation for such purpose is arranged pursuant to Articles . . . and . . . of Part I of the Disarmament Convention. . . ." (*Ibid.*, pp. 495–6.) The consultation referred to in the British draft convention and in the American declaration evidently had a preventive as well as repressive character in that it would take place not only in case of a threat of a breach but also in case of an actual breach of the Pact of Paris.

The Argentine Anti-War Treaty of non-aggression signed at Rio de Janeiro 10 October 1933, to which the United States was a contracting party, contained in Article 3 the following provision: "In case of noncompliance by any state engaged in a dispute, with the obligations contained in the foregoing articles, the contracting states undertake to make every effort for the maintenance of peace. To that end they will adopt in their character as neutrals a common and solidary attitude; they will exercise the political, juridical or economic means authorized by international law; they will bring the influence of public opinion to bear but will in no case resort to intervention either diplomatic or armed; subject to the attitude that may be incumbent on them by virtue of other collective treaties to which such states are signatories." The first two Articles of the Treaty were similar to the first two Articles of the Kellogg-Briand Pact. *Cf.* Jessup, *International Security*, p. 76.

3. *Cf.* Cooper, *op. cit.*, pp. 348 ff.

4. Article 4, paragraph 5, of the Covenant of the League of Nations expressly provided that any member of the League not represented on the Council should be invited to send a Representative to sit as a member at any meeting of the Council during the consideration of matters especially affecting the interests

of that member of the League. Thus, consultation among the disinterested members was secured along with consultation with the interested member. Article 31 of the Charter of the United Nations stipulates that any member of the United Nations which is not a member of the Security Council may participate, without vote, in the discussion of any question brought before the Security Council whenever the latter considers that the interests of that member are specially affected. Article 32 provides that any member of the United Nations which is not a member of the Security Council, if it is a party to a dispute under consideration by the Security Council, shall be invited to participate, without vote, in the discussion relating to the dispute.

5. According to Article 32 of the Charter, a state which is not a member of the United Nations, if it is a party to a dispute under consideration by the Council, shall be invited to participate, without vote, in the discussion.

6. *Cf.* Cooper, *op. cit.*, p. 352.

7. There are still a number of states not members of the United Nations, and, according to Article 2, paragraph 6, of the Charter, the Organization shall ensure that these states act in accordance with the Principles of the Charter so far as this may be necessary for the maintenance of international peace and security. As far as the principle of settling disputes by peaceful means is concerned, consultation with the non-member state involved in a dispute is secured by Article 32. With respect to enforcement measures to be directed against a non-member state in case of threat to or breach of the peace, no previous consultation with this state is provided for by the Charter; nor is any consultation with a non-member state obligatory which, according to the principle laid down in Article 2, paragraph 5, is supposed to give the United Nations every assistance in any action the Organization takes in accordance with the Charter and to refrain from giving assistance to any state against which the United Nations is taking preventive or enforcement action. However, it may be assumed that consultation with the non-member state, especially in the latter case, is not excluded.

8. Cooper, *op. cit.*, p. 349.

9. *Ibid.*, p. 352.

10. The first treaties by which the United States legally committed itself to consult with other states under certain conditions were the Four-Power Treaty, signed 13 December 1921 by the United States, the British Empire, France and Japan concerning insular possessions in the Pacific and the Nine-Power Treaty, signed 6 February 1922 by the United States, Belgium, the British Empire, China, France, Italy, Japan, the Netherlands and Portugal concerning the principles and policies to be followed in matters concerning China. Recently, the United States accepted special obligations of consultation in defense treaties such as the North Atlantic Treaty signed at Washington on 4 April 1949 which contains in Article 4 the following provision: "The Parties will consult together whenever, in the opinion of any of them, the territorial integrity, political independence or security of any of the Parties is threatened"; the Security Treaty concluded by Australia, New Zealand, and the United States of America, signed at San Francisco on 1 September 1951, Article III of which stipulates: "The Parties will consult together whenever in the opinion of any of them the territorial integrity, political independence or security of any of the Parties is threatened in the Pacific"; the South-East Asia Collective Defense Treaty, signed on 8 September 1954 by the United States, Great Britain, France, Australia, New Zealand, the Philippines, Thailand and Pakistan, which contains the following provisions: Article 4, paragraph 2: "If, in the opinion of any of the

parties, the inviolability or the integrity of the territory or the sovereignty or political independence of any party in the treaty area or of any other state or territory to which the provisions of paragraph 1 of this Article from time to time apply is threatened in any way other than by armed attack or is affected or threatened by any fact or situation which might endanger the peace of the area, the parties shall consult immediately in order to agree on the measures which would be taken for the common defense." Article 5: "The parties hereby establish a Council, on which each of them shall be represented, to consider matters concerning the implementation of this treaty. The Council shall provide for consultation with regard to military and any other planning as the situation obtaining in the treaty area may from time to time require. The Council shall be so organized as to be able to meet at any time" (*Disarmament and Security*, pp. 611 ff.) ; and in the Treaties for Mutual Defense Assistance concluded on the basis of the Mutual Defense Assistance Act of 1949 (Public Law 329, 81st Congress; 63 Stat. 714). For instance, Article VI, paragraph 1, of the Mutual Defense Assistance Agreement between the United States of America and France, signed at Washington on 27 January 1950 (Department of State Publication 3769), stipulates: "The two Governments will, upon the request of either of them, consult regarding any matter relating to the application of this Agreement or to operations or arrangements carried out pursuant to this Agreement." Similar provisions are contained in other Mutual Defense Assistance Agreements.

Consultation as a means for the preservation of peace has played an important part in the Pan-American movement. The Inter-American Conference for the Maintenance of Peace, Buenos Aires, 1936, recommended: "The procedure of mutual consultation in order to find means of peaceful cooperation in the event of war or threat of war between American countries," and recognized "that every act susceptible of disturbing the peace of America affects each and every one of the American Nations and justifies the initiation of the procedure of consultation." At the Eighth International Conference of American States, Lima, 1938, these states declared: "That in case the peace, security or territorial integrity of any American republic is threatened by acts of any nature that may impair them, they proclaim their common concern and their determination to make effective their solidarity, coordinating their respective sovereign will by means of the procedure of consultation, using the measures which in each case the circumstances may make advisable." Declaration Fourth of the Act of Chapultepec, 8 March 1945, reads as follows: "That in case that acts of aggression occur or there may be reasons to believe that an aggression is being prepared by any other State against the integrity or inviolability of the territory, or against the sovereignty or political independence of an American State, the states signatory to this declaration will consult amongst themselves in order to agree upon measures they think it may be advisable to take." The Inter-American Treaty of Reciprocal Assistance, Rio de Janeiro, 2 September 1947, to which the United States of America is a contracting party, stipulates: "*Art.* 7. In the case of the conflict between two or more American States, without prejudice to the right of self-defense in conformity with Article 51 of the Charter of the United Nations, the High Contracting Parties, meeting in consultation shall call upon the contending States to suspend hostilities and restore matters to the *status quo ante bellum*, and shall take in addition all other measures necessary to re-establish or maintain inter-American peace and security and for the solution of the conflict by peaceful means. The rejection of the pacifying action will be considered in the determination of the aggressor and in the application of the measures which the consultative meeting may agree upon. *Art.* 8. For the purposes of this Treaty, the measures on which the Organ of

Consultation may agree will comprise one or more of the following: recall of chiefs of diplomatic missions; breaking of diplomatic relations; breaking of consular relations; partial or complete interruption of economic relations or of rail, sea, air, postal, telegraphic, telephonic, and radio-telephonic or radio-telegraphic communications; and use of armed force. *Art 9.* In addition to other acts which the Organ of Consultation may characterize as aggression, the following shall be considered as such: *a.* Unprovoked armed attack by a State against the territory, the people, or the land, sea or air forces of another State; *b.* Invasion, by the armed forces of a State, or the territory of any American State, through the trespassing of boundaries demarcated in accordance with a treaty, judicial decision, or arbitral award, or, in the absence of frontiers thus demarcated, invasion affecting a region which is under the effective jurisdiction of another State. *Art. 10.* None of the provisions of this Treaty shall be construed as impairing the rights and obligations of the High Contracting Parties under the Charter of the United Nations. *Art. 11.* The consultations to which this Treaty refers shall be carried out by means of the meetings of the Ministers of Foreign Affairs of the American Republics which have ratified the Treaty, or in the manner or by the Organ which in the future may be agreed upon. *Art. 12.* The Governing Board of the Pan American Union may act provisionally as an organ of consultation until the meeting of the Organ of Consultation referred to in the preceding Article takes place. *Art. 13.* The consultations shall be initiated at the request addressed to the Governing Board of the Pan American Union by any of the Signatory States which has ratified the Treaty. *Art. 14.* In the voting referred to in this Treaty only the representatives of the Signatory States which have ratified this Treaty may take part. *Art. 15.* The Governing Board of the Pan American Union shall act in all matters concerning this Treaty as an organ of liaison among the Signatory States which have ratified this Treaty and between these States and the United Nations. *Art. 16.* The decisions of the Governing Board of the Pan-American Union referred to in Articles 13 and 15 above shall be taken by an absolute majority of the members entitled to vote. *Art. 17.* The Organ of Consultation shall take its decisions by a vote of two-thirds of the Signatory States which have ratified the Treaty. *Art. 18.* In the case of a situation or dispute between American States, the parties directly interested shall be excluded from the voting referred to in the two preceding Articles. *Art. 19.* To constitute a quorum in all the meetings referred to in the previous Articles, it shall be necessary that the number of States represented, shall be at least equal to the number of votes necessary for the taking of the decision. *Art. 20.* Decisions which require the application of the measures specified in Article 8 shall be binding upon all the Signatory States which have ratified this Treaty, with the sole exception that no State shall be required to use armed force without its consent. *Art. 21.* The measures agreed upon by the Organ of Consultation shall be executed through the procedures and agencies now existing or those which may in the future be established."

The Charter of the Organization of American States, Bogota, March 30–May 2, 1948, contains the following provisions: "*Chapter XI: The Meeting of Consultation of Ministers of Foreign Affairs. Art. 39.* The Meeting of Consultation of Ministers of Foreign Affairs shall be held in order to consider problems of an urgent nature and of common interest to the American States, and to serve as the Organ of Consultation. *Art. 40.* Any Member State may request that a Meeting of Consultation be called. The request shall be addressed to the Council of the Organization, which shall decide by an absolute majority whether a meeting should be held. *Art 41.* The program and regulations of the Meeting of Consultation shall be prepared by the Council of the Organization and submitted to the Member States for consideration. *Art. 42.* If, for exceptional reasons, a Minister of Foreign Affairs is unable to attend the meeting, he shall be represented by a special delegate. *Art 43.* In case of an armed attack within the territory of an American State or within the region of security delimited by treaties in force, a Meeting of Consultation shall be held without delay. Such Meeting shall be called immediately by the Chairman of the Council of the Organization, who shall at the same time call a meeting of the Council itself. *Art. 44.* An Advisory Defence Committee shall be established to advise the Organ of Consultation on problems of military cooperation that may arise in connection with the application of existing special treaties on collective security. *Art. 45.* The Advisory Defence Committee shall be composed of the highest military authorities of the American States participating in the Meeting of Consultation. Under exceptional circumstances the Governments may appoint substitutes. Each State shall be entitled to one vote. *Art. 46.* The Advisory Defence Committee shall be convoked under the same conditions as the Organ of Consultation, when the latter deals with matters relating to defence against aggression. *Art. 47.* The Committee shall also meet when the Conference or the Meeting of Consultation or the Governments, by a two-thirds majority of the Member States, assign to it technical studies or reports on specific subjects."

An obligation of consultation is imposed upon the contracting parties by the Treaty of Economic, Social and Cultural Collaboration and Collective Self-Defense, signed at Brussels on 17 March 1948 by Belgium, France, Luxembourg, the Netherlands and the British Empire, which contains the following provisions: "*Art. 1.* Convinced of the close community of their interests and of the necessity of uniting in order to promote the economic recovery of Europe, the High Contracting Parties will so organize and coordinate their economic activities as to produce the best possible results, by the elimination of conflict in their economic policies, the coordination of production and the development of commercial exchanges.—The cooperation provided for in the preceding paragraph, which will be effected through the Consultative Council referred to in Article 7 as well as through other bodies, shall not involve any duplication of, or prejudice to, the work of other economic organizations in which the High Contracting Parties are or may be represented but shall on the contrary assist the work of those organizations. *Art. 2.* The High Contracting Parties will make every effort in common, both by direct consultation and in specialized agencies, to promote the attainment of a higher standard of living by their peoples and to develop on corresponding lines the social and other related services of their countries. The High Contracting Parties will consult with the object of achieving the earliest possible application of recommendations of immediate practical interest relating to social matters, adopted with their approval in the specialized agencies. They will endeavour to conclude as soon as possible conventions with each other in the sphere of social security." "*Art. 7.* For the purpose of consulting together on all the questions dealt with in the present Treaty, the High Contracting Parties will create a Consultative Council, which shall be so organized as to be able to exercise its functions continuously. The Council shall meet at such times as it shall deem fit. At the request of any of the High Contracting Parties, the Council shall be immediately convened in order to permit the High Contracting Parties to consult with regard to any situation which may constitute a threat to peace, in whatever area this threat should arise, with regard to the attitude to be adopted and the steps to be taken in case of a renewal by Germany of an aggressive policy; or with regard to any situation constituting a danger to economic stability."

Other treaties concluded for the purpose of economic and cultural cooperation, also contain the obligation of consultation. An example is the Agreement establishing the South Pacific Commission concluded by Australia, France, the Netherlands, New Zealand, United Kingdom and the United States, Canberra, on 6 February 1947 for cooperation in promoting the economic and social welfare advancement of the peoples of the non-self-governing territories in the South Pacific region administered by them. According to Article IV: "The Commission shall be a consultative and advisory body to the participating Governments in matters affecting the economic and social development of the non-self-governing territories within the scope of the Commission and the welfare and advancement of their peoples."

11. *London Naval Conference: Speeches and Press Statements by Members of the American Delegation, January 20–April 29, 1930* (Department of State Publication, Conference Series, No. 3), p. 35.

12. *New York Times*, 28 March 1930.

13. *Ibid. Cf.* Jessup, *International Security*, p. 70.

14. John Bassett Moore, "An Appeal to Reason," *Foreign Affairs*, Vol. 11 (July 1933), pp. 571–2.

(bb) *The peaceful settlement of international disputes.*

An international dispute exists if one state claims that another state should behave in a certain way, and the latter rejects the claim of the former.

Disputes between states, just as disputes between human beings,[1] may be settled peacefully either by agreement of the parties to the dispute or by the decision of an agency which is binding upon the parties.

The agreement may be brought about through direct negotiation by the states, parties to the dispute, or through the friendly intervention of a third state or some third states. This friendly intervention is called good offices or mediation. The purpose of both procedures is to bring about an agreement of the parties to the dispute. Some writers speak of mediation, in contradistinction to good offices, if one or more third states try to bring about an agreement of the parties to the dispute on the basis of concrete proposals made by the mediator. In both cases the suggestions made to the parties to the dispute are not binding.

If a dispute arises from a difference of opinion on points of fact it may be submitted to an international commission of inquiry established by a special agreement between the parties to the dispute. The function of the commission of inquiry is restricted to a statement of facts. The parties to the dispute may or may not accept this statement.

If the commission is competent not only to ascertain disputed facts but also to make recommendations for the settlement of the dispute, one speaks of conciliation. The commission of conciliation may be composed as follows: each party to the dispute appoints one or an equal number of members and, by agreement, these members appoint a chairman.[2] The commission may adopt its decision by majority vote, but settlement of the dispute is brought about only if the parties accept the recommendations of the commission, which implies that they have come to an agreement.

Within a more or less universal security organization the function of conciliation is conferred by the constituent treaty upon a central agency of the organization composed of representatives of all, or only of some, of the members of the organization. The party to a concrete dispute, which is not a member of the agency, may be authorized to send a representative to participate in the discussion of the case. The representatives of the parties may or may not be entitled to participate in the decision.[3]

The function of the agency has the character of conciliation if its decisions constitute only recommendations which are not legally binding upon the parties.[4] If its decisions are binding upon the parties, the function has a quasi-judicial character and differs from that of a tribunal insofar as its members are not, as in the case of a tribunal, independent judges but representatives of the governments by which they are appointed and hence bound by instruction given to them by their governments.

The constituent treaty of an international security organization may impose upon its members the obligation to submit their disputes—even disputes with non-members—to the conciliation procedure provided for by the treaty. This means that if one party to a dispute submits a case to the competent organ the other party is obliged to recognize the jurisdiction of this organ. In other terms: the constituent treaty may establish compulsory jurisdiction of a special organ for the pacific settlement of disputes by conciliation. If the conciliation procedure does not lead to an agreement among the parties and hence to a settlement of the dispute, the constituent treaty may leave it to the parties to submit the case to an arbitral tribunal established by their agreement or to an international tribunal established by the constituent treaty itself as a judicial organ of the security organization organized as a permanent court.[5] The parties to the dispute may even be obliged to submit their disputes to the tribunal if the conciliation procedure fails; or they may be obliged to submit only certain disputes, normally so-called legal disputes, to the judicial procedure either in case of the failure of a conciliation procedure or without such a procedure being necessary at all.[6]

The judicial organ of the security organization,[7] its permanent court, may be composed of members elected by the assembly or by the council of the organization or by both.[8] Since these organs are composed of the representatives of the member-states appointed by the governments concerned, these governments have a considerable influence on the composition of the court, especially if the organs of the security organization have to elect the judges from a list of candidates nominated directly or indirectly by the governments of the member states.[9] If, in order to achieve the highest possible degree of independence for the judges, this influence is to be eliminated as far as possible, a procedure may be adopted in which the decisive function within the process of the appointment of the judges is not conferred on the governments of the states but on their supreme courts, law schools, or international scientific organizations for international law and the like.[10] For the same purpose, the judges should be elected for life or until they reach a certain age limit but not for a limited period of time so that the question of a possible re-election does not arise.[11] Only the professional and moral qualification of the candidate should be required. The president of the court may be elected by its members or this office may be filled by rotation.[12]

As to the procedure of the court, it stands to reason that it must adopt its decision by majority vote.[13] Collective security is guaranteed most effectively if its jurisdiction is compulsory.[14] That it is compulsory means that if one party to a dispute submits the case to the court the other party is obliged to recognize the court's jurisdiction, even if there is no previous agreement by the parties to the dispute concerning the jurisdiction of the court in this case. The constituent treaty may even authorize the court to proceed under certain circumstances and with respect to certain matters *ex officio*, on its own initiative without its jurisdiction being invoked by any party. The court should be open not only to states and international organizations but also to private individuals, not only as plaintiffs in case of a violation of their rights established by treaties, but also as defendants especially if they are accused of having committed punishable violation of international law; that is to say, the court should have criminal jurisdiction.[15]

Either the treaty constituting an international security organization or the statute of its permanent court may stipulate that in settling a dispute brought before it, this court must apply the rules of existing international law unless the parties to the dispute agree upon the application of principles of justice or equity. By such an agreement, the tribunal is authorized to create within its discretion new law for the case at hand.[16] However, the constituent treaty or the statute of the court may distinguish two categories of disputes—namely, legal and political disputes—and provide that, without regard to the wishes of the parties, legal disputes shall be settled in accordance with positive law and political disputes in accordance with justice or equity.[17]

There are two ways to define the concept of legal disputes. One is the general definition adopted by the so-called Locarno Treaties—that is, the treaties of conciliation and arbitration signed by Germany on the one hand and by Belgium, Czechoslovakia, France and Poland on the other, in London on 1 December 1925. In Article 1 of these treaties, legal disputes are defined as disputes with regard to which the parties are in conflict as to their respective rights. This formula is not quite satisfactory, because it refers only to "rights," and "rights" may or may not be "legal" rights, and especially because it does not refer to legal obligations which are mainly involved. One state has a right only if the other has a corresponding obligation; and there is a dispute only if one claims to have a right and the other denies being under a corresponding obligation. The legal character of a dispute depends on the attitude of the parties: whether one party justifies its claim and the other party rejects this claim by referring to existing international law, which implies that the parties agree to have their dispute settled by the application of existing international law. The other way consists in enumerating certain categories of disputes—namely, disputes concerning the interpretation of a treaty; any question of international law; the existence of any fact which if established would constitute a breach of an international obligation; the nature or extent of the reparation to be made for the breach of an international obligation. This enumerative definition is adopted in Article 13, paragraph 2, of the Covenant of the League of Nations and in Article 36, paragraph 2, of the Statute of the International Court of Justice.[18] The enumeration is, logically, very problematical, since one of the enumerated matters, "any question of international law," covers the three others. Besides, the legal character of a dispute does not depend on its subject matter but on the norms to be applied to it. It is legal if it is to be settled by the application of the rules of existing law. It is not legal (i. e., political) if it is to be settled by the application of other principles, such as justice or equity, or if, as a consequence of the attitude of the parties, it is not to be settled in a peaceful way at all. The political question as to whether or not a dispute should be settled as a legal dispute—that is, by the application of existing international law—must not be confused with the legal question as to whether or not a dispute can be settled by the application of existing international law—that is, whether a dispute is justiciable or not justiciable. It has been pointed out in a previous connection[19] that there are no disputes which, by their very nature, are not justiciable—that is to say, which, as a consequence of the subject matter to which they refer, cannot be settled by the application of existing law because these subject matters are not regulated by the existing law or, what amounts to the same thing, because there are gaps in the existing law. It has been shown that there is no objective criterion at the basis of the distinction between legal and political, justiciable and non-justiciable disputes, and that the distinction between disputes which are to be settled in accordance with existing law and disputes which are to be settled in accordance with justice or equity—that is, in accordance with new law to be created by the court for the concrete case—can be justified only if the application of the existing law, although legally possible, is, according to the opinion of the parties concerned or the competent tribunal, politically not satisfactory; and that the flexibility of the legal system, which is evidently the purpose of such a distinction, can be achieved only at the expense of the security to be guaranteed by it.

The doctrine that there are international conflicts which, by their very nature, cannot be settled by judicial means has recently been presented in a new version. There are, this new version asserts, conflicts of such a nature that "they will generally be not even formulated in legal terms," [20] that is to say, in terms of concrete obligations and rights, and hence they will not be settled by international tribunals because a tribunal can settle a conflict only by deciding the question of whether or not a definite state has a concrete obligation and, consequently, whether or not another state has the corresponding right. Such "unformulated" conflicts are those which stand in relation to a general "tension" between two states, the issue of which is "the overall distribution of power" between them, the opposition between "the maintenance of the *status quo* and its overthrow." The situation which existed in the relation between Germany and Czechoslovakia in 1938 is an example of such a "tension." The real issue of the conflict between these two states was not sovereignty over the Sudetenland but Hitler's claim to the military and political domination of Central Europe.

The conflicts in question are "unformulated" not because they cannot be formulated at all—in the example just given the "unformulated" conflict is precisely formulated—but because they cannot be formulated in legal terms. This simply means that a state which intends to overthrow the *status quo* of the distribution of power by extending its control over territories legally under the sovereignty of other states, or over an entire continent, or even over the whole world is not in a position to present its claim in conformity with existing international law. If such a conflict were subjected to a judicial procedure, the tribunal applying the existing law could come to no other conclusion but to reject the claim and to condemn any attempt to realize it by force as a violation of international law. This is the reason why a state will never submit such a claim to a judicial procedure. This is self-evident. But the statement that such "unformulated conflicts," the issue of which is a "tension"—that is, the "political" conflicts of the new doctrine—"cannot be settled by judicial means," i. e., by the application of existing law, is incorrect if it means more than the truism that if there is no court with compulsory jurisdiction such conflicts will actually not be settled by judicial means. It is just as incorrect as the analogous statement concerning political disputes within the meaning of the old doctrine. From a scientific point of view, the only statement that can be made with respect to "tension" conflicts is exactly the same as that which can be made with respect to political conflicts of the old doctrine. This is the statement that a judicial settlement of such conflicts, although legally possible, is politically not satisfactory to the state whose claim to overthrow the *status quo* of distribution of power creates the "tension."

The "tension" theory of political conflicts does not contribute a new aspect to the problem of judicial settlement. It may be that a state which wishes to overthrow the existing *status quo* of the distribution of power will refuse to submit the "unformulated" conflict even to an international agency competent to apply principles other than those of existing international law, principles of justice or equity, because the state concerned cannot assume that its claim is justifiable even according to these principles, just as a band of gangsters who want to rob a bank will not "formulate" the conflict which exists between their interest and that of the bank and hence will not submit it to a tribunal of law or equity but will simply try to get what they want by force. Just as the function of a national legal order is to prevent the crime and, if this is not possible, to punish the criminals, the very purpose of an international security organization is to prevent a state which intends to overthrow the *status quo* by force from realizing its intention and, if prevention is not possible, to react against it by enforcement measures effective enough to restore the law. The "tension" doctrine of political conflicts may be correct as a mere description of international relations as they actually exist, but it is not correct as a justification of the thesis that these conflicts are not justiciable.

If an international dispute is settled by the decision of an international agency binding upon the parties, the latter are obliged to carry out the decision. If, in violation of its obligation, one party within an international security organization does not comply with the decision, the enforcement of the decision should not be left to the other party but should be a function of the organization itself performed by its executive organ. This may be the same organ as the one which has settled the dispute by its decision so that both functions: the decision by which the dispute is settled and the enforcement of this decision, are conferred upon one and the same organ of the organization, composed of representatives of the members. If, however, the dispute must be settled in conformity with existing law, the competent organ should have the character of a tribunal. An agency composed of representatives of states and not of independent judges always has the tendency to settle conflicts in accordance with political convenience rather than by applying the rules of existing law. If a dispute is settled by the court of an international security organization, the judgment may be enforced against the recalcitrant party by the executive agency of the organization on the request of the other party or of the court. Since non-compliance with the decision of the court is a violation of the constituent treaty, the action taken for the purpose of enforcing the decision has the character of a sanction. On the other hand, all enforcement measures of an international security organization, especially those involving the use of armed force, should, as a rule, be taken only as the execution of a judicial decision—that is, only as a reaction against a violation of the law ascertained in an objective and impartial procedure. The executive organ of the security organization should, as a rule, act only as the sheriff of the court.[21] The usual objection to this suggestion, that if enforcement measures are to be preceded by a judicial procedure they may be too late to restore the law, especially in case of an armed attack, has been discussed in a previous chapter.[22]

NOTES

1. *Cf.* pp. 15 ff.

2. Article 14 of the Treaty signed by Germany and Switzerland at Berne on 3 December 1921 is typical: "The contracting parties shall appoint one member each of their own choice, and nominate three other members by mutual agreement. These three members shall not be nationals of the contracting parties, nor shall they be domiciled on their territory, nor employed in their service. The contracting parties shall by mutual agreement elect the president from among these three members."

3. Article 4, paragraph 5, of the Covenant of the League of Nations stipulated: "Any Member of the League not represented on the Council shall be invited to send a Representative to sit as a member at any meeting of the Council during the consideration of matters specially affecting the interests of that Member of the League."

Article 32 of the Charter of the United Nations provides: "Any Member of the United Nations which is not a member of the Security Council or any state which is not a Member of the United Nations, if it is a party to a dispute under consideration by the Security Council, shall be invited to participate, without vote, in the discussion relating to the dispute. The Security Council shall lay down such conditions as it deems just for the participation of a state which is not a Member of the United Nations."

According to Article 27, paragraph 3, members of the Security Council which are parties to a dispute shall abstain from voting on a decision taken for the purpose of the pacific settlement of disputes under Chapter VI of the Charter.

4. According to the Covenant of the League of Nations, the Council was competent to make only recommendations for the settlement of a dispute. However, a recommendation unanimously adopted by the Council had a certain legal effect. In this respect, Article 15, paragraph 6, provided: "If a report by the Council is unanimously agreed to by the Members thereof other than the Representatives of one or more of the parties to the dispute, the Members of the League agree that they will not go to war with any party to the dispute which complies with the recommendations of the report."

According to the Charter, too, the Security Council is authorized to make only recommendations for the settlement of disputes. These recommendations may be adopted, according to Article 27, by an affirmative vote of seven (of the eleven) members including the concurring votes of the permanent members. It must, however, be taken into consideration that the Security Council, according to Article 39, may consider the non-compliance of a party with its recommendations as a threat to the peace and hence may take enforcement measures in order to maintain international peace. If these measures are to be considered as sanctions, the so-called recommendations of the Security Council have the character of a decision which may be binding upon the parties.

5. Under the Covenant, the members had the choice of submitting their dispute to the conciliation procedure of the Council or to the decision of an international tribunal (tribunal of arbitration or the Permanent Court of International Justice). Article 12 stipulated:

"1. The Members of the League agree that, if there should arise between them any dispute likely to lead to a rupture, they will submit the matter either to arbitration, *or judicial settlement* or to inquiry by the Council, and they agree in no case to resort to war until three months after the award by the arbitrators *or the judicial decision*, or the report by the Council. 2. In any case under this Article the award of the arbitrators *or the judicial decision* shall be made within a reasonable time, and the report of the Council shall be made within six months after the submission of the dispute." Article 15, paragraph 1: "If there should arise between Members of the League any dispute likely to lead to a rupture, which is not submitted to arbitration *or judicial settlement* in accordance with Article 13, the Members of the League agree that they will submit the matter to the Council. Any party to the dispute may effect such submission by giving notice of the existence of the dispute to the Secretary-General, who will make all necessary arrangements for a full investigation and consideration thereof."

The Charter provides in Article 33, paragraph 1: "The parties to any dispute, the continuance of which is likely to endanger the maintenance of international peace and security, shall, first of all, seek a solution by negotiation, enquiry, mediation, conciliation, arbitration, judicial settlement, resort to regional agencies or arrangements, or other peaceful means of their own choice."

Article 37, paragraph 1: "Should the parties to a dispute of the nature referred to in Article 33 fail to settle it by the means indicated in that Article, they shall refer it to the Security Council."

As far as settlement by judicial means is concerned, the members have the choice of submitting the dispute to the International Court of Justice or to an arbitral tribunal established by their agreement. Article 92 of the Charter provides: "The International Court of Justice shall be the principal judicial organ of the United Nations. It shall function in accordance with the annexed Statute, which is based upon the Statute of the Permanent Court of International Justice and forms an integral part of the present Charter." Article 95: "Nothing in the present Charter shall prevent Members of the United Nations from entrusting the solution of their differences to other tribunals by virtue of agreements already in existence or which may be concluded in the future."

6. The General Act for the Pacific Settlement of International Disputes adopted by the Ninth Assembly of the League of Nations on 26 September 1928 stipulated that legal disputes shall be submitted to arbitration or judicial settlement and that other disputes, provided that conciliation does not lead to an agreement of the parties, shall be submitted to an arbitral tribunal. The most important provisions of the General Act were: Article 1: "Disputes of every kind between two or more Parties to the present General Act which it has not been possible to settle by diplomacy shall, subject to such reservations as may be made under Article 39, be submitted, under the conditions laid down in the present Chapter, to the procedure of conciliation." Article 2: "The disputes referred to in the preceding article shall be submitted to a permanent or special Conciliation Commission constituted by the parties to the dispute." Article 17: "All disputes with regard to which the parties are in conflict as to their respective rights shall, subject to any reservations which may be made under Article 39, be submitted for decision to the Permanent Court of International Justice, unless the parties agree, in the manner hereinafter provided, to have resort to an arbitral tribunal. It is understood that the disputes referred to above include in particular those mentioned in Article 36 of the Statute of the Permanent Court of International Justice." Article 20, paragraph 1: "Notwithstanding the provisions of Article 1, disputes of the kind referred to in Article 17 arising between parties who have acceded to the obligations contained in the present Chapter shall only be subject to the procedure of conciliation if the parties so agree." Article 21: "Any dispute not of the kind referred to in Article 17 which does not, within the month following the termination of the work of the Conciliation Commission provided for in Chapter I, form the object of an agreement between the parties, shall, subject to such reservations as may be made under Article 39, be brought before an arbitral tribunal which, unless the parties otherwise agree, shall be constituted in the manner set out below." Article 28: "If nothing is laid down in the special agreement or no special agreement has been made, the Tribunal shall apply the rules in regard to the substance of the dispute enumerated in Article 38 of the Statute of the Permanent Court of International Justice. In so far as there exists no such rule applicable to the dispute, the Tribunal shall decide *ex aequo et bono*." The last sentence of Article 28 presupposed that there were gaps in existing international law which could be filled by principles of equity. *Cf.* pp. 19 f., 32, 189. Article 39 of the General Act contained an extensive enumeration of the reservations which a state might make in acceding to the Act. By these reservations the following disputes might be excluded from the procedure described in the Act: "(a) Disputes arising out of facts prior to the accession either of the Party making the reservation or of any other Party with whom the said Party may have a dispute; (b) Disputes concerning questions which by international law are solely within the domestic jurisdiction of States; (c) Dis-

putes concerning particular cases or clearly specified subject-matters, such as territorial status, or disputes falling within clearly defined categories."

The Resolution 268 (III) A (Restoration to the General Act of 26 September 1928, of its original efficacy) adopted by the General Assembly at its 199th Plenary Meeting on 28 April 1949, instructed the Secretary-General "to prepare a revised text of the General Act," including certain amendments mentioned in the resolution, "and to hold it open to accession by States, under the title 'Revised General Act for the Pacific Settlement of International Disputes.'" The amendments mentioned in the resolution "will only apply as between States having acceded to the General Act as thus amended and, as a consequence, will not affect the rights of such States, parties to the Act as established on 26 September 1928, as should claim to invoke it in so far as it might still be operative."

Neither the Covenant nor the Charter imposes upon the members of the security organization an obligation to submit disputes to a judicial procedure. The Member states may do so by agreement, and they are free to submit the dispute either to the Permanent Court of the Organization or to an arbitral tribunal established by their agreement.

7. The judicial organ of the League of Nations was the Permanent Court of International Justice established in accordance with Article 14 of the Covenant by the Protocol of Signature of the Statute of the Permanent Court of International Justice of 16 December 1920. The judicial organ of the United Nations is the International Court of Justice established by the Charter. Its Statute forms an integral part of the Charter. It is not very different from that of the Permanent Court of International Justice.

8. According to Article 2 of the Statute of the International Court of Justice, the Court is composed of a body of independent judges, elected regardless of their nationality from among persons of high moral character, who possess the qualifications required in their respective countries for appointment to the highest judicial offices, or who are jurisconsults of recognized competence in international law. According to Article 3, the Court consists of fifteen members, no two of whom may be nationals of the same state. According to Article 4, the members are elected by the General Assembly and by the Security Council from a list of persons nominated by the national groups in the Permanent Court of Arbitration. A "national group" is formed by the persons (four at most) selected by the contracting parties to the Hague Convention for the Pacific Settlement of International Disputes of 1907, according to Article 44 of this Convention. In the case of members of the United Nations not represented in the Permanent Court of Arbitration, candidates are nominated by national groups appointed for this purpose by their governments under the same conditions as those prescribed for members of the Permanent Court of Arbitration by Article 44 of the Hague Convention of 1907. No national group may nominate more than four persons, not more than two of whom shall be of their own nationality (Article 5). Those candidates who obtain an absolute majority of votes in the General Assembly and in the Security Council are considered as elected (Article 10).

9. The members of the "national groups," competent to nominate the candidates which may be elected members of the International Court of Justice, are appointed by the governments concerned.

10. Article 6 of the Statute of the International Court of Justice only recommends that each national group should consult its highest court of justice, its legal faculties and schools of law, and its national academies and national

sections of international academies devoted to the study of law before making the nomination of candidates.

11. According to Article 13 of the Statute, the members of the Court are elected for nine years and may be re-elected. Their independence and impartiality is guaranteed by the following provisions: no member of the Court may exercise any political or administrative function, or engage in any other occupation of a professional nature (Article 16, paragraph 1); no member of the Court may act as agent, counsel, or advocate in any case; no member may participate in the decision of any case in which he has previously taken part as agent, counsel, or advocate for one of the parties or as a member of a national or international court, or of a commission of enquiry or in any other capacity (Article 17, paragraphs 1 and 2); no member of the Court can be dismissed unless, in the unanimous opinion of the other members, he has ceased to fulfill the required conditions (Article 18, paragraph 1). The members of the Court, when engaged on the business of the Court, enjoy diplomatic privileges and immunities (Article 19). Every member of the Court shall, before taking up its duties, make a solemn declaration in open court that he will exercise his powers impartially and conscientiously (Article 20). If, for some special reason, a member of the Court considers that he should not take part in the decision of a particular case, he shall so inform the President. If the President considers that for some special reason one of the members of the Court should not sit in a particular case, he shall give him notice accordingly. If in any such case the member of the Court and the President disagree, the matter shall be settled by the decision of the Court (Article 24). Judges who are of the nationality of the parties to the case before the Court are not excluded from sitting in the case. However, if "the Court includes upon the Bench a judge of the nationality of one of the parties, any other party may choose a person to sit as judge. Such person shall be chosen preferably from among those persons who have been nominated as candidates as provided in Articles 4 and 5. If the Court includes upon the Bench no judge of the nationality of the parties, each of these parties may proceed to choose a judge as provided in paragraph 2 of this Article" (Article 31, paragraphs 2 and 3). This is the institution of "national judges."

12. According to Article 21 of the Statute, the Court elects its President and Vice-President; they may be re-elected.

13. According to Article 55 of the Statute, all questions shall be decided by a majority of the judges present. In the event of an equality of votes, the President or the judge who acts in his place shall have a casting vote.

14. The International Court of Justice has no compulsory jurisdiction. As pointed out, the members of the United Nations, and other states which may become parties to the Statute on conditions to be determined (according to Article 93 of the Charter) by the General Assembly upon recommendation of the Security Council, are not obliged to submit disputes to the Court. But they may do so. A case may be brought before the Court by a special agreement of the parties to the dispute. In this way any dispute whatsoever may be submitted to the Court. Such a special agreement is not necessary and the case may be brought before the Court by a written application addressed by one party to the Court (Article 40, paragraph 1), if the parties to the dispute have previously made a declaration determined in Article 36, paragraph 2, of the Statute, which provides: "The states parties to the present Statute may at any time declare that they recognize as compulsory *ipso facto* and without special agreement, in relation to any other state accepting the same obligation, the jurisdiction of the Court in all legal disputes concerning: a. the interpretation of a

treaty; b. any question of international law; c. the existence of any fact which, if established, would constitute a breach of an international obligation; d. the nature or extent of the reparation to be made for the breach of an international obligation". This declaration "may be made unconditionally or on condition of reciprocity on the part of several or certain states, or for a certain time" (Article 36, paragraph 3).

The jurisdiction of the Court recognized by a declaration made under Article 36, paragraph 2, of the Statute is not a true compulsory jurisdiction as it is called in this article, for if a state which has made such a declaration brings a dispute with another state before the Court by a unilateral application in conformity with Article 40 of the Statute, the other party is obliged to recognize the jurisdiction of the Court only if it, too, has made the same declaration. This means that the jurisdiction of the Court in this case is based, not on a special agreement referring to this concrete case, but on a general agreement of the parties to the dispute constituted by their declarations made under Article 36, paragraph 2. Declarations under Article 36, paragraph 2, of the Statute have been made by several states, some of them under reservations which deprive them of almost all practical value.

Thus, e. g., the United States recognized the jurisdiction of the Court in disputes concerning the matters enumerated in Article 36, paragraph 2, of the Statute "*Provided*, that this declaration shall not apply to (a) disputes the solution of which the parties shall entrust to other tribunals by virtue of agreements already in existence or which may be concluded in the future; or (b) disputes with regard to matters which are essentially within the domestic jurisdiction of the United States of America as determined by the United States of America; or (c) disputes arising under a multilateral treaty, unless (1) all parties to the treaty affected by the decision are also parties to the case before the Court, or (2) the United States of America specially agrees to jurisdiction; and *Provided further*, that this declaration shall remain in force for a period of five years and thereafter until the expiration of six months after notice may be given to terminate this declaration." That the jurisdiction of a court recognized under these reservations is not "compulsory" is quite evident.

15. According to Article 34, paragraph 1, of the Statute, only states may be parties before the International Court of Justice.

16. Article 38 of the Statute of the International Court of Justice provides: "1. The Court, whose function is to decide in accordance with international law such disputes as are submitted to it, shall apply: a. international conventions, whether general or particular, establishing rules expressly recognized by the contesting states; b. international custom, as evidence of a general practice accepted as law; c. the general principles of law recognized by civilized nations; d. subject to the provisions of Article 59, judicial decision and the teachings of the most highly qualified publicists of the various nations, as subsidiary means for the determination of rules of law. 2. This provision shall not prejudice the power of the Court to decide a case *ex aequo et bono*, if the parties agree thereto."

That the Court has to apply the existing conventional and customary law (clauses [a] and [b]) is self-evident and did not need to be stipulated. As to "the general principles of law recognized by civilized nations" (clause [c]), it is doubtful whether such principles common to the legal orders of the civilized nations exist at all, especially in view of the ideological antagonism which separates the communist from the capitalist and the autocratic from the democratic legal systems. If the Court assumes that a general principle of law recognized by civilized nations exists, the question of under what conditions the Court is supposed to apply this principle to the case at hand arises. If there is a treaty to which the states involved in the dispute are contracting parties, and if the treaty refers to the dispute, the treaty is to be applied (clause [a]). If there is no treaty, general customary international law is to be applied (clause [b]). This, as pointed out, is always possible, but clause (c) evidently presupposes the idea that there are gaps in international law. This means that the Court is authorized to apply a rule which the Court considers to be a general principle of law in case the Court deems the application of particular conventional or general customary international law not to be satisfactory, which implies an almost unlimited discretion on the part of the Court.

It is, however, doubtful whether the framers of the Statute really intended to confer such an extraordinary power upon the Court. Article 38, paragraph 1, expressly stipulates that the function of the Court is "to decide in accordance with international law."

Hence, it might be argued that "the general principles of law" are applicable only if they are part of international law, and that means part of the law referred to in clauses (a) and (b) of Article 38. Then, clause (c) is superfluous. Clause (d) does not refer to rules of international law to be applied by the Court; it establishes only a principle of interpretation. Article 59, to which clause (d) refers, stipulates that the decision of the Court has binding force only between the parties and only in respect to the particular case. Hence, a decision of the Court cannot have the character of a precedent.

17. *Cf.* pp. 16, 31 f. The Charter of the United Nations, just as the Covenant of the League of Nations, only recommends to the members that they refer their legal disputes to a judicial procedure. Article 13 of the Covenant provided: "1. The Members of the League agree that, whenever any dispute shall arise between them which they recognize to be suitable for submission to arbitration *or judicial settlement*, and which can not be satisfactorily settled by diplomacy, they will submit the whole subject-matter to arbitration *or judicial settlement*. 2. Disputes as to the interpretation of a treaty, as to any question of international law, as to the existence of any fact which, if established, would constitute a breach of any international obligation, or as to the extent and nature of the reparation to be made for any such breach, are declared to be among those which are generally suitable for submission to arbitration *or judicial settlement*. 3. *For the consideration of any such dispute, the court to which the case is referred shall be the Permanent Court of International Justice, established in accordance with Article 14, or any tribunal agreed on by the parties to the dispute or stipulated in any convention existing between them.* 4. The Members of the League agree that they will carry out in full good faith any award *or decision* that may be rendered, and that they will not resort to war against a Member of the League which complies therewith. In the event of any failure to carry out such an award *or decision*, the Council shall propose what steps should be taken to give effect thereto."

Article 36 of the Charter stipulates: "1. The Security Council may, at any stage of a dispute of the nature referred to in Article 33 or of a situation of like nature, recommend appropriate procedures or methods of adjustment. 2. The Security Council should take into consideration any procedures for the settlement of the dispute which have already been adopted by the parties. 3. In making recommendations under this Article the Security Council should also take into consideration that legal disputes should as a general rule be referred by the parties to the International Court of Justice in accordance with the provisions of the Statute of the Court."

As to the definition of legal disputes, Article 36, paragraph 2, of the Statute (*cf.* p. 191) follows Article 13, paragraph 2, of the Covenant.

18. *Cf.* p. 191.

19. *Cf.* pp. 19 f.

20. *Cf.*, Morgenthau, *op. cit.*, pp. 400–10.

21. Under the Covenant of the League of Nations, the enforcement of judicial decisions against a recalcitrant party was left to the other party. The Council had the power only to make recommendations. Article 13, paragraph 4, stipulated: "The Members of the League agree that they will carry out in full good faith any award or decision that may be rendered, and that they will not resort to war against a Member of the League which complies therewith. In the event of any failure to carry out such an award or decision, the Council shall propose what steps should be taken to give effect thereto." Enforcement measures to be taken as reactions against violations of the Covenant (Article 16) were not to be preceded by a judicial decision.

The Charter of the United Nations stipulates: "Article 94. 1. Each Member of the United Nations undertakes to comply with the decision of the International Court of Justice in any case to which it is a party. 2. If any party to a case fails to perform the obligations incumbent upon it under a judgment rendered by the Court, the other party may have recourse to the Security Council, which may, if it deems necessary, make recommendations or decide upon measures to be taken to give effect to the judgment."

The Security Council is only authorized, not obliged, to enforce the judgment of the Court. Instead of enforcing the judgment of the Court, the Council may even settle the dispute concerned by a recommendation made in accordance with principles of political convenience. As far as decisions of other tribunals are concerned (Article 95), the Security Council has no competence, but it may consider non-compliance with such a decision as a threat to the peace and take enforcement measures in conformity with Article 39.

22. *Cf.* pp. 121 f.

(cc) *The peaceful change of legally established international relations.*

Closely connected to the problem of the peaceful settlement of international disputes is a problem which is usually presented as the peaceful change of legally established international relations. If the relations are established by international agreements, one speaks of the revision of treaties. It is a widespread view that, in order to prevent war, an international security organization should have institutions to alter situations which are so unbearable to one or the other state that they may endanger the peace. If the dangerous situation manifests itself in a concrete dispute between two states, the problem may be solved by settling the dispute in one of the ways just described. However, such a situation may exist without materializing as a concrete dispute. The situation may have a more or less general character, with not only one or two but many states being involved in it as a consequence of the actual status of general international law, although the situation becomes an imminent danger to the peace only in the relation between two definite states. In this event, the only radical solution of the problem lies in a change of the general rules of international law which are at the basis of the situation. This is possible under existing international law only by a general agreement, and to reach such an agreement is so difficult that it is practically out of the question. Only an international legislative organ competent to adopt general rules of law by a majority vote decision could fulfil such a function. If only two states are involved in the situation, especially if the situation is constituted by a treaty concluded by these states, the problem is not the changing of a general rule of international law but the altering or abolishing of a concrete obligation of one state and the corresponding right of the other. This is possible under existing law only by an agreement of the states concerned, but it is just the fact that such an agreement cannot be reached that creates the danger to the peace. If the constitutent treaty of a security organization should institute a legislative organ—that is, an agency composed of representatives of all or some of its members, competent to adopt by a majority vote decision general rules of law binding upon the members—the organization would assume the character of a super-state, and it is more than likely that for the time being most states, and particularly the great powers, would refuse to become parties to such a treaty. Only an organ with a power restricted to altering or abolishing the concrete obligation and the corresponding right of a definite state has a chance, and even then only a very modest chance, of being accepted as an institution of an international security organization. This organ may be the assembly of the organization, composed of representatives of all the members; or its council, composed only of representatives of some of them; or it may be a special organ established for this particular purpose and composed in a way similar to the assembly or the council. The organ may act on its own initiative or only if it is requested to act by a party. The more important question is whether it may adopt its decision, binding upon the parties, by a majority vote or whether unanimity is required. It stands to reason that only in the former case can an effective function of the organ be expected.[1] There can be no doubt that the establishment of an international agency endowed with the power to deprive a state of a right acquired under existing law or to impose upon a state an obligation without its consent constitutes a considerable limitation of the sovereignty of this state, and that for this reason many states will be reluctant to submit their relations with other states to the authority of such an international agency. However, they may be willing to confer this power on an international court in order to effect a peaceful change of established legal relations. Sovereignty is essentially the principle that a state can be legally bound only by, and not against, its own will, but international courts are—as a matter of fact—the only organs the procedure of which is not subjected to this principle. States do not consider their submission to the decision of an international court to be incompatible with their sovereignty. This may be due to the fact that international courts—unless expressly authorized to decide *ex aequo et bono*—are bound to apply only existing international law and hence it is assumed that their decision has a declarative, rather than a constitutive, character. They cannot abolish or create obligations and rights but can only ascertain in an authoritative way which obligations or rights a state has under the existing law. As pointed out in a previous connection,[2] this assumption is an illusion. Even in applying a general norm of positive law, a court creates new law, an individual legal norm which did not exist prior to its decision. No application of a general norm is possible without interpretation, and there is no clear borderline between a mere interpretation and an alteration of the law. The history of law shows that the most remarkable changes of the existing law have been brought about by its interpretation. This is especially true if the law-applying organ is a court of last resort endowed with compulsory jurisdiction. There can be little doubt that a court with compulsory jurisdiction, established by the constitution of an international security organization, would serve not only as a most adequate organ for a peaceful settlement of disputes but would also fulfill the function of effecting a peaceful change of established legal relations.

NOTES

1. Article 19 of the Covenant of the League of Nations stipulated: "The Assembly may from time to time advise the reconsideration by Members of the League of treaties which have become inapplicable, and the consideration of international conditions whose continuance might endanger the peace of the world." This provision proved to be entirely inefficient, first, because the Assembly had the power only to "advise" and, secondly, because unanimity was required. In Article 14, the Charter of the United Nations authorizes the General Assembly to "recommend measures for the peaceful adjustment of any situation, regardless of origin, which it deems likely to impair the general welfare or friendly relations among nations, including situations resulting from a violation of the provisions of the present Charter setting forth the Purposes and Principles of the United Nations." A decision of the General Assembly under Article 14 may be made by a two-thirds majority of the members present and voting. However, the decision is not binding upon the members; it is merely a recommendation.

2. *Cf.* pp. 17 f.

(dd) *Disarmament.*

DISARMAMENT AND SECURITY

Disarmament is not an isolated problem.[1] It is essentially connected with the problem of international security.[2] It can be solved only within an effective international security organization.[3] During the discussions of the reduction and limitation of armament which took place within the League of Nations and later within the United Nations, the relation between disarmament and security was generally recognized. In particular, the French government insisted and still insists on this aspect of the problem.[4] Resolution XIV adopted by the Assembly of the League of Nations in September, 1922, expressly ascertained the fact that "in the present state of the world many governments would be unable to accept the responsibility for a serious reduction of armaments unless they received in exchange a satisfactory guarantee of the safety of their country." This means that security is a condition of disarmament and that there can be no disarmament without security. However, on the other hand, it is no less true that there can be no perfect security without disarmament. Hence, Resolution XIV suggested the conclusion of a defensive treaty of mutual guarantee open to all states but provided that "previous consent" to a general reduction of armaments should be "the first condition for the Treaty," that is to say, the guarantee would apply only after the reduction of armaments had been carried out according to a general plan.[5] Article 1 of Lord Robert Cecil's Draft Treaty of Mutual Assistance submitted to the Permanent Advisory Committee and included in the report of the Temporary Mixed Commission of 30 August 1923 stated that if any one of the signatories was attacked, "all the others will forthwith take such action as they may respectively have agreed to take in accordance with this Treaty and any Treaty supplementary hereto, provided that this obligation shall be conditional upon the reduction of the military forces of the party attacked."[6] The Geneva Protocol[7] of 2 October 1924 (1) prohibited war in any circumstance; (2) established means for determining the aggressor whereby the aggressor should be presumed to be that state which refused to resort to arbitration, or to comply with an award, or refused to comply with the provisional measures prescribed by the Council; (3) made the applications of sanctions compulsory after the determination of the aggressor; (4) provided that all disputes should be terminated by a binding decision pronounced by the Permanent Court of International Justice, the Council of the League or a board of arbitrators. It also contained in Article 21 the following clauses: "If within such period after the adoption of the plan for the reduction of armaments as shall be fixed by the said Conference [International Conference for the Reduction of Armament, provided for in Article 17], the plan has not been carried out, the Council shall make a declaration to that effect. This declaration shall render the present Protocol null and void. . . . A signatory State which, after the expiration of the period fixed by the Conference, fails to comply with the plan adopted by the Conference, shall not be admitted to benefit by the provisions of the present Protocol." The General Assembly of the United Nations, too, recognized the relation between disarmament and security. Its Resolution 41 (I) concerning Regulation and Reduction of Armaments, adopted on 14 December 1946 contains the following statements: "The General Assembly, regarding the problem of security as closely connected with that of disarmament, recommends the Security Council to accelerate as much as possible the placing at its disposal of the armed forces mentioned in Article 43 of the Charter." [8] It must be noted that Article 43 of the Charter is still not implemented since it proved impossible to conclude the special agreements determining the contingents of the armed forces which the members were to place at the disposal of the Security Council. Hence, the security system intended by the Charter is still a fragment.

As is the case with the more general problem of international security, the problem of disarmament has two different aspects: a political aspect and a technical one. The political forces, responsible for the fact that the serious efforts during a quarter of a century to solve this problem have been without result, are well known and do not need to be discussed. The work of the League, continued by the United Nations, has shown that no insurmountable technical difficulties stand in the way of a satisfactory legal solution. With regard to the most difficult topic technically, that of the control of atomic energy, the Scientific and Technical Committee of the Atomic Energy Commission declared: "We do not find any basis in the available scientific facts for supposing the effective control [of atomic energy] is not technologically feasible." [9]

PHYSICAL DISARMAMENT

It is usual to distinguish between physical disarmament—referring to the external means by which war is waged, such as men, material and money; and moral disarmament—referring to the state of mind which tolerates and even leads to war. However, it is generally recognized that there is no physical disarmament without moral disarmament and no moral disarmament without physical disarmament.

Direct and indirect disarmament.—Physical disarmament may be brought about indirectly or directly. The indirect method consists in attempting to remove the causes of war and thus to create a situation in which disarmament will take place, so to speak, by itself.[10] As pointed out in a previous connection,[11] this is a utopian scheme. However, there is a particular cause of war upon which disarmament has a direct bearing: armament itself. There can be no doubt that armaments, although certainly not the only cause, are one of the causes of war, especially if the manufacture of war materials is in the hands of private firms.[12] This view is evidently at the basis of Article 8, paragraph 5, of the Covenant of the League of Nations: "The Members of the League agree that the manufacture by private enterprise of munitions and implements of war is open to grave objections." It has been argued that the armaments of one country are caused by and hence directed against the armaments of a definite other country. They have the immanent tendency of increasing steadily and thus of imposing a financial burden upon the respective countries. When this burden becomes unbearable it may lead to the desperate attempt by one party to unburden itself by waging war against the other in the hope of disarming the opponent and forcing him to remain disarmed, thus removing, at least for a certain time, the main cause of the financially disastrous armaments race. The principle of preventing war by armaments—the slogan generally opposed to disarmament, *si vis pacem para bellum*—is in the author's opinion rather problematical. It cannot be denied that its application may in some cases have the desired effect; but neither can it be denied that it may under certain circumstances bring about just the opposite result.[13]

If armaments are a possible cause of war, the direct method of disarmament must be considered to be appropriate. It consists of bringing about the reduction, limitation and even prohibition and elimination of armaments by an international convention imposing upon the contracting parties corresponding obligations the fulfillment of which is guaranteed by adequate measures of control and sanctions.

The object of disarmament: armaments defined.—What is the meaning of the term "armaments"? What are the facts, factors or elements constituting armaments? There are three: a *personal*, a *material* and a *financial* element: the men (effectives), the materials and establishments used by them, and the expenditures required. With respect to disarmament, the distinction between peacetime and wartime armaments is of importance in so far as reductions, limitations and prohibitions may be restricted to peacetime armaments, or those referring to wartime armaments may differ from those referring to peacetime armaments. In this respect, as far as the personal element is concerned, it is necessary to distinguish between the forces in actual service in peacetime—that is, the permanently organized armed forces—and the forces prepared for wartime—namely, the trained reserves; and, as far as the material element is concerned, to distinguish the war material and establishments actually used in peacetime from the material in reserve—that is, the stock of war material and preparations of every description undertaken with a view to war. As to the trained reserves and the material in reserve, there are two opposite views. According to one, trained reserves and material in reserve are to be considered as wartime armaments and hence not to be subject to restriction and limitation. According to the other view, they are to be considered as peacetime armaments and hence to be subject to reduction and limitation. This divergence of opinion played an important role in the disarmament discussions within the League of Nations.[14]

In addition to the forces and material used in peacetime and prepared for wartime, those ultimate war forces must be considered which are created during hostilities by means of the general resources at the disposal of each country. These resources are not themselves armaments so-called.[15] The forces of a country which can be transferred from peace to war aims are the elements which constitute the so-called war potential. In addition, there are other factors which must be taken into consideration in order to judge the war power of a nation, such as the size of the territory; the number of inhabitants; the military system—whether there is a voluntary and professional army or a conscript army based on obligatory military service; and certain imponderables such as patriotism, religious faith, internal cohesion, physical and moral courage, general and technical intelligence, tradition and strength of institutions and the like.[16] There is a strong tendency to restrict disarmament efforts to permanent peace armaments whether they are dealing with effectives, materials or expenditures, since only these factors are susceptible to effective control.[17]

The "trained reserves" may include all persons who receive military (naval, air) or pre-military training either under or not under the control of the government and so-called para-military forces, men in the service of the merchant marine and in civil aviation. Men in arms factories may also be considered as belonging to the armed forces.[18]

An important distinction is that between reducible and irreducible effectives. As "irreducible" effectives, the police force is considered to be necessary for the maintenance of internal order,[19] but the police force may be included in the total of effectives if it has one or more of the following characteristics: "(a) Arms other than individual (machine-pistols, Lewis guns, machine-guns and weapons of accompaniment, etc.); (b) Training of a military nature, other than close-order drill, physical training or technical training in the use of individual arms; (c) Transport, signalling or engineer equipment of a suitable nature and on a sufficient scale to enable it to be employed by units in tactical operations." Cases which might appear to be doubtful may be decided by taking into account the following conditions: "(i) Quartering in barracks; (ii) Training in groups of 100 men or more; (iii) Organization on a military basis; (iv) Previous military training; (v) The possession of the arms referred to in sub-paragraph (a) above in such number as to permit of the tactical employment of the forces possessing them as military units." [20]

With respect to the stationing of armed forces, those stationed in the homeland may be distinguished from those stationed overseas and those stationed in foreign countries.

War materials consist of arms (weapons), munitions and implements of war, as well as the raw material from which they are manufactured. There are three categories of arms and munitions: arms and munitions designed exclusively for land, sea and aerial warfare; arms and munitions capable of being used both for military and for other purposes; and arms and munitions having no military value. It is usual to distinguish between conventional armaments in contradistinction to atomic armaments and other armaments adopted to mass destruction.[21]

At present, arms of mass destruction are in the foreground of disarmament discussions. Arms of mass destruction are weapons "capable of destroying at a single blow a total number of human lives greatly exceeding, by a ratio to be established, those which a single conventional armament could destroy, or those which render the enemy incapable of fighting by means other than the effect of metals or of explosives." [22] In particular, disarmament discussions revolve around nuclear (atomic and hydrogen) weapons as well as the raw or source material necessary for their manufacture: uranium and thorium, whether containing or not containing other important constituents, and the nuclear fuel, whether produced for beneficial or destructive purposes. Bacterial and chemical weapons and material also occupy an important place in contemporary disarmament proposals.

In order to be effective, disarmament conventions must deal not only with the use of arms, munitions and implements of war, but also with their manufacture and trade as well as with the production of the raw material, especially the location, mining, milling and dumping of nuclear source material (uranium and thorium ores).

As war is waged on land, at sea and in the air, land, sea and air armaments may be distinguished from each other but their interdependence must not be ignored. Nevertheless, there are tendencies to restrict disarmament to one of them or to apply different principles to the three different types of armaments.[23] As a consequence of the differentiation between defensive and aggressive wars, armaments for defensive purposes may be distinguished from armaments for aggressive purposes. This distinction is of importance in so far as the aim of disarmament is considered to be to decrease the offensive power of arms, but to leave untouched the defensive power.[24] Thus, the problem arises as to how to establish a reliable method of ascertaining that a force is organized for aggression or for defense only and especially how to find a criterion to distinguish between weapons whose character is offensive and those whose character is defensive, so that only the former can be prohibited and eliminated or reduced and limited.[25] However, it has been argued that weapons of aggression *per se* do not exist, and that only weapons of mass destruction, whether tactical or strategic,[26] should be defined and abolished. As to atomic weapons, there is a divergence of opinion. According to one view, atomic weapons are weapons of mass destruction but not weapons of aggression; they may be used for defensive purposes. According to the other, atomic weapons are not weapons of defense but weapons of aggression, for they are intended not for use in the defense of one's own territories, but in foreign territories; they are a threat not so much to armies in the field as to civilian populations.[27]

A more general aspect of the problem is the distinction between the quantity and the quality of armaments and, consequently, between quantitative and qualitative disarmament—that is, between reducing and limiting only the numerical strength of the armed forces and the quantity of war material on the one hand or reducing, limiting or even prohibiting certain categories of armaments (armed forces and war material) on the other.[28]

As far as the financial aspect of disarmament is concerned, it is generally recognized that there is a certain relation between the size of armaments and the armaments expenditure—that is, the sums spent on the personal and material element of armaments, the so-called national defense expenditure or military budget. Reduction and limitation of expenditure are the most tangible proof of a reduction and limitation of armaments. This problem will be discussed later.[29]

THE AIM OF DISARMAMENT

Total or partial disarmament. There is a fundamental conflict between the view that disarmament should include not only peacetime but also wartime armaments and the view that disarmament efforts should be restricted to permanent peacetime armaments (effectives, material and expenditure) and not affect wartime armaments.[30] Restriction to peacetime armaments has been justified by the assertion that only this kind of armament is capable of effective control. For this reason, trained reserves, to be considered as part of wartime armaments, should not be prohibited or limited, and the question of war potential should not be considered.[31]

Another difference of opinion concerns the question of whether disarmament should refer to land, sea and air armaments or only to one or the other.[32]

The disarmament effort may aim at a complete abolition—that is, the prohibition and elimination—of all kinds of armaments. If successful, it would thus affect all states of the world.[33] The disarmament effort may aim only at a reduction and limitation of armaments.[34] It would thus affect only states possessing substantial armaments. Reduction presupposes a final level of armaments and especially of armed forces. The aim of reduction is to bring armaments down to a minimum, recognized as necessary, representing the final military position of each state. Limitation means that, as of a certain date, no increase in armaments and especially no increase in armed forces is permitted, and total strength and total amount of equipment is frozen at a level determined by disclosure and verification.[35]

The reduction and limitation of armaments may be combined with the complete prohibition of certain types of armaments or of specific categories of arms and their use in warfare such as nuclear weapons and other weapons adaptable to mass destruction;[36] chemical and bacterial weapons;[37] submarines,[38] tanks and large mobile guns;[39] and aircraft, especially bombers.[40]

A kind of partial disarmament is so-called geographic disarmament—that is, the limitation or prohibition of armaments and armed forces in certain definite territorial areas or the establishment of demilitarized zones.[41]

There are two reasons why total disarmament is not considered to be possible: first, the need of each state to have at its disposal a certain armed force for the maintenance of internal order—that is to say, a national police force, a so-called irreducible component; second, the necessity of sanctions, especially enforcement measures involving the use of armed force as reactions against violations of the legal order constituting the security organization and in particular as reactions against violations of the provisions concerning the reduction and limitation of armaments.[42] As long as these sanctions are to be executed by the members of the organization employing their

370624—57——14

own national armed forces, no real disarmament is possible. The establishment of an international police force—that is, an armed force at the direct disposal of the international organization and different from, as well as independent of, the armed forces of the members—is an essential condition of an effective attempt to reduce and limit the latter. The only question is whether the abolition—that is, the prohibition and elimination—of certain types of armaments or categories of arms mentioned above, must be restricted to national or may be extended to international armed forces. If the abolition were extended, certain armaments or arms, e. g., nuclear, chemical, bacterial weapons, and bombardment from the air, would be prohibited even in the execution of international sanctions. If the abolition were not extended, there would not be an absolute abolition but rather an internationalization of these types of armaments or of the production, possession, and use of such weapons. In this respect, the internationalization of military aviation plays an important part in the discussion of disarmament.[43]

Immediate, complete or gradual (progressive) disarmament. One of the most important conflicts of views in the discussion of the disarmament problem is the conflict between immediate and complete disarmament and gradual (progressive) disarmament. It is understandable that a state, and especially a great power, would be reluctant to accept the obligation of immediate disarmament because it would be afraid to become the victim of another state, especially, a great power, which would not fulfil its obligation. Hence, a plan of gradual disarmament would have a far better chance of being successful.[44] In this respect, the question arises as to the relationship between the reduction of armaments and the establishment of an effective organization for its control. There is a divergence of opinion between those who suggest that a convention for the reduction and limitation, or even for the total or partial prohibition and elimination of armaments, should precede the organization of control, and those who prefer a reverse procedure because they think it a hopeless attempt to impose upon states the obligation to disarm without having previously established a legal system guaranteeing the fulfillment of this obligation. The question of the priority of control plays a decisive role in the discussion of nuclear (atomic and hydrogen) disarmament.[45] A kind of compromise between these opposite views is the proposal to put into force a convention for the reduction and limitation of armaments and for the abolition of nuclear weapons, simultaneously with the establishment of an effective control machinery.[46]

Proportional or balanced disarmament. In contradistinction to proportional[47] reduction, the balanced reduction of armaments aims at avoiding the dangerous situation of disequilibrium between the different categories of armaments of one state and between the total armaments—and hence the war power—of different states. Only if this disequilibrium is avoided, it has been argued by the representative of France in Committee 1 of the United Nations Disarmament Commission, might countries "pass from one stage to another without any danger to or even any lessening of their security. Each intermediate step after the initial balance should be marked by increasing security until a final balance was reached in which no state could menace the life of its neighbors. Balanced reduction was inconsistent with proportional reduction. The essential task was to render war impossible. If peace was threatened by a disequilibrium between certain armaments, it was not evident how proportional reduction could lead to security."[48]

GEOGRAPHICAL DISARMAMENT

The term "geographical disarmament" has been suggested by J. H. Marshall-Cornwall[49] to designate "the restriction or prohibition of armaments and armed forces in certain definite territorial areas," that is to say, the demilitarization of particular zones of territory. There are two types of demilitarization: 1) the prohibition imposed upon states against erecting fortifications and stationing troops in certain zones of their territories in time of peace; 2) the exclusion of a certain part of state territories from any military operations in time of war.[50] The purpose of the first type of demilitarization is to prevent a future conflict by a regime maintained during time of peace. The purpose of the second is to restrict and localize hostilities once they have broken out.[51] This second type is sometimes termed the "neutralization" of a definite zone of territory (to be distinguished from the permanent neutralization of an entire state territory, such as the neutralization of Switzerland) or, to use a terminology suggested by Marshall-Cornwall, the "immunization" of a definite zone of territory from war.[52] Both types of demilitarization may be effected by international agreement or by the decision of the agency of an international security organization.

Demilitarized zones are normally placed on the frontier between two states.[53] They may be restricted to the territory of one state only, as in the case of the unilateral demilitarization of the Rhineland in the peace treaty of Versailles,[54] or they may be established on the territories of two neighboring states on both sides of their common frontier so that the demilitarized zone is determined, as

Marshall-Cornwall [55] formulates it, by three lines: the political frontier between the two states and, parallel to it and at a certain distance on either side, the boundaries of the demilitarized zone. "Although the zone boundaries are in principle parallel to and equidistant from the political frontier, they must in practice conform to the local topographic, economic, and military circumstances and must be precisely demarcated on the ground." [56]

REDUCTION AND LIMITATION OF EXPENDITURES

The reduction and limitation of armaments may be brought about not only directly by the reduction and limitation of effectives and war material but also indirectly by the reduction and limitation of the sums to be spent on armaments—that is, by the reduction and limitation of the armaments expenditures or, as it is usually termed, the national defense expenditures. This term may be defined as "all expenditure necessitated or entailed by the creation, maintenance and training in time of peace of armed forces and formations organized on a military basis and by measures immediately connected with the preparation for national mobilization." [57] Although the reduction and limitation of expenditure are the most tangible proof of the reduction and limitation of armaments, there can be little doubt that the limitation of expenditure is not in itself an adequate measure of disarmament. Hence, a combination of the reduction and limitation of effectives and war material and a reduction and limitation of expenditure is advisable.[58] There may be a limitation of the total expenditure or limitation by categories—that is, by the separate limitation of expenditure for land, sea, air armaments or the separate limitation of expenditure for effectives as distinguished from expenditure for material, the expenses in manufacture, purchase, and upkeep of weapons and other war material.[59] As far as the distinction between peacetime and wartime armaments is concerned, it would seem that budgetary limitations can be effectively established only for peacetime armaments.

Some writers hold that an essential condition for an effective limitation of expenditure is publishing the budget, either the military budget only or the total budget. Some governments which have not been in favor of budgetary limitations have wished to restrict budgetary regulations of a disarmament convention to publishing the budget. There is a divergence of opinion with respect to the question of whether budgetary limitations should be introduced immediately or should be preceded by a period of years during which only a system of budgetary publicity is established. The working of such a system would show to what extent budgetary limitation is feasible.[60] The difficulties with which the establishment of budgetary limitations is confronted are, in the main, the fluctuations in the purchasing power of currency and the differences in the budgetary systems of the different states. Consequently, unification of the military budget has been suggested.[61]

In connection with budgetary publicity and limitation, the abolition of secret funds has been suggested.

On 29 August 1955, the French government submitted to the Subcommittee of the United Nations Disarmament Commission a draft agreement on the financial supervision of disarmament and the allocation for peaceful purposes of the funds made available. In this proposal reductions of military expenditures are combined with the allocation of the funds made available by these reductions for the improvement of levels of living and the development of underdeveloped areas.[62]

DEROGATIONS

It is generally recognized that under certain circumstances a party to the disarmament convention may be permitted to go beyond the limits of armaments laid down in the convention. There is a tendency to restrict such permission to the case of an unprovoked aggression. To provide derogation for any war without any qualification whatsoever makes any limitation of armaments illusory. Other circumstances under which it has been suggested that derogation might take place are: a civil war, a threatened attack by another state, an unforeseen circumstance such as a new weapon, a radical change in military laws, a radical change in the political organization of a neighboring state, an alteration in the value of money. Such derogation may be possible only with the consent of the central organ of the security organization competent to decide the question as to whether these circumstances exist in the concrete case.[63] If the decision is left to the state concerned the provisions of the disarmament convention concerning the reduction and limitation of armaments can hardly be considered to be effective.

CONTROL

Another condition of an effective disarmament convention is an appropriate measure of control or supervision. In view of the close connection between control and sanctions it is understandable that the antagonism of opinions regarding the latter applies also to the former. There is a view that treaties rest on mutual confidence and that their fulfillment should not be supervised because any such attempt would only cause suspicion between states, while according to another view a disarmament convention which does not provide for the establishment of a well organized control system is a blank cartridge. It does not guarantee that degree of security which is a necessary prerequisite for disarmament.[64] Control implies two functions: disclosure and verification. The international control agency must get all the necessary information concerning their armaments from the states concerned and must have the power to verify them by inspection and investigation in order to know not only the declared but also the clandestine activities of the states which are parties to the disarmament convention. The term "control," especially if applied to atomic disarmament, is sometimes used in a wider sense meaning not only disclosure and verification by inspection but also certain measures constituting participation of the international control agency in the direction or management of the undertakings, especially international ownership of the material essential for the production of atomic energy.[65]

It stands to reason that full knowledge of all the facts relevant to the armaments or disarmament of states is an essential condition of all disarmament efforts. Hence, the states must be obliged to furnish the necessary information to the international control agency which may publish it.[66] This information can be verified effectively only by an inspection carried out on the territory of the state whose armaments are to be investigated. The most important question in this respect is whether such investigations should have an obligatory character with the states which as parties to the disarmament convention are obliged to allow on-the-spot inspection, or whether inspection by the international control agency should be possible only with the consent of the state concerned given in each concrete case. Inspection may be organized as a regular institution on a continuous basis, involving investigating at least once a year and whenever the control agency considers it necessary, or it may consist only of occasional investigations conducted by the control agency in case of suspicion, especially at the request of one or more members of the security organization and/or the suspected member itself. It may be conducted not only as a field inspection but also by aerial surveys and operated by a corps of technically qualified inspectors partly stationed permanently in the countries adhering to the disarmament program.[67]

The reduction and limitation of armaments are not possible without the control of the manufacture of, and the trade in, arms, ammunition, and other war material. There are two different ways of organizing this control: direct national control of manufacture and trade exercised by the government of each state within its country under the supervision of an international control agency—that is, indirect international control; or direct international control of manufacture and trade without the interposition of direct national control.

If the manufacture of arms and ammunition remains in the hands of private enterprise, it may be controlled by a system of licensing, with the licenses issued by the national government responsible for the strict handling of this system to an international control agency which must be kept informed by the national governments through detailed reports covering the production by value, number and weight of licensed private manufacture. The results of these reports should be published. Publishing the results of private manufacture is an essential element of this system.

National control of the manufacture of arms and ammunition is perfect if private manufacture is abolished and a state monopoly of manufacture established. Publicizing state manufacture is a prerequisite of its international control. The reports submitted to the international control agency may be verified by inspection on the spot, but the international control agency may be authorized to call for explanation only if it has reason to believe that the information is not reliable or, in case the national manufacture is limited by convention, that the imposed limits have been exceeded.

National control of the trade in arms and ammunition may be exercised by a system of export and import licenses to be issued by the government. As to publishing and verifying these licenses, the same principles apply as in the case of manufacture.

Direct international control of private manufacture may be exercised by a system of licenses to be issued not by the national governments but by the international control agency. International control of this phase of the armaments process reaches its highest degree in the internationalization of the manufacture of arms and ammunition. Direct international control of the trade in arms and ammunition may be exercised by having the international control agency issue export and import licenses; by completely prohibiting the export and import of war material, except that states unable to manufacture the quantities allotted to them should be permitted to import the necessary quantities from abroad; by prohibiting the export and import of certain categories of arms and ammunition, or the import to certain territories; by prohibiting the export to private persons and permitting such export only to governments. In this case, the question of the recognition of government arises which, in case of a civil war, may be answered in different ways by different authorities. The principle of publicity applies also to a direct international control of the trade in arms and ammunition. In order to be effective, inspection on the spot is indispensable.[68]

As far as the main organ competent to carry out the disarmament program is concerned, the first question is: should this organ be different from the central organ of the international security organization, and, if so, what should be the relationship between them? In view of the fact that disarmament is an essential and probably the most important function of a security system, subordinating the disarmament organ to the central security agency would seem to be adequate. If a special organ for the control of atomic energy is established, the same principle applies to the relationship between this organ and the disarmament agency. The composition of these organs may follow the patterns which have been indicated with respect to the composition of the central organ of a security organization.[69]

A highly disputed issue is that of the procedure in the disarmament agency. In particular, there is the question of whether or not the principle of the unanimity of the permanent members—the so-called veto right—should apply to the decisions of the atomic energy control agency. It seems that, with the exception of the Soviet Union and of some other communist governments, most governments agree that the application of sanctions to be directed against a state which violates its obligations under the convention concerning control of atomic energy should not be prevented by the exercise of a veto right.[70]

MORAL DISARMAMENT

Since in the course of the social evolution of civilized nations the almost general conviction has been formed that destroying human life is immoral, except as a sanction, it may be possible to bring the mass of the people to the belief that war, like murder, is a detestable crime. If this is achieved, the fundamental principle of the Charter of the United Nations may become not only the content of an international convention but also the content of the conscience of mankind. This is the ultimate goal of moral disarmament.[71]

As a means of achieving this goal, an international agreement might be concluded in which the contracting states would assume the obligation to take certain legislative and administrative measures in the fields of social and especially political life—that is, in the fields of press, broadcasting, stage, cinema and, above all, education—for the purpose of influencing public opinion in favor of the maintenance of a durable peace. The most drastic measure in this agreement would be the application of penal law to certain acts dangerous to the peace. As punishable acts of this kind the following might be considered: undertakings calculated to disturb international relations, especially those whose purpose is incitment to war; propaganda against peace; agitation with a view to exerting pressure on the government in favor of war while negotiations for the peaceful settlement of a conflict are in progress; founding or directing or even only belonging to an association whose aims are dangerous to the peace; publishing in the press false and tendentious reports on the international situation. In addition to a law providing for the punishment of those responsible for such reports, there would have to be legal provisions stipulating the right of having a reply to such reports published in the newspaper concerned or even authorizing the government to suppress the selling or spreading of the press products containing such reports. Governmental control of broadcasting, theatrical performances, and cinema shows with a view to preventing any abuse of these instruments of public opinion for the purpose of political propaganda incompatible with the idea of moral disarmament would also be necessary.

The most important means for effecting such disarmament is the organization of the education of youth and the training of teachers in a way that they may inspire the ideal of international peace and mutual respect between nations. In this connection, it would be necessary to control schoolbooks, especially those dealing with history, with a view to eliminating everything capable of arousing hatred of other peoples, and instruction in the basic principles of international law and in the organization and purposes of the United Nations would have to be compulsory.[72]

Some of these measures would constitute a radical restriction of the individual freedoms guaranteed by the constitutions of democratic states, especially the freedom of opinion and its expression. It may be very difficult to find a satisfactory compromise between this political ideal and that of moral disarmament. A still more serious difficulty confronting every intellectual movement directed against international war is the fact that, in almost all of the states of the world, there are political parties fostering a revolutionary ideology. As long as the actual circumstances of social life are such that a considerable part of the population considers, rightly or wrongly, civil war to be justifiable or even to be a necessary and inevitable means of improving their economic and political situation, the attempt to convince them that international war should be condemned under all circumstances remains problematical.

NOTES

1. *Cf.* Salvador De Madariaga, *Disarmament* (1929), pp. 217 ff.: "It is therefore hopeless to try to solve the problem of armaments in isolation from the remaining problems of the world. . . . There is only one way of solving the problem of disarmament, and that is by considering it, in the admirable French saying, as *the organization of peace.*"

2. Some modern writers in the field of international law and politics are rather sceptical about the possible effect of disarmament on international security. Stone, *op. cit.*, p. 100, speaks ironically of "the slogan 'arbitration, security and disarmament'." He agrees with the opinion that this "slogan" was "one of the reactions to the messianic view that arbitration might be a specific against war. From this aspect the insistence of the slogan that all three elements were interdependent was a brilliant diplomatic device for shaking off the hounds of pacifist idealistic public opinion." Morgenthau, *op. cit.*, pp. 383 ff., says: "At the foundation of the modern philosophy of disarmament there is the assumption that men fight because they have arms"; but, so he objects, "Men do not fight because they have arms. They have arms because they deem it necessary to fight. . . . Reducing the quantity of weapons actually or potentially available at any particular time could have no influence upon the incidence of war; it could conceivably affect its conduct. Nations limited in the quantity of arms and men would concentrate all their energies upon the improvement of the quality of such arms and men as they possess. They would, furthermore, search for new weapons that might compensate them for the loss in quantity and assure them an advantage over their competitors. The elimination of certain types of weapons altogether would have a bearing upon the technology of warfare and, through it, upon the conduct of hostilities. It is hard to see how it could influence the frequency of war or do away with war altogether." This pessimistic evaluation of a policy aiming at disarmament starts from a wrong premise. Such a policy is not necessarily based on the illusion that disarmament will have the effect of making war impossible. Its reasonable aim is to make war as a profitable enterprise more difficult, and, as far as qualitative disarmament is concerned, to make the conduct of war more human. Disarmament is not *the* condition of peace but, as Marion W. Boggs (*Attempts to Define and Limit "Aggressive" Armament in Diplomacy and Strategy.* The University of Missouri Studies, Vol. XVI, no. 1, 1941, p. 104) states, "only one among the several indispensable conditions of peace." Morgenthau admits: "Disarmament or at least regulation of armaments is an indispensable step in a general settlement of international conflicts. It can, however, not be the first step. Competition for armaments reflects, and is an instrument of, competition for power. So long as nations advance contradictory claims in the contest for power, they are forced by the very logic of the power contest to advance contradictory claims for armaments. Therefore, a mutually satisfactory settlement of the power contest is a precondition for disarmament. Once the nations concerned have agreed upon a mutually satisfactory distribution of power among themselves, they can then afford to reduce and limit their armaments. Disarmament, in turn, will contribute greatly to the general pacification." However, an agreement on "a mutually satisfactory distribution of power" necessarily implies an agreement concerning a mutually satisfactory "disarmament or at least regulation of armaments." For, as Morgenthau says (p. 27): "In international politics . . . armed strength as a threat or a potentiality is the most important material factor making for the political power of a nation." His attempt to distinguish political power from military power is of no avail. He defines political power as "the mutual relations of control among the holders of public authority" (p. 26); and by "control" he understands "a psychological relation between two minds" (p. 27). This relationship, he says, "is of the essence of political power." From this assumption he concludes that political power "must be distinguished from force in the sense of the actual exercise of physical violence." But if—as he affirms—armed strength, that is military power, is essential to political power, political power cannot be separated from military power.

On the other hand, even the "actual exercise of physical violence" implies "a psychological relation between two minds," that is, political power. Weapons, prisons, electric chairs are dead things. As instruments of military or police power they must be operated by men directed by the holders of public authority. If military power is an essential element of political power, the settlement of the power contest cannot be a precondition for disarmament, because the former is not possible without the latter.

3. The idea that disarmament is an essential element of an effective system of international security was at the basis of the Covenant of the League of Nations in which the provisions concerning disarmament were placed immediately after those concerning the organization of the League and preceded those concerning the settlement of conflicts. They read as follows:

"ARTICLE 8. 1.—The Members of the League recognize that the maintenance of peace requires the reduction of national armaments to the lowest point consistent with national safety and the enforcement by common action of international obligations. 2. The Council, taking account of the geographical situation and circumstances of each State, shall formulate plans for such reduction for the consideration and action of the several Governments. 3. Such plans shall be subject to reconsideration and revision at least every 10 years. 4. After these plans shall have been adopted by the several Governments, the limits of armaments therein fixed shall not be exceeded without the concurrence of the Council. 5. The Members of the League agree that the manufacture by private enterprise of munitions and implements of war is open to grave objections. The Council shall advise how the evil effects attendant upon such manufacture can be prevented, due regard being had to the necessities of those Members of the League which are not able to manufacture the munitions and implements of war necessary for their safety. 6. The Members of the League undertake to interchange full and frank information as to the scale of their armaments, their military, naval and air programs and the condition of such of their industries as are adaptable to warlike purposes. *Article 9.* A permanent Commission shall be constituted to advise the Council on the execution of the provisions of Articles 1 and 8 and on military, naval and air questions generally."

In this respect there is a remarkable difference between the Covenant and the Charter of the United Nations. The Charter does not, as the Covenant did, recognize that the maintenance of peace requires disarmament. It contains, however, two Articles which deal with this problem. One is Article 11, paragraph 1, which authorizes the General Assembly to "consider the general principles of cooperation in the maintenance of international peace and security, including the principles governing disarmament and the regulation of armaments" and to "make recommendations with regard to such principles to the Members or to the Security Council or to both." The other is Article 26, which runs as follows: "In order to promote the establishment and maintenance of international peace and security with the least diversion for armaments of the world's human and economic resources, the Security Council shall be responsible for formulating, with the assistance of the Military Staff Committee referred to in Article 47, plans to be submitted to the Members of the United Nations for the establishment of a system for the regulation of armaments." The Charter recognizes that a certain relationship exists between peace and disarmament, but only in so far as the maintenance of peace should be promoted with the "least diversion for armaments of the world's human and economic resources." Consequently, in the same sentences in which it refers to disarmament, it provides for the establishment of principles or the formulation of plans for the regulation of armaments.

Nevertheless, an interpretation of the Charter is possible according to which the members of the United Nations may be subjected to much stricter obligations with respect to their disarmament than were the members of the League. The latter could be obliged to disarm only under the "plan" formulated by the Council under Article 8, paragraphs 3 and 4, that is to say, the obligation of a member to reduce its own armaments could be established only with its consent. The same seems to be true with respect to Article 26 of the Charter. The "plans" formulated by the Security Council "for the establishment of a system for the regulation of armaments" may provide for reduction of armaments; they must be "submitted to the Members of the United Nations." That means that they are binding upon the members only if accepted by them. The obligation is established by a treaty concluded by the Members with the Organization. Unlike Article 8, paragraph 4, of the Covenant, Article 26 does not provide expressly for the "adoption" of the plan by the member, but if the plan of the Security Council is to be submitted to the members, it can be only for the purpose of being adopted by them. According to Article 26—if interpreted as an isolated provision of the Charter—the members are free to accept or not accept the plan formulated by the Security Council and submitted to them. The situation appears in a different light if Article 39 is taken into consideration. The fact that a member refuses to accept the plan providing for a reduction of its armament may, in the opinion of the Security Council, constitute a threat to the peace and consequently may lead directly or indirectly (through the intermediate stage of a non-accepted recommendation of the Security Council) to an enforcement action. If this measure is interpreted as a sanction and if the obligation to behave in a certain way is considered to be constituted by a sanction to be executed in case of contrary behavior, the Security Council, in submitting the plan referred to in Article 26 to a member, may impose upon it the obligation to act in conformity with this plan; in other terms, the Security Council has the power to enforce its plans for the establishment of a system for the regulation of armaments which may provide for disarmament.

The same interpretation may be applied to Article 11, paragraph 1. According to the wording of this provision, the members are free to accept or not to accept the "recommendations" made to them by the General Assembly with regard to the principles governing disarmament and the regulations of armaments. However, under Article 39, the Security Council may determine that the refusal to accept the recommendation of the General Assembly is a threat to the peace and may enforce this "recommendation." Such enforcement of the disarmament plans of the Council was impossible under the Covenant.

4. A memorandum on "French Opinion and the Problem of Collective Security" by Georges Scelle and René Cassin [*Collective Security*, pp. 66 ff.] contains the statement that: "the French government upholds the formula: security first, then disarmament or at least disarmament in proportion to the degree of security obtained," and at the 32nd meeting of the First Committee of the General Assembly of the United Nations on 3 December 1946 the representative of France declared: "It must be recognized that disarmament is impossible without security organized along parallel lines. The French position on this point between the two World Wars was well known and had been justified by subsequent events". *Journal of the United Nations*, No. 48, pp. 197–8.

5. The full text of Resolution XIV runs as follows:

"(*a*) The Assembly, having considered the report of the Temporary Mixed Commission on the question of a general Treaty of Mutual Guarantee, being of opinion that this report can in no way affect the complete validity of all the Treaties of Peace or other agreements which are known to exist between States; and considering that this report contains valuable suggestions as to the methods by which a Treaty of Mutual Guarantee could be made effective, is of the opinion that:

1. No scheme for the reduction of armaments, within the meaning of Article 8 of the Covenant, can be fully successful unless it is general. 2. In the present state of the world many Governments would be unable to accept the responsibility for a serious reduction of armaments unless they received in exchange a satisfactory guarantee of the safety of their country. 3. Such a guarantee can be found in a defensive agreement which should be open to all countries, binding them to provide immediate and effective assistance in accordance with a prearranged plan in the event of one of them being attacked, provided that the obligation to render assistance to a country attacked shall be limited in principle to those countries situated in the same part of the globe. In cases, however, where, for historical, geographical, or other reasons, a country is in special danger of attack, detailed arrangements should be made for its defense in accordance with the above-mentioned plan. 4. As a general reduction of armaments is the object of the three preceding statements, and the Treaty of Mutual Guarantee the means of achieving that object, previous consent to this reduction is therefore the first condition for the Treaty. This reduction could be carried out either by means of a general Treaty, which is the most desirable plan, or by means of partial treaties designed to be extended and open to all countries. In the former case, the Treaty will carry with it a general reduction of armaments. In the latter case, the reduction should be proportionate to the guarantees afforded by the Treaty. The Council of the League, after having taken the advice of the Temporary Mixed Commission, which will examine how each of these two systems could be carried out, should further formulate and submit to the Governments for their consideration and sovereign decision the plan of the machinery, both political and military, necessary to bring them clearly into effect.

(*b*) The Assembly requests the Council to submit to the various Governments the above proposals for their observations, and requests the Temporary Mixed Commission to continue its investigations, and, in order to give precision to the above statements, to prepare a Draft Treaty embodying the principles contained therein."

6. Cf. the *Historical Survey of the Activities of the League of Nations regarding the Questions of Disarmament 1920–1937.* United Nations, General Assembly, Doc. A/AC.50/2, 18 June 1951 (hereafter referred to as Doc. A/AC.50/2), p. 27.

7. *Cf.* pp. 85, 100.

8. The full text of Resolution 41 (I) of the General Assembly runs as follows:

"1. In pursuance of Article 11 of the Charter and with a view to strengthening international peace and security in conformity with the Purpose and Principles of the United Nations,

The General Assembly,

Recognizes the necessity of an early general regulation and reduction of armaments and armed forces.

"2. *Accordingly,*

The General Assembly,

Recommends that the Security Council give prompt consideration to formulating the practical measures, according to their priority, which are essential to provide for the general regulation and reduction of armaments and armed forces and to assure that such regulation and reduction of armaments and armed forces will be generally observed by all participants and not unilaterally by only some of the participants. The plans formulated by the Security Council shall be submitted by the Secretary-General to the Members of the United Nations for consideration at a special session of the General Assembly. The treaties or conventions approved by the General Assembly shall be submitted to the signatory States for ratification in accordance with Article 26 of the Charter.

"3. As an essential step toward the urgent objective of prohibiting and eliminating from national armaments atomic and all other major weapons adaptable now and in the future to mass destruction, and the early establishment of international control of atomic energy and other modern scientific discoveries and technical developments to ensure their use only for peaceful purposes,

The General Assembly,

Urges the expeditious fulfilment by the Atomic Energy Commission of its terms of reference as set forth in section 5 of the General Assembly resolution of 24 January 1946.

"4. In order to ensure that the general prohibition, regulation and reduction of armaments are directed towards the major weapons of modern warfare and not merely towards the minor weapons,

The General Assembly,

Recommends that the Security Council expedite consideration of the reports which the Atomic Energy Commission will make to the Security Council and that it facilitate the work of that Commission, and also that the Security Council expedite consideration of a draft convention or conventions for the creation of an international system of control and inspection, these conventions to include the prohibition of atomic and all other major weapons adaptable now and in the future to mass destruction and the control of atomic energy to the extent necessary to ensure its use only for peaceful purposes.

"5. *The General Assembly,*

Further recognizes that essential to the general regulation and reduction of armaments and armed forces, is the provision of practical and effective safeguards by way of inspection and other means to protect complying States against the hazards of violations and evasions.

Accordingly,

The General Assembly,

Recommends to the Security Council that it give prompt consideration to the working out of proposals to provide such practical and effective safeguards in connection with the control of atomic energy and the general regulation and reduction of armaments.

"6. To ensure the adoption of measures for the early general regulation and reduction of armaments and armed forces, for the prohibition of the use of atomic energy for military purposes and the elimination from national armaments of atomic and all other major weapons adaptable now or in the future to mass destruction, and for the control of atomic energy to the extent necessary to ensure its use only for peaceful purposes,

There shall be established, within the framework of the Security Council, which bears the primary responsibility for the maintenance of international peace and security, an international system, as mentioned in paragraph 4, operating through special organs, which organs shall derive their powers and status from the convention or conventions under which they are established.

"7. *The General Assembly,*

Regarding the problem of security as closely connected with that of disarmament,

Recommends the Security Council to accelerate as much as possible the placing at its disposal of the armed forces mentioned in Article 43 of the Charter;

Recommends the Members to undertake the progressive and balanced withdrawal, taking into account the needs of occupation, of their armed forces stationed in ex-enemy territories, and the withdrawal without delay of their armed forces stationed in the territories of Members without their consent freely and publicly expressed in treaties or agreements consistent with the Charter and not contradicting international agreements;

Further recommends a corresponding reduction of national armed forces, and a general progressive and balanced reduction of national armed forces.

"8. Nothing herein contained shall alter or limit the resolution of the General Assembly passed on 24 January 1946, creating the Atomic Energy Commission.

"9. *The General Assembly,*

Calls upon all Members of the United Nations to render every possible assistance to the Security Council and the Atomic Energy Commission in order to promote the establishment and maintenance of international peace and collective security with the least diversion for armaments of the world's human and economic resources."

9. Atomic Energy Commission. *Official Records.* Special Supplement. Report to the Security Council (New York, 1946), p. 37.

10. *Cf.* Madariaga, *op. cit.*, p. 84.

11. *Cf.* p. 23.

12. *Cf.* Madariaga, *op. cit.*, pp. 8 ff.

13. Madariaga, *op. cit.*, pp. 11 ff. says: " 'If you want peace, prepare for war.' That is, if you want something, get ready for the reverse of it. Such is the slogan generally opposed to disarmament efforts. Now, there was a time when circumstances may have given some practical justification to this theoretically untenable position. Nations small and sparsely distributed over unorganized territories, small armies, simple weapons, little or no international faith, unstable compacts, personal influence on international policies, may have made the method of preparedness the cheapest, safest, and most practicable, nay, the only one available. To-day, the situation is the very reverse. The world has grown small for our power and resources. Only one opinion and only one market cover the face of the earth. Wars absorb the whole population of the countries which engage in them, exact all their resources and consume all the raw materials which human ingenuity has wrung from the recesses of the earth. In this condition, preparing for war means securing indefinite stocks of food and raw materials of all kinds and/or absolute control over the sources of supply and communications. Short of that, preparing for war is a worthless slogan or a misleading falsehood. Preparedness leads therefore to the scramble for raw materials and territories, and thence to increasing causes of friction and possibilities of war."

14. Doc. A/AC.50/2, p. 40.

15. *Cf.*, *ibid.*, p. 39.

16. *Cf.*, Madariaga, *op. cit.*, pp. 42 ff.

17. *Cf.* Doc. A/AC.50/2, p. 49.

18. The Problem of pre-military training and military training given outside the army was considered by the Technical Committee of the League of Nations

Disarmament Conference in connection with the question of effectives. The Technical Committee gave the following definition of pre-military training:

"Pre-military training shall be deemed to mean all kinds of training involving military instruction given in any form whatsoever (voluntary or compulsory) to young men aged 18 years at least, prior to their possible incorporation in the armed forces."

The Technical Committee defined military training elsewhere than in the army as being training having the following principal characteristics:

"(1) Technical and tactical training in the use of individual and collective arms used in war;

(2) Training for field service in varied terrain.

In addition, individual cases will have to be examined, taking into account especially the following criteria:

(1) Training of cadres in indoor (on the map) and outdoor exercises;

(2) Use of military means of liaison and signalling."

Doc. A/AC.50/2, p. 104.

The Draft Convention adopted in the first reading by the General Commission of the League of Nations Disarmament Conference (Conf. D, 163 (1) Geneva, Sept. 22nd, 1933. *Series of League of Nations Publications* IX. Disarmament, 1935, IX/4, pp. 600 ff. [hereafter referred to as Draft Convention]), contained in Part II, Disarmament, Section 1, Effectives, the following provision: "*Article 9.* It is understood that effectives consist of: (a) all officers, officer cadets, N. C. O.s, soldiers, sailors, airmen, reservists and all other persons (such as military officials of the administrative, sanitary or veterinary services or military agents) of equivalent status who perform a day's duty in the land, sea and air armed forces; (b) Persons who perform a day's duty in police forces or similar formations under the conditions prescribed in Article 12; (c) All other persons of at least 18 years of age who receive military training under the control of the State. Military training is taken to mean any training given to persons of at least 18 years of age under the military regulations in force in each country or under regulations containing similar provisions, with a view to preparing those who receive it for performing military duty in the armed forces. The main characteristics of this training are as follows: (1) Technical and tactical training in the use of individual and other than individual arms used in war; (2) training in field service over broken ground. Furthermore, in the examination of special cases, account will be taken, in particular, of the following criteria: (1) theoretical (by map) and field training of cadres; (2) use of military methods of communication and signalling. Physical and sports training in the strict sense of the term, for whatever purpose given, shall not be regarded as military training." As to Article 12, *cf.* p. 200 and note 20.

19. According to a proposal made on 20 June 1932 by President Hoover to the General Commission of the Conference for the Reduction and Limitation of Armaments. Doc. A/AC.50/2, p. 88.

20. According to the Draft Convention, Part II, Section I, Article 12. Article 13 ran as follows: "The following naval effectives should be included among effectives of the land armed forces: (a) Effectives employed in land coast defense; (b) Marines who are normally in excess of those assigned to, or destined for, service afloat; (c) Effectives coming within the classification of similar formations (as defined in Article 12). Naval personnel serving ashore in the fleet services (training, administrative, etc.), as well as those assigned to, or destined for, service afloat, will be included in the effectives of the sea armed forces."

21. On 12 August 1948, the Commission for Conventional Armament resolved to advise the Security Council "1. that it considers that all armaments and armed forces, except atomic weapons and weapons of mass destruction, fall within its jurisdiction and that weapons of mass destruction should be defined to include atomic explosive weapons, radio-active material weapons, lethal chemical and biological weapons, and any weapons developed in the future which have characteristics comparable in destructive effect to those of the atomic bomb or other weapons mentioned above. 2. that it proposes to proceed with its work on the basis of the above definition." Doc. S/C.3/32/Rev. 1. 18 August 1948.

22. This definition was formulated by the representatives of France in Committee 1 of the United Nations Disarmament Commission on 4 April 1952. United Nations Disarmament Commision. *Official Records.* Special Supplement No. 1. Second Report of the Disarmament Commission (hereafter referred to as Second Report of the United Nations Disarmament Commission), pp. 49–50.

23. Treaties on limitation of naval armaments are: the Treaty signed by the United States of America, Great Britain, France, Italy and Japan at Washington on 6 February 1922; the Treaty signed by the same Parties at London on 22 April 1930; the Treaty signed by the United States of America, France and Great Britain at London on 25 March 1936; the Agreement concerning Limitation of Naval Armament and the Exchange of Information concerning Naval Construction between Great Britain and Germany, London, 17 July 1937; and the Agreement signed at the same date between Great Britain and the Soviet Union.

24. *Cf.* Doc. A/AC.50/2, p. 68.

25. *Cf.* Boggs, *op. cit.*, *passim* and p. 99.

26. Second Report of the United Nations Disarmament Commission, p. 50.

27. *Ibid.*, pp. 50, 59.

28. Boggs, *op. cit.*, pp. 13 f.: "When quantitative disarmament is applied, the absolute magnitude of the various categories of the armed forces is fixed at certain levels, all forces in excess of that limit being disbanded or destroyed, and their re-establishment prohibited. This involves at the outset definition of an armament ratio, or determination of the relative quantities of armaments permitted to various states after the entry into force of a disarmament convention." The qualitative principle "involves the abolition or reduction, or alternatively, the internationalization in a world police force, of those classes of weapons and forms of military organization deemed 'aggressive,' or 'offensive,' or of greater utility to the attack than to the defense."

29. *Cf.* pp. 206 f.

30. In its report to the Assembly of the League of Nations on 7 September 1922 the Temporary Mixed Commission established by the Council on 25 February 1921 laid down the principle that limitation of armaments must be based on peacetime strength. *Cf.* Doc. A/AC.50/2, p. 16.

31. Principles at the basis of the French Draft Convention submitted to the Preparatory Commission on 23 March 1927. *Cf.* Doc. A/AC.50/2, pp. 49–50; *Cf. also loc. cit.*, p. 39.

32. The first concrete proposal for disarmament considered by the Temporary Mixed Commission and submitted by Lord Esher (United Kingdom) suggested a definite scale of reduction of peace effectives to be adopted by the various governments of Europe and was based on a fixed ratio of standing military and air forces. It did not refer to sea armament. *Cf.* Madariaga, *op. cit.*, p. 89, and Doc. A/AC.50/2, p. 16.

370624—57——15

33. At the fourth session of the Preparatory Commission for the Disarmament Conference (established on 12 December 1925 by the Council of the League of Nations) which opened on 30 November 1927 the delegation of the U.S.S.R. proposed measures for the complete and immediate abolition of all land, naval and air forces along the following lines: "(a) The dissolution of all land, sea and air forces and the non-admittance of their existence in any concealed form whatsoever; (b) The destruction of all weapons, military supplies, means for chemical warfare and all other forms of armament and means of destruction in the possession of troops or in military or general stores; (c) The scrapping of all warships and military air vessels; (d) The discontinuance of calling up citizens for military training either in armies or public bodies; (e) Legislation for the abolition of military service, either compulsory, voluntary or recruited; (f) Legislation prohibiting the calling-up of trained reserves; (g) The destruction of fortresses and naval and air bases; (h) The scrapping of military plans and factories and of war industry equipment in general industrial works; (i) The discontinuance of assigning funds for military purposes both on State budgets and those of public bodies; (k) The abolition of military, naval and air ministeries, and the dissolution of general staffs and military administrations, departments and institutions of every kind; (l) The legislative prohibition of military propaganda and military training of the population and of military education both in State and public bodies; (m) The legislative prohibition of the patenting of all kinds of armaments and means of destruction with a view to the removal of incentives to the invention of the same; (n) Legislation making the infringement of any of the above stipulations a grave crime against the State; (o) The withdrawal or corresponding alteration of all legislative acts, both of national or international scope, infringing the above stipulations." Doc. A/AC.50/2, pp. 51–2.

34. The President of the League of Nations Preparatory Commission, opening the general discussion of the problem of disarmament on 21 March 1927 declared that the Commission's task was to consider reduction of armaments and not "disarmament" which has a false ring, as in the present state of affairs it must be regarded as difficult of achievement. Doc. A/AC.50/2, p. 47.

35. Second Report of the United Nations Disarmament Commission, p. 50.

36. Resolution 1 (I) of the General Assembly concerning the establishment of the Atomic Energy Commission, adopted on 24 January 1946, provided: "The Commission shall proceed with the utmost despatch and enquire into all phases of the problem, and make such recommendations from time to time with respect to them as it finds possible. In particular, the Commission shall make specific proposals: (a) for extending between all nations the exchange of basic scientific information for peaceful ends; (b) for control of atomic energy to the extent necessary to ensure its use only for peaceful purposes; (c) for the elimination from national armaments of atomic weapons and of all other major weapons adaptable to mass destruction; (d) for effective safeguards by way of inspection and other means to protect complying States against the hazards of violations and evasions.—The work of the Commission should proceed by separate stages, the successful completion of each of which will develop the necessary confidence of the world before the next stage is undertaken." And in Resolution 808 (IX), adopted on 4 November 1954, the General Assembly, "Reaffirming the responsibility of the United Nations for seeking a solution of the disarmament problem . . . . 1. Concludes that a further effort should be made to reach agreement on comprehensive and coordinated proposals to be embodied in a draft international disarmament convention providing for: (a) The regulation, limitation and major reduction

of all armed forces and all conventional armaments; (b) The total prohibition of the use and manufacture of nuclear weapons and weapons of mass destruction of every type, together with the conversion of existing stocks of nuclear weapons for peaceful purposes; (c) The establishment of effective international control, through a control organ with rights, powers and functions adequate to guarantee the effective observance of the agreed reductions of all armaments and armed forces and the prohibition of nuclear and other weapons of mass destruction, and to ensure the use of atomic energy for peaceful purposes only;—The whole programme to be such that no State would have cause to fear that its security was endangered . . ."

37. The Protocol for the Prohibition of the Use in War of Asphyxiating, Poisonous or other Gases and of Bacteriological Methods of Warfare signed at Geneva 17 June 1925 contains the following provisions: "Whereas the use in war of asphyxiating, poisonous or other gases, and of all analogous liquids, materials or devices, has been justly condemned by the general opinion of the civilized world; and whereas the prohibition of such use has been declared in Treaties to which the majority of Powers of the world are Parties; and to the end that this prohibition shall be universally accepted as a part of International Law, binding alike the conscience and the practice of nations; [the signatories] declare: That the High Contracting Parties, so far as they are not already Parties to Treaties prohibiting such use, accept this prohibition, agree to extend this prohibition to the use of bacteriological methods of warfare and agree to be bound as between themselves according to the terms of this declaration.—The High Contracting Parties will exert every effort to induce other States to accede to the present Protocol. Such accession will be notified to the Government of the French Republic, and by the latter to all signatory and acceding Powers, and will take effect on the date of the notification by the Government of the French Republic."

The League of Nations Preparatory Commission for the Disarmament Conference adopted on 23 April 1929 the following text to be included in a draft convention on disarmament: "The High Contracting Parties undertake, subject to reciprocity, to abstain from the use in war of asphyxiating, poisonous or similar gases and of all analogous liquids, substances or processes. They undertake unreservedly to abstain from the use of all bacteriological methods of warfare." Doc. A/AC.50/2, p. 57.

The Draft Convention contained in Part IV.—Chemical Warfare, among others, the following provisions: "Article 47. The following provision is accepted as an established rule of International Law: The use of chemical, incendiary or bacterial weapons as against any State, whether or not a party to the present Convention, and in any war, whatever its character, is prohibited. This provision does not, however, deprive any party which has been the victim of the illegal use of chemical or incendiary weapons of the right to retaliate, subject to such conditions as may hereafter be agreed." "Article 51. All preparations for chemical, incendiary or bacterial warfare shall be prohibited in time of peace as in time of war."

A United States Working Paper (DC/15) setting forth a summary of proposals made by the United States representative in the United Nations Disarmament Commission on 15 August 1952 contains the following passage: "It is proposed that appropriate stages in an effective system of disclosure and verification agreed measures should become effective providing for the progressive curtailment of production, the progressive dismantling of plants, and the progressive destruction of stockpiles of bacterial weapons and related appliances. Under this programme, with co-operation in good faith by the principal States concerned, all bacterial weapons and all facilities and appliances connected therewith should be completely eliminated from national armaments and their use prohibited." Second Report of the Disarmament Commission, pp. 154–5.

38. On 22 February 1932 the United Kingdom submitted to the League of Nations Conference for the Reduction and Limitation of Armaments the prohibition and abolition of submarines as a humanitarian measure. Doc. A/AC.50/2, p. 83.

39. On 22 June 1932 the United States delegation proposed the abolition of all tanks, of chemical warfare and of large mobile guns to the Conference. Doc. A/AC.50/2, p. 88.

40. The United Kingdom draft convention submitted to the League of Nations Conference for the Reduction and Limitation of Armaments provided for the complete abolition of bombing from the air except for police purposes in certain outlying regions. It was recognized that a complete abolition of military and naval aircraft must depend on an effective supervision of civil aviation. Doc. A/AC.50/2, p. 106.

41. *Cf.* pp. 205 f.

42. On 24 April 1952 the representative of the United States submitted to the United Nations Disarmament Commission proposals entitled "Essential Principles for a disarmament programme" (DC/C.1/1). Point 3, referring to the goal of disarmament, reads as follows: "To reach and keep this goal, international agreements must be entered into by which all States would reduce their armed forces to levels, and restrict their armaments to types and quantities, necessary for (a) The maintenance of internal security, (b) Fulfilment of obligations of States to maintain peace and security in accordance with the United Nations Charter." Second Report of the Disarmament Commission, p. 63. *Cf.* note 46.

During the debate on the program of work in committee 1 of the United Nations Disarmament Commission, the representative of France declared the forces strictly necessary to a state within the framework of a collective security system may be determined as follows: "(a) police forces required for the security of metropolitan territory; (b) forces required for the security of geographically separated dependent territories; (c) reserves for the foregoing forces, and (d) forces to be placed at the disposal of the United Nations." Second Report of the United Nations Disarmament Commission, p. 51.

43. The Report on *International Sanctions* contains, on p. 125, the following statements: "Many believers in the idea of an international police have been led to concentrate on the air arm by a knowledge of the tremendous advance that has been made in the technique of aviation since this weapon was first employed for military purposes in the Great War. The greatest preoccupation in the minds of governments and peoples to-day is fear of an attack from the air—an attack which can be launched at almost a moment's notice, which can strike immediately at the heart of a nation, and against which many military experts and responsible statesmen have declared there can be no sure defence. It is felt that the danger of such an attack can be removed only by the abolition of national air forces, but that nations cannot be expected to renounce the use of the air weapon unless they are assured of the support of an international air force in case of unprovoked aggression on their territory."

44. On 24 March 1928 the Preparatory Commission for the League of Nations Disarmament Conference adopted the following resolution: "The Preparatory Commission for the Disarmament Conference: Having examined the bases of the Draft Convention for Immediate, Complete and General Disarmament sub-

mitted by the Union of Socialist Soviet Republics, notes that the immense majority of its members are of opinion that this draft, while in harmony with the ideals of mankind, is under existing world conditions incapable of being carried into execution, that it can only be realized when international organization is strengthened in respect both of methods of pacific procedure and the system of sanctions, and that, consequently, the said draft cannot be accepted by the Commission as a basis for its work, which work must be pursued along the lines already mapped out." Doc. A/AC.50/2, pp. 54, 55. On 19 April 1932 the General Commission of the Disarmament Conference, created on 8 February 1932, adopted the following resolution: "In view of the opinions expressed during the discussion at the Conference for the Reduction and Limitation of Armaments, the General Commission considers that the reduction of armaments, as provided for in Article 8 of the Covenant of the League of Nations, shall, after this Conference has taken the first decisive step of general reduction to the lowest possible level, be progressively achieved by means of successive revisions at appropriate intervals.' *Loc. cit.* p. 89.

In a draft resolution submitted to the Subcommittee of the UN Disarmament Commission (Doc. DC/SC. 1/15/Rev. 1, 8 March 1955, and DC/SC. 1/22, 1 April 1955), Canada, France, the United Kingdom and the United States suggested that the disarmament program should be carried out in the following stages:

"I. After the constitution and positioning of the control organ which shall be carried out within a specified time, and as soon as the control organ reports that it is able effectively to enforce them, the following measures shall enter into effect: (a) conventional armament and overall military manpower shall be limited to levels existing on 31 December 1954, or such other date as may be agreed at the World Disarmament Conference, (b) overall military expenditure, both atomic and nonatomic, shall be limited to amounts spent in the year ending 31 December 1954, or such other date as may be agreed at the World Disarmament Conference.

II. As soon as the control organ reports that it is able effectively to enforce them, the following measures shall enter into effect: (a) one-half of the agreed reductions of conventional armaments and armed forces shall take effect; (b) on completion of (a): the manufacture of all kinds of nuclear weapons and all other prohibited weapons shall cease.

III. As soon as the control organ reports that it is able effectively to enforce them, the following measures shall enter into effect: (a) The second half of the agreed reductions of conventional armaments and armed forces shall take effect; (b) On completion of (a): i. The total prohibition and elimination of nuclear weapons and the conversion of existing stocks of nuclear materials for peaceful purposes shall be carried out; ii. The total prohibition and elimination of all other prohibited weapons shall be carried out; The measures mentioned in subparagraphs II and III above shall be accompanied by consequent reductions in over-all military expenditure."

Second Report of the Subcommittee of the Disarmament Commission, Annexes 4 and 11.

On 4 May 1956, Canada, France, the United Kingdom and the United States of America submitted to the Subcommittee of the Disarmament Commission a Declaration (DC/SC.1/46), which contains the following statements: "(1) The programme [of disarmament] should proceed by stages. Progress from one state to another must depend upon the satisfactory execution of the preceding stage and upon the development of confidence through the settlement of major political problems. (2) The programme should begin, under effective international control, with significant reductions in armed forces, to such levels as are feasible in present unsettled world conditions. There should be corresponding reductions in conventional armaments and in military expenditures. Further reductions would be carried out as world conditions improved. (3) The programme should provide that, at an appropriate stage and under proper safeguards, the build-up of stockpiles of nuclear weapons would be stopped and all future production of nuclear material devoted to peaceful uses. (4) The programme should provide for a strong control organization with inspection rights, including aerial reconnaissance, operating from the outself and developing in parallel with the disarmament measures. The control measures should also provide against major surprise attack. This is particularly important so long as it is impossible to account for past production of nuclear material. (5) Preliminary demonstrations of inspection methods on a limited scale would help to develop an effective control system and could bring nearer agreement on a disarmament programme. (6) Provision should be made for the suspension of the programme, in whole or in part, if a major State failed to carry out its obligations or if a threat to peace under Chapter VII of the United Nations Charter should occur." Third Report of the Sub-Committee of the Disarmament Commission (Doc. DC/83, 4 May 1956), Annex 10.

45. In its Third Report, adopted on 17 May 1948 (AEC/31), the Atomic Energy Commission declared that it had reached an impasse in its work caused by the fact that the U. S. S. R. held that a convention outlawing atomic weapons and providing for the destruction of existing weapons must precede any control agreement on the ground that the prohibition of atomic weapons would be the only valid reason for the establishment of a control system, whereas the majority of the Commission considered that such a convention, without safeguards, would offer no protection against non-compliance.

46. The majority of the members of the United Nations was always of the opinion that effective control is an essential condition of reduction and limitation of armaments and especially of the prohibition of nuclear weapons. Resolution 192 (III), adopted by the General Assembly on 19 November 1948, contains the statement "that the aim of the reduction of conventional armaments and armed forces can only be attained in an atmosphere of real and lasting improvement in international relations, which implies in particular the application of control of atomic energy involving the prohibition of the atomic weapon." In Resolution 299 (IV) adopted on 23 November 1949, the General Assembly "Calls upon Governments to do everything in their power to make possible, by the acceptance of effective international control, the effective prohibition and elimination of atomic weapons"; and in Resolution 290 (IV) adopted on 1 December 1949, the General Assembly "Calls upon every nation" "To agree to the exercise of national sovereignty jointly with other nations to the extent necessary to attain international control of atomic energy which would make effective the prohibition of atomic weapons and assure the use of atomic energy for peaceful purposes only." By resolution 502 (VI) adopted by the General Assembly on 11 January 1952 the Atomic Energy Commission was dissolved and the Disarmament Commission of the United Nations established. In this resolution the General Assembly declared that "in a system of guaranteed disarmament there must be progressive disclosure and verification on a continuing basis of all armed forces—including para-military, security and police forces—and all armaments including atomic"; and that the implementation of this disclosure and verification "is recognized as a *first and indispensable step in carrying out the disarmament programme envisaged in the present resolution*" (Italics supplied). In its Resolution

914 (X), adopted on 16 December 1955, the General Assembly declared that "a control system" "is the keystone to any disarmament agreement."

47. On 23 March 1928 the delegation of the U.S.S.R. submitted to the Preparatory Commission for the League of Nations Disarmament Conference a draft convention for the reduction of armaments, the principles of which were stated by the representatives of the U.S.S.R. on 17 April 1929 as follows: "(1) The substantial reduction of existing armaments; (2) the carrying out of reduction on proportional principles, with certain deviations in favour of less protected and smaller countries; (3) the establishment at once of a coefficient for proportional reduction." In response, the Commission declared on 19 April 1929 that it "has not seen its way to adhere to the method of reduction based on the proportional principle" and to accept "numerical coefficients for the reduction of armaments" constituting this method. (Doc. A/AC.50/2, p. 55) The Resolution 502 (VI) adopted by the General Assembly of the United Nations on 11 January 1952 required a "balanced" reduction of all armed forces and all armaments.

48. The representative of France declared also: "The security of a State or group of States was indivisible. Effectives and conventional armaments could not be separated from atomic armaments because the latter contributed to national security as long as they were not prohibited. Proportional reduction could not be considered since there was neither—(1) equilibrium between atomic armaments nor (2) equilibrium between conventional armaments and armed forces. The existing disequilibrium in one area compensated for the disequilibrium in the other. The U.S.S.R. proposals for prohibition of atomic weapons and proportional reductions of conventional weapons would reduce the security of some instead of increasing the security of all. The only way to meet the problem was to group atomic and conventional elements and to take the precarious initial balance resulting from the excess of atomic bombs on one side, and the excess of divisions on the other, as a point of departure. If there were an excess of one thousand atomic bombs on one side and an excess of one hundred divisions on the other, the suppression of the atomic bomb should involve the dissolution of the hundred divisions. By this means a first balanced reduction would have been effected with a general increase of security. After that, matters would be simpler, since all armaments would be conventional. Reduction might take place in three stages, in each of which each country would reduce its arms by one-third of the difference between the minimum levels set for it and the forces existing on the completion of the first reduction." Second Report of the United Nations Disarmament Commission, pp. 51, 52.

On 28 May 1952 France, the United Kingdom and the United States submitted to the United Nations Disarmament Commission a Working Paper setting forth proposals for fixing numerical limitations of all armed forces. (United Nations Disarmanent Commission Doc. DC/10, 28 May 1952.) It contained the following working formula fixing numerical ceilings for China, France, the Union of Soviet Socialist Republics, the United Kingdom, and the United States of America:

"(a) There should be fixed numerical ceilings for China, France, the Union of Soviet Socialist Republics, the United Kingdom, and the United States of America which should be worked out with a view to avoiding a disequilibrium of power dangerous to international peace and security among themselves or with other States and thus reducing the danger of war. It is tentatively suggested that the maximum ceilings for the Union of Soviet Socialist Republics, the United

States of America and China should be the same and fixed, at, say, between 1 million and 1.5 million, and the maximum ceilings for the United Kingdom and France should be the same and fixed at, say, between 700,000 and 800,000.

(b) For all other States having substantial armed forces there should be agreed maximum ceilings fixed in relation to the ceilings agreed upon for the Five Powers. Such ceilings should be fixed with a view to avoiding a disequilibrium of power dangerous to international peace and security in any area of the world and thus reducing the danger of war. The ceilings would normally be less than one per cent of the population. Moreover, they should be less than current levels except in very special circumstances."

A Supplement to this Working Paper (DC/12, 12 August 1952) reads as follows:

"I. It is contemplated that any agreement for the numerical limitation of armed forces would necessarily comprehend:

(a) provisions to ensure that production of armaments and quantities of armaments bear a direct relation to the amounts needed for permitted armed forces;

(b) provisions for composition of permitted armed forcas and armaments in order to prevent undue concentration of total permitted armed forces in a manner which might prejudice a balanced reduction;

(c) procedures in conformity with the directive contained in paragraph 6 (b) of General Assembly Resolution 502 (VI) of 11 January 1952, for the negotiation within overall limitations of mutually agreed programmes of armed forces and armaments with a view to obtaining early agreement on these matters among States with substantial military resources.

Procedures should be worked out to facilitate the development under the auspices of the Disarmament Commission, of mutually agreed programmes of armed forces and armaments to be comprehended within the treaty or treaties referred to in General Assembly Resolution 502 (VI) of 11 January 1952.

II. One possible procedure, advanced for the purpose of initiating discussions, might be:

(a) Upon acceptance of the proposals set forth in Working Paper DC/10 with respect to fixing numerical limitation of all armed forces, arrangements might be made for a conference between China, France, Union of Soviet Socialist Republics, United Kingdom and the United States of America with a view to reaching tentative agreement among themselves, by negotiation, on:

(1) the distribution by principal categories of the armed forces that they would consider necessary and appropriate to maintain within the agreed numerical ceilings proposed for their armed forces;

(2) the types and quantities of armaments which they would consider necessary and appropriate to support permitted armed forces within the proposed numerical ceilings;

(3) the elimination of all armed forces and armaments other than those expressly permitted, it being understood that provision will be made for the elimination of all major weapons adaptable to mass destruction, and for the effective international control of atomic energy to ensure the prohibition of atomic weapons and the use of atomic energy for peaceful purposes only.

The distribution of armed forces within stated categories and the types and volumes of armaments would not necessarily be identic, even for States with substantially equal aggregate military strength, inasmuch as their needs and responsibilities may be different. The objective of the agreements would be to reduce the possibility and fear of aggression and to avoid a disequilibrium of power dangerous to international peace and security. Such agreements would necessarily be tentative, as they would have to be reviewed in the light of further tentative agreements to be reached, as indicated in the following paragraph.

(b) When tentative agreement is attained at the conference referred to in paragraph II (a), regional conferences might be held, to be attended by all governments and authorities having substantial military forces in the respective regions, for the purpose of reaching similar tentative agreement on

(1) the overall numerical ceilings for the armed forces of all such governments and authorities, as proposed in paragraph 5 (b) of the Tripartite Working Paper on numerical limitations,

(2) the distribution of the permitted armed forces within stated categories,

(3) the type and volume of armaments necessary and appropriate to support the permitted armed forces, and

(4) the elimination of all armed forces and armaments other than those expressly permitted, it being understood that provision will be made for the elimination of all major weapons adaptable to mass destruction, and for the effective international control of atomic energy to ensure the prohibition of atomic weapons and the use of atomic energy for peaceful purposes only.

(c) Thereafter a draft treaty might be worked out, as contemplated in operative paragraph 3 of General Assembly Resolution 502 (VI) of 11 January 1952, comprehending and bringing into a balanced relationship all essential components of the programme.

III. The timing and co-ordination of the reductions, prohibitions and eliminations should ensure the balanced reduction of overall armed strength and should avoid creating or continuing any disequilibrium of power dangerous to international peace and security during the period that the reductions, prohibitions and eliminations are being put into effect. In particular, the initial limitations or reductions in armed forces and permitted armaments and the initial steps toward elimination of prohibited armaments should commence at the same time. Subsequent limitations and reductions should be synchronized with subsequent progress in elimination of prohibited armaments. An international control authority should be established at the commencement of the programme and it should be in a position to assume progressively its functions in order to ensure the carrying out of such limitations, reductions, curtailments and prohibitions. Thus, when the limitations and reductions in armed forces and permitted armaments provided by the treaty or treaties are completed, production of prohibited armaments will have ceased, existing stockpiles of prohibited armaments and facilities for their production will have been disposed of, atomic energy will be utilized for peaceful purposes only, and the international control authority will have assumed its full functions."

49. J. H. Marshall-Cornwall, *Geographic Disarmament*, A Study of Regional Demilitarization (London, 1935), pp. v, vi.

50. *Cf.* Oppenheim-Lauterpacht, *International Law*, 7th Ed., Vol. II, p. 244; Marshall-Cornwall, *op. cit.*, p. 49; John Fischer Williams, *Chapters on Current International Law and the League of Nations*, 1929, p. 111.

51. Marshall-Cornwall, *op. cit.*, p. 49.

52. Marshall-Cornwall, *op. cit.*, p. 50.

53. It has been asserted (*cf.* Paul de Lapradelle, *La Frontiere*, 1928, pp. 14 ff.; and Marshall-Cornwall, *op. cit.*, p. 174) that an international frontier cannot be expressed by a line, that it is, from a fiscal and especially from a military-

strategic point of view, by its very nature a zone which may extend to a depth of several miles.

54. The provisions of the Treaty of Versailles concerning the demilitarization of the Rhineland ran as follows: "Art. 42. Germany is forbidden to maintain or construct any fortifications either on the left bank of the Rhine or on the right bank to the west of a line drawn 50 kilometres to the east of the Rhine. Art. 43. In the area defined above the maintenance and the assembly of armed forces, either permanently or temporarily, and military manoeuvres of any kind, as well as the upkeep of all permanent works for mobilization, are in the same way forbidden. Art. 44. In case Germany violates in any manner whatever the provisions of Articles 42 and 43, she shall be regarded as committing a hostile act against the Powers signatory of the present Treaty and as calculated to disturb the peace of the world." Example of provisions by which the prohibition of fortifications is imposed upon a defeated state, is Article 47 of the Peace Treaty with Italy, 10 February 1947, which runs as follows: "1. (a) The system of permanent Italian fortifications and military installations along the Franco-Italian frontier, and their armaments, shall be destroyed or removed. (b) This system is deemed to comprise only artillery and infantry fortifications whether in groups or separated, pillboxes of any type, protected accommodation for personnel, stores and ammunition, observation posts and military cableways, whatever may be their importance and actual condition of maintenance or state of construction, which are constructed of metal, masonry or concrete or excavated in the rock. 2. The destruction or removal, mentioned in paragraph 1 above, is limited to a distance of 20 kilometers from any point on the frontier as defined by the present Treaty, and shall be completed within one year from the coming into force of the Treaty. 3. Any reconstruction of the above-mentioned fortifications and installations is prohibited. 4. (a) The following construction to the east of the Franco-Italian frontier is prohibited: permanent fortifications where weapons capable of firing into French territory or territorial waters can be emplaced; permanent military installations capable of being used to conduct or direct fire into French territory or territorial waters; and permanent supply and storage facilities emplaced solely for the use of the above-mentioned fortifications and installations. (b) This prohibition does not include other types of non-permanent fortifications or surface accommodations and installations which are designed to meet only requirements of an internal character and of local defence of the frontiers. 5. In a coastal area 15 kilometers deep, stretching from the Franco-Italian frontier to the meridian 9° 30′ E., Italy shall not establish any new, nor expand any existing, naval bases or permanent naval installations. This does not prohibit minor alterations to, nor the maintenance in good repair of, existing naval installations provided that their overall capacity will not thereby be increased." Other examples of demilitarization of defeated states in: *Disarmament and Security*, pp. 449 ff.

55. Marshall-Cornwall, *op. cit.*, p. 175.

56. In April, 1923, with reference to the proposed Treaty of Mutual Guarantee, Lord Robert Cecil submitted to the Temporary Mixed Commission on the Reduction of Armaments a memorandum which contained the following provisions:

"1. One of the principal difficulties in connection with the proposed Treaty of Mutual Guarantee, which is under the consideration of the Temporary Mixed Commission, consists in devising means for deciding at a moment of international crisis, when hostilities between two States may have begun, which State is the aggressor. It is proposed, in the draft Treaty of Mutual Guarantee which the Commission is studying, that the Council should decide this point and that, failing other evidence, that State should be considered the aggressor whose troops have violated the territory of another. 2. It is clear that decision on this point would be greatly facilitated if, on the frontier between the two States about to go to war, there existed a demilitarized frontier zone into which both of them had undertaken not to send their military forces. If, further, the supervision of such a zone were in the hands of a Commissioner or Commissioners appointed by the League of Nations, who could, if either State sent its forces into the zone, so report to the Council of the League, the decisions of the Council would be immensely facilitated. 3. The establishment of such demilitarized zones under League supervision might, in other ways, give definite and concrete security against the danger of sudden attack to the States on both sides of them. In the agreements under which such zones would be established, provisions might be inserted which would have the effect of rendering military concentrations, preparatory to attack, very difficult, if not impossible, to carry out. These provisions, although they would not render attack impossible, might cause such delay to the aggressor as to make the position of the State attacked much stronger than it otherwise would be. It is therefore perhaps worth while for the Temporary Mixed Commission to examine how such zones might be established. 4. It may be suggested that an agreement for the establishment of such a frontier zone might include some or all of the following stipulations: (a) The zone should be at least thirty miles in width. (b) In this zone, no military fortifications or works of any sort should be constructed. (c) The conscription or military training of the population of the zone should be forbidden. (d) No military camps or barracks should be situated in the zone. (e) No depots of military stores or ammunition should be allowed. (f) No manufacture of arms or munitions of any sort should be carried out—For ensuring that these obligations were effectively carried out in the whole zone, the Council of the League should appoint an impartial Commissioner or Commissioners who should reside in the zone and who should have the necessary rights of inspection and inquiry. Such Commissioners should be directly responsible to the Council and removable by them alone." The memorandum contains also suggestions concerning the use of railways in the demilitarized zones and the organization of a permanent international police force to render more effective the provisions establishing the demilitarized zones.

The Draft Treaty of Mutual Assistance submitted by the Fourth Assembly of the League of Nations on 25 October 1923 to the Governments concerned contained the following article: "Article 9. In order to facilitate the application of the present treaty, any High Contracting Party may negotiate, through the agency of the Council, with one or more neighbouring countries for the establishment of demilitarized zones. The Council, with the co-operation of the representatives of the parties interested, acting as members within the terms of Article 4 of the Covenant, shall previously ensure that the establishment of the demilitarized zone asked for does not call for unilateral sacrifices from the military point of view on the part of the High Contracting Parties interested."

The General Convention to Improve the Means of Preventing War, signed at Geneva, 26 September 1931, contains the following provisions: "*Article 2.* If, in circumstances which, in the Council's opinion, do not create a state of war between the Powers at issue which are parties to the present Convention, the forces of one of those Powers enter the territory or territorial waters of the other or a zone demilitarized in virtue of international agreements or fly over them, the Council may prescribe measures to ensure their evacuation by those forces. The High Contracting Parties undertake to carry out without delay the measures so prescribed, without prejudice to the other powers vested in the Council under Article 11 of the Covenant. *Article 3.* If the circumstances referred to in Article 2 have arisen, or if, in the event of a threat of war, special conditions, and in particular the possibilities of contact between the forces of the parties to the dispute, render it necessary, the Council may fix lines which must not be passed by their land, naval, or air forces and, where necessary in order to avoid incidents, by their civil aircraft. The High Contracting Parties undertake to comply with the Council's recommendations in this matter. The lines referred to in the previous paragraph shall, if possible, be fixed by agreement with the parties at issue. Failing such agreement, the Council shall fix the lines with the consent of the party whose forces are affected, provided always that this does not involve the withdrawal of the forces further back than the exterior lines of the defense organizations existing on the frontier of the High Contracting Parties concerned at the time when the Council of the League of Nations takes its decision, and that the lines do not involve the abandonment of any other work, position or line of communication essential to the security or the supplies of the party concerned. It shall, in every case, rest with the Council to determine the period within which the said lines shall be fixed under the conditions specified above. The High Contracting Parties further agree to give strict orders to the commanders of their forces, if the Council so recommends, to take all necessary precautions to avoid incidents."

57. This is the definition which was presented by the Technical Committee appointed by the National Defense Expenditure Commission established by the General Commission of the League of Nations Disarmament Conference on 25 February 1932. *Cf.* Preliminary Report on the Work of the Conference. *Series of League of Nations Publications.* IX Disarmament, 1936, IX. 3 (hereafter referred to as: Preliminary Report on the Work of the Conference) p. 96.

58. As to the question of the limitation of defense expenditures, the Committee of Experts on Budgetary Questions constituted on 29 November 1926 by Sub-Commission B of the Preparatory Commission for the League of Nations Disarmament Conference was of the opinion "that a limitation of armaments through limitations of expenditures only would be an inadequate basis for a convention. The Committee of Experts wondered whether the limitation of expenditure could not be regarded as a subsidiary measure forming a useful supplement to the direct method of disarmament. . . ." Doc. A/AC.50/2, p. 43.

The Draft Convention framed by the Preparatory Commission for the Disarmament Conference contained only one Article referring to limitation of the material of land armament—namely Article 10—which ran as follows: "The annual expenditure of each High Contracting Party on the upkeep, purchase and manufacture of war material for land armaments shall be limited to the figures laid down for such Party, and in accordance with the conditions prescribed in the annex . . . to this Article." The Article embodied a decision taken by the Preparatory Commission to apply to land war material the principle of indirect or budgetary limitation. Preliminary Report on the Work of the Conference, p. 58.

59. Certain members of the Committee of Experts preferred total limitation because it would involve less uncertainty than a limitation by categories. Doc. A/AC.50/2, p. 43.

60. *Cf.* Preliminary Report on the Work of the Conference, p. 97. The Draft Convention contains in Part II, Section III (Expenditure) the following pro-

vision formulated by the Technical Committee of the National Defense Expenditure Commission: "Article 1. The High Contracting Parties undertake to give full publicity periodically to their national defense expenditure on a basis of reciprocity and in the manner and by the dates stipulated in the following articles and in the Annex to this part of the Convention which includes a general definition and a conventional list of such expenditure.—Such publicity shall apply to all national defence expenditure, irrespective of the nature and origin of the resources out of which such expenditure is met."

61. "The most important part of the system submitted (by the Technical Committee) for approval consisted of the Model Statement, in which all national defense expenditure would be entered in a uniform manner for all States. The scheme had been unanimously adopted by the Technical Committee as a framework in which both limitation and publicity might operate." Preliminary Report on the Work of the Conference, p. 98.

62. The principles of this draft agreement (DC/SC.1/27) are formulated as follows: "1. The purpose of the present agreement is to institute financial supervision of military expenditure, together with a system of penalties, for the purpose of encouraging disarmament. It provides for the allocation of the funds thus made available for the improvement of levels of living and the development of underdeveloped areas. 2. This form of financial supervision has an economic purpose. By ensuring the automatic transfer of part of the savings effected on military expenditure to orders for goods for peaceful purposes, the agreement averts the threat of an economic crisis which might be brought about by mass disarmament carried out within a short period of time. 3. The agreement provides certain advantages for States which, in a form recognized as accurate and complete by the supervisory body, submit evidence of the implementation of the budgetary reductions which they have agreed to make. States will agree to reduce their total military expenditure by a percentage that will increase from year to year, the increase in the percentage from one year to the next being based on the amount of the original defence budget. However, once evidence of the reductions has been accepted as being accurate and complete, this percentage will, for the current budgetary year, refer only to the actual amount of expenditure—that is to say, to a lower sum. 4. The amounts thus made available will be transferred to an international fund which will ensure that they are used in accordance with the criteria laid down by the agreement. 5. The computation, administration and distribution of these resources will be assured by an international fund for development and mutual assistance, hereinafter called 'the Fund'. 6. Upon the entry into force of the convention for the reduction of conventional armaments and armed forces, the abolition of weapons of mass destruction and the setting up of a control, the percentage reductions in military expenditure envisaged in the agreement will be calculated in such a way as to correspond to the reductions in conventional armaments and armed forces and the abolition of weapons of mass destruction as provided for in connexion with each stage of the disarmament convention." Second Report of the Sub-Committee of the Disarmament Commission, DC/71, Annex 16.

63. The Draft Convention contained the following provision in Part V, Section II (Derogations):

"Article 88. Should any of the High Contracting Parties become engaged in war, or should a change of circumstances constitute, in the opinion of any High Contracting Party, a menace to his national security, such party may suspend temporarily, in so far as he is concerned, any provision or provisions of the present Convention, other than those contained in Articles 30, 34 and 47 to 62, provided that: (a) such High Contracting Party shall immediately notify the other High Contracting Parties, and at the same time the Permanent Disarmament Commission, of such temporary suspension and of the extent thereof; (b) in the event of the suspension's being based upon a change of circumstance, the High Contracting Party concerned shall, simultaneously with the said notification, communicate to the other High Contracting Parties and to the Permanent Disarmament Commission a full explanation of such change of circumstances.—Thereupon the other High Contracting Parties shall promptly advise as to the situation thus presented.—When the reasons for such temporary suspension have ceased to exist, the said High Contracting Party shall reduce his armaments to the level agreed upon in the Convention and shall make immediate notification to the other High Contracting Parties."

64. Sub-Commission A of the Preparatory Commission for the League of Nations Disarmament Conference "reported complete disagreement on the question of the supervision and control of armaments. The delegations of Chile, Italy, Japan, Sweden, the United Kingdom and the United States were of the opinion 'that any form of supervision or control of armaments by an international body is more calculated to foment evil and suspicion between States than to foster international confidence.' In their opinion, the execution of the provisions of any convention for the reduction and limitation of armaments 'must depend upon the good faith of nations scrupulously to carry out their great obligations.' The delegations of Chile, Italy, Japan and the United States were of the opinion that the inquiries contemplated would in general prove 'fruitless and illusory' and that, to be successful, such inquiries would have to be carried out under strict and definite rules which would involve serious commitments in regard to military secrecy on the part of the State subjected to the inquiry. The same delegations, except the United States, recalled the opinion expressed by the Permanent Advisory Commission that 'the undertakings contained in Article 8 are based on a belief in the pledged word and the Permanent Advisory Commission does not consider that it is either opportune or conducive to great efficiency to substitute mistrust for this belief.' The French delegation, together with a number of others, did not agree that inquiries would be 'illusory and ineffective.' They recalled the precedent of the Opium Convention, which had introduced a system of supervision, and that of the Treaty for the Pacific Settlement of Disputes between American States, signed at Santiago de Chile on 3 May 1923. They also mentioned the League's right of investigation under the clauses of the Treaties of Peace relating to the disarmament of the defeated States, which showed that it was technically possible for armaments to be placed under supervision. They concluded that all States must be given a guarantee that the convention would be strictly observed, 'because, in the absence of such a guarantee, those States which regulated their armaments in strict accordance with the provisions of the convention would lack that adequate security upon which such limitation of armaments as were accepted should properly be based.'" Doc. A/AC.50/2, p. 45.

The Draft Constitution of International Organization, prepared by the Special Committee appointed in 1943 by Secretary of State Hull (*cf. supra*, p. 137), contained in Article 10 the following provisions: "6. Members of the International Organization undertake to keep the general level of their armaments at the lowest point consistent with the effective discharge of their respective obligations for maintaining international security, and consistent with their internal domestic security. They accordingly agree that the Council, acting on the advice of the General Security and Armaments Commission, and taking into account the special responsibilities for security assumed by some states, and the collective responsibility assumed by all, shall establish the minimum and maximum limitations on armaments and the regulations of previously agreed categories of armaments potential to be observed by all members. These limitations and regulations shall be subject to modification and amendment by the Council. 7. The limitations and regulations established under paragraph 6 shall be enforced by a system of inspection carried out by the Armaments Inspection Commission under the direction of the General Security and Armaments Commission. Member States agree freely to accord to the Commission every facility for the effective discharge of its mission." (*Postwar Foreign Policy*, pp. 478 f.)

65. In Committee 1 of the United Nations Disarmament Commission, the French representative, discussing the concept of "control" found one of the difficulties "to be the different meanings of the word in different languages. In French 'control' comported the establishment of fact for a higher authority which wished to know and verify the accuracy of what subordinate authorities reported in the exercise of their duties. In the USSR the separation of action from control was even more clear-cut. On the other hand, in English-speaking countries control implied an idea of direction and was, therefore, not so clearly separated from action. In the Commission for Conventional Armaments, France had argued for its conception of control, i. e., without participation in the direction or management of the undertakings. The United Nations plan for the control of atomic energy, however, used the word 'control' to include participation in management. It might be useful to set down either in the Commission or in a small committee the various meanings of the word "control," in order to determine to what extent it might be possible to devise a plan better or no less effective than the United Nations plan. That alternative could not be the USSR plan of 1947 which had already been judged to be less effective." Second Report of the United Nations Disarmament Commission, p. 52. The representative of the U.S.S.R. declared that the "USSR, like the French delegation, understood 'control' to mean verification and inspection, not management and ownership, as it was understood by the United States." *Ibid.*, p. 57.

In Resolution 191 (III), adopted on 4 November 1948, the General Assembly approved the general findings (part II C) and recommendations (part III) of the first report and the specific proposals of part II of the second report of the Atomic Energy Commission "as constituting the necessary basis for establishing an effective system of international control of atomic energy to ensure its use only for peaceful purposes and for the elimination from national armaments of atomic weapons in accordance with the terms of reference of the Atomic Energy Commission." This is the so-called United Nations plan for control of atomic energy. The recommendations of the Atomic Energy Commission follow, in principle, the so-called Baruch Plan, that is, the United States Proposal for the International Control of Atomic Energy presented to the United Nations Atomic Energy Commission by the United States Representative, Mr. Bernard Baruch, on 14 June 1946. In this plan the United States proposed "the creation of an International Atomic Development Authority, to which should be entrusted all phases of the development and use of atomic energy, starting with the raw material and including:

1. Managerial control or ownership of all atomic-energy activities potentially dangerous to world security.
2. Power to control, inspect, and license all other atomic activities.
3. The duty of fostering the beneficial uses of atomic energy.
4. Research and development responsibilities of an affirmative character intended to put the Authority in the forefront of atomic knowledge and thus

to enable it to comprehend, and therefore to detect, misuse of atomic energy. To be effective, the Authority must itself be the world's leader in the field of atomic knowledge and development and thus supplement its legal authority with the great power inherent in possession of leadership in knowledge."

The following measures were submitted as representing the fundamental features of the Baruch Plan:

"1. *General.*—The Authority should set up a thorough plan for control of the field of atomic energy, through various forms of ownership, dominion, licenses, operation, inspection, research and management by competent personnel. After this is provided for, there should be as little interference as may be with the economic plans and the present private, corporate and state relationships in the several countries involved.

2. *Raw Materials.*—The Authority should have as one of its earliest purposes to obtain and maintain complete and accurate information on world supplies of uranium and thorium and to bring them under its dominion. The precise pattern of control for various types of deposits of such materials will have to depend upon the geological, mining, refining, and economic facts involved in different situations.

The Authority should conduct continuous surveys so that it will have the most complete knowledge of the world geology of uranium and thorium. Only after all current information on world sources of uranium and thorium is known to us all can equitable plans be made for their production, refining, and distribution.

3. *Primary Production Plans.*—The Authority should exercise complete managerial control of the production of fissionable materials. This means that it should control and operate all plants producing fissionable materials in dangerous quantities and must own and control the product of these plants.

4. *Atomic Explosives.*—The Authority should be given sole and exclusive right to conduct research in the field of atomic explosives. Research activities in the field of atomic explosives are essential in order that the Authority may keep in the forefront of knowledge in the field of atomic energy and fulfil the objective of preventing illicit manufacture of bombs. Only by maintaining its position as the best-informed agency will the Authority be able to determine the line between intrinsically dangerous and nondangerous activities.

5. *Strategic Distribution of Activities and Materials.*—The activities entrusted exclusively to the Authority because they are intrinsically dangerous to security should be distributed throughout the world. Similarly, stockpiles of raw materials and fissionable materials should not be centralized.

6. *Non-Dangerous Activities.*—A function of the Authority should be promotion of the peacetime benefits of atomic energy.

Atomic research (except in explosives), the use of research reactors, the production of radioactive tracers by means of non-dangerous reactors, the use of such tracers, and to some extent the production of power should be open to nations and their citizens under reasonable licensing arrangements from the Authority. Denatured materials, whose use we know also requires suitable safeguards, should be furnished for such purposes by the Authority under lease or other arrangement. Denaturing seems to have been over-estimated by the public as a safety measure.

7. *Definition of Dangerous and Non-Dangerous Activities.*—Although a reasonable dividing line can be drawn between dangerous and non-dangerous activities, it is not hard and fast. Provision should, therefore, be made to assure constant reexamination of the questions and to permit revision of the dividing line as changing conditions and new discoveries may require.

8. *Operations of Dangerous Activities.*—Any plant dealing with uranium or thorium after it once reaches the potential of dangerous use must be not only subject to the most rigorous and competent inspection by the Authority, but its acual operation shall be under the management, supervision, and control of the Authority.

9. *Inspection.*—By assigning intrinsically dangerous activities exclusively to the Authority, the difficulties of inspection are reduced. If the Authority is the only agency which may lawfully conduct dangerous activities, then visible operation by others than the Authority will constitute an unambiguous danger signal. Inspection will also occur in connection with the licensing functions of the Authority.

10. *Freedom of Access.*—Adequate ingress and egress for all qualified representatives of the Authority must be assured. Many of the inspection activities of the Authority should grow out of, and be incidental to, its other functions. Important measures of inspection will be associated with the tight control of raw materials, for this is a keystone of the plan. The continuing activities of prospecting, survey, and research in relation to raw materials will be designed not only to serve the affirmative development functions of the Authority, but also to assure that no surreptitious operations are conducted in the raw materials field by nations or their citizens.

11. *Personnel.*—The personnel of the Authority should be recruited on a basis of proven competence but also so far as possible on an international basis.

12. *Progress by Stages.*—A primary step in the creation of the system of control is the setting forth, in comprehensive terms, of the functions, responsibilities, powers and limitations of the Authority. Once a Charter for the Authority has been adopted, the Authority and the system of control for which it will be responsible will require time to become fully organized and effective. The plan of control will, therefore, have to come into effect in successive stages. These should be specifically fixed in the Charter or means should be otherwise set forth in the Charter for transitions from one stage to another, as contemplated in the resolution of the United Nations Assembly which created this Commission.

13. *Disclosures.*—In the deliberations of the United Nations Commission on Atomic Energy, the United States is prepared to make available the information essential to a reasonable understanding of the proposals which it advocates. Further disclosures must be dependent, in the interests of all, upon the effective ratification of the treaty. When the Authority is actually created, the United States will join the other nations in making available the further information essential to that organization for the performance of its functions. As the successive stages of international control are reached, the United States will be prepared to yield, to the extent required by each State, national control of activities in this field to the Authority.

14. *International Control.*—There will be questions about the extent of control to be allowed to national bodies, when the Authority is established. Purely national authorities for control and development of atomic energy should to the extent necessary for the effective operation of the Authority be subordinate to it. This is neither an endorsement nor a disapproval of the creation of national authorities. The Commission should evolve a clear demarcation of the scope of duties and responsibilities of such national authorities."

With respect to violations, the Baruch Plan suggested: "In the agreement, penalties of as serious a nature as the nations may wish and as immediate and certain in their execution as possible, should be fixed for:

1. Illegal possession or use of an atomic bomb;

370624—57——16

2. Illegal possession, or separation, of atomic material suitable for use in an atomic bomb;

3. Seizure of any plant or other property belonging to or licensed by the Authority;

4. Wilful interference with the activities of the Authority;

5. Creation or operation of dangerous projects in a manner contrary to, or in the absence of, a license granted by the international control body."

The International Control of Atomic Energy. Growth of a Policy. The Department of State. Publication 2702, pp. 141 ff.

The Recommendations of Part III of the First Report of the Atomic Energy Commission, approved by the Resolution 191 (III) of the General Assembly, contain a statement to the effect that the Convention should include provisions "specifying the means and methods of determining violations of its terms, setting forth such violations as shall constitute international crimes, and establishing the nature of the measures of enforcement and punishment to be imposed upon persons and upon nations guilty of violating the terms of the treaty or convention.

The judicial or other processes for determination of violations of the treaty or convention, and of punishments therefor, should be swift and certain. Serious violations of the treaty shall be reported immediately by the international control agency to the nations parties to the treaty, to the General Assembly, and to the Security Council." Less serious infringements may be dealt with by the control agency itself. Chapter 3 of Part II of the Second Report of the Atomic Energy Commission (Official Records, Second Year, Special Supplement, p. 37) contains the following special proposal: "The Agency shall reserve the power to modify regulations and to suspend or revoke licenses in case of violation by the licensee. In case of refusal by the agency to grant a license applied for by a nation, or in case of suspension or revocation of a license granted, the applicant or licensee shall have the right of appeal to an international court, and the agency shall have the right to maintain its control measures."

66. In a resolution adopted by the first Assembly of the League of Nations in 1920, it was recognized that, while the final and general limitation of armaments was subordinate to certain preliminary conditions, the first step towards disarmament should, nevertheless, be taken without delay. The Temoprary Mixed Commission, considering that the ascertaining of the military strength of different States was one of the preliminary conditions for the final and general limitation of armaments, decided to carry out a statistical investigation on the armaments of the various countries for the years 1913-1921. Under the direction of the Temporary Mixed Commission, the Secretariat prepared the "Statistical Enquiry on Armaments, First Series of Data," and the "Budget Expenditure on National Defence, 1913 and 1920–1922." The Third Committee, in the report it presented to the Assembly on 22 September 1922 took the view that the "Statistical Enquiry on Armaments" was of great scientific interest but of no practical value to the subsequent work of the Temporary Mixed Commission. The Committee found that the national security of each country depended very largely on the existing military strength of other countries. It therefore proposed to the Assembly that the subject of the statistical inquiry should be the existing military strength. While expressing the view that potential military strength should perhaps be studied at a later date, it proposed that for the time being the investigation should be limited to the two following points: peacetime armaments and expenditure on armaments. Doc. A/AC.50/2, p. 18.

In accordance with the Assembly resolution of 27 September 1922 concerning the exchange of military information between States, the Temoprary Mixed Commission suggested on 15 August 1923 that:

"The engagements undertaken by the signatories of the Covenant in the last paragraph of Article 8 might now be begun by giving instructions to the Secretariat periodically to publish a year-book containing a certain number of data regarding the matters referred to in the last paragraph of Article 8."

Pursuant to that suggestion, the Council adopted a resolution authorizing the Secretariat to publish a year-book beginning with an experimental volume dealing with the figures for 1923, it being understood that the information would be drawn solely from official publications. The objectives aimed at in the exchange of information were summarized by the Commission in its report for 1923. "Article 8 of the Covenant," declared the Commission, "was not drawn up with a view to facilitating the work of general staffs. Its object was to improve the political atmosphere by creating confidence." The Commission also considered that the exchange of information "would render it possible to nip in the bud any campaign started by an alarmist Press and based upon the armaments of countries considered as potential enemies."

The first edition of the Armaments Year-Book was published in September 1924, and the last in May 1940. The first volume contained information on thirty-six countries, including all the great Powers, members and non-members of the League. The next edition included practically all the countries of the world, members and non-members of the League, all Colonies, Protectorates and Mandated Territories. Doc. A/AC.50/2, pp. 19–20.

A resolution adopted by the Council in 1931 requested the Secretariat to prepare a special edition of the Armaments Year-Book for the use of the Disarmament Conference. That edition was based not only on official publications of various governments but also on their replies to a special questionnaire approved by the Council relating to the numerical strength of their respective forces.

At the request of the Temporary Mixed Commission, the Secretariat also published regularly a year-book containing statistical information on the trade in arms, ammunition and implements of war. That request was made in connection with the view expressed by the Temporary Mixed Commission, as early as 1921, "that it was imperative to establish a control over the export and import of arms and implements of war, and that it was essential for the League of Nations to receive complete information as to the extent and character of the trade in arms." The Year-Book on the Trade in Arms, Ammunition and Implements of War included statistical information on practically all States, Colonies, Protectorates and other territories of the world. The tables contained data on exports and imports of arms and ammunition by categories and according to countries of destination or of origin. The monographs were prepared by the Secretariat on the basis of official publications and not as a result of any questionnaires. Doc. A/AC.50/2, pp. 20–21.

On the question of the exchange of military information, as provided for under Article 8 of the Covenant of the League of Nations, Sub-Commission A of the Preparatory Commission for the Disarmament Conference submitted a text which was unanimously accepted. That text provided for the collection and periodical publication by the Secretariat of the League of military information in an enlarged "Armaments Year-Book." In addition to the Year-Book itself, Sub-Commission A considered the possibility of publishing a number of bulletins in the course of the year. The delegation of Belgium, France and some others proposed, in addition to the "Armaments Year-Book" and the periodical bulletins, the preparation of objective reports on the carrying out of the convention for the limitation of armaments, on the basis of periodic uniform statistical returns by governments on their armaments, whether subject to limitation or not. The reports prepared on the basis of those returns were to be discussed by a commission to be set up by the Conference. The delegations of Chile, Italy, Japan, Spain, Sweden, the United Kingdom and the United States objected that that proposal would raise the question of supervision or control. In their declaration concerning supervision of armaments by an international organization, those delegations, except Spain, pointed out that "most unfortunate results, both political and technical, would follow from these inquiries." They continued: "It is impossible to disregard the possibility that, in certain circumstances, one country might bring a charge against another in order to obtain, unjustifiably, information about the secret defensive organizations of the country accused. Moreover, the delegations of Chile, Italy, Japan, the United Kingdom and the United States are entirely unable to accept for their own governments anything in the nature of itinerant inquisitorial commissions." Doc. A/AC.50/2, p. 46.

The Draft Convention framed by the Preparatory Commission contained in Part IV three articles concerning information to be annually communicated in respect to effectives. Article 30 provided for information to be exchanged through the Secretary-General of the League of Nations in regard to the average daily number of effectives reached during the course of the preceding year in the land, sea and air armed forces and formations organized on a military basis of each of the contracting parties, to be accompanied by an explanatory note showing the elements on which the figures supplied were based. Article 31 provided for information to be exchanged as to the number of units compulsorily receiving preparatory military training during the preceding year. Article 32 provided for an exchange of information at the end of the year concerning the provisions of the respective laws of the contracting parties relating to the total number of days comprised in the first period of service of effectives recruited by conscription and the total duration in days of the ensuing periods. Preliminary Report on the Work of the Conference, p. 42.

67. At the first meeting of Committee 2 of the United Nations Disarmament Commission, the representative of the United States submitted a Working Paper (DC/C.2/1) containing proposals for progressive and continuing disclosure and verification of armed forces and armaments on a continuing basis.

Under the heading "C. Inspection" the following statements are made:

"The system of disclosure and verification is an integral part of the system of safeguards which must be established to ensure observance of the overall programme of regulation, limitation and balanced reduction of armed forces and armaments so as to provide for the prompt detection of violations while at the same time causing the minimum degree of interference in the internal life of each country. It will not be adequate to provide merely for the verification of disclosed information. In addition, provision must be made for determining the adequacy of the disclosed information, through broad general powers of 'on-the-spot' inspection, through access to statistical data permitting independent confirmation of required reports and through aerial surveys. Extensive aerial reconnaissance is obviously essential to the verification procedure in order completely to determine the adequacy of disclosed information. It will be obvious that aerial reconnaissance furnishes the easiest method of determining the existence of large undisclosed facilities and installations. Aerial Survey will be essential in all stages of the disclosure and verification procedure. It is contemplated that 'on-the-spot' inspection will take place in all stages as a part of the verification procedure. Its use, however, will be less extensive in the first than in the later stages because of the greater ease of verification through other methods of the items disclosed in the first stage. It will of course be necessary at each stage to regulate inspection in such a way as to prevent disclosure of information which is to be withheld from disclosure and verification during the particular stage. Certain principles governing limitations on the right of 'on-the-spot' inspections in early stages are set forth in Annex I and II. Each State at the commencement of each stage should submit to the Commission a general description of the nature and location of facilities falling within the terms of reference for that stage. Access to such locations, reasonably sufficient to verify the information disclosed, should be granted to inspectors. Inspection in each stage should proceed in accordance with a previously accepted plan. It is essential to an effective system of verification that the international inspectors, in addition to examining declared installations and facilities, be permitted in all stages to have access to the entire national territory in order that the Commission may determine within reasonable limits the accuracy and adequacy of the information disclosed. Accordingly, each State should be required during each stage of the process of disclosure and verification to permit the international inspectors such freedom of movement and to give them access to such installations and facilities, records and data as may reasonably be required, including the right to inspect physical dimensions of all facilities and installations wherever situated. Each State should facilitate the activities of the international inspectors and furnish to them such assistance as they may reasonably require. Procedure should be set up in order to permit a determination by the Commission of the necessity for inspection of any facilities or installations access to which is denied to the inspectors and where in the judgment of the inspectors such inspection is required. The inspectors should report to the Commission any information indicating a major violation of any provisions of the treaties or agreements respecting disclosure and verification. In the event of a Commission determination confirmed by the Security Council, by the affirmative vote of any seven members, of such a major violation during any stage and the failure of the State guilty of violation to repair the same within a reasonable specified period, other States should be free to suspend the operations of the disclosure and verification system." Second Report of the United Nations Disarmament Commission, pp. 25, 26.

On 21 April 1955, Canada, France, the United Kingdom of Great Britain and Northern Ireland and the United States of America submitted to the Sub-Committee of the Disarmament Commission a Joint Draft Resolution on the Principles of Control, in which the following principles were formulated: "A. The control organ shall have, to the extent necessary to ensure implementation of the treaty by all States, full responsibility for supervising and guaranteeing effective observance of all the provisions of the disarmament treaty including: 1. The limitations on levels of conventional armaments and over-all military man-power, and on over-all military expenditures, both atomic and non-atomic (paragraphs 6 (i) (a) and (b) of the four-Power draft resolution of 8 March 1955 [DC/SC.1/15/Rev.1]); 2. The major reductions in armed forces and conventional armaments (paragraphs 6 (ii) (a) and 6 (iii) (a) of the four-Power draft resolution of 8 March 1955); 3. The total prohibition of manufacture and use, and the elimination of nuclear weapons and all other weapons of mass destruction, as well as conversion of existing stocks of nuclear materials to peaceful uses (paragraphs 6 (ii) (b) and 6 (iii) (b) of the four-Power draft resolution of 8 March 1955); 4. The continued supervision of permitted atomic energy installations and facilities; B. In order to enable it to carry out these responsibilities and functions, the control organ shall be accorded powers to be exercised in accordance with the terms of the disarmament treaty and which shall include the following: 1. To determine, within the limits established by the disarmament treaty, the details of the methods and processes of supervising and guaranteeing the effective observance of the various phases of agreed limitations, reductions, and prohibitions, in order to ensure that the disarmament programme is carried out as rapidly as possible and with safety and equity for all; 2. To supervise and verify the disclosures of information required at each stage of the disarmament programme laid down in the four-Power draft resolution of 8 March 1955, with respect to all armaments and armed forces and related installations and facilities; 3. To ensure that installations, facilities, equipment, and materials, including stocks of nuclear materials, are disposed of or utilized in accordance with the terms of the disarmament treaty; 4. To organize and conduct field and aerial surveys in connexion with the above functions and for the purpose of determining whether all installations and facilities have been disclosed; 5. To conduct such research as is necessary to keep itself in the forefront of nuclear knowledge and to enable it to be fully effective in eliminating the destructive uses of nuclear energy, so that such energy shall be used only for peaceful purposes; 6. To report and provide information to the Security Council, the General Assembly and the States signatories and to make recommendations concerning appropriate action by them in the event of violation of the disarmament treaty; 7. To take such measures provided for in the treaty as may be necessary to deal with violations of the disarmament treaty pending action by the Security Council, the General Assembly or the States signatories, and to call upon the party concerned and its agents to comply with such measures, without prejudice to the rights, claims or position of the party concerned; C. In order to ensure that the international officials of the control organ are continuously in a position to fulfil their responsibilities, they will be granted the right: 1. To be stationed permanently in the countries adhering to the disarmament treaty; 2. Of unrestricted access to, egress from and travel within the territory of participating States, and unrestricted access to all installations and facilities as required by them for the effective performance of their responsibilities and functions; 3. Of unrestricted use of communication facilities necessary for the discharge of their responsibilities; 4. Of inviolability of person, premises, property and archives; D. The control organ shall remain in being in order to ensure that the reductions, prohibitions and eliminations are faithfully and permanently observed." Second Report of the Sub-Committee of the Disarmament Commission, Annex 14.

On 21 July 1955, at the Geneva meetings of the Heads of Government of France, USSR, the United Kingdom and the United States, the President of the United States made a statement in which he declared "that the priority attention of our combined study of disarmament should be upon the subject of inspection and reporting," and proposed "to give each other a complete blueprint of our military establishments, from beginning to end, from one end of our countries to the other, lay out the establishments and provide the blueprints to each other. Next, to provide within our countries facilities for aerial photography to the other country—we to provide you the facilities within our country, ample facilities for aerial reconnaissance, where you can make all the pictures you choose and take them to your country to study, you to provide exactly the same facilities for us and we to make these examinations, and by this step to convince the world that we are providing as between ourselves against the possibility of great surprise attack, thus lessening danger and relaxing tension." Doc. DC/SC. 1/28, 29 August 1955. Second Report of the Sub-Committee of the Disarmament Commission. DC/71, 7 October 1955, Annex 17.

In its Resolution 914 (X), adopted at its 559th plenary meeting on 16 December 1955, the General Assembly "Recognizing . . . that inspection and control of disarmament can best be achieved in an atmosphere which is free of fear and suspicion, 1. urges that the States concerned and particularly those on the Sub-Committee of the Disarmament Commission . . . should, as initial steps, give priority to early agreement on an implementation of: (i) Such confidence-building measures as the plan of Mr. Eisenhower, President of the United States of America, for exchanging military blueprints and mutual aerial inspection, and the plan of Mr. Bulganin, Prime Minister of the Union of Soviet Socialist Republics, for establishing control posts at strategic centers, (ii) All such measures of adequately safeguarded disarmament as are now feasible."

68. The Special Committee for the Regulation of the Trade in and Private and State Manufacture of Arms and Implements of War, set up on 22 September 1932 by the General Commission of the League of Nations Disarmament Conference, presented the results of its discussions in a report of which the following brief analysis is contained in the Preliminary Report on the Work of the Conference, pp. 125 ff.:

"(a) *General Obligations and Definition of Categories.*—The Special Committee unanimously adopted texts stipulating that each contracting party would assume, in the territories under its jurisdiction, full responsibility for the supervision to be exercised over the manufacture of and trade in arms, with a view to ensuring the regular communication and accuracy of the information to be supplied under the Convention. Each of the contracting parties, for the purpose of securing publicity, undertook to forward to the Permanent Disarmament Commission the texts of all laws, regulations or other legal provisions enacted for the purpose of ensuring the execution of the Convention.—The categories of arms, ammunition and implements of war proposed by the Special Committee did not secure unanimity. A Technical Committee on Categories, reporting to the Special Committee, submitted the results of its work as an attempt at solution of a purely technical character, accepted by its members with reservations as to the assent of their respective Governments.—Five categories were proposed by the Special Committee comprising: (I) military armaments; (II) naval armaments; (III) air armaments; (IV) arms and ammunition capable of being used for both military and non-military purposes; and (V) aircraft other than those in category III.

(b) *Manufacture.*—Texts unanimously adopted by the Special Committee provided that the contracting parties should forbid in their respective territories the manufacture of arms and implements of war as set forth in categories I, II and III, unless the manufacturers had, in the case of private establishments, obtained a license to manufacture issued by the government. The license to manufacture was to be valid for a definite period, to be revocable at any time and to be renewable for further periods at the discretion of the Government concerned. Licenses to manufacture would give the name and address of the manufacture, or the name, head office and principal works of the firm, together with a designation of the articles by headings in categories I, II and III whose manufacture was authorized by the license. Further, it was unanimously agreed that the contracting parties should send to the Permanent Disarmament Commission, within three months from the entry into force of the Convention, a copy of the licenses to manufacture already issued to private establishments and, within the thirty days following the end of each quarter, a return showing copies of all licenses to manufacture granted, amended, renewed or revoked during the previous quarter.—In regard to naval armaments, the Committee unanimously adopted texts under which the contracting parties undertook to forward to the Permanent Disarmament Commission, within thirty days of the laying-down of a war vessel in State or private shipyards within their jurisdiction, a return showing the date of the laying-down of the keel, the classification of the vessel, for whom the vessel was built, its standard displacement and principal dimensions and the calibre of its largest gun. They further undertook, within thirty days of the date of the completion of each war vassel, to send a return giving the date of completion, together with the foregoing particulars.—The above provisions in regard to the regulation of the manufacture of arms represented the minimum position adopted in the Committee. Texts provisionally approved by the majority of the members of the Committee, on the basis of the United States text, provided for a stricter system of control and a more extended publicity. It was stipulated, for example, that the manufacture of articles appearing in categories I, II and III should not take place in private establishments unless the producer was in possession of *bona fide* orders, in each case duly notified in advance to the government, and further stipulated that licenses accorded to manufacturers should state that all orders received by them were to be communicated immediately to the Government which had granted the license. These provisions were not accepted by the delegations of the United Kingdom, Italy and Japan.—Further, the texts approved by the majority provided that the contracting parties should send to the Permanent Disarmament Commission, among other particulars, a return at the beginning of each financial year showing the quantities of articles in categories I, II and III whose manufacture or purchase was contemplated in the course of the year; a return showing the national defense expenditure proposed in respect of the manufacture and purchase of articles in categories I, II and III; a return within fifteen days of orders placed with State or private establishments for articles in categories I, III and V, with their description, number and type, the name of the Government on whose account the order was given, and the name and address of the private manufacturer a description of the State establishment; and, finally, a return within the month following the end of the civil year of manufactures completed during the year of articles in categories I to V. These provisions were not accepted by the delegations of the United Kingdom, Italy and Japan.—Texts going beyond these provisions in respect of the returns to be made to the Permanent Disarmament Commission were submitted by the delegations of France, Turkey, Afghanistan, Iraq, Spain, Czechoslovakia, the Union of Soviet Socialist Republics and China.—An alternative text proposed by the United Kingdom, Italian and Japanese delegations provided that, within sixty days of the end of the quarter, a quarterly return of the total value under each heading of the categories of the articles whose manufacture had been completed during the previous quarter should be forwarded to the Permanent Disarmament Commission.

(c) *Trade.*—The texts of the provisions concerning the trade in arms and implements of war were adopted subject to declarations by the minority delegations. Texts approved by the majority provided that the contracting parties should prohibit, in their territories, the export of articles in categories I to V inclusive, and the import of articles in categories I to III inclusive, without an export or import permit issued by the Government. The export permit was to contain a description of the articles, giving their number, aggregate weight and type, with the name and address of the exporter and a reference to the original order in cases where the order had been notified to Geneva and was for arms manufactured in the country of export. It was also to give the name and address of the importing consignee, with a reference to the import permit for articles in categories I, II and III. The import permit was to contain a description of the articles in categories I to III inclusive whose import was authorized, giving their number, aggregate weight and type, the name and address of the importer, a reference to the order and the name and address of the exporter.—The contracting parties further undertook to forward to the Permanent Disarmament Commission copies of all import or export permits prior to the entry or despatch of articles in categories I to III and similarly copies of all export permits in respect of articles in categories IV and V. Moreover, within a period of one month from the end of the year, the contracting parties were to forward a statement of all imports and exports effected during the year.—The provisions relating to naval armanents provided that, within thirty days of the end of each quarter, the contracting parties would furnish a return in respect of each vessel of war acquired during the quarter other than those constructed for their own account within their respective jurisdictions. The delegations of the United Kingdom, Italy, Japan and Switzerland submitted alternative texts from which all references to orders for manufacture were omitted. Further, the delegations of the United Kingdom, Italy and Japan submitted an alternative text, as a substitute for the above provisions relating to returns, under which the contracting parties would furnish to the Permanent Disarmament Commission, within sixty days of the end of each quarter, a quarterly return giving the total values of the articles falling within categories I to V imported and exported during the previous quarter, showing the countries of origin and destination. Finally, the Soviet delegation, supported in principle by the delegations of France, Spain and China, submitted a proposal that the contracting parties should undertake not to issue import, export or transit permits for implements of war in excess of qualitative or quantitative limits to be fixed under agreements binding on the parties responsible for the permits."

Concerning supervision the Special Committee suggested the establishment of a Permanent Disarmament Commission and the appointment of experts by the Commission "to accompany its representatives and for the constitution of regional committees to be entrusted with the duty of permanently following the execution of the Convention by the different States included in each of the regional groups within their respective jurisdictions. They further provided that the Commission, for the purpose of its investigations, might take into account any information reaching it from a responsible source which it might consider as pertinent to the execution of its duties, and that it should have the right to hear such witnesses as might voluntarily appear before it or consult any person able to throw any light on a question under examination. The Commission, moreover, might proceed annually, or more often if it so determined, to examine on the spot the conditions in which the national control exercised by each government over the manufacture of and trade in arms was organized and the accuracy of the information furnished by the governments, such inspections being effected through the regional committees. The regional committees, if notified in the course of their inspections of certain facts which appeared to call for the attention of the Permanent Disarmament Commission, would be authorized to establish such facts and to report upon immediately to the Permanent Disarmament Commission. Any contracting party would be entitled to request the Commission to conduct, in its territory, such investigations as might be necessary, in order to verify the execution of its obligations, and any contracting party of opinion that the provisions of the Conventions had been infringed might address a complaint to the Commission. The Commission, on receiving such requests or complaints, would be bound to consider the matter and determine whether a special investigation was necessary. Special investigations undertaken under these provisions would be carried out by a special committee created for the purpose, and the result of such investigations would be embodied in a special report by the Permanent Disarmament Commission, which might make recommendations addressed to the contracting party. The procedure to be followed in carrying out such local investigations was defined in detail.

The delegations of the United Kingdom, Italy, Japan and Poland were unable to accept the articles which provided for a system of continuous and automatic inspection and supervision on the spot. These delegations submitted, in substitution for the texts adopted by the Committee, a general article providing that the Permanent Disarmament Commission might call for explanations in the event of it having reason to believe that an infringement of the Convention had occurred or that information supplied to it by a contracting party was incomplete or inaccurate. The contracting party would in that case furnish explanations, either verbally by responsible officials or in writing as desired by the Permanent Commission, and the Commission would draw up, as soon as possible, a report embodying the result of its examination. The French delegation, in addition to the measures adopted by the Committee, proposed that each regional committee should apoint agents who would reside permanently in the territories of each of the states for which the committee was competent. These agents would be accredited to the local authorities and would have the necessary means of action to proceed at any moment to effect such local inspection as might be required for the discharge of the duties of supervision imposed on the regional committees. The Polish and Latvian delegations, moreover, proposed that the attention of the Permanent Disarmament Commission might be drawn by any one of the contracting parties to unexpected increases in the manufacture, import or export of arms and munitions or implements of war which seemed to it to indicate a threat to peace, the Commission being in such an event required to consider the matter and to call for such explanations as it might consider necessary." Preliminary Report on the Work of the Conference, p. 138.

69. *Cf.* pp. 13 ff, 104 ff. The Draft Convention contained in Part V the following provisions:

ARTICLE 64. There shall be set up at the seat of the League of Nations a Permanent Disarmament Commission composed of representatives of the Governments of the High Contracting Parties. Each such Government shall appoint one member of the Commission. Each member may be a accompanied by substitutes and experts. . . .

ARTICLE 69. It will be the duty of the Commission to watch the execution of the present Convention. The Commission shall receive all the information which the High Contracting Parties are bound to communicate to the Secretary-General of the League of Nations in pursuance of their international obligations in this respect. The Commission may request the High Contracting Parties to supply, in writing or verbally, any supplementary particulars or explanations in regard to the said information which it may consider necessary.

ARTICLE 72. Any High Contracting Party whose observance of the execution of the present Convention may have been the subject of criticism shall be entitled to request the Commission to conduct in its territory such investigations as may be necessary in order to verify the execution of the obligations of the said party under the present Convention.—On receipt of such a request, the Commission shall meet at once in order to give effect to it, to determine the scope of the investigation within the limits of the criticism which has been made, and to lay down the conditions in which the investigation is to take place.

ARTICLE 73. At the request of one or more of the High Contracting Parties, the Commission may decide to have investigations of alleged infractions of the Convention conducted on the territory of any High Contracting Party.—On the receipt of such a request, the Commission shall meet at once in order to take a decision upon it.—The decision which will determine the scope of the investigation, if such is decided upon, shall be taken by a two-thirds majority of all the members of the Commission, whether present at the meeting or not.

ARTICLE 74. The result of the investigations decided upon in accordance with Articles 72 and 73 shall be embodied in each case in a special report by the Commission.—The High Contracting Parties shall promptly advise as to the conclusions of the report.

The United States Working Paper on Methods of Implementing and Enforcing Disarmament Programmes, submitted to the Sub-Committee of the Disarmament Commission on 25 May 1954 (DC/SC. 1/5) suggested the establishment of a United Nations Disarmament and Atomic Development Authority and, under this Authority a Disarmament and an Atomic Development Division. The Authority should be composed in the same manner as the Disarmament Commission, that is, only one representative from each of those states represented on the Security Council (and Canada when that State is not a member of the Security Council) ; but the inclusion of a limited number of representatives of additional states should be possible. "Any State not a member of the Authority would have an automatic right to participate, without vote, in Authority discussions of charges of violations by that State of provisions of the disarmament programme treaty. Any State not a member of the Authority would have the right to participate, without vote, in Authority discussions of any question brought before the Authority whenever the latter considers that the interests of that State are specially affected. . . . The Disarmament Division would be under the supervision and control of a Director-General, who might be appointed for a fixed term, by the Authority. While the Director-General would be subject to control by the Authority, he should be allowed sufficient discretion in carrying out the terms of the disarmament programme treaty and the instructions of the Authority to ensure effective operation of the Disarmament Division. The Director-General would be required to refer to the Authority charges of violations and other important developments but not routine day-to-day decisions concerning the operations of the Disarmament Division. . . . The Atomic Development Division would be under the supervision and control of a Board of Governors. Each permanent member of the Authority would appoint a member of the Board. Not less than six nor more than eight additional members of the Board would be appointed by the Authority. Appointees would be expected to possess outstanding technical qualifications and would be appointed for a term of five years. While the Board of Governors would be subject to control by the Authority, it should be allowed sufficient discretion in carrying out the terms of the disarmament programme treaty and the instructions of the Authority to ensure effective operation of the Atomic Development Division."

The relations of the Authority to the main organs of the United Nations are determined as follows:

"*To the Security Council.*—The Authority would be required to submit such reports as might be requested by any seven members of the Security Council. The Authority's findings in respect to violations, evasions, discrepancies or pertinent omissions should be referred, as appropriate with certification of facts to the Security Council. Findings would be accompanied by such recommendations as the Authority might deem appropriate. In this regard, provision would have to be made for specific steps to be taken by the Security Council and/or the General Assembly to bring about rectification of violations of the disarmament programme treaty.

To the General Assembly.—The Authority would transmit to the General Assembly periodic reports and any findings in respect to violations, evasions, discrepancies or pertinent omissions which are submitted to the Security Council. The Authority would be required to submit such reports as might be requested by the General Assembly.

To the International Court of Justice.—The Authority would be authorized by the General Assembly to request of the International Court of Justice advisory opinions on legal questions arising within the scope of the Authority's activities. Proceedings before the Court, however, would not be permitted to delay the taking of measures necessary to maintain international peace and security.

To the United Nations Secretariat.—The Authority would use the services of the United Nations Secretariat to the extent mutually agreed upon.

Reports and other communications from the Authority to other organs of the United Nations would be transmitted through the Secretary-General."

On 3 April 1956, the United States of America submitted to the Subcommittee of the Disarmament Commission a Draft Working Paper for the First Phase of a Comprehensive Agreement for Disarmament (DC/SC.1/42) which contains among others the following provisions: "1. Without delay and pending the report on the preliminary steps, the five Powers members of the Subcommittee, while continuing their work in the Subcommittee of the Disarmament Commission of the United Nations, agree to organize a preparatory armaments regulation commission. All decisions of the preparatory armaments regulation commission shall be taken by unanimous vote. 2. The preparatory armaments regulation commission shall agree upon the reduced level of conventional armaments, armed forces and military expenditures of the five members to be accomplished in the first phase. (a) The reduced level of armaments shall be fixed by an agreed application of the manpower levels as a basis for measurement applied to all conventional armaments. (b) The reduced manpower level at the first phase for illustrative purposes shall be: France—750,000, U.S.S.R.—2.5 million, United Kingdom—750,000, United States—2.5 million. (c) The application of the manpower measurement to the composition of the arms of each State shall be at the discretion of the State involved, but such application as is decided upon by the States shall be communicated to the preparatory armaments regulation commission prior to the beginning of any reductions. (d) The reduced level of military expenditures shall be an agreed reflection of the reduced level of armaments and manpower. 3. A control and inspection plan will be agreed upon which will include the Geneva proposals of the President of the United States and of the Chairman of the U.S.S.R., and will include ground control posts at ports, railway terminals, airfields and main highways; aerial survey; mobile units; and an effective communications method. This control and inspection system shall be reciprocally extended in an appropriate and effective manner with consent of the States concerned to forces and facilities which the five Powers have outside their own borders. This control and inspection system shall be designed to be capable of providing against surprise attack by any State and to be capable of verifying the agreed levels of conventional armaments, armed forces and military expenditures. 4. A committee of jurists shall be appointed to prepare a draft treaty to carry out the first phase of a disarmament programme and to prepare for subsequent phases. The draft treaty will include a clause for suspension, partial suspension, countering steps, or termination in the event of violation or upon the occurrence of circumstances adverse to the continued successful operation of the treaty. The draft treaty will also include a clause for appropriate reports to the United Nations Security Council and General Assembly. 5. The preparatory armaments regulation commission will prepare for the control and inspection responsibilities principally through the use of member States as executive agents designated for specific assignments. The executive agents, in the carrying out of their assignments, shall use the nationals of at least five States of which at least one State shall not be associated in any mutual defence agreements with the executive agent. Sixty percent of the personnel used by an executive agent on an assignment may be nationals of the executive agent's State. The assignments as executive agent shall be made with the consent of the State to be inspected and of the executive agent to be designated. 6. An effective world-wide control communications network shall be established with major control communications centres. 7. Upon the agreement of the members of the preparatory armaments regulation commission on the reduced level of conventional armaments and armed forces and military expenditures to be accomplished in the the first phase; and upon agreement on the system of control and inspection to be installed to provide against surprise attack and to verify reductions in levels of armaments, armed forces, and military expenditures; the following three steps will be taken interdependently and concurrently: (a) Each State will provide to the preparatory armaments regulation commission a 'blueprint' of its military establishments consisting of the identification, strength, command structure, and disposition of personnel units and equipment of all major land, sea, and air forces including organized reserves and para-military; and a complete list of conventional military plant facilities and installations with their locations; and the relevant budgetary and appropriation documents for the year ended 31 December 1955 and for the current year. (b) Each State will carry out measures of a stabilizing nature relating to the limitation of the main types of armaments and armed forces, and accordingly will take steps not to increase its appropriations for armed forces and armaments above the level of the expenditures effected for those purposes during the year ended 31 December 1955. (c) The installation of the inspection and control system will be initiated and expeditiously completed. 8. The praparatory armaments regulation commission will notify the member States when the control communications centres are prepared to function and thereafter each member State will give advance notice to the control communication centres of all projected movements of land, sea, or air armed forces through international air or water or over foreign soil. The method and extent of the notice will be in accordance with detailed reciprocal arrangements drawn up for the purpose of increasing the effectiveness and reliability of the safeguards against surprise attack by any State upon any other State. 9. The Disarmament Commission of the United Nations will be requested to invite other States having a significant military potential to join in an armaments regulation organization. (a) In each instance an agreed first phase reduced level of armaments, armed forces, and military expenditures will be established, which should be considerably below the levels fixed for the four major members of the preparatory armaments regulation commission, account being taken of agreed criteria including demographic, geographic, economic and political factors, and providing that the first phase levels of the armed forces of these States shall not exceed 500,000 men unless special circumstances require an agreed exception, and except that the first stage level of the armed forces of China shall not exceed 2,500,000 men. (b) Each State will be required to take appropriate corresponding obligations for inspection, control, limitation, and reporting in all respects similar to the obligations taken by the members of the praparatory armaments regulation commission. 10. An armaments regulation organization will be established, with an armaments regulation council including all signatories, an executive committee consisting of permanent and non-permanent elected members, and a director-general. All decisions of the executive committee will be taken by a unanimous vote of the permanent members plus a majority vote of the non-permanent members. (a) Upon the establishment of the armaments regulation organization the preparatory armaments regulation commission will transfer all of its functions and activities to the appropriate bodies of the armaments regulation organization and will cease to exist. 11. All signatory States will report to the director-general in the affirmative or negative on the following four points: (a) The possession of fissionable materials; (b) The production of fissionable materials; (c) The possession of nuclear weapons; and (d) The planning of tests of nuclear weapons. 12 The control and inspection system will be expanded so that it becomes capable of accounting for future production of fissionable materials and of monitoring the future testing of nuclear weapons. 13. Upon the report of the director-general that the system is prepared to verify the reductions in levels of armaments, armed forces, and military expenditures, and is prepared to provide against surprise attack; and upon the acceptance of the report of the director-general by the executive committee; and upon the adherence to the treaty of the States considered by the executive committee as essential for a sound system; the first phase reductions will be carried out in all signatory States in accordance with an agreed and parallel time schedule. (a) The destruction of existing armaments required by each State to reduce to the agreed first phase levels will be done under the supervision of the inspectors of the armaments regulation organization, and the salvage material will be used for peaceful national purposes. 14. Appropriations by States for armaments and armed forces will be reduced correspondingly to reflect in an agreed manner the first phase reductions, and the funds available through this reduction shall be used both to improve the well-being of the peoples of these States and to furnish assistance particularly to the economically less-developed countries. 15. Upon the report of the director-general that the inspection and control system is prepared to account for future production of fissionable materials, and upon the acceptance of this report by the executive committee, all signatory States agree that future production of fissionable materials will not be used for the manufacture of explosive weapons. 16. All signatory States possessing nuclear weapons will begin to make agreed regular reciprocal and equitable transfers from past production of fissionable materials over to the use of such transferred material for exclusively peaceful purposes, thereby progressively reducing the amount of fissionable materials available for nuclear weapons purposes. 17. The testing of nuclear weapons will be limited and monitored in an agreed manner under the control of the armaments regulation council. 18. Upon a report of the inspector-general that the first phase of the disarmament programme has been successfully completed, and upon the acceptance of this report by the executive committee, the executive committee will call a plenary session of the armaments regulation council. The council will appraise the status of world tensions, review the situation affecting major issues between the States, consider the feasibility of further reductions of armaments, armed forces, and military expenditures, study the possibilities for further decreasing or eliminating the nuclear threat, and make recommendations to the executive committee for further phases in a comprehensive disarmament programme. 19. The executive committee will take account of the recommendations of the armaments regulation council, consider scientific, military, economic, and political factors, and decide upon further phases of a comprehensive disarmament programme, which will best serve the objective of a just and durable peace, for recommendation to the signatory States." Third Report of the Sub-committee of the Disarmament Commission, Annex 6.

70. The Baruch Plan contained the following statement: "There must be no veto to protect those who violate their solemn agreements not develop or use atomic energy for destructive purposes." *The International Control of Atomic Energy*, p. 142. The Recommendations of Part III of the first Report of the United Nations Atomic Energy Commission, approved by the Resolution 191 (III) adopted on 4 November 1948 of the General Assembly, contains the following passage: The treaty concerning control of atomic energy "shall provide that the rule of unanimity of the permanent members, which in certain circumstances exists in the Security Council, shall have no relation to the work of the international control agency. No Government shall possess any right of 'veto' over the fulfilment by the international control agency of the obligations imposed upon it by the treaty nor shall any government have the power, through the exercise of any right of 'veto' or otherwise, to obstruct the course of control or inspection."

71. Georg Cohn, in a memorandum submitted to the International Studies Conference on Collective Security (*Collective Security*, pp. 287 ff.), wrote: "It may be that the tendency to war and to murder are innate in mankind. In that case, considering the frightful consequences entailed in the carrying out of this tendency, a much more energetic action should be undertaken with a view to suppressing it and rooting it out from childhood. But it is also possible that we have here an unhealthy perversion of tendencies which are in themselves healthy and useful, and that it may therefore be possible to combat the madness of war also by medical means. Aside from this pedagogical and medical struggle against the war spirit, it is possible, finally, to consider combating it by means of repressive measures of an international character against incitement to war, either by parallel national legislation in the different countries, or by the establishment of penal dispositions of an international order against States which do not repress with sufficient effectiveness the incitement to war on their own territory."

72. Most of the measures mentioned above were suggested in a Memorandum submitted by the Polish Government to the Disarmament Conference of the League of Nations on 17 September 1931 (*Series of League of Nations Publications* IX. Disarmament 1931. IX, 19, pp. 1 f.) and Proposals of the Polish Delegation with regard to the gradual attainment of Moral Disarmament (*Series of League of Nations Publications* IX. Disarmament 1932. IX, 18, pp. 1 f.)

The Political Commission of the League of Nations Disarmament Conference appointed on 15 March 1932 a special committee of 22 members selected for their personal qualifications to study the question of moral disarmament. This committee adopted on 17 November 1933 the following Draft of a Convention on Moral Disarmament:

"The High Contracting Parties, considering that moral disarmament is one of the essential aspects of the general work of disarmament; considering that the reduction and limitation of armaments depend to a large extent upon the increase of mutual confidence between nations; considering that, as far as public opinion is concerned, a sustained and systematic effort to ease tension may contribute to the progressive realization of material disarmament; considering that the interdependence of States calls, not only for their cooperation in the political sphere, but also for an effort of mutual understanding between the peoples themselves; being resolved to do whatever lies in their power to induce their nationals to display in any public discussion a spirit of tolerance and mutual respect; being convinced that the success of the measures adopted in one country to ensure moral disarmament is largely dependent on the application of similar measures in other countries; recognizing that the League of Nations has placed at the disposal of the various States the Intellectual Cooperation Organization, which is particularly suited to the accomplishment of certain tasks connected with moral disarmament, although a different procedure may have to be adopted to meet special situations:

ARTICLE 1. The High Contracting Parties undertake to use their powers or their influence to see that education at every stage, including the training of teachers, is so conceived as to inspire mutual respect between peoples and to emphasize their interdependence, which makes international collaboration a necessity.

ARTICLE 2. The High Contracting Parties will also do whatever lies in their power to see that teachers are guided by these principles. School text-books should be prepared in the same spirit; those which are at variance with that spirit should be revised. The High Contracting Parties likewise agree to recommend to their competent authorities the inclusion of the following subjects in the syllabus prescribed for entrance examinations to official posts which entail relations with other countries: fundamental principles of international law, legal bases of international relations, and outlines of the efforts made to consolidate peace between nations. They undertake to recommend to their competent authorities that their country's history is taught in relation to the history of other countries.

ARTICLE 3. The High Contracting Parties undertake to encourage, in accordance with the special system in force in their respective countries, the use of the cinematograph and broadcasting with a view to increasing the spirit of good-will between nations. With this end in view, they will also support any action taken by the Intellectual Cooperation Organization, as well as by organizations having the same object. In accordance with the special system in force in their respective countries, they will use their influence to avoid the showing of films, the broadcasting of programmes and the organization of performances obviously calculated to wound the legitimate sentiments of other nations.

ARTICLE 4. The High Contracting Parties will endeavor to facilitate, by the most appropriate means, the cooperation in the work of moral disarmament of government departments, intellectual circles and others working for peace on a larger scale. With this end in view, they agree to encourage the creation and activities of national committees for intellectual cooperation or other organizations collaborating in the work of moral disarmament." (*Series of League of Nations Publications* IX. Disarmament 1936. IX, 4, pp. 925 f.)

At its meeting on 25 June 1932 the Committee for Moral Disarmament decided to set up a Legal Committee. This Committee drew up a questionnaire on the various points to which its attention had particularly been directed and attached to this questionnaire the draft of some articles, which ran as follows:

Article 1. (First Alternative): "The High Contracting Parties agree to consider, within the limits of the possibilities afforded by their public law, the adoption of constitutional rules formally embodying the obligation to refrain from recourse to force as an instrument of national policy and not to attempt the solution of any difference or dispute by other than pacific means. The High Contracting Parties who are Members of the League of Nations assume the same obligation in respect of the stipulations of the Covenant of the League of Nations." (Second Alternative): "The High Contracting Parties undertake to recognize as fundamental laws the stipulation of the Pact of Paris, the Covenant of the League of Nations (in the case of Members of the League of Nations) and of such articles as may subsequently be specified of the General Convention for the Reduction and Limitation of Armaments. Each party further undertakes to ensure that none of its laws, regulations or other provisions shall conflict or be at variance with the stipulations of the aforesaid international agreements. . . .

Article 2. The High Contracting Parties undertake to adopt legislative measures empowering them to penalize: 1. The preparation and carrying-out in their respective territories of acts directed against the security of a foreign power. 2. (First Alternative): Direct public propaganda urging the State to be the first to commit, contrary to its international undertakings, any of the following acts: (a) declaration of war upon another state; (b) invasion by its armed forces, even without declaration of war, of the territory of another State; (c) attack by its land, naval or air forces, even without declaration of war, upon the territory, vessels or aircraft of another State; (d) naval blockade of the coasts or ports of another State; (e) assistance given to armed bands, organized in its territory, which have invaded the territory of another State, or refusal, in spite of the request of the invaded State, to take in its own territory all possible steps to deprive the aforesaid bands of all assistance or protection. (Second Alternative): Direct public propaganda urging the State to commit any one of the acts of aggression enumerated in Article . . . of the present Convention relative to the definition of the aggressor. (Third Alternative): Inciting public opinion by direct public propaganda with a view to forcing the State to embark upon a war of aggression. 3. Participation in or support of armed bands, organized in the territory of the State, which have invaded the territory of another State. 4. The dissemination of false news, reports or of documents forged, falsified or inaccurately attributed to third parties, whenever such dissemination has a disturbing effect upon international relations and is carried out in bad faith. 5. Causing prejudice to a foreign State by maliciously attributing to its acts which are manifestly untrue and thus exposing it to public resentment or contempt. 6. Acts contrary to the prohibitions laid down in Articles . . . of the Convention. (This text should be completed by provisions dealing more especially with the case of persons who, contrary to the undertakings given by the State, have been guilty of the private manufacture of or trade in arms or implements of war and also of preparations, contrary to the provisions of the Convention, for chemical, incendiary or bacterial warfare, etc.).

Article 3. The High Contracting Parties further undertake: (1) to prevent the activities of organizations committing any of the acts enumerated in Article 2 and to treat them as organizations pursuing illegal aims under the municipal laws of the country; (2) to incorporate in their laws the necessary provisions to permit of their giving effect to any provisions which may be embodied in the Convention on the subject of immunities (the reference here is to the provisions of the Convention which may be elaborated in consequence of the French delegation's proposals)." *Series of League of Nations Publications* IX. Disarmament 1935. IX, 4, pp. 701 ff.

The General Assembly of the United Nations adopted at its 108th plenary meeting on 3 November 1947 a Resolution 110 (II) concerning measures to be taken against propaganda and the inciters of a new war which runs as follows:

"*Whereas* in the Charter of the United Nations the peoples express their determination to save succeeding generations from the scourge of war, which twice in our lifetime has brought untold sorrow to mankind, and to practice tolerance and live together in peace with one another as good neighbours, and

Whereas the Charter also calls for the promotion of universal respect for, and observance of, fundamental freedoms which include freedom of expression, all Members having pledged themselves in Article 56 to take joint and separate action for such observance of fundamental freedoms,

The General Assembly

1. *Condemns* all forms of propaganda, in whatsoever country conducted, which is either designed or likely to provoke or encourage any threat to the peace, breach of the peace, or act of aggression;

2. *Requests* the Government of each Member to take appropriate steps within its constitutional limits:

(a) To promote, by all means of publicity and propaganda available to them, friendly relations among nations based upon the Purposes and Principles of the Charter;

(b) To encourage the dissemination of all information designed to give expression to the undoubted desire of all peoples for peace;

3. *Directs* that this resolution be communicated for the forthcoming Conference on Freedom of Information."

The Resolution 176 (II) adopted by the General Assembly at its 123rd plenary meeting on 21 November 1947 contains the following statement: "*The General Assembly Resolves* to request the Governments of the Member states:

1. To take appropriate measures to extend the teaching of international law in all its phases, including its development and codification, in the universities and higher educational institutions of each country that are under government control or over which Governments have some influence, or to initiate such teaching where it is not yet provided;

2. To promote similar teaching regarding the aims, purposes, structure and operation of the United Nations in conjunction with paragraph 1 above and in accordance with Resolution 137 (II) adopted by the General Assembly on 17 November 1947, on the teaching of the purposes and principles, the structure and activities of the United Nations in the schools of Member States."

A Resolution, 290 (IV), concerning essentials of peace, adopted by the General Assembly at its 261st plenary meeting on 1 December 1949 contains the statement: "The General Assembly calls upon every nation. . . . 8. To *remove* the barriers which deny to peoples the free exchange of information and ideas essential to international understanding and peace."

On 17 November 1950 the General Assembly adopted at its 308th plenary meeting Resolution 381 (V) concerning the condemnation of propaganda against peace, which runs as follows:

"*The General Assembly*,

1. *Reaffirms* its resolutions 110 (II) and 290 (IV), paragraph 8, which condemn all propaganda against peace and recommends the free exchange of infor-

mation and ideas as one of the foundations of good-neighbourly relations between the peoples;

2. *Declares* that such propaganda includes:

(1) Incitement to conflicts or acts of aggression;

(2) Measures tending to isolate the peoples from any contact with the outside world, by preventing the Press, radio and other media of communication from reporting international events, and thus hindering mutual comprehension and understanding between peoples;

(3) Measures tending to silence or distort the activities of the United Nations in favour of peace or to prevent their peoples from knowing the views of other States Members."

In this connection also the International Convention concerning the Use of Broadcasting in the Cause of Peace, 23 September 1936, and the Resolution of the General Assembly 424 (V) of 14 December 1950, are to be mentioned. *Cf. supra*, p. 89, note 8.

(ee) *Economic cooperation.*

If war is caused not only by political but also by economic circumstances, a universal or quasi-universal international security organization must have institutions to bring about, as far as possible, satisfactory economic conditions throughout the world, and thus its constituent treaty must provide for so-called economic cooperation.[1] The main question of the exact nature of the relationship between economic circumstances and war is highly disputed. It is a specific Marxian theory that the occurrence of war is exclusively, or at least predominantly, due to economic causes, especially to the capitalistic system. This view is rejected by an outstanding English economist, Lionel Robbins, who tries to show that, although it would be an exaggeration to say that wars have no economic causes or to deny that conflicts of national economic interests may lead to war, these conflicts are not the root cause. "The ultimate condition giving rise to those clashes of national economic interest which lead to international war is the existence of independent national sovereignties. Not capitalism, but the anarchic political organization of the world is the root disease of our civilization."[1a] He says further: "We know today that unless we destroy the sovereign state, the sovereign state will destroy us."[2] Hence, according to Robbins, the main purpose of an international security organization is to restrict national sovereignty by imposing upon its members definite obligations, the fulfillment of which is guaranteed by effective sanctions. However, another and no less outstanding writer, Edward H. Carr, advocates the opinion that international security is only a by-product of a definite social organization. "International peace . . . cannot be achieved by the signing of pacts or covenants 'outlawing' war any more than revolutions are prevented by making them illegal. A generation which makes peace and security its aim is doomed to frustration. . . . If the victors in the present war [the second World War] are able to create the conditions for an orderly and progressive development of human society, peace and security will be added unto them."[3] Further, he suggests that this "orderly and progressive development of human society" may be brought about by a "new democracy" which differs from "liberal" democracy by the fact that the ideals of equality and liberty are "re-interpreted in predominantly economic terms,"[4] by restricting the self-determination of the states,[5] which are to be placed within a more or less universal international organization, and, last but not least, by abandoning the *laissez-faire* policy of economic liberalism and adopting a policy of planned economy,[6] that is to say, by socialism.

However that may be, it is now an almost generally accepted opinion that economic cooperation is an important preventive measure which may be applied by an international security organization.[7]

That economic cooperation is a purpose of an international security organization means that this organization should bring about, as far as possible, a coordination of the economic policies of its members. The activities of different subjects can be coordinated only with a view to a definite goal. Economic cooperation of the members of an international security organization is achieved if the governments of these states adapt their activity to a certain pattern of economic policy which is characterized by its end as well as by the means to be applied with a view to realizing the end. There is no difficulty in answering the question as to the end of economic cooperation. It is a satisfactory economic situation of the states, an adequate status of world economy. The usual formulas by which this goal is described are: "economic health of every country,"[8] "economic prosperity" (the opposite of economic depression), "social security,"[9] "economic stability and well being," "high standard of living,"[10] "economic advancement,"[11] "economic progress," "full employment,"[12] and the like. All these formulas are meaningless unless the specific means are indicated by which these ideals may be realized. There is, in general, agreement concerning the ultimate ends of social life: the greatest possible happiness of the greatest possible number of individuals. The real problem, and the main cause of conflict of opinion, is not the end but the means by which the generally accepted end is to be realized. There are two fundamentally different and directly opposite views concerning the appropriate method of bringing about satisfactory economic conditions: economic liberalism, postulating private property in the means of production and complete freedom of economic life, and rejecting any governmental intervention; and economic socialism, postulating the nationalization of the means of production, and the authoritative regulation of economic life, especially in the organization of economic production and in the distribution of products.[13] If there is no agreement with respect to the specific methods determining the economic pattern to which the members of an international security organization are to adapt their policy—and there is evidently not only no agreement but the most passionate antagonism in this respect—there is not very much left to the activity of an international security organization in the field of economic cooperation. Even apart from this fundamental antagonism, economic cooperation is hampered by the conflict of interests between states which are forced to secure their national economy by protective tariffs and those the economy of which requires a free trade. The most serious limitation of economic cooperation results from the principle that the international organization must not intervene in matters which are within the domestic jurisdiction of its members; and economic matters are usually considered to be within the domestic jurisdiction of the states.[14]

In view of these circumstances, it is not astonishing that the only effective way of achieving economic cooperation within an international security organization: the establishment of a special organ competent to impose by its decisions definite obligations upon the member states with respect to their economic policy, is practically out of the question. The organ or organs concerned may be endowed only with the power of discussing the problems involved, of giving advice, of making recommendations, of collecting and disseminating useful information.[15] Positive results may be—and actually have been—achieved on a more or less voluntary basis, especially through agencies established by special conventions, in the fields of relief and reconstruction,[16] international lending and monetary regulation,[17] food and agricultural organization.[18]

The treaty constituting an international security organization may provide not only for economic but also for social cooperation—that is, for cooperation in the fields of labor, health, drug control, education, and human rights in general.[19] It may contain provisions concerning the treatment of non-self-governing peoples, especially colonies, by placing their administration under a system of international control.[20] However, these functions are not directly connected with its main purpose—the prevention of war [21]—and therefore not essential elements of a system of collective security in the strict sense of this term.

NOTES

1. Article I of many Mutual Defense Assistance Agreements refers to "the principle that economic recovery is essential to international peace and security and must be given clear priority."

1[a]. Lionel Robbins, *The Economic Causes of War*, (1939), p. 99; *cf.* also pp. 15 ff, 57.

2. Robbins, *op. cit.*, p. 105.

3. Edward Hallett Carr, *Conditions of Peace* (1942), p. xxiii.

4. Carr, *op. cit.*, pp. 11, 30 ff.

5. Carr, *op cit.*, pp. 12, 39 ff.

6. Carr, *op cit.*, pp. 13 ff.

7. Economic cooperation was not a main purpose of the League of Nations. The only provision of the Covenant referring to this subject matter was Article 23 (e) which provided: "the Members of the League . . . will make provisions to secure and maintain freedom of communications and of transit and equitable treatment for the commerce of all Members of the League. In this connection the special necessities of the regions devastated during the war of 1914–1918 shall be borne in mind." However, as a matter of fact, the activity of the League in the field of economic cooperation went far beyond the narrow limits of this provision, and in December 1939, the Assembly approved the report of a special committee—the so-called Bruce Committee, named for its Chairman, S. M. Bruce, Australian High Commissioner—which suggested the establishment of a Central Committee for Economic and Social Questions (The Development of International Co-operation in Economic and Social Affairs. Report of the Special Committee. Special Supplement to the Monthly Summary of the League of Nations, August 1939). The outbreak of the Second World War prevented the realization of this plan.

In the Charter of the United Nations, economic cooperation plays an important part. The preamble proclaims that the United Nations are determined "to promote social progress and better standards of life in larger freedom" and to "employ international machinery for the promotion of the economic and social advancement of all peoples." Article 1, paragraph 3, declares that it is a Purpose of the United Nations "To achieve international cooperation in solving international problems of an economic, social, cultural, or humanitarian character . . ." Article 13, paragraph 1, letter b, confers upon the General Assembly the power to "initiate studies and make recommendations for the purpose of . . . promoting international cooperation in the economic, social, cultural, educational, and health fields . . ." and two Chapters (IX and X) containing Articles 55–72 are devoted to "International Economic and Social Cooperation" and "The Economic and Social Council." The most characteristic provisions of these two chapters are:

"ARTICLE 55. With a view to the creation of conditions of stability and well-being which are necessary for peaceful and friendly relations among nations based on respect for the principle of equal rights and self-determination of peoples, the United Nations shall promote:

a. higher standards of living, full employment, and conditions of economic and social progress and development;

b. solutions of international economic, social, health, and related problems; and international cultural and educational cooperation; and

c. universal respect for, and observance of, human rights and fundamental freedoms for all without distinction as to race, sex, language, or religion.

ARTICLE 61. 1. The Economic and Social Council shall consist of eighteen Members of the United Nations elected by the General Assembly. 2. Subject to the provisions of paragraph 3, six members of the Economic and Social Council shall be elected each year for a term of three years. A retiring member shall be eligible for immediate reelection. 3. At the first election, eighteen members of the Economic and Social Council shall be chosen. The term of office of six members so chosen shall expire at the end of one year, and of six other members at the end of two years, in accordance with arrangements made by the General Assembly. 4. Each Member of the Economic and Social Council shall have one representative.

ARTICLE 62. 1. The Economic and Social Council may make or initiate studies and reports with respect to international economic, social, cultural, educational, health, and related matters and may make recommendations with respect to any such matters to the General Assembly, to the Members of the United Nations, and to the specialized agencies concerned. 2. It may make recommendations for the purpose of promoting respect for, and observance of, human rights and fundamental freedoms for all. 3. It may prepare draft conventions for submission to the General Assembly, with respect to matters falling within its competence. 4. It may call, in accordance with the rules prescribed by the United Nations, international conferences on matters falling within its competence.

ARTICLE 67. 1. Each member of the Economic and Social Council shall have one vote. 2. Decisions of the Economic and Social Council shall be made by a majority of the members present and voting."

8. President Franklin D. Roosevelt said in his address to the Monetary and Financial Conference, Washington, D. C., on 29 June 1944: "Economic diseases are highly communicable. It follows, therefore, that the economic health of every country is a proper matter of concern to all its neighbors, near and distant." In: Louise W. Holborn, Ed., *War and Peace Aims of the United Nations* (Boston: World Peace Foundation, 1948), p. 288.

9. Atlantic Charter (14 August 1941): "The President of the United States of America and the Prime Minister, Mr. Churchill, representing His Majesty's Government in the United Kingdom, being met together, deem it right to make known certain common principles in the national policies of their respective countries on which they base their hopes for a better future of the world. . . . Fourth. They will endeavor . . . to further the enjoyment by all states, great and small, victor or vanquished, of access, on equal terms, to the trade and to the raw materials of the world which are needed for their economic prosperity. Fifth, They desire to bring about the fullest collaboration between all nations in the economic field, with the object of securing, for all, . . . economic advancement and social security. . . ."

10. Article 55 of the U.N. Charter.

11. Preamble to the U.N. Charter.

12. Article 55 of the U.N. Charter.

13. When after the First World War the problem of the cooperation of the United States and the United Kingdom for the economic reconstruction of Europe became urgent, Bernard Baruch, on behalf of the United States, advocated the following opinion: "The salvation of the world must rest upon the initiative of individuals" (H. R. G. Greaves, *The League Committees and World Order*, 1931, p. 66.) This is a typical expression of economic liberalism. From this point of view, economic cooperation as a function of an international organization is possible only in a negative sense: Its main purpose is to induce the governments of the members to remove all economic barriers. This was also the view of President Wilson who in point three of his fourteen points program of January, 1918, called for the "removal, so far as possible, of all economic barriers and the establishment of an equality of trade conditions among all the

nations consenting to the peace . . ." (*Cf.* Daniel S. Cheever and H. Field Haviland, Jr., *Organizing for Peace*, 1954, pp. 159, 160 ff.)

14. Article 2, paragraph 7, of the Charter of the United Nations stipulates: "Nothing contained in the present Charter shall authorize the United Nations to intervene in matters which are essentially within the domestic jurisdiction of any state or shall require the Members to submit such matters to settlement under the present Charter; but this principle shall not prejudice the application of enforcement measures under Chapter VII." In its *Report to the President on the Results of the San Francisco Conference* (Department of State Publication 2349, Washington, 1945, p. 44), Secretary of State Stettinius justified this provision as desirable "because of the amplification of the power and authority given to the Assembly and, particularly, to the Economic and Social Council. Without this general limitation . . . it might have been supposed that the Economic and Social Council could interfere directly in the domestic economy, social structure, or cultural or educational arrangements of the member states. Such a possibility is now definitely excluded." *Cf.* also Cheever and Haviland, *op. cit.*, pp. 212, ff.

15. *Cf.* Article 13, paragraph 1 (b), and Article 62 of the U.N. Charter, p. 256 f.

16. In this respect the United Nations Relief and Rehabilitation Administration (UNRRA) should be mentioned.

17. The International Monetary Fund and the International Bank for Reconstruction and Development were established for these purposes.

18. The Food and Agricultural Organization of the United Nations.

19. The following agencies operate for these purposes: the International Labor Organization, the World Health Organization (specialized agencies brought in relationship with the United Nations); the Commission on Narcotic Drugs of the Economic and Social Council, which took the place of the Advisory Committee on Traffic in Opium and other Dangerous Drugs of the League of Nations); the United Nations Educational, Scientific and Cultural Organization (a specialized agency); the Human Rights Commission of the Economic and Social Council.

20. Such as the mandate system of the League of Nations (Article 22 of the Covenant) and the trusteeship system of the United Nations (Chapters XI and XII of the Charter.)

21. Article 73 (c) of the U.N. Charter stipulates as an obligation of the members which have or assume responsibilities for the administration of territories whose people have not yet attained a full measure of self-government, the obligation "to further international peace and security," and Article 76 (a) characterizes one of the objectives of the trusteeship system by the same formula. However, this is an obligation incumbent upon all members and not a specific element of the political system established for non-self-governing territories in general and trust territories in particular.

(ff) *Universalism and regionalism.*

In spite of their tendency towards universality, the Covenant of the League of Nations and the Charter of the United Nations both authorize the establishment of regional security organizations. However, they do not contain a definition of this concept.[1] As a matter of fact, there are different views as to the meaning of the term "regional."[1a] According to one, a regional organization is an association of neighboring states, that is, of states which are united by the fact that their territories are contiguous. According to another, the geographical element is not essential. States may form a regional organization even if their territories are separated by the territories of states not belonging to the organization or by the ocean. Their unity is constituted by a common interest, e. g., by the fact that they have a common enemy. That their organization is "regional" means that it is not a universal but a partial association of states, comprising only several but not all (or not almost all) the states of the international community. An additional criterion may be that the realization of the purpose for which the organization is established is limited to an area precisely defined in the constituent treaty.[2]

It stands to reason that territorial contiguity in itself is not capable of constituting a political unity. If states *A*, *B* and *C* may form a regional organization even though the territory of *A* is contiguous only to that of *B* and not to that of *C* whose territory is contiguous only to that of *B*, then there is no reason to exclude state *D* whose territory is contiguous only to that of *A* or state *E* whose territory is contiguous only to that of *C*, and so forth. There is no answer to the question of where the territorial contiguity, which is to be considered as the basis of a "regional" organization, ends. There must be an additional factor constituting the unity of a regional organization, a common interest uniting the neighboring states, but such a common interest, as for instance defense against a potential aggressor, may unite states whose territories are far distant from one another. It may be only the territory of the potential aggressor which separates the states united by an international organization established for the purpose of collective defense. Such an organization is "regional" but not in the geographical sense of this term.[3]

There can be little doubt that a universal or quasi-universal organization is the ideal solution of the problem of international security. Regional security organizations are at best only partial solutions and to some extent they are even a danger to international security. For this reason the framers of the Covenant as well as of the Charter were not in favor of regional security organizations which were suspected of being the old alliances in the disguise of mutual assistance agreements.[4] In order to differentiate alliances from regional security organizations, the doctrine has been expounded that the latter are by their very nature directed against an aggression which takes place within the organization whereas the former are directed against an aggression from the outside[5] and hence may be misused for offensive purposes. There is, however, no sufficient reason to deny a treaty, concluded by some states and imposing upon the parties the obligation to assist one another in case of an aggression on the part of a state not a contracting party, the character of a regional security agreement. On the contrary, only a regional—in the sense of a non-universal—organization can be directed against aggression on the part of a state not belonging to the organization; and even an agreement which restricts the obligation of the parties to mutual assistance in case of internal aggression may be misused for offensive purposes. A state, party to such an agreement, may very well be attacked on the part of other parties under the pretext of being guilty of an aggression. A defensive alliance is always a regional security organization, and even if restricted to the case of internal aggression, a regional security organization is a defensive alliance of the non-aggressors against the potential aggressor among them. It is true that an "alliance," in the specific sense of the term—that is, a regional defense organization directed against aggression from the outside—arouses the suspicion of aggressive intentions and leads, therefore, to counter alliances and thus to a situation which is just the contrary of international security. However, it should not be ignored that the strongest motive of uniting several states in a regional organization is the common danger of aggression on the part of a third state and that the most important regional organizations are thus defensive "alliances" in the specific sense of the term. To refuse to call them "regional" is hardly more than a terminological paradox.

Regional security organizations outside or within a universal or quasi-universal security organization are justifiable in so far as the latter, for some reason, does not work satisfactorily and hence needs to be supplemented or strengthened by the former. If, or to the extent that, a universal or quasi-universal security organization does not fulfill its task to guarantee international peace, regional security organizations may be useful. In addition, there are some functions which regional organizations may perform without impairing the security to be guaranteed by the universal or quasi-universal organization. Among these functions are, first, the peaceful settlement of strictly local disputes, especially if the treaty constituting the universal organization does not establish a court with compulsory jurisdictions,[6] and, secondly, collective self-defense. Regional agreements imposing upon the parties the obligation to assist one another in case of aggression until a competent agency of the universal organization takes action against the aggressor can hardly be excluded if the universal organization does not have its own armed force ready for immediate action at its disposal.[7] Within the limits just mentioned, such regional agreements may even establish a central executive organ for the purpose of collective self-defense. However, enforcement measures to be taken as sanctions which go beyond this limit should be reserved to the universal organization, which may—if appropriate—use the coercive machinery of regional organizations to execute sanctions against a violator of the constituent treaty.[8] Such an action taken by a regional organization under the authority of the universal organization is to be considered as a function of the latter, and not as a regional action.

The most important preventive measure—disarmament—can be effected successfully only on a universal basis. Regional disarmament as a permanent political system is possible only within a partial area which is safe against aggression from the outside. Since there is no longer such an area, regional disarmament is hardly a practical consideration.[9]

NOTES

1. Article 21 of the Covenant of the League of Nations refers to "regional understandings." It runs as follows: "Nothing in this Covenant shall be deemed to affect the validity of international engagements, such as treaties of arbitration or regional understandings like the Monroe doctrine, for securing the maintenance of peace."

Chapter VIII (Articles 52–54) of the Charter of the United Nations deals with "regional arrangements." It provides:

"*Article 52.* 1. Nothing in the present Charter precludes the existence of regional arrangements or agencies for dealing with such matters relating to the maintenance of international peace and security as are appropriate for regional action, provided that such arrangements or agencies and their activities are consistent with the Purposes and Principles of the United Nations. 2. The Members of the United Nations entering into such arrangements or constituting such agencies shall make every effort to achieve pacific settlement of local disputes through such regional arrangements or by such regional agencies before referring them to the Security Council. 3. The Security Council shall encourage the development of pacific settlement of local disputes through such regional arrangements or by such regional agencies either on the initiative of the states concerned or by reference from the Security Council. 4. This Article in no way impairs the application of Articles 34 and 35.

Article 53. 1. The Security Council shall, where appropriate, utilize such regional arrangements or agencies for enforcement action under its authority. But no enforcement action shall be taken under regional arrangements or by regional agencies without the authorization of the Security Council, with the exception of measures against any enemy state, as defined in paragraph 2 of this Article, provided for pursuant to Article 107 or in regional arrangements directed against renewal of aggressive policy on the part of any such state, until such time as the Organization may, on request of the Governments concerned, be charged with the responsibility for preventing further aggression by such a state. 2. The term enemy state as used in paragraph 1 of this Article applies to any state which during the Second World War has been an enemy of any signatory of the present Charter.

Article 54. The Security Council shall at all times be kept fully informed of activities undertaken or in contemplation under regional arrangements or by regional agencies for the maintenance of international peace and security."

1a. *Cf.* pp. 229 ff.

2. Pierre Vellas, *Le Régionalisme International et l'Organisation des Nations Unies* (Paris, 1948), pp. 32 ff., 147, referring to declarations made by Latin-American delegations at the San Francisco Conference (U. N. C. I. O., Vol. XII, p. 792, 802), advocates the doctrine that a regional organization is the expression of sociological solidarity, the legal order constituting the organization being the effect of the social reality. If the solidarity is effective, the legal order is superfluous. If it does not exist, the legal order is ineffectual. It is true that there must be a common interest and, in this sense, a certain solidarity inducing states to enter an agreement establishing a legal order regulating the mutual behavior of the contracting state. However, the sociological doctrine overlooks the fact that the legal order may not only be the effect of a certain solidarity, but may, as a fact in the minds of the men concerned, in itself have the effect of strengthening the solidarity so that there is a correlation between solidarity as a social reality and legal order, which is itself a social reality.

3. Neither the Covenant nor the Charter restricts regional organizations to states whose territories are contiguous.

4. *Cf.* p. 39 ff.

5. Vellas, *op. cit.*, p. 46.

6. Article 21 of the Covenant expressly mentions treaties of arbitration; and, according to Article 52, paragraph 2, of the Charter, regional arrangements shall provide for the pacific settlement of local disputes. Article 95 authorizes the members to entrust the solution of their differences to other tribunals than the International Court of Justice, which implies that regional agreements for arbitration are compatible with the Charter.

7. The question as to whether treaties for the implementation of the provisions of Article 51 concerning collective self-defense are to be considered as "regional arrangements" within the meaning of Chapter VIII of the Charter is answered in the negative as well as in the affirmative. The main arguments for a negative answer are that Article 51 is not inserted into Chapter VIII, and that enforcement actions in the exercise of self-defense are not mentioned in Article 53, paragraph 1, among the enforcement actions which may be taken under regional arrangements without the authorization of the Security Council. However, there can be no doubt at all that at the San Francisco Conference the right of collective self-defense, as stipulated in Article 51, was considered by many delegates, especially by the South American delegates, as a specific subject of regional arrangements. (*Cf.* the declaration of the representative of Colombia, U. N. C. I. O., Vol. XII, p. 680.)

Whether a treaty for the implementation of Article 51 is or is not a regional arrangement within the meaning of Chapter VIII of the Charter, it is certainly a regional agreement within the meaning of the definition of this concept presented above. Such a treaty may—in accordance with Article 51—provide for mutual assistance not only in case of an aggression within the organization but also in case of an aggression from the outside. It may even provide for collective action against an aggressor which is not a member of the United Nations; for the wording of Article 51 does not restrict the right of individual and collective self-defense to the case of an armed attack on the part of a member state; and Article 53, paragraph 1 refers to enforcement actions "taken under regional arrangements or by regional agencies," that is, by regional organizations, against former enemy states, which may not be members of regional organizations and even not members of the United Nations. If a treaty concluded for the implementation of Article 51 of the Charter does not constitute a "regional" arrangement in the sense of Chapter VIII of the Charter, Article 54, providing that "the Security Council shall at all times be kept fully informed of activities undertaken or in contemplation" under the treaty, does not apply. This may explain the tendency to interpret Chapter VIII of the Charter in a restrictive sense, so that treaties such as the North Atlantic Treaty do not fall under the provisions of this Chapter.

Julius Stone, *op. cit.*, pp. 247 ff., considers as an essential element of a regional organization that some relation to a "region" must be implied in the arrangement, "but what it is is obscure." He expressly rejects the view that the treaty constituting a regional security organization may provide for collective measures "against attack from another region." The state against which the enforcement action is directed may not be a contracting party to the constituent treaty, but it must be "within the region" if the organization constituted by the treaty is to be considered as a "regional" organization within the meaning of Articles 52–54 of the Charter. That the state must be "within the region" can only mean that its territory must be within the region determined by the constituent treaty. Stone justifies his interpretation first, by stating that "this is the natural meaning of the phrase 'appropriate for regional action' in Article 52 [not 53, as misprinted], paragraph 1." However, an action may be regional—in the "natural" meaning of this term—not only when the state against which it is directed is within the area determined in the constituent treaty but also when the action is restricted to this area insofar as it is conditioned by an act of aggression which has taken place within this area, even by a state whose territory is not within this area. This may be the case when the attack takes place on the open sea on vessels of one of the contracting parties, a case expressly referred to in Article 6 of the North Atlantic Treaty. Secondly, Stone says "if an arrangement for common action of one region against a threat to peace from another region were within the articles, the provision of Article 53, paragraph 1, that the Security Council may use regional arrangements as agencies for enforcement under its authority, would mean that the Council would invoke the military aid of one regional alliance against another region." Although Stone admits that "such a situation is conceivable," he asserts that "it certainly seems inconsistent with the 'Purposes and Principles of the United Nations' as Article 52, paragraph 1, requires. It would arise as a stage in the breakdown of the Charter, not of its application." If the Security Council may authorize an enforcement action to be taken by a regional organization against an aggressor state which is within the region, without violating the provisions of the Charter concerning the Purposes and Principles of the United Nations, it is not understandable why the Security Council could not, without violating these provisions, authorize an enforcement action to be taken by a regional organization against an aggressor state which is not "within the region." All the more so as no provision of Chapter VIII restricts enforcement action by a regional organization to actions directed against states within the region. Article 53 expressly refers to enforcement actions "taken under regional arrangements or by regional agencies" against former enemy states, whether these states are or are not "within the region." Since the Charter does not restrict enforcement actions to be taken by a regional organization to actions against a state "within the region," the Security Council may, in *applying* Article 53, paragraph 1 of the Charter, authorize a regional organization to take an enforcement action against a state which is not "within the region." Such an authorization would be quite "natural" if in case of a conflict between a state member of a regional organization and a state which is not within the region, the Security Council considered an enforcement action involving the use of armed force to be directed against the state which is not within the region as adequate, but still has not yet at its disposal the armed forces referred to in Article 43, whereas the regional organization disposes of such an armed force. There is no reason to assume that such a situation "would arise as a stage in the breakdown of the Charter, not of its application."

The provision of Article 53, paragraph 1, that enforcement action may be taken by a regional organization only with the authorization of the Security Council, must be interpreted as restricted by Article 51. If a state, member of a regional organization, is the victim of an armed attack by a state which is not "within the region," the regional organization, in the exercise of the right of collective self-defense, may take a collective enforcement action against the aggressor until the Security Council intervenes. The latter may if it considers this action adequate, applying Article 53, paragraph 1, authorize the regional organization to continue its action. In this way Article 53, paragraph 1 may be interpreted as complementing the provision of Article 39 concerning action to be taken by the Security Council in case of a threat to or breach of the peace.

The third argument set forth by Stone runs as follows: "The disputes, the pacific settlement of which parties to regional arrangements are to assume, and the Security Council is to encourage them to assume, are specified by Article 52, paragraphs 2 and 3, to be 'local' only. It would be strange to limit the delegation of the settlement function to intra-regional disputes, without a similar limit on delegated peace enforcement." By "local disputes" Article 52, paragraph 2 can only mean disputes between parties to the treaty constituting the regional organization. For this treaty can impose only upon the contracting parties the obligation to settle their disputes in a definite way, prescribed by the treaty. A state which is "within the region," but not a contracting party, cannot be bound by it. Hence "local" cannot mean "intra-regional." That a treaty constituting a regional organization regulates only the settlement of disputes between the members of the organization, but does not limit enforcement actions to be taken by the organization to actions against an aggressor which is a member of the organization, is not strange at all. For also an enforcement action to be directed against an aggressor which is not a member of the organization—whether it is or is not within the region—may be provided for by the stipulation of obligations imposed upon the member states. The provision concerning "local disputes" does not support Stone's statement: "The real question is not whether the State against which enforcement action is directed is within the *arrangement;* it is rather whether it is within the *region.*" Finally, Stone states that only if his interpretation of the term "regional" is accepted the absurdity could be avoided to apply Article 54 to organizations constituted by treaties providing for military action against external aggression. "If an alliance for defence against a Permanent Member from *outside* the region were a 'regional arrangement,' even military staff plans would have to be disclosed in advance to the potential aggressor; and the potential aggressor's own consent obtained before he could be resisted. On the present view these absurdities are avoided, and such outwardly orientated arrangements must justify themselves as preparation for measures of self-defence, reportable only after they are taken, under Article 51." If security organizations protecting their members against aggression on the part of states not members of the organization or not being within the region are not considered to be "regional," then, indeed, Article 54 does not apply to them. That its non-application to the organizations concerned is desirable, can certainly not be denied. But from this fact does not follow that the organizations concerned are not regional within the meaning of the Charter. Such an interpretation can be based neither on the wording, nor on the intention of those who drafted the provisions, of Articles 51–54.

8. Article 53, paragraph 1, of the Charter contains such a provision.

9. In 1922 the Assembly of the League of Nations did not share this opinion. On 27 September it adopted a resolution (XV) which runs as follows: "The Assembly, whilst declaring that the reduction of armaments contemplated by Article 8 of the Covenant cannot achieve its full effect for world peace unless it be general, desires to emphasize the importance of regional agreements for the purpose of reducing armaments—agreements which, if necessary, might even go beyond the measures decided upon in respect of general reduction; and requests the Council to ask the Temporary Mixed Commission to take into consideration, during its subsequent work, the possibility of recommending the conclusion of similar agreements to States which might be concerned."

A regional agreement for the purpose of reducing armaments was the Convention signed on 7 February 1923 by Guatemala, El Salvador, Honduras, Nicaragua, and Costa Rica. It is characteristic that among the derogations expressly recognized by the treaty were "impending invasion by another state" (Article I), and "threatened attack by a foreign state" (Article IV).

INDEX

A

Absolute or relative security, 7, 10 f., 23
Acts of state, 123 f.
Aggression, 10, 24, 27 f., 29 f., 35 f., 37, 40, 55, 58 ff., 60 f., 63 ff., 65 ff., 67 ff., 69 ff., 73 ff., 75 ff., 78 ff., 80 ff., 83 ff., 85 ff., 88 f., 90 ff., 93 ff., 98 f., 115, 118
armed attack as, 60 f., 88
including or not including the use of armed force, 63 ff.
as unprovoked attack, 86
definition of, 60, 66 ff., 69 ff., 73 ff., 78 ff., 83 ff., 87, 93 ff., 89 f.
and determination of the aggressor, 83 ff.
general, enumerative or mixed, 78 ff., 98 f.
direct and indirect, 61, 63 ff., 80, 82, 89
economic, 65, 81 f.
elimination of the problem of, 67 ff., 90 ff.
external and internal, 24, 29 f., 61, 64, 115, 118
ideological, 65, 81 f.
intention of, 63, 85, 88, 93, 94
under general international law, 35 f., 37
legal or political concept, 75 ff.
major or minor, 66
military and legal concept of, 58 f.
revolution as internal aggression, 64, 88
and self-defense, 27 f., 59 ff., 68, 86, 118
Aggressive or defensive war, 35 f., 58 f., 89, 90 f., 110, 202
weapons, 202, 219
Aggressor, definition of the, 79 ff.
determination of the, 67 f., 70, 72 f., 75, 120, 121 f., 146 f.
by an international court, 121 f.
Alliances, 39 ff., 259 f., 262 ff.
and regional security organizations, 39 ff., 259 f., 262 ff.
Armaments, *see also* Disarmament
abolition of, 203 f.
aggressive and defensive, 202
bacterial and chemical, prohibition of, 201, 203 f., 221 f.
as cause of war, 199
control of, 26, 232. *See also* Disarmament, control of
conventional and atomic, 201, 219
definition (elements of), 199 ff.
differentiation of, 120
expenditure, 202, 206 f.
internationalization, 204
land, sea and air, 202 f.
nuclear, 201 f., 203 f., 210, 220 f., 224
control of, 204, 208, 210, 220 f., 224
peacetime and wartime, 199 f., 202 f., 206, 219
quantity and quality of, 202
reduction and limitation of, 118 f., 120, 197 ff., 203, 206 f., 231 f.
derogations, 207, 231 f.

Armed force, *see* Force, armed
use of, *see* Force, armed, use of
Arms and ammunition, manufacture, internationalization of, 209
nationalization of (state monopoly), 209
Arms and ammunition, manufacture and trade of, 201, 209, 241 ff.
Arms of mass destruction, 201 f., 203
Assistance, mutual, 24, 40
Assistance (defense), right or obligation of, 24 ff., 61
Attack, armed, 60 f., 88
Atomic energy, control of, 198, 210, 220 f., 224, 233 ff.
Aviation, civil and military, internationalization of, 120, 145, 204

B

Balance of power, 39, 41 f., 51
Baruch Plan, 233 ff., 249
Bellum justum principle, 30, 34 ff., 38 f., 41, 49, 53, 59 f., 65, 86, 110, 153, 158
Blockade, pacific, 35, 53, 109
Boycott, international, 92, 107 ff., 133 f.
Budget, military, 202, 206 f., 231
publication of, 206 f.

C

Case method, 31
Causes of illegal use of force, 22 f.
war, 23, 46, 54, 199, 253
Centralization and decentralization, 2, 7 ff., 11, 12 ff., 24 ff., 28 f., 38, 43, 105, 110
Change, peaceful, of established legal relations, 28 f., 43, 194 ff.
Civil execution, 102
Coercive (enforcement) measures as sanctions, 5 f., 11, 23 ff., 53 ff., 69, 101 ff.
Coercive measures not having the character of sanctions, 102
Collective security, *see also* International security
concept of, 1 ff., 11
of communism, 23
degrees of, 9, 10 ff.
and democracy, 9
and individual security, 1 ff.
and law, 5 ff., 10, 34 ff.
and flexibility of law, 16, 22, 43, 46, 75, 77 f., 82, 97, 185
under general international law, 34 ff.
under national and under international law, 23, 34 ff.
under particular international law, 53 ff.
under primitive law, 7 ff.
Compulsory jurisdiction, 13 f., 21, 28, 43, 182 f., 191 f., 196
Conciliation, 181 f.
Conflicts, *see* Disputes
Consultation, 171 ff.
Contigent or quota system, 112 ff., 119 f., 135, 138 f.
Control of atomic energy, 198, 210, 220 f., 224, 233 ff.
Control of disarmament, 204, 207 ff., 224 f., 232 f.
Cooperation, economic, 253 ff.
social, 255
Criminal law and international law, 91 f.
Custom as a decentralized creation of law, 28

D

Decentralization, *see* Centralization
Delict and sanction, 6, 8, 10, 92, 101 ff.
Demilitarization of territorial areas, 205 f., 228 ff.
Democracy and collective security, 9
Denationalization of organs of an international security organization, 117, 144
Differentiation of armaments, 120
Diplomatic sanctions, 104, 106
Disarmament, 26, 120, 197 ff., 202 ff., 205 f., 207 ff., 210, 212 ff., 219, 222 ff., 224 f., 232 f., 244 ff., 249 f., 261, 265
  aim of, 202 ff.
  control of, 204, 207 ff., 224 f., 232 f.
  derogations, 207, 265
  direct and indirect, 199
  geographical, 203, 205 f.
  immediate, complete or gradual (progressive), 204, 222 ff.
  organization of, 210, 244 ff.
  physical and moral, 198 ff., 210 ff., 249 f.
  proportional or balanced, 205, 225
  quantitative and qualitative, 202, 219
  regional, 261, 265
  and security, 197 ff., 212 ff.
  total or partial, 202 f.
Dispute, concept of, 19, 181, 184
Disputes (conflicts), legal (justiciable) and political (non-justiciable), 19 ff., 182 ff., 189, 191 f., 193
  local, 260, 264
  peaceful settlement of, 15 ff., 181 ff., 260
Disputes, international, judicial procedure for the settlement, 182 ff., 190
Domestic affairs (jurisdiction), intervention by an international security organization in the domestic affairs (jurisdiction) of its members, 118 f., 189, 192, 255, 258

E

Economic sanctions, 67 f., 91, 92, 104, 106 ff., 111, 122, 125 f., 160, 162 f.
Economic security, 1, 22 f.
Effectives, reducible and irreducible, 200 f., 203, 222
Egotism of the state and international security, 42, 47 f.
Enforcement (execution) of judicial decision, 187
Enforcement measures (actions), *see also* Force, sanction
  involving and not involving the use of armed force, 53, 57 f., 104
Equity and justice, 16, 31 f., 183 f., 185 f.
Expenditure, armaments, 202, 206 f., 230 f.
  defense, 202, 206 f., 230 f.
  reduction and limitation, 202, 206 f., 230 f.
Expulsion from international security organization, 113, 125, 151

F

Financial sanctions, 104, 106 ff., 133
Flexibility of law and collective security, 16, 22, 43, 46, 75, 77 f., 82, 97, 185
Force, armed, definition of the concept, 79
    international, 113 f.
  concept of, 11 f., 31, 53 ff., 57 f.

Force—Continued
and law, 6
monopoly, 6 ff, 26, 35 ff., 119, 120
of the international security organization, 119 f.
physical and non-physical, 11
thread of, 64
use of, causes of illegal, 22 ff.
centralization and decentralization, 11, 14, 23 ff.
legal and illegal, 6, 22
to be prohibited within an international security organization, 53 ff.
repression and prevention of the illegal use of force, 15 ff., 171 ff.
(enforcement action), as sanction, 5 ff., 11, 14, 23 ff., 53 ff., 69, 101 ff.
as a sanction, centralization, 23 ff.
security as protection against, 1 ff.
and self-defense, 27
Force, use of armed force as war, 1, 53 ff., 57 f.
short of war, 53 ff., 57 f.
Forfeiture of rights as a sanction, 102, 125, 151 f.

G

Gaps in law, 19 ff., 32 f., 185, 189, 193
Government, form of government of international security organization, 119

I

Ideology, legal, international security as, 42, 44 f.
"Ideology" in Marxian sociology, 44 f.
Illegal use of force, causes of, 22 ff.
Independence, political, protected by international law, 36, 62
Individual and collective responsibility, *see* Responsibility
Individual and collective security, *see* Collective security
Informations, military, 208, 236 ff.
Integrity, territorial, protected by international law, 36, 62
Interest of the state and international security, 46 ff.
International criminal jurisdiction, 123
International law, collective security under general international law, 34 ff.
and criminal law, 91 f.
nature of, 34 ff., 45
neutrality under general international law, 36 f., 152 ff.
peace treaties under general international law, 36 ff., 152 ff.
primitive character of the sanctions of, 103 f.
self-defense under general international law, 35 f., 59 f.
International legislative organ, 195
International security, 1 ff., 5, 23, 34 ff., 42, 44 f., 46 ff., 51 f., 54 f., 90 ff., 110, 117, 154 ff., 195 f. *see also* Collective security
as a legal ideology, 42, 44 f.
and national security, 3 ff., 23
and neutrality, 90 ff., 117, 154 ff.
opposition to, 5, 42 ff., 51 f., 54
and interest of the state (national interest), 46 ff.
and egotism of the state, 47 f.
as security of the state, 1 ff.
and sovereignty of the states, 42, 45, 55, 110, 117 f., 195 f.

Internationalization of armaments, 204
of aviation (civil and military), 120, 145, 204
manufacture of arms and ammunition, 209
territories of security organizations, 117
Inquiry, 181
Interpretation of law, 18, 77, 196

J

Judicial decision, declaratory or constitutive character of, 17 f., 196
enforcement (execution) of, 187, 194
Judicial function, application of law as, 13, 16
Judicial procedure for the settlement of international disputes, 182 ff., 190
Jurisdiction, compulsory, *see* Compulsory jurisdiction
domestic, 118 f., 189, 192, 255, 258
international criminal, 123
over states, 123 f.
Justice and equity, 16, 31 f., 183 f., 185 f.
Justice and law, 31 f.
Justice and peace, 44
Justiciable and non-justiciable conflicts (disputes), 19 ff., 182 ff., 189, 193

K

Kellogg-Briand Pact (Pact of Paris), 39, 50, 87, 164 f., 174 f.
Korea, police action of the United Nations in, 142 f.

L

Law, application of, two stages, 12 ff.
creation and application of, centralization and decentralization, 12 ff., 28 f.
criminal, *see* Criminal law
and force, 6
gaps in, 19 ff., 32 f., 185, 189, 193
international, *see* International law
interpretation of, 18, 77, 196
and justice, 31 f.
and peace, 6 f.
primitive, collective security under, 7 ff.
as a decentralized coercive order, 7 ff., 12 f.
and security, 5 ff., 10, 34 ff.
and state, 1 f.
League of Nations, 30, 38, 42, 43, 47, 50, 55 ff., 67, 88, 100, 108 f., 125 ff., 134 f., 136 f., 143, 168, 172, 175 ff., 187 f., 189 f., 193, 196, 197 f., 213, 217 f., 220 ff., 225 f., 228 f., 230 ff., 236 ff., 241 ff., 249 ff., 256, 261 f., 265
Legal and political concepts (norms), 75 f.
Legal and political conflicts (disputes), 19 ff., 182 ff., 189, 191 f., 193
Legal and political considerations, 75 f., 105, 106, 121, 187
Legal security, 3 f., 5 f., 9, 16, 71
Legislation as a centralized creation of law, 28
Legislative organ, international, 195
Liberalism, economic, and socialism, 254 f., 257 f.

M

Mass destruction, arms of, 201, 203
Mediation, 181
Military bases of international security organization, 117
Military informations, 208, 236 ff.
Military organization as centralization, 24
Military and non-military sanctions, 68, 104 ff., 106 ff., 110 ff., 125 f., 160, 163
Moral disarmament, 210 f., 249 f.

N

National security and international security, 3 ff., 23
Nationalization of manufacture of arms and ammunition (state monopoly), 209
Natural-law doctrine, 3, 27, 38, 46, 87
Neutrality and *bellum justum* principle, 157 f.
  concept of, 154 ff.
  and impartiality, 154 ff.
  under general international law, 36 f., 152 ff.
  and non-belligerency, 154 ff.
  obligations and rights, 157
  and international security, 90 ff., 117, 154 ff.
  within an international security organization, 154 ff.
  permanent, 9, 117, 168 f.
  qualified, 163 f.
Neutralization of zones of territory, 205 f.
Neo-neutrality, 90 f.
Non-aggression pacts, 40, 158
Non liquet, 20, 32
Nulla poena sine lege, 74 f., 123
Nullum crimen sine lege, 74 f.

O

Organization, security, *see* Security organization

P

Pacific blockade, 35, 53, 109
Peace, breach of, and threat to, 68
  and justice, 44
  and law, 6 f.
  and security, 6 f.
  treaties under general international law, 36 ff., 152 ff.
  treaties within an international security organization, 152 ff.
Police action, 37, 93, 114 f., 143
  force, 26, 30, 112 ff., 115 ff., 142 f., 203 f., 222
    international, 112 ff., 203 f.
      composition of, 118
      financial problems, 118 f.
      location, 117
      nationality (denationalization) of its members, 117, 144
      recruitment, 116 f., 143 f.
    national, 203, 222
Political independence protected by international law, 36, 62
Political and legal concepts (norms), 75 f.
Political and legal conflicts (disputes), 19 ff., 182 ff., 189, 191 f., 193

Political and legal considerations, 75 f., 105, 106, 121, 187
Political security, 4
Power policy, 44
Precedent, 29, 31
Preventive measures, 171 ff.
Preventive war, 60, 62, 88
Prevention and repression of the illegal use of force, 15 ff., 171 ff.
Primitive law, collective security under, 7 ff.
as a decentralized coercive order, 7 ff., 12 f.
Provisional measures applied in the procedure for the determination of the aggressor, 68, 120, 122, 146 f.
Provocation, 86
Publicity, budgetary, 206 f.
Punishment, concept of, 102 ff., 123
Punitive character of the sanctions of international law, 103 f.

Q

Quota or contingent system, 112 ff., 119 f., 135, 138 f.

R

Rechtssicherheit, 9, 16
Regional arrangements, 127, 262 ff.
and collective self-defense, 262 ff.
Regional disarmament, 261, 265
Regional security organizations and alliances, 39 ff., 259 f., 262 ff.
Regional and universal security organizations, 29 f., 40 f., 106, 120, 258 ff., 262 ff.
Regionalism and universalism, 29 ff., 113, 258 ff.
Repression and prevention of the illegal use of force, 15 ff., 171 ff.
Reprisals, 34 ff., 53, 57, 103 f., 109, 159, 165
as sanction, 35, 53, 57, 103 f., 109, 159
Responsibility, collective and individual, for violations of international law, 74, 103, 111, 122 ff.
individual criminal, for violations of international law by acts of state, 123 ff., 147 ff.
of states, 63
Revision of treaties, 194 f.
Revolution as internal aggression, 64, 88
Rule-of-law principle, 9, 16, 22, 32, 71, 74 f.

S

Sanction, concept of, 5 f., 69, 101 ff.
and delict, 6, 8, 10, 92, 101 ff.
forfeiture of rights as, 102, 125, 151 f.
as use of force, centralization and decentralization, 11, 14, 23 ff.
as coercive (enforcement) measure, 5 f., 11, 23 ff., 53 ff., 69, 101 ff.
diplomatic, 104, 106
economic, 67 f., 91, 92, 104, 106 ff., 111, 122, 125 f., 160, 162 f.
execution of, centralization, 14, 23 ff.
within an international security system, 104 ff.
procedure preceding, 120 ff.
financial, 104, 106 ff., 133
military and non-military, 68, 104 ff., 106 ff., 110 ff., 125 f., 160, 163
opposition to, 110 f., 122
organization of, 111 ff.

Security, absolute or relative, 7, 10 f., 23
collective, *see* Collective security
economic, 1, 22 f.
external and internal, 24, 29
individual, 1 ff.
international, *see* International security
and law, 5 ff., 10, 34 ff.
legal, 3 f., 5 f., 9, 16, 71
national, and international, 3 ff., 23.
and peace, 6 f.
political, 4
Security organization, international, denationalization of organs, 144
expulsion from 113, 125, 151
force monopoly of, 119 f.
form of government, 119
military bases of, 117
neutrality within, 154 f.
legal status of its organs, 117, 144
peace treaties within, 152 ff.
prohibition of war within, 53 ff.
execution of sanctions within, 104 ff.
sovereignty of, 117
internationalization of territories, 117
use of force to be prohibited within, 53 ff.
withdrawal from, 113, 143
Security organizations, regional and universal, 29 f., 40 f., 106, 120, 258 ff., 262 ff.
Security as protection against the use of force, 1 ff.
Self-defense, 25, 26 ff., 31, 35, 53, 59 ff., 62, 68, 86, 87 ff., 91, 105, 118, 127 ff., 161 ff., 262 ff.
and aggression, 27 f., 59 ff., 68, 86, 118
collective, and regional arrangements, 262 ff.
individual and collective, 25, 61, 87 f., 105, 118, 127 ff., 161 f.
under general international law, 35 f., 59 f.
and use of force, 27
Self-help, 8, 25 ff., 86
Self-preservation, right of, 27, 60
Separation of powers, 22
Si vis pacem para bellum, 199, 217
Social contract, 3
Social cooperation, 255
Socialist doctrine, 20, 22, 253
Socialism and economic liberalism, 254 f., 257 f.
Sovereignty of the state, 35, 42, 45, 55, 62, 110, 117 f., 195 f.
and international security, 42, 45, 55, 110, 117 f., 195 f.
Sovereignty of international security organization, 117
State, acts of, 123 f.
concept of, 1 f., 25, 35, 42, 45
egotism, 42, 47 f.
interest, 42, 46 ff.
jurisdiction over, 123 f.
and law, 1 f.
responsibility of, 63

State—Continued
and international security, *see* International security
security of the state as international security, 1 ff.
sovereignty of, *see* Sovereignty of the state
Status quo, change or preservation of, 28, 39, 41, 42 ff., 185 f.
Stimson doctrine, 133
Superior order, individual responsibility for acts committed at, 124, 149 f.

T

"Tension" conflicts, 185 f.
Territorial integrity protected by international law, 36, 62
Territories, internationalization of territories of international security organizations, 117
Treaties, revision of, 194 f.

U

United Nations, 25, 30, 31, 39, 42, 43, 47, 50, 57 f., 61, 71, 74, 80 ff., 83, 87 ff., 93 ff., 96 ff., 126 ff., 132, 134 f., 138 ff., 140 ff., 144 ff., 167, 169 ff., 172, 177, 187 ff., 190 ff., 196, 198, 207, 210, 213 f., 215 ff., 219 ff., 225 ff., 231, 233 ff., 238 ff., 245 ff., 252 f., 256 ff., 261 ff.
Universal and regional security organization, 29 f., 40 f., 106, 120, 258 ff., 262 ff.
Universalism and regionalism, 29 ff., 113, 258 ff.
Use of force *see* Force

V

Veto right, 105, 210, 249

W

War, acts of, 49, 53 ff., 57, 58
aggressive or defensive, 35 f., 58 f., 89, 90 f., 110, 202
causes of, 23, 46, 54, 199, 253
concept of, 37, 49 ff.
and counterwar, 35, 37, 158
legal or illegal, 35 f., 37, 58 f.
localization of, 42, 49
material, 199, 200, 208 f.
manufacture and trade of, 199, 208 f.
potential, 200
preventive, 60, 62, 88
prohibition of, conditional or unconditional, 53, 55 f.
within an international security organization, 53 ff.
as sanction, 35 ff., 53, 103 f.
as use of armed force, 1, 53 ff., 57 ff.
universal (world war) as a consequence of international security organization, 47, 49
Weapons, aggressive or defensive, 202, 219
Withdrawal from the security organization, 113, 143
World public opinion, 174
World state, 29 f., 52

www.ingramcontent.com/pod-product-compliance
Lightning Source LLC
Chambersburg PA
CBHW020044260926
51874CB00001B/3
* 9 7 8 1 5 8 4 7 7 1 4 4 9 *